CROSS-CULTURAL ROOTS
OF MINORITY CHILD DEVELOPMENT

Voluntary immigrants, eager to learn how to cross cultural/language boundaries. Bellagio Road Newcomers School, Los Angeles, California, USA, 1993 (see chapter 18).
Photograph by Lauren Greenfield

CROSS-CULTURAL ROOTS OF MINORITY CHILD DEVELOPMENT

Edited by

Patricia M. Greenfield
University of California, Los Angeles

Rodney R. Cocking
National Institute of Mental Health

LEA LAWRENCE ERLBAUM ASSOCIATES, PUBLISHERS
1994   Hillsdale, New Jersey   Hove, UK

The cover design and legend have been adapted with permission from *Dancing Colors: Paths of Native American Women* by C. J. Brafford & Laine Thom. San Francisco: Chronicle Books, © 1992. Photograph courtesy of San Diego Museum of Man.

Lawrence Erlbaum Associates, Inc., Publishers
365 Broadway
Hillsdale, New Jersey 07642

Library of Congress Cataloging-in-Publication Data

Cross-cultural roots of minority child development / edited by
    Patricia M. Greenfield, Rodney R. Cocking.
        p.   cm.
    Includes bibliographical references and index.
    ISBN 0-8058-1223-7 (cloth). — ISBN 0-8058-1224-5 (paper)
    1. Socialization—Cross-cultural studies. 2. Child psychology—
Cross-cultural studies. 3. Child development—Cross-cultural
studies. 4. Ethnopsychology. 5. Minorities—United States—Canada—France—
Psychology. I. Greenfield, Patricia M. II. Cocking, Rodney
R.
    GN510.C78 1994
    303.3′2—dc20   93-24098
                                                                  CIP

Books published by Lawrence Erlbaum Associates are printed on acid-free paper, and their bindings are chosen for strength and durability.

Printed in the United States of America
20 19 18 17 16 15 14 13 12

CONTENTS

II. AFRICAN ROOTS

III. ASIAN ROOTS

IV. CONCLUDING PERSPECTIVES

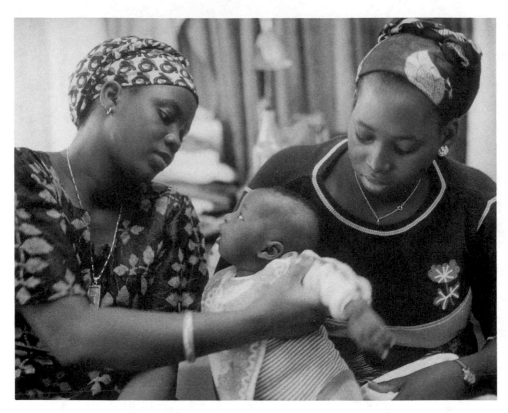

West African immigrants in Paris, France. Mother–child triad (see chapter 8).
Photograph by Martine Barrat

PREFACE

The field of developmental psychology is an ethnocentric one dominated by a Euro-American perspective. Interaction with a wider international community can provide perspectives on goals, conditions, and paths of development that differ from those we too often take for granted. Only in this way will our field be decentered and our collegial relationships internationalized. At international conferences, all too often, colonial and other hierarchical power relations are replicated at the intellectual level. Cross-cultural and racial/ethnic findings are evaluated in terms of established mainstream Euro-American evidence. Little attention is paid to how different behaviors serve their respective users. Consequently, a major goal of the international workshop for which the following chapters were written was to bring scholars from every part of the world together to work on a common theme, to which each could contribute on an inherently equal footing.

The goal of two of our sponsoring bodies, the Developmental Psychology Division of the American Psychological Association (APA) and the International Society for the Study of Behavioral Development, was to internationalize the field of developmental psychology. From the perspective of the APA, it seemed that developmental psychologists in the United States would be most interested in an international perspective, if such a perspective could solve a problem of central importance to the field and to society. Minority child development and socialization seemed to be just such an issue.

Although cultures sometimes coincide with national borders, conquest and immigration have made this state of affairs the exception rather than the rule.

At the end of the 20th century, the mixture of cultures within nation–states is a fact that is gaining increasing recognition and importance in both national and international affairs. The United States is far from unique in representing a confluence of voluntary immigrants, involuntary immigrants, and conquered indigenous peoples. In the United States, as in many countries such as France, England, Canada, and Australia, this mixture has left physically identifiable subcultural groups termed *minorities*. Importantly, each minority group has its own cultural history and roots. Moreover, except for Native Americans, the cultural background of each minority in the United States and Canada comes from another part of the world. These facts raise critical issues for understanding the development and socialization of minority children.

THE PROBLEM OF PERSPECTIVE

As with most contemporary psychology, the methodological ideology of psychology is objectivity. Yet when one studies development in one's own culture, in fact, one has an insider's cultural perspective. Partly because this fact runs counter to the very ideological assumptions of psychological science, the insider's perspective almost always goes unacknowledged (cf. Rogoff & Morelli, 1989). A basic assumption of our workshop was that the insider's perspective is valuable for studying developmental issues in every culture and every subculture in the world.

Recently, mainstream developmental psychology has begun to recognize that a key aspect of development is the acquisition of culture. Because most developmental psychologists are not trained in the study of culture, they necessarily fall back on their unacknowledged insider's perspective when studying development and socialization issues. However, the dominant knowledge base of current developmental psychology comes from Euro-American researchers studying the development of children from their own cultural experience. Significantly, a largely unacknowledged consequence is that our developmental knowledge is primarily knowledge of the acquisition of Euro-American culture as this process transpires in the United States.

Our workshop sought to redress this situation by enlisting insiders' perspectives on socialization and development in a diverse sampling of the world's cultures, including developing regions that often lack the means to speak for themselves in the arena of international social science. We also redressed the balance by including outsiders' perspectives on socialization and development in the United States.

When one group, the majority, has the exclusive power, through science, to define the nature of itself and all the other groups in a society, all minority groups are *ipso facto* disempowered. When members of minority groups gain the power to define themselves and the broader society in which they live, they are *ipso facto* empowered. With reference to his or her own group, the insider understands the meanings and motives behind in-group behaviors that may be misinterpreted or devalued by outsiders looking through the lenses of their own cultural values. With reference to the dominant majority, an out-group member can see, and therefore study, aspects of the dominant culture that insiders have taken for granted or even repressed. The outsider can also serve as a cultural intermediary in making one culture more understandable to members of another. The issues of insider and outsider perspectives that reflect and influence relations between less powerful and more powerful groups in a single society also reflect and influence the relations between less powerful and more powerful nations in the world.

This volume provides an opportunity for the development of Africans, African Americans, Mexicans, Mexican Americans, Asians, Asian Americans, and Native Americans to be studied through the lenses of insiders (Nsamenang, Oloko, Blake, Tapia Uribe, Delgado-Gaitan, Kim, Choi, Azuma, Hieshima, Lee, Lebra, Takanishi, Ho, Suina, & Joe), sometimes in collaboration with Euro-American outsiders (Lamb, R. LeVine, S. LeVine, Schneider, Plank, and Smolkin). It also provides an opportunity for Euro-American society and its impact on child development to be studied through the lenses of outsiders whose origins are neither American nor European (Ogbu, a Nigerian immigrant to the United States; Lebra, a Japanese immigrant to the United States; Kim, a Korean immigrant to Canada and the United States; Choi, a Korean immigrant to Canada; and Azuma, Japanese by birth and residence). Some of our insiders have the perspectives of multiple generations in the United States as members of an involuntary minority group (Blake, an African American) and a voluntary minority group (Takanishi, a Japanese American from Hawaii). Nor have we excluded the more usual cross-cultural perspective—that of a European or Euro-American who "crosses over" to a different culture (Rabain-Jamin, Stevenson). We also have one author with a dual perspective on the cultures (Native American) he studies (Tharp). As Tharp (1991) puts it, he is "by blood and affection" one-fourth Cherokee, by culture Euro-American. These multiple perspectives bring us several steps closer to a truly multicultural model of development—one in which the acquisition and construction of culture is a primary component.

CROSS-CULTURAL ROOTS OF MINORITY CHILD DEVELOPMENT

For too long, minority child development has been viewed exclusively as a series of responses to negative environmental forces, such as poverty, discrimination, and slavery. It is equally important to consider the positive heritage that minority socialization practices owe to their cultures of origin.

By examining the roots of cognitive socialization in their cultures of origin, it is hoped that this volume will contribute to knowledge of cultural sources of learning styles in African-American, Mexican-American, Asian-American, and Native-American children. In this project, we expand a tradition manifest in the work of a small but diverse group of researchers in psychology and anthropology: Boykin (1986; Boykin & Toms, 1985); Diaz-Guerrero (1987); Harrison, Wilson, Pine, Chan, and Buriel (1990); John-Steiner and Osterreich (1975); Lewis (1975); Phillips (1983); Sudarkasa (1988); Tharp and Gallimore (1989); and Schneider and Lee (1990).

Our workshop and its subsequent publications (this volume; Greenfield & Cocking, 1993) constitute the first time in the field of developmental psychology that cross-cultural roots of minority child development have been studied in their ancestral societies in a systematic way and by an international group of researchers. Rather than focus exclusively on the maladaptiveness of particular socialization practices for conditions in the dominant society, it is time to consider and understand their adaptive roles in their cultures of origin. Such understanding was the primary goal of our major sponsor, the National Institute of Mental Health, in the United States. The Institute sponsored a workshop entitled "Continuities and Discontinuities in the Cognitive Socialization of Minority Children." Each chapter in the present volume represents a presentation to that workshop. In addition, chapter 1 attempts to capture the richness of the discussion and commentary that occurred during the workshop.

To what extent can the development and socialization of minority children be seen as continuous with their ancestral cultures? To what extent have cultural and political conditions in the United States (or other countries) modified developmental and socialization processes, yielding discontinuities with ancestral cultures? To what extent have the ancestral cultures changed, yielding cross-generational discontinuities in the development and socialization of immigrants from the same countries? These questions provided the unifying theme for the workshop. Participants in the workshop contributed perspectives on the Asian, West-African, Mexican, and Native-American roots to minority child development in the United States and, in the West African case, to minority child development in France as well.

HOW SHOULD ETHNIC GROUPS BE LABELED?

Berry (in press), a Canadian, noted that the term *minority group* implies relative powerlessness and discrimination. He recommended the term *ethnocultural group*, with its implication that all groups are equal in a multicultural society. This ideal reflects Berry's own Canadian background. The official social policy in Canada is multiculturalism, whereas in the United States, Europe, and many other parts of the world, a dominant culture is officially sanctioned. The distinction between minority and majority also implies that the majority group controls most resources and provides the context of acculturation for the minority groups. In addition, all the groups termed *minority* in this book have racial as well as cultural markers, making it impossible to hide group status or hide from racial discrimination no matter what your precise cultural origin (e.g., African Americans of African slave origin vs. African Americans who have come to the United States as voluntary immigrants from Africa or the West Indies). This fact is as true in Canada as it is in the United States. For all of these reasons, the term *minority group*, with its connotations of little power and object of considerable discrimination, unfortunately, seems to be an accurate one for the groups we consider.

Nonetheless, we have struggled with labels. Recognizing that race is as much a social category as a biological one, we have eschewed racial labels such as Black, White, Caucasian, and Oriental. Recognizing that not all members of the dominant majorities in North America are of English origin, we have eschewed the term *Anglo* in favor of *Euro-American*. We consider this term to cover Canadians of European origin because they also inhabit North America. However, where it is necessary to make a distinction (Kim & Choi, this volume), we use the term *Euro-Canadian*.

Although we have logical scientific reasons for these choices, there is a price: We lose the ethnolinguistic culture-specific flavor of the labels that groups in contact use with each other. Thus our labels fail to recognize the fact that Hispanics call Euro-Americans *Anglos*, whereas African Americans call them *Whites*, and Asian Americans call them *Caucasians*. What seemed important was to have a set of labels that provides accuracy and clarity for a work that considers multiple groups in a multicultural society. The adequacy of our group labels should be assessed in the light of this goal.

CULTURAL ANTHROPOLOGY, SOCIOLOGY, AND CULTURAL PSYCHOLOGY: THE VALUE OF MULTIPLE DISCIPLINES IN STIMULATING FURTHER RESEARCH IN DEVELOPMENTAL PSYCHOLOGY AND EDUCATION

Because most psychologists are not trained in cultural analysis, it is difficult for them to take an intellectually rigorous approach to exploring cultural factors in childrearing and child development. At the same time, it can be difficult for developmental and educational psychologists to relate to the work of anthropologists and sociologists because the methods and definitions of data are so different in these fields. The primary data of cultural anthropology and sociology are dismissed as "background information" in psychology.

Even worse, psychology often reduces culture to a label dividing one group from another (e.g., Black and White groups compared), omitting background information altogether. In addition, these ethnocultural labels do not get connected by the research to any psychological process in which we might be interested (Betancourt & Lopez, 1993). Because of this lack in our conceptual apparatus and the resulting studies, culture is often rejected by our colleagues in psychology and education as uninteresting.

Yet accepted methods in the field of psychology do not include the ethnographic fieldwork and qualitative interviews that would enable us to identify either the precise cultural processes behind observed behavioral differences or the meaning of such differences in the lives and value systems of the subjects. Therefore, we are in a scientific bind.

The field of cultural psychology (Cole, 1989; Price-Williams, 1980) has begun to remove this bind with its Vygotskian emphasis on cultural tools of cognitive socialization (e.g., Greenfield, 1993; Greenfield & Childs, 1977; Price-Williams, Gordon, & Ramirez, 1969; Saxe, 1991; Scribner, 1984; Scribner & Cole, 1981) and interactional processes in the transmission of culture (e.g., Greenfield, 1984; Rogoff, 1990; Wertsch, Minick, & Arns, 1984). Cultural psychology transforms questions concerning cultural influences into questions about psychological processes.

However, the approach from cultural psychology has not yet been applied to minority cultures in which the mix of tools and interaction styles may reflect a mixture of cultural origins—some from the ancestral culture, some from the dominant society, and some from the power relations between ethnic minority and dominant society. Clearly, the relations between culture, socialization, and development are much more complex for ethnic minorities immersed in a dominant majority culture. Because cultural psychology tends to look at the proximal aspects of culture (Cocking, this volume), that is, those that are part of an individual's immediate stimulus situation, it is not conceptually ready to deal with the more distal layers of cultural and social structure that are required to explain the development of minority children in a majority culture.

As a consequence, in our workshop and book we found it necessary to draw on anthropologists and sociologists, as well as psychologists and specialists in education, to begin our investigation of the cross-cultural roots of minority child development. We want to alert developmental and educational psychologists to the value of these fields in stimulating richer and more meaningful psychological research. Where the methods of data collection and data analysis are different from those used in psychology (e.g., ethnography and qualitative description), the studies often provide a conceptual orientation that could stimulate future research using psychological methods.

A good example of this potential stimulation is Delgado-Gaitan's ethnographic study of preschool socialization in Mexican-American homes. Her conceptualization of cultural values in Mexican-American homes and her examples of the interaction patterns that these values engender could well form the basis for a quantitative and even comparative developmental psychology study of family–child interaction in Mexican-American and Euro-American homes, both immigrant and later generations. Because of Delgado-Gaitan's ethnographic groundwork, such a study would look not just at mother–child interaction, the typical ethnocentric methodology in developmental psychology, but at child–family interaction more generally. The ethnographic groundwork could lead a subsequent study in developmental psychology to look at the interrelationship between communicative socialization and cultural values such as respect for elder family members. As a result, psychology researchers would be able to go beyond a precise quantitative description of cultural differences across generations and across ethnic groups to understand the participants' values and goals, as well as the historical processes, that generate the differences.

At the same time, this volume contains research done by interdisciplinary teams or by investigators knowledgeable in multidisciplinary methodology. These authors have managed to combine data from historical, sociological, cultural, and psychological sources to explore multiple levels of causality of developmental phenomena. A good example of such a multilevel approach is the chapter by Tapia Uribe, LeVine, and LeVine on childrearing and socialization in Mexico. Their studies combine census data, ethnography, interviews, and observations of mother–child interactions. Another example is Oloko's chapter on children's street work in Nigeria, in which she combines large-scale questionnaires and smaller scale interviews with ethnographic observation and information on the history of the relevant sociopolitical context. A different sort of example is the chapter by Schneider, Hieshima, Lee, and Plank in which large-scale national surveys, smaller scale parental interviews, and ethnographic observation in schools are combined to provide a multifactor approach to socialization and school achievement among Japanese Americans, Chinese Americans, and Korean Americans.

VALUES, SOCIALIZATION, AND DEVELOPMENT

How do family interactions transmit values and skills that influence learning and cognitive development in young children? A major focus of this volume is the learning consequences of two value themes that characterize and contrast Euro-American culture in North America and much of Western Europe with that in African, Asian, Latin-American, and Native-American societies. The first is the dimension of an individualistic, private, or independent orientation (Western) versus a collective, social, or interdependent orientation (Africa, Asia, Latin America). A second theme is the contrast between the early socialization goal of maximizing educational development (commercial societies) versus the socialization goal of infant survival and childhood subsistence skills in hunting/gathering and agricultural societies (LeVine, 1977, 1987). It was thought that these contrasting cultural adaptations would also have their consequences in the child's learning styles and cognitive development.

The particular value dimensions around which we organized the workshop and the book, selected in collaboration with J. Rabain-Jamin, were chosen for two interrelated reasons. First, they are fundamental and therefore integrative dimensions. They influence and unify many otherwise disparate facts of socialization and development. Second, when a minority group is similar to the pole of each dimension valued in the dominant society, there is harmony and continuity between majority and minority socialization. In contrast, dissimilarities with the value pole in the dominant society lead to conflict and discontinuity.

PLANS AND GOALS FOR THIS BOOK

Our strategy was (a) to invite empirical articles about cognitive socialization in societies that, for one reason or another, now have substantial groups of descendants in the United States and, often, in other countries as well; (b) to invite empirical articles about cognitive socialization in the corresponding minority groups in the United States, as well as other countries such as France and Canada; and (c) to ask the authors to use the value dimensions of individualism/collectivism and survival/education as organizing themes. In this way, we hoped to facilitate conceptual comparison between socialization patterns in minority groups and their ancestral cultures.

Therefore, we invite the reader to consider the connections in socialization patterns and values (a) between Mexican (Tapia Uribe, LeVine, & LeVine) and Mexican-American (Delgado-Gaitan) settings; (b) between African (Nsamenang & Lamb; Oloko), African-French (Rabain-Jamin), and African-American (Blake) settings; and (c) between East-Asian (Ho; Stevenson; Lebra; Azuma; Kim & Choi) and Asian-American settings (Schneider, Hieshima, Lee, & Plank; Takanishi). To facilitate this kind of comparative reading, we organized the book by geographic/cultural origins; the three sections are entitled "American Roots," "African Roots," and "Asian Roots." The order of the three sections reflects (approximately) the order in which particular racial groups appeared on the American continent.

Note a cultural connection that is even older: Native peoples in all of the Americas arrived on this continent from Asia. Therefore, going back farther, native peoples and Asians share both cultural roots and a biological heritage. The native heritage is particularly strong in Mexican society.

We hope that the comparative reading of separately conceived studies using different methods will stimulate coordinated comparative research in the future. In this way, implicit connections between minority and ancestral cultures can become explicit. One example of such research appears in the book. It is the cross-sectional research of Kim, summarized in the chapter by Kim and Choi, in which developmental and socialization patterns of Korean youth are compared with those of Korean Americans and Korean Canadians. Another example is the longitudinal comparison of Luis Laosa in which he follows Puerto Rican families back and forth from Puerto Rico to the New York area. We very much regret that Laosa was unable to participate in the workshop.

Because Native Americans are conquered peoples, immigrants in their own land (Attneave, 1982), a different approach had to be taken. We have included three chapters that analyze and discuss the developmental and educational implications of value contrasts between Euro-American and Native-American cultures: (a) Pueblo (Suina & Smolkin), (b) Navajo (Joe, Tharp), and (c) Native Hawaiian (Tharp). Perhaps future studies might explore the role of ancestral culture by comparing Native-American socialization and development on and off reservations.

The ultimate goals are to contribute (a) to a historical reconstruction of the cross-cultural roots of minority child development, (b) to a cultural-historical approach to developmental psychology, and (c) to a more universal developmental theory in which Euro-American patterns of socialization are seen to represent a particular set of developmental alternatives.

—Patricia M. Greenfield

ACKNOWLEDGMENTS

This book stems from an initiative of Herbert Pick, then-president of APA Division 7, to internationalize our field by forming an International Committee in Division 7, of which Greenfield was named chair. The members of the International Committee were Barbara Rogoff, Lonnie Sherrod, and Ellen Skinner. Richard Lerner, then-secretary of the International Society for the Study of Behavioral Development (ISSBD), obtained support from ISSBD for an international workshop; Lonnie Sherrod hosted a major planning meeting at the New School for Social Research for the workshop, ultimately entitled "Continuities and Discontinuities in the Cognitive Socialization of Minority Children." This planning meeting was also attended by David Palermo and Linda Burton of Penn State University. Harold Stevenson, then-president of ISSBD and also present at the meeting, later provided valuable assistance in identifying workshop participants. Kenneth Rubin, ISSBD treasurer, served as a second representative of ISSBD. The U.S. National Institute of Mental

Health sponsored the international workshop, which took place in Washington, DC. It was at this workshop that draft papers were circulated, critiqued, debated, and discussed, and the refined chapters for this volume emerged. Additional funding was provided by the Grant Foundation and the University of California at Los Angeles. Helpful comments on material that ultimately became this preface and the introductory chapter that follows were provided by R. R. Cocking, I. Blake, J. Jacobs, M. Tapia Uribe, B. Nsamenang, and A. B. Oloko. Useful critiques of several draft chapters were contributed by members of Greenfield's 1991 seminar on culture, social change, and development.

A. C. Mundy-Castle provided a stimulating discussion at the workshop. C. Merrill-Mirsky presented a multicultural and participatory ethnomusicology evening. Both made extremely valuable contributions to the workshop. Hopefully, all of their spirit and some of their substance have been incorporated into the introductory chapter that follows.

Thanks to Lauren Greenfield, Jean Jamin, Joyce Hieshima, Sarah LeVine, Martha Bardach, and Michelle Bonnice for help with photographs and to Leslie Devereaux, Terry Marks-Tarlow, Steven Guberman, and Michelle Bonnice for contributions to the cover design. Thanks also to the San Diego Museum of Man and Chronicle Books for permission to adapt the cover from a photograph in *Dancing Colors: Paths of Native American Women* by C. J. Brafford and L. Thom.

Very special thanks and appreciation are due to Lisa Kendig Black, who so ably and enthusiastically assisted with the manuscript preparation and editing of the entire book.

—Patricia M. Greenfield
—Rodney R. Cocking

REFERENCES

Attneave, C. (1982). American Indians and Alaskan Native families: Emigrants in their own homeland. In M. McGoldrick, J. K. Pearce, & J. Giordano (Eds.), *Ethnicity and family therapy*. New York: Guilford.

Berry, J. W. (in press). An ecological perspective on cultural and ethnic psychology. In E. Trickett (Ed.), *Human diversity: Perspectives on people in context*. San Francisco: Jossey-Bass.

Betancourt, H., & Lopez, S. R. (1993). The study of culture, ethnicity and race in American psychology. *American Psychologist, 48*, 629–637.

Boykin, A. W. (1986). The triple quandary and the schooling of Afro-American children. In U. Neisser (Ed.), *The school achievement of minority children: New perspectives*. Hillsdale, NJ: Lawrence Erlbaum Associates.

Boykin, A. W., & Toms, F. D. (1985). Black child socialization: A conceptual framework. In H. P. McAdoo & J. L. McAdoo (Eds.), *Black children: Social, educational, and parental environments* (pp. 33–51). Newbury Park, CA: Sage.

Cole, M. (1989). Cultural psychology: A once and future discipline. In J. Berman (Ed.), *Nebraska Symposium on Motivation: Cross-cultural perspectives* (Vol. 37, pp. 279–335). Lincoln: University of Nebraska Press.

Diaz-Guerrero, R. (1987). Historical sociocultural premises and ethnic socialization. In J. S. Phinney & M. J. Rotherham (Eds.), *Children's ethnic socialization* (pp. 239–250). Newbury Park, CA: Sage.

Greenfield, P. M. (1984). A theory of the teacher in the learning activities of everyday life. In B. Rogoff & J. Lave (Eds.), *Everyday cognition: Its development in social context* (pp. 117–138). Cambridge, MA: Harvard University Press.

Greenfield, P. M. (1993). Representational competence in shared symbol systems: Electronic media from radio to video games. In R. R. Cocking & K. A. Renninger (Eds.), *The development and meaning of psychological distance* (pp. 161–183). Hillsdale, NJ: Lawrence Erlbaum Associates.

Greenfield, P. M., & Childs, C. P. (1977). Weaving, color terms and pattern representation: Cultural influences and cognitive development among the Zinacantecos of Southern Mexico. *Inter-American Journal of Psychology, 11*, 23–48.

Greenfield, P. M., & Cocking, R. R. (Eds.). (1993). International roots of minority child development. *International Journal of Behavioral Development* [Special Issue].

Harrison, A. O., Wilson, M. N., Pine, C. J., Chan, S. Q., & Buriel, R. (1990). Family ecologies of ethnic minority children. *Child Development, 61*, 347–362.

John-Steiner, V. P., & Osterreich, H. (1975). *Learning styles among Pueblo children: Final report to National Institute of Education*. Albuquerque: University of New Mexico, College of Education.

LeVine, R. A. (1977). Child rearing as cultural adaptation. In P. H. Leiderman, S. R. Tulkin, & A. Rosenfeld (Eds.), *Culture and infancy: Variations in the human experience* (pp. 15–27). New York: Academic Press.

LeVine, R. A. (1987). Women's schooling, patterns of fertility, and child survival. *Educational Researcher*, 21–27.

Lewis, D. K. (1975). The black family: Socialization and sex roles. *Phylon, 36*, 221–237.

Phillips, S. U. (1983). *The invisible culture: Communication in classroom and community on the Warm Springs Indian Reservation*. New York: Longman.

Price-Williams, D. (1980). Toward the idea of a cultural psychology: A superordinate theme for study. *Journal of Cross Cultural Psychology, 11*, 75–88.

Price-Williams, D., Gordon, W., & Ramirez, M. III. (1969). Skill and conservation: A study of pottery-making children. *Developmental Psychology, 1*, 769.

Rogoff, B. (1990). *Apprenticeship in thinking: Cognitive development in social context*. New York: Oxford University Press.

Rogoff, B., & Morelli, G. (1989). Perspectives on children's development from cultural psychology. *American Psychologist, 44*, 343–348.

Saxe, G. B. (1991). *Culture and cognitive development: Studies in mathematical understanding*. Hillsdale, NJ: Lawrence Erlbaum Associates.

Schneider, B., & Lee, Y. (1990). A model for academic success: The school and home environment of East Asian students. *Anthropology and Education Quarterly, 21*(4), 358–377.

Scribner, S. (1984). Studying working intelligence. In B. Rogoff & J. Lave (Eds.), *Everyday cognition: Its development in social context* (pp. 9–40). Cambridge, MA: Harvard University Press.

Scribner, S., & Cole, M. (1981). *Psychology of literacy*. Cambridge, MA: Harvard University Press.

Sudarkasa, N. (1988). Interpreting the African heritage in Afro-American family organization. In H. P. McAdoo (Ed.), *Black families* (2nd ed.; pp. 27–43). Newbury Park, CA: Sage.

Tharp, R. G. (1991, June/July). *Continuities and discontinuities in the cognitive socialization*. In P. M. Greenfield & R. R. Cocking (Chairs), Proceedings of a workshop, Department of Health and Human Services, Public Health Service, Alcohol, Drug Abuse and Mental Health Administration.

Tharp, R. G., & Gallimore, R. (1989). *Rousing minds to life: Teaching and learning in social context*. New York: Cambridge University Press.

Wertsch, J. V., Minick, N., & Arns, F. J. (1984). The creation of context in joint problem-solving. In B. Rogoff & J. Lave (Eds.), *Everyday cognition: Its development in social context* (pp. 151–171). Cambridge, MA: Harvard University Press.

With their children, two African immigrant mothers—one from Senegal, the other from Ivory Coast—meet every day to enjoy time together. Paris, France (see chapter 8). *Photograph by Martine Barrat*

1

Independence and Interdependence as Developmental Scripts: Implications for Theory, Research, and Practice

Patricia M. Greenfield
University of California, Los Angeles

Developmental psychology, like other branches of psychology, desires to establish a universal science of the person. Yet we are in constant danger of mistaking the particular for the universal. This chapter moves toward the construction of a truly universal theory of development through the empirical and theoretical understanding of cultural diversity. The roles of cultural history and social history are emphasized in this account of development. It is argued that central components of cultural history are value orientations or cultural scripts. These are essential to understand the cultural variability of developmental goals and the acquisition of culture in different societal contexts. However, the study of cultural scripts and their effects on development requires some new methodological assumptions for psychology.

Minority child development provides an important topic that requires all of these conceptual elements for its empirical understanding: cultural history, social history, and new methodological paradigm. In this chapter, I develop each element in turn, drawing on concepts and data from this volume and the workshop that preceded it. As the chapter progresses, it becomes clear that these elements are relevant to the development of all children, not only minority children. The chapter concludes by discussing implications of concepts and data for minority mental health, educational practice, future research, and developmental theory.

IMPACT OF CULTURAL HISTORY
ON SOCIALIZATION AND DEVELOPMENT

Minority Child Development and Cultural History

Although recent developmental theory in the Russian tradition has stressed the important role of cultural history in individual development (e.g., Scribner, 1985), proponents of this theory have not applied it to the cultural roots of minority child development. (An important exception to this generalization is Vera John-Steiner.) The present book, in its conception and actualization, makes cultural history a central component of minority child development.

Kim (1991) noted that ethnic groups result from the interaction of the heritage culture and the dominant culture. As Berry (1987) pointed out, minority research up to now has paid too much attention to the "contact culture" and not enough to the culture of origin. A principal aim of this chapter and this book is to redress this balance.

Within ethnic groups, there are variable perspectives on the role of ancestral cultural history. These vary with the time and manner in which a particular ethnic group becomes incorporated into a particular society. At one extreme in the United States are Japanese Americans: They place so much importance on ancestral history that they label every generation since emigration from Japan with a distinctive name. At another extreme are African Americans, among whom the notion of African roots is quite controversial. One view is that the experience of slavery and subsequent discrimination are entirely responsible for a distinctive African-American culture; African culture was wiped out by the slave masters. Yet details of culture, such as African-American handclapping games, are practically identical in West Africa, as Merrill-Mirsky (1991) demonstrated. Sudarkasa (1988) took a sensible position that acknowledges both the historical influence of slavery and the fact that the Africans who adapted to and survived slavery had a culture that must have affected the nature of their adaptation.

Value Orientations: A Key Aspect
of Cultural History

Development and socialization in different cultures may originate as adaptations to different ecological/economic conditions (e.g., Berry, 1967, in press; Draper & Cashdan, 1988), the material side of culture. However, the need to create meaning intrinsic to human culture means that these differing adaptations are reflected and rationalized in different value orientations, the symbolic side of culture. Kim (1991) joined these two sides by viewing culture as a collective way to attach meaning to ecological conditions.

The material circumstances of minority children in the United States (or other Western countries) are often very different from those of children growing up in the societies of their ancestral origin. Therefore, it seemed that value orientations, with their attendant goals of development (an aspect of symbolic culture), would be more likely than cultural adaptations to ecological conditions (the material side of culture) to provide evidence of ancestral cultural roots as a source of continuity in the developmental processes of minority children. Although both material and symbolic levels are seen as part and parcel of both culture and human development, the value orientations inherent in cultural scripts were selected as our theoretical starting point.

The key fact about human culture is its intergenerational transmission through the socialization process. Socialization is used in its broadest sense to include informal education in the family as well as formal education. Most important for this chapter and the chapters that follow, value orientations incorporate different goals or endpoints of development, which become the developmental scripts for intergenerational socialization.

Only by viewing behavior and thought processes in relation to people's goals and values is it possible to go beyond the identification of cultural or other group differences and understand the adaptive function and meaning of those differences for the actors. By inserting a value dimension, we are able to go beyond differences to people's own reasons for those differences (Kim & Choi, chapter 11, this volume). In this chapter and this volume, interdependence/independence (often termed *collectivism/individualism*) is the primary value theme and subsistence survival/schooling is the secondary theme.

Independence/Interdependence:
Two Contrasting Developmental Scripts

Psychology as the science of the individual was born and nourished by the philosophical foundations of individualism. We now discover that the independent individual is not a universal fact, but a culture-specific belief system about the development of a person. There is an important alternative belief system that is held by about 70% of the world's population (Triandis, 1989); it is called *interdependence* or *collectivism*. Choi (1992) cogently observed that "the socio-cultural themes that came out of the individualistic culture and historical background of the West have the natural bearings of their intellectual heritage, and can never be the alternative view of human beings" (p. 2).

Nonetheless, developmentalists from interdependence-oriented societies can help to balance the ethnocentric picture of individualistic development with an alternative view of interdependent development.

> There are increasing voices pointing to a need to derive some intellectual nourishment from the Asian traditions. In the West, the social sciences have been encapsulated by their focus on the individual as the unit of analysis . . . the Asian contribution would be to refocus the attention on not just the individual, but on relationships. (Ho, 1991, p. 319)

Because every human society must deal with the relationship between person and group, this is a universal developmental issue. To what extent does a culture idealize personhood in terms of individual achievement and autonomy? To what extent does a culture idealize personhood in terms of interdependence with family and community? This choice, with its implications for socialization and development, provides a unifying conceptual framework for considering the relationship between cultural values and developmental pathways. This framework relates closely to the second value dimension, socialization for subsistence/socialization for schooling.

What difference does it make for socialization and development whether the members of a group define the preferred endpoint of human development as independence or interdependence? How does the dialectic (Ho, 1991) between independence and interdependence relate to preferred methods of socialization and education? To answer these questions is a major goal of this chapter and the book that follows.

Independence and Interdependence as Intertwined Phenomena

All human beings are both individuals and members of a social group. Therefore, no one is exclusively independent or interdependent (cf. Turiel, 1994). However, in focusing on values, we are pointing to the ideals of a society. **The tension between independence and interdependence generates a continuum of idealized cultural scripts.** Although no society can eliminate either the separate individual or the interdependent group, the nature of the ideal has important implications for what is responded to, emphasized, and sanctioned in the socialization process and for the character of social relations. By these means, cultural ideals influence the trajectory of individual development.

Each society strikes a particular balance between individual and group, between independence and interdependence. Every group selects a point on the independence/interdependence continuum as its developmental ideal. The major mode of one society is the minor mode of another. The balance is never perfect; each emphasis, whether it be independence or interdependence, has its own psychological cost (Kim, 1987). Kim noted that, in socially oriented societies, the cost of interdependence is experienced as suppression of individual development, whereas in individualistically oriented cultures, the cost of independence is experienced as alienation. In extreme cases, these costs can become cultural pathologies on either an individual or group level. It is because no society has found the perfect balance between the individual and the group that this theme has such universal fascination.

Intellectual History of Independence/Interdependence

The origins of the independence/interdependence (or individualism/collectivism) dimension lie in the observations of colonialized people who were educated in Western ways and noticed a profound difference in world view. For example, Aimé Cesaire, a subject of French colonization, developed the concept of *negritude*. In contrast to individualism, a key value of Western civilization, *negritude* involves "solidarity, born of the cohesion of the primitive clan" (Kesteloof, 1962, p. 84). Individuals as well as physical objects were subordinated to a social collectivity in the world view of sub-Saharan Africa (Greenfield, 1966).

Soon, anthropologists who immersed themselves in African cultures experienced the dichotomous world views. As Lewis (1975) pointed out, an interesting example is the anthropologist Robin Horton (1967):

> Horton describes his childhood when he felt most at ease, not with his family or friends, but with his Bunsen burners and chemicals: "Potassium hydroxide and nitric acid were my friends; sodium phosphate and calcium chloride my brothers and sisters." He continues: ". . . the image of the man happier with things than with people is common enough in modern Western literature (and) shows that what I am talking about here is the sickness of the times" (Horton, 1967, p. 64).
>
> Horton tried to explain to a group of Nigerian students how life in an urban industrial West differed from life in the students' own traditional communities by telling them of his childhood ease with objects and sense of alienation from people. He writes: "What I was saying about a life in which things might seem a welcome haven from people was just so totally foreign to their experience that they could not begin to take it in. They just stared. Rarely have I felt more of an alien than in that discussion." (Lewis, 1975, p. 231)

The first psychologist to recognize this profound dimension of cultural difference was Mundy-Castle (1968, 1974), who formulated the distinction between social and technological intelligence. This formulation was based on observations concerning the relative importance of people and things in Africa compared with the Western world. Whereas people and social skills seemed more important in Africa, things and technology seemed more important in countries such as the United States, with corresponding differences in strategies of socialization.

Following in the path of researchers such as Wober (1974), Dasen (1984) and Serpell (1993) gave this idea a firm empirical foundation with their investigations of Baoulé intelligence in Ivory Coast and Chewa intelligence in Zambia. Dasen found that what is valued in the Baoulé's indigenous conception of intelligence are social skills such as helpfulness, obedience, respect, and familial responsibility. "More technological skills, such as a sense of observation, quick learning, memory, or manual dexterity are also valued, but only if they are put into the service of the social group" (Dasen, 1984, p. 130). Hence, one can see that it is not a question of social intelligence instead of technological intelligence, but rather an integration of technological intelligence as a means to social ends, not an end in itself. In contrast, in Western society, technological intelligence is generally considered as an end in itself.

In Mundy-Castle's (1968, 1974) original formulations, literacy, with its abstractions removed from a social context, was considered a key to the primacy of technological intelligence. Wober (1967) in turn found a connection between print literacy and the independent individual in Nigeria. There, some workers rejected traditional African housing, with its dense, noisy social environment, in favor of quiet European-style housing, with houses separated by yards, because they wanted to be alone to read. These were signs that European literacy had brought with it the stress on solitude and privacy that is characteristic of an independence orientation (Triandis, 1989; Wober, 1967). In this way, technology in general and literacy in particular are seen as forces that moved African society away from its traditional script of interdependence.

The first application of the independence/interdependence conceptualization to development can be seen in work by Barry, Child, and Bacon (1959), social anthropologists who related subsistence mode to socialization values: Independence and self-reliance are valued in hunting/gathering societies, and obedience and social responsibility are valued in societies based on agriculture or animal husbandry. (Tharp's chapter identifies variation on this dimension within agricultural societies based on their particular ecology.)

In psychology, Berry (1967) took up the theme of Barry et al. (1959) and extended it to cognitive socialization (1968, 1971). Hofstede (1980) did a major multinational study of individualism/collectivism, with subsequent theoretical and empirical contributions in various domains and cultures by Shweder and colleagues (Shweder, 1982; Shweder & Bourne, 1982), Triandis and colleagues (Marin & Triandis, 1985; Triandis, 1989; Triandis, Leung, Villareal, & Clack, 1985), Kagitçibasi (1985, 1987), Ito (1985), Sampson (1988), and Markus and Kitayama (1991; Kitayama & Markus, 1992). We decided to use the *independence/interdependence* terminology because of its less ideological and more developmental connotations, in comparison with *individualism/collectivism*.

Independence/Interdependence: A Key
to the Cross-Cultural Roots of Minority Child Development

The contrast between an independence script, on the one hand, and an interdependence script, on the other, was in fact the most useful theoretical framework for integrating the findings on cognitive socialization and development that emerged in our workshop and are presented in this book. It provided a broader framework that encompassed and superseded the contrast between social and technological intelligence.

We hypothesized that a value orientation stressing interdependence would characterize the cultural and cross-cultural roots of socialization practices and developmental goals for the minority groups studied in the chapters that follow: Native Americans, African Americans, African French, Mexican Americans, Asian Americans, and Asian Canadians. A further corollary was that, because of their cultural and cross-cultural roots, the developmental scripts of all of these minority cultures would contrast with the independence scripts that characterize the cultural roots of Euro-American, Euro-Canadian, and European socialization and developmental goals.

At the same time, we also recognized that there is more than one variety of individualism or independence orientation and more than one variety of collectivism or interdependence orientation across cultures. An extremely useful typology of varying relationships between individuals and groups characteristic of both individualistic and collectivistic societies is presented by Kim and Choi (chapter 11, this volume). Their scheme graphically shows that both individuals and collectivities exist in all societies. It also shows how a differential emphasis on the social group or the individual yields collectivistic or individualistic social structures. These social structures are in turn both cause and effect of different patterns of socialization and development, elucidated in the chapters that follow.

Interdependence and Independence as Belief Systems and Cultural Scripts.
In addition to contrasting sets of practices, interdependence and independence are integrated with contrasting philosophies of life. As an example, Kim and Choi contrast Confucianism as a social philosophy in Korea with the dominant social philosophy of the United States. The former is part of a virtue-based society in which virtue is defined as serving others through benevolence, sharing, and caring. The dominant social philosophy in the United States is, in contrast, grounded in self-protection and individual rights.

However, the philosophies are not mutually exclusive, but recognize the constant interplay between individual and group. For example, Confucianism emphasizes serving others precisely because people do not do it naturally (Kim, 1991).

Each philosophy both rationalizes and produces a cultural script concerning favored patterns of thought and action—favored methods of socializing the next generation to attain these cultural ideals. **This is the cultural construction of development. However, the choices of methods of socialization are not infinite, nor are they arbitrary. The importance of the independence/interdependence dimension is shaped by the nature of the human species; the particular point on the continuum is very much influenced by ecology.**

When groups move from a homeland to a new country, the scripts move with them. They become a major source of continuity in the transition. Whether they are in conflict or harmony with the scripts of the new sociocultural environment, the ancestral scripts influence the nature of adaptation to it—the balance of assimilation and accommodation, to use Piaget's terminology. These are major themes of this chapter and the book that follows.

The Nature of Cultural Scripts. In essence, the interdependence and independence scripts have a contrasting cast of characters. Each cast expresses a cultural view of the ideal person and how that person develops.

As we would expect from the agrarian roots of African culture and the history of the interdependence concept, African researchers find evidence of a developmental script that features interdependence. For the people of the Bamenda Grasslands in Cameroon, the very definition of developmental stages is social, as we learn from Nsamenang and Lamb's chapter (chapter 7, this volume). The Bamenda child is seen as being capable of different forms of social interdependence as development progresses. This culturally constructed developmental path contrasts with the motor- and object-oriented stages of Euro-American developmental psychology.

Unlike the Euro-American ideal of the independent self (Kitayama & Markus, 1992; Markus & Kitayama, 1991), the Bamende consider that human offspring need others to attain full selfhood, and that a sense of self cannot be attained without reference to the broader community. "Socialization in the Bamenda Grass Fields, as in much of West Africa, is not organized to train children for individuality outside ancestral culture but primarily to teach responsibility and competence within the family system" (Nsamenang, 1991, p. 448).

Consequences of the Independence and Interdependence Scripts for Socialization and Development

Transmission of Interdependence Through Mother–Child Contact and Communication. In East Asia, Kim and Choi (chapter 11, this volume) describe a primary interdependence between Korean mothers and their children, in which the devoted mother feels at one with her children. This is reflected in mother–child co-sleeping arrangements, which are typical of cultures that stress interdependence rather than independence (Morelli, Rogoff, Oppenheim, & Goldsmith, 1992). Lebra's (chapter 12, this volume) description of mother–child empathy (social closeness) and naturalism (physical closeness) in Japan generalizes this theme to a second East-Asian society.

These modes of physical closeness between mother and child in a society oriented toward interdependence have implications for mother–child communication, as Azuma (1991) points out. He contrasts teaching by osmosis, emphasized in Japan, with verbal teaching, emphasized in the United States. He sees osmosis as based on the closeness that is obtained in a milieu of interdependence, whereas he sees verbal teaching as a method that can bridge the separation between mother and child that occurs in a society oriented toward independence.

Ho (1991) makes a value judgment, seeing verbalization as more important. He criticizes maternal closeness and soothing as dampening verbal assertiveness of East-Asian children.

Also, related to this theme, Blake's chapter (chapter 9) examines the communicational aspects of an interdependence script in her study of early mother–child communication and language development in African-American children. In the context of overall similarities in African-American and Euro-American child language, she finds a greater emphasis on interpersonal and emotional themes in African-American children—an emphasis that reflects their mothers' communication with them.

Mother–Child Communication: Continuity of the Interdependence Scripts Across Societal Contexts. Rabain-Jamin (chapter 8, this volume), echos the interpersonal theme in the way in which African mothers who have immigrated to France communicate with their young children. Most notable is their use of linguistic communication with the young child to establish a social relationship between child and others in the family, both present and absent. Hence, there is a similarity in the social emphasis of African-French mothers, recent immigrants to Paris, and African-American mothers, descendants of slaves who were taken out of Africa centuries ago.

Interdependent Forms of Family Responsibility. The model of the interdependent self (Kitayama & Markus, 1992; Markus & Kitayama, 1991) leads as well to interdependent forms of family responsibility. Unlike the European and Euro-American models of the independent self, responsibility within the family is not limited to doing one's own work. For example, if a girl fails to do her assigned chores, African children say that her sister must do them for her. In contrast, Euro-American children say that it is not right for a girl to have to do her sister's chores and that they would refuse to do so (Mundy-Castle, 1991).

Respect for Elders: An Element of Socialization for Interdependence.   Respect for elders is an important element in the collectivistic or interdependent socialization complex (Triandis, 1989). It provides good examples of cultural continuities and changes from an ancestral culture to minority status in a different nation.

In terms of ecology, respect for elders may have originated under agrarian conditions in which older people controlled resources and there was a desire to maintain the status quo (Collier, 1991). Hence, it is not surprising to find respect for elders as a valued quality, a target of socialization, among the Bamende Grasslands people, an agricultural group residing in Cameroon (Nsamenang & Lamb, chapter 7, this volume), or among Mexicans and Mexican Americans of agrarian origin (Delgado-Gaitan, chapter 3, this volume; Tapia Uribe, LeVine, & LeVine, chapter 2, this volume).

Respect for Elders: A Source of Cultural Continuity in New Societal Contexts. Respect for elders may be less adaptive in an entrepreneurial commercial society that values innovation. Nonetheless, when societies or immigrants move from agriculture to commerce, respect for elders often remains as a value residue of an interdependence script, contrasting with the youth-oriented culture of Euro-American society. As Nsamenang and Lamb (chapter 7, this volume) show, the ideology of respect endures across two generations, despite schooling and other influences of European origin, just as it does across the two generations of Mexican Americans studied by Delgado-Gaitan (chapter 3, this volume).

According to Suina and Smolkin (chapter 6, this volume), respect for elders is an important aspect of Native-American socialization among the Pueblos; Suina eloquently describes the disparate standards by which respect is gained in Native-American and Euro-American cultures. In the former, it is wisdom and knowledge possessed by elders; in the latter, it is educational achievement, which often elevates younger over older.

Respect for elders is similarly important in Ho's chapter (chapter 14, this volume) on the influence of Confucianism on the cognitive socialization of Chinese children. However, in contrast to the others, Ho looks at respect for elders quite negatively. Is this because he is adopting the perspective of Western culture with its value on the creative, independent individual, or does respect actually function differently in Chinese society than it does in Bamenda, Mexican-American, or Native-American societies? Perhaps the multiple cultural perspectives of a postmodern world in general, and Ho's native Hong Kong in particular, simply engender cultural self-criticism, a characteristic of Stevenson's chapter (chapter 15, this volume) as well.

One manifestation of respect for elders is obedience to them, as outlined by Nsamenang and Lamb (chapter 7, this volume) in Cameroon. When a culture that values respect and obedience to authority figures is conquered, this leads to cultural ambiguity, as Tapia Uribe (1991) pointed out with reference to the Spanish conquest of indigenous Mexico. Respect and obedience to the conquerors becomes an undesirable sort of cultural subordination, a collaboration with one's own cultural conquest. These issues are still being sorted out in Mexico, with its important Mestizo (Spanish-Indian) culture.

Family Relations and Interdependence. Extended families are extremely important in cultures oriented around interdependence. Joe (1991) noted that a Navajo child will have multiple mothers, both fictive and real. In the world of the dominant Euro-American society, the extended family of Native Americans serves as a buffer against poverty and isolation. Whereas the Euro-American locates others in the world of professions ("What do you do?"), the Navajo locates others in the familial world ("What clan do you belong to?").

Independence/Interdependence: The Relation Between Culture and Gender. Like Sampson (1988), Lebra (chapter 12, this volume) points out that the interdependence complex, focused as it is on relationality, interdependence, and connection, corresponds to the female qualities conceptualized by Chodorow (1978), Gilligan (1982), and others (Lykes, 1985; Miller, 1976; Noddings, 1984). The individualistic complex, with its emphasis on separation, independence, individuation, and self-creation, corresponds to the masculine culture identified by these theorists. Yet it is also the case that gender roles tend to be most rigidly defined and differentiated in societies oriented toward interdependence. Can we speak of "masculine" and "feminine" cultures? What is the relationship between the "gender" of a culture and its gender role differentiation of individuals? What exactly is the relationship between societal culture and gender culture? How does this relationship affect the socialization process?

Socialization for Survival/Socialization for Educational Development: A Related Value Dimension

Based on studies in five cultures, LeVine and colleagues (LeVine, 1987; Richman et al., 1988) concluded that maternal interaction emphasizing close physical contact occurs in societies with the highest infant mortality (and correspondingly high birthrates), where the immediate perceived need is to protect infants, rather than to educate them. This is infant socialization for survival. Mexico and Kenya provide examples of such societies in their research.

In contrast, maternal interaction emphasizing distal modes of communication, notably vocalization and talking, characterize societies such as the

United States, Sweden, and Italy, societies with low infant mortality and low birthrates, where immediate survival is not usually in question and the perceived need is to invest in a long-term educational process. This is infant socialization for educational development.

Like Azuma, LeVine (1991) also saw a connection between the socialization of independence and an emphasis on verbal communication: Physical separation of infant and mother makes the mother more likely to use verbal rather than tactile communication. In the physical closeness characteristic of interdependence-oriented societies, tactile communication is facilitated.

In Mexico, as in Africa, maternal education appears to act as the trigger, provoking a change from the first mode of socialization to the second (Tapia Uribe, LeVine, & LeVine, chapter 2, this volume; Richman et al., 1988). In the second mode, there is a similarity between the mother's interactive style at home and the teacher's interactive style in formal schooling. Hence, one would expect that the change in maternal interactive style would also have consequences for children's learning and cognitive development. This book explores this issue, and investigates the existence and characteristics of these two styles beyond the infancy period.

In Mexico, Tapia Uribe, LeVine, and LeVine (chapter 2, this volume) describe a historical transition from adaptation to a society in which infant survival depends on maternal care to one in which it depends on use of medical facilities and medical knowledge.

Subsistence/Schooling.   This transition has a number of related elements. It is part of a transition from adaptation to a society in which adult economic survival and reproductive success depend on subsistence skills learned in everyday life to one in which success increasingly depends on the skills acquired in school. As Oloko (chapter 10, this volume) points out, it is also part of a transition from child as subsistence worker and economic asset to child as economic liability because of his or her need for educational resources. Oloko discusses this latter transition in West Africa through her studies of children's street trading and schooling in urban Nigeria.

Our hypothesis is that societies orienting interaction toward survival in infancy stress the development of subsistence survival skills in childhood. We were forced to expand the original value theme concerning survival because we learned that, beyond infancy, it is not a question of an orientation toward survival versus an orientation toward educational development. Instead, it is much more a question of changing the definition of survival skills to move from a subsistence to a market economy (Kim, 1991).

Dissociating High Mother–Infant Contact from Subsistence Socialization.   Ho (chapter 14, this volume) further criticizes the dichotomy of socialization for survival versus socialization for educational development. He points out that, in Asian cultures, babies have a high degree of physical contact with their mothers even though infant survival is no longer a major concern. According to LeVine's theory, the same high-contact mothers should not be oriented toward their children's educational development. But Asian mothers are so oriented. Or, if these mothers are highly educated (as they often are), they should concentrate on verbal communication rather than proximal contact. Yet they remain higher on proximal contact than on vocal contact. Historically, in China, Ho (chapter 14, this volume) points out, "the early concern with survival was to ensure that the hope for later educational achievement by the child could remain alive."

The resolution of this theoretical conflict can be partly resolved with new data from Asia: It is necessary to look at within-culture variability to answer the question. Do more highly educated mothers hold their babies less or talk to them more? Are more fragile babies held more? It would also be useful to compare Asian with Mexican and African mothers with respect to both distal and proximal communication. Perhaps, in the end, the case of China will force us to consider a concern for early survival and later socialization goals theoretically independent although often empirically linked. This example illustrates how even broad comparative study (the five-cultures study of Richman et al., 1988) sometimes requires additional cultures (China, in this instance) to make sure that seemingly universal principles of causation are not an artifact of particular sociocultural contexts.

Ho challenges LeVine and colleagues' formulation in another way. He demonstrates that, in China, maternal education has no relationship to children's educational socialization. My interpretation of this interesting paradox is that, for Mexicans of primarily Indian descent, as for Africans, school-based education is not part of traditional, indigenous practices or values. Instead, it was an imposition of colonial conquest. Therefore, school experience is required for mothers to develop the value of formal education, which is not part of their indigenous cultures. In China, in contrast, scholarship and education are indigenous to the culture, and therefore are instilled in all members of society at all social levels, independent of their particular experience with formal education. This example illustrates how relationships between socialization variables and outcomes vary as a function of sociocultural history. This illustrates the importance of the historical perspective, all too often missing from developmental science.

Schooling and the Independent Individual

There is another fundamental connection between our two value dimensions. As John and Beatrice Whiting, pioneers in the cross-cultural study of socialization, pointed out in a seminar many years ago, schooling entails and engenders individualism because in school assessment, cooperation receives powerful negative sanctions: It is called cheating. Consequently, there seems to be a link between school-based skill development and individualism on the one hand versus subsistence skill socialization and interdependence on the other.

An illustration of the oppositional nature of schooling and the interdependence script comes from Africa. There, informal education emphasizing subsistence skills and the sharing of resources among the extended family is the indigenous tradition. Schooling, with its emphasis on developing the potential of separate individuals, was of foreign origin, imposed by Africa's European conquerors. Empirical evidence of this opposition has been provided by Dozon (1986), who found that school attendance develops aspirations to be released from the duties of the lineage (extended family).

Similarly, Nsamenang (1991) noted that, in Cameroon, schooling, in the absence of suitable jobs, causes alienation from the family—an inability to make the traditional contribution to family welfare through subsistence work. Based on her research in Nigeria, Oloko (chapter 10, this volume) observes that it is the parents with the most formally educated children who are most deprived. Unlike children educated informally according to the indigenous tradition, they do not take care of their parents when they are old and sick. This most certainly is one of the social costs of the independent individual.

Another example comes from Mexico, where Tapia Uribe, LeVine, and LeVine (chapter 2, this volume) inform us that school attendance is seen as a challenge to parental authority. Finally, Joe (chapter 5 this volume) notes that when Native-American children were, often forcibly, sent to government boarding schools, or when they attended missionary schools, they were taught to be ashamed of their own culture. Therefore, they returned from these schools lacking basic attributes of Native-American culture, such as respect for elders.

School-Based Literacy Undermines Interdependence. The fundamental commitment of schooling to print literacy provides a more intrinsic factor in the opposition between schooling and an interdependence value orientation. Suina (1991) gives shape to Mundy-Castle's (1974) insight that literacy undermines social intelligence, an important component of the interdependence script. In the Pueblo world view, parents and grandparents are the repositories of knowledge, and this fact provides a social connection between the generations. The introduction of encyclopedias, reference books, and the like undermines "the very fiber of the connectedness" (Suina, 1991, p. 153). Things, rather than people, become the authorities for knowledge.

Or, following Kim and Choi's chapter (chapter 11, this volume), we would connect reading and writing to the fact that, in individualistic societies, people have many encounters and relations with people whom they do not know. Such encounters, along with the ideology of individualism, are typical of a market economy. Reading in school is almost always an encounter with an unknown person: the author. **Hence, school-based literacy, independent of the particular arrangements in the classroom or the culture-specific goals of schooling, undermines an interdependence developmental script by undermining known people as sources of knowledge.**

Schooling Undermines the Family as an Educational Institution. Closely related is the fact that, in Pueblo society as in many societies in which formal schooling is not part of indigenous education, learning takes place by being around adult family members who are carrying out essential tasks (Suina, 1991); this is what Lave and Wenger (1991) called *legitimate peripheral participation.* It is the apprenticeship model of learning. A job structure based on the credentials of formal schooling undermines the economic importance of apprenticeship and reduces the amount of time spent with adult family members, thus undermining the educational role and life importance of close familial and community relationships.

As Suina (1991) pointed out, for the Pueblo learning is not separated from the larger social context. This is what Tharp (chapter 4, this volume) calls a wholistic style of learning: going from whole to part. He contrasts this style with the analytic style assumed and developed in Euro-American schools, in which knowledge progresses from part to whole. Phonetic literacy, in which wholes are constructed out of the atoms that are letters, is the paradigm case.

These contrasting learning styles can operate at various levels from perceptual problem solving to real-life activities. In some of Tharp's examples, wholism is manifest by placing a technical skill, such as making moccasins, in social-historical context. Mundy-Castle (1991) found that perceptual wholism, as assessed in Africa by the Gestalt Continuation Test, is transformed into analyticity by school-based literacy. Thus, *technological intelligence*, as defined by Mundy-Castle (1968, 1974), is analytic thinking removed from its larger social context.

Indeed, wholism seems to be a cognitive outgrowth of an interdependence script. Kim (1991) pointed out that it is also typical of the Confucian theory of knowledge. According to Confucianism, one starts inquiry into any subject by understanding its relationship to one's ancestors and one's family before proceeding to the analytic level. At the same time, Confucian societies are a sort of intermediate case: The impersonality of textual authority has been traditionally used to support philosophy of interdependence.

The Development of Logical Argumentation Undermines Respect for Authority. Delgado-Gaitan's (chapter 3, this volume) observations point to other ways in which the development of school skills may undermine the requirements of culturally defined social skills. For example, she shows that the development of critical thinking, which requires children to articulate and even argue their views with older family members, may be in conflict with, and therefore undermine, respect for elders—an important value in the culture of Mexican-American immigrants.

From the point of view of mainstream values for cognitive socialization, American teachers might (and have been known to) criticize Mexican-American children as relatively nonverbal and inarticulate. However, what Delgado-Gaitan's sensitive ethnographic observations show is that this communicative style does not result from a negative practice. Instead, it is the result of a positive value—respect for elders—stemming from the Mexican culture of origin.

Schooling Reduces Willingness to Share Resources with the Extended Family. Oloko (chapter 10, this volume) articulates an important paradox with her data, one that must also be operative for a large number of Mexican Americans, particularly immigrants: Although schooling becomes increasingly important to survival in an urban, industrial society, schooling by itself decreases a person's willingness to share school's economic rewards with an extended family group. Thus, school reduces the size of the functional social unit from the extended family to the nuclear family and, perhaps ultimately, to the independent individual.

Oloko found that Nigerian children's subsistence street-trading activities counteracted this tendency: Highly educated adults who had been street traders as children more consistently maintained that rewards from professional progress should be used to fulfill obligations to the extended family than did other professional adults who lacked the trading experience. At the same time, Oloko found that, under modern urban conditions, child trading may undermine school progress.

Hence, it may be impossible to attain the rewards of formal schooling while retaining the willingness to share these rewards broadly. For minority families who look upon a child's education as an investment for the whole extended family, this conclusion points up a paradox: The very process of becoming highly educated may make the recipient of the investment much less willing to share his or her fruits with the extended family.

Ways to Integrate Socialization for Schooling and Orientation to Interdependence

Nonetheless, other relationships between the two value dimensions are possible. Although West African and Mexican cultures combine an interdependence orientation with an orientation toward subsistence survival, contrasting in both dimensions with the dominant Euro-American model, the East Asian cultures combine an interdependence orientation with an orientation toward educational development, thus providing a midway point between the West African and Mexican models on the one hand, and the Euro-American model on the other hand. Given the oppositional nature of schooling and the interdependence script, what are some means by which an integration can take place?

Positional and Empathy Socialization. Lebra (chapter 12, this volume) elaborates empathy and positional socialization as central to the socialization of Japanese children. Both are means that involve and imply social interdependence. Whereas empathy is emphasized at infancy, positional socialization becomes increasingly important as children get older. Positional socialization involves verbal instruction about one's position in every social situation, schooling being one such situation. As Azuma (chapter 13, this volume) notes, it therefore can be used to socialize the independent and individual achievement required by school. Takanishi (chapter 17, this volume) points out that positional socialization among Japanese Americans may make Western schooling intrinsically compatible with Japanese culture because the desirability of adapting to each distinct social situation is built into positional socialization.

But empathy socialization can also be used to encourage academic achievement. For example, Hieshima (chapter 16, this volume) conducted an interview with a Japanese American child in which she asked, "If you brought home a bad report card, what would your parents do?" The reply was: "Oh, I don't know that they would do anything because they would know how bad I would feel already."

Emphasis on Social Skills. LeVine (1991) pointed out that Japanese education, unlike education in the United States, is based on the premise that social skills and social relations with the teacher must precede school-based learning. This premise provides another mechanism for an integration between an interdependence developmental script and a strong orientation toward schooling.

For example, Catherine Lewis, a cross-cultural researcher specializing in Japan, found that Japanese preschool education is based on the

> sense that there are a variety of social skills that have to come first before you can focus fruitfully . . . on the intellectual development of the child. . . . In almost every Japanese setting where education goes on, . . . the greatest attention is first given to the building of the teaching-learning relationship, and, secondly, to making that relationship motivating for the child, and only after that to the actual . . . promotion of cognitive development. (LeVine, 1991, p. 92)

Given the high level of educational attainment in Japan, LeVine went on to speculate about the validity of our cultural assumptions about what is necessary in infancy and early childhood for children to become good learn-ers in school.

Familial and Community Goals for Formal Education.   Schneider, Hieshi-ma, Lee, and Plank (chapter 16, this volume) point to the intrinsic respect for education in Chinese, Korean, and Japanese cultures and the continuity of this respect in Chinese, Korean, and Japanese Americans. However, these authors note that, in the Asian and Asian-American contexts, a major goal of education is to bring honor to the family. Suina and Smolkin (chapter 6, this volume) note that the Pueblo Indians see schoolwork as providing pride, cohesion, and future sustenance to the group as a whole. Tapia Uribe (1991) also indicated that the goal of schooling in Mexico is to provide aid to the group as a whole. Such goals insert socialization for educational development into an interdependence developmental script.

Ho (chapter 14, this volume) makes an argument for a style in Asian class-rooms that reflects the respect for authority typical of an interdependence orientation. He views this respect as emanating from the Confucian tradition of filial piety. In this view, schooling is not intrinsically individualistic; schools can be either individualistic or collectivistic, depending on their social or-ganization.

Based on his research on elementary classrooms in China, Japan, and the United States, Stevenson (chapter 15, this volume) disagrees with Ho that Asian teachers operate in an authoritarian way. As Stevenson points out, a possi-ble reason for the conflict between himself and Ho is that he and his col-leagues have studied elementary education, whereas Ho has focused on secondary education. Each researcher may simply be viewing a different point on a single developmental trajectory.

In societies oriented toward an interdependence script, children start out life as individuals but are expected to become increasingly integrated with the group and its social structure as they grow (cf. Rabain, 1979). Hence, it is possible that, in East Asia, elementary school children may be treated more as individuals, whereas secondary school students may be treated more as subordinates in hierarchical power relations with the teacher. Perhaps Steven-son has studied an earlier, more individualistic period of a person's develop-ment, whereas Ho has studied a later stage of greater interdependence orien-tation.

Suina and Smolkin's (chapter 6, this volume) analysis of Pueblo classrooms offers ideas for pedagogical techniques that can introduce interdependence values into school learning. Opportunities to make decisions by consensus rather than by vote, opportunities for one child to help another in learning, and opportunities for collaborative projects are some examples they provide.

In summary, the East-Asian and Native-American cases provide some cul-tural means by which the school with its emphasis on individual achievement and competition can become integrated into an interdependence-oriented value system: (a) Education can be seen as a means to bring honor and aid to the family rather than the individual, (b) socialization to teachers' requirements for student behavior can be part of a positional socialization process in which children are taught their roles in every socially defined relationship, and (c) student behavior can become assimilated into the Confucian role of filial piety as development progresses into the secondary school years.

Bringing an Interdependence Developmental Script to an Independence-Oriented Society: Adaptation and Biculturalism

Lambert, Hammers, and Frasure-Smith (1979) found in a cross-national study that childrearing values persist over several generations, even when samples from cultures oriented toward interdependence raise their children in a society favoring independence as its developmental script. Schneider, Hieshima, Lee, and Plank (chapter 16, this volume) also point to the continuity of the emphasis on family interdependence in Japanese Americans, despite three generations of adults growing up in an individualistic country. The findings of continuity in socialization values despite new economic and ecological conditions in the United States validates our decision to focus on value orientations and cultural scripts in studying cross-cultural roots of minority child development.

Nonetheless, the behavioral expression of ancestral continuities becomes increasingly constrained over the generations, as Delgado-Gaitan's (chapter 3, this volume) comparison of immigrant and first-generation Mexican-American parents shows. This is because there is a genuine value conflict between the independence script required for educational and economic success and the interdependence script required for social success in the family. Delgado-Gaitan shows how, in the parenting style of the first generation of Mexican Americans who are raised and educated in the United States, critical thinking, necessary for school success, expands its sphere of influence. At the same time, respect becomes correlatively more restricted in its contexts of socially required operation. In essence, her comparative study of family communication patterns in immigrant and first-generation Mexican-American families documents the emergence of successful bicultural socialization.

We learn that the same basic conflict between independence and interdependence occurs as a result of conquest (Suina and Joe's chapters on Native-American socialization), of immigration now (Delgado-Gaitan's chapter on Mexican-American socialization, Kim and Choi's chapter on Korean-American and Korean-Canadian socialization, Rabain-Jamin's chapter on African-French socialization), and of immigration in the past (Schneider, Hieshima, Lee, & Plank's study of Japanese-American socialization).

When interdependently oriented people are minority members of a dominant society oriented toward independence, an unequal meeting of values occurs. There is a tendency for members of the dominant individualistic society to evaluate negatively members of a minority whose behavior, goals, and attitudes reflect an emphasis on interdependence. For example, the dominant Euro-American society treats Native Americans as hampered by communal values (Joe, 1991).

Furthermore, in the case of involuntary minorities, discussed in the next section, societal force is often used to weaken or eradicate collective social structures. Joe reported that there have been many outside pressures to transform the extended family systems of Native Americans into a nuclear family system. For example, historically there has been no recognition of the rights of extended family members in Native-American adoption or foster cases. Native-American tribes have resisted the imposition of individualistic social norms and structures. One example of successful resistance is the relatively recent Indian Child Welfare Act, which recognizes the Native-American child as a member of an extended family and community in adoption and foster care cases.

Cultures of Origin: A Moving Target

Ancestral cultures do not stand still; the immigrants of today are not necessarily coming with the same cultural background as their compatriots did in past generations. This is a particularly compelling point for African Americans, most of whose ancestors were brought to the United States as slaves hundreds of years ago; they came from societies organized around subsistence farming.

Current immigrants from African countries such as Nigeria reflect very different conditions. In fact, they are coming from a society that is very much in transition from a subsistence orientation to a schooling orientation. For this reason, Nigerian mothers, for example, do not all agree on what the most adaptive skills are. Oloko (chapter 10, this volume) notes that some busy Nigerian mothers criticize their children's attempt to study, demanding that children terminate "abstract studies" and attend to "sustenance matters"; this view comes out of a subsistence mentality and does not at all agree with the official view of the modernizing nation–state. It is a working-class view in a society that has already created a middle class that places a strong value on formal education.

The same issue of cultural change is also stressed by Tapia Uribe, LeVine, and LeVine (chapter 2, this volume). They point out that the Mexican immigrants of today have more schooling than immigrants of previous generations. Thus, these immigrants come with greater social capital to facilitate their adjustment. This may be one reason why the immigrant parents studied by Delgado-Gaitan (chapter 3, this volume) have taken a more active role vis-à-vis the schools than did immigrants of earlier generations.

A historical perspective on the immigration process, such as Delgado-Gaitan takes in her chapter, is extremely important. In considering her analysis of two generations of Mexican immigrants to Carpinteria, California, along with emigration from the Mexican perspective (Tapia Uribe, LeVine, & LeVine, chapter 2, this volume), it is clear that, as LeVine (1991) pointed out, nothing stands still: Carpinteria changes, Mexico changes, and the immigrants change. But once immigrants have arrived in their new country, their ancestral culture can freeze and fossilize when there is a lack of further contact.

SOCIAL HISTORY AND UNEQUAL SOCIAL POWER

Historical Power Relations Between Majority and Minority Groups

In contrast to the other chapter authors, Ogbu (chapter 18, this volume) points out the role of an entirely different factor in minority child development—the history and nature of power relations between minority and majority. Ogbu reminds one that study of the cultural roots of minority child development must add to, **but not replace**, an appreciation of the importance of the historical power relations between minority and majority groups. Even with an appreciation of diverse cultural roots, minority children must still cope with the effects of varying sorts of sociopolitical relations with the dominant majority group.

As Ogbu points out, the origin and therefore nature of these relations is not a function of minority culture per se. Instead, it varies with each minority–majority group pair. For example, West-Indian immigrants have one relationship with majority culture in the United States, and a quite different one in the United Kingdom. Coping with these unequal power relations, whatever their precise nature, exerts a tremendous influence on minority child development.

Involuntary minority groups (those who enter a country through conquest, slavery, or colonization) tend to define themselves and their cultures in opposition to the cultural values of the majority. This is because conquerors, enslavers, and colonizers try to wipe out indigenous cultures. In reaction, involuntary minorities feel they cannot adopt any of the majority's ways without losing their own. In this they differ from voluntary minorities, whose cultures are tolerated by the societies to which they immigrate. African Americans (through slavery), Native Americans (through conquest), and, to some extent, Mexican Americans (through conquest of the American Southwest from Mexico) fall under the definition of *involuntary minorities* (Ogbu, chapter 18, this volume).

Involuntary Minority Status Undermines Socialization for Schooling

Ogbu's (chapter 18, this volume) formulation provides an explanation for why those writing about Native-American education (Suina & Smolkin, chapter 6, this volume; Tharp, chapter 4, this volume) emphasize the importance of creating a culturally compatible learning environment in U.S. schools, whereas those writing about Asian-American education are either unconcerned about this issue (Schneider, Hieshima, Lee, & Plank, chapter 16, this volume) or feel that the cultural differences of the North-American classroom exert a positive influence on the learning and educational achievement of Asian-American students (Ho, chapter 14, this volume).

The explanation is that Native Americans are involuntary minorities, whereas Asian Americans are voluntary. Because early Mexican Americans experienced the conquest of the U.S. Southwest, whereas later generations were defined as voluntary immigrants, one would expect the Mexican-American perspective to fall somewhere in between on the issue of cultural compatibility. This is exactly what we find in the chapter by Delgado-Gaitan (chapter 3, this volume), where she stresses the role of community organizations as mediators between Euro-American schools and Mexican-American parents.

Voluntary immigrants are secure in their ethnic identities but want to learn the new ways that will enable them to take advantage of opportunities in the new country (Ogbu, chapter 18, this volume). Unlike the experience of involuntary minorities, such as African Americans, Native Americans, and Mexican Americans, the dominant culture has never actively interceded to eradicate the culture and language of voluntary immigrants. For example, Native-American children were forcibly put into government boarding schools, a major goal of which was to eradicate Native culture and languages. For this reason, the most successful schooling for Native Americans has been their own community-run institutions.

Therefore, involuntary minorities have strong historical justification for the belief that their ancestral or ethnic culture and Euro-American culture are mutually exclusive. Here is an important source of the oppositional frame of reference of involuntary minorities identified by Ogbu (chapter 18, this volume).

CHANGING PARADIGMS: TOWARD A SCIENCE OF MULTIPLE PERSPECTIVES

Objectivity or Perspective?

In developmental psychology, as in psychology as a whole, we have, as part of our attempt to conform to the scientific method, ratified and reified objectivity as opposed to subjectivity. A corollary of this scientific value is that the less involved you are in a psychological phenomenon, the more accurately you can study it. The absence of involvement allows you to be objective.

However, this view is naive at best. In studying their own culture, psychologists or other social scientists are **unacknowledged** insiders. Acknowledging the insider's perspective, we see that the advantage for research is that methodological procedures and interpretations of data are unconsciously adapted to the culture of the subjects. It follows that an insider's perspective is essential to the valid description of socialization and development. As a consequence, we have included an insider's perspective on socialization and development in every culture and society represented in this book. Our goal is to redress the situation in which many groups and societies in the world have been studied almost exclusively by European and Euro-American outsiders.

But the insider's perspective is not perfect either; it has its own weaknesses. Its disadvantage is that it breeds a lack of awareness of culture. What is culturally specific to one's homeland is taken as universal. Kim (1991) pointed out that for Japanese in Japan, Americans have culture but they themselves do not. For Americans, Japanese have culture but they themselves do not. Kim pointed further to a need to look at U.S. culture and see how ethnic cultures interact with it to produce either adaptation or problem behavior.

> It is only when Americans realize that what they believe in is cultural, then they can recognize what African Americans or Native Americans are experiencing is also cultural. However, when Americans feel that their standard or their view is not cultural and is universal, and that it is the Japanese Americans or Native Americans who are clinging to culture, then . . . there is a problem of discourse. (Kim, 1991, p. 187)

Lebra (1991) reminded us that Euro-American culture is not a single monolith and that there is a need to study the variability among the various Euro-American ethnic groups.

When psychologists leave their own culture to study another, the lack of acknowledgment of culture generally leads to disaster. All too often we are completely unaware that we are imposing assumptions about conditions, values, and pathways of socialization and development that are foreign to the people being studied. This point holds as much for studying different ethnic groups within the researcher's own society as it does for development in another country.

However, when an outsider goes through the process of getting to know another culture by participating in it, the outsider's viewpoint has its own special strengths. As cultural insiders, we take for granted basic cultural assumptions about life in general and socialization in particular. Having to adapt to these differences, the outsider is forced to perceive and recognize them. Because of his or her comparative perspective, the outsider sometimes identifies patterns that an insider would not see. Two excellent examples in the present volume are Lebra's (chapter 12, this volume) view of male adolescence as a trope or model for U.S. relationships in general, and Ogbu's (chapter 18, this volume) distinction between the psychology of voluntary and involuntary minorities.

For Lebra, an anthropologist and Japanese immigrant to the United States, adolescence in the United States revealed itself in this culturally central position **by contrast with** the mother–child relationship in Japan, which she analyzes as the culturally central model for Japanese relationships. For Lebra, male adolescence in the United States actualizes and symbolizes both the establishment of independence through rebellion from the preceding generation and the priority of the romantic couple relationship over the intergenerational relationship between parents and children.

This state of affairs contrasts strongly with the mother–child relationship as cultural trope in Japan, where intergenerational continuity and intergenerational relationships have cultural priority. I add that it is perhaps the history of the United States, as a country of immigrants who in fact do leave their parents thousands of miles behind, that both requires and supports adolescent separation as a central cultural model (Lebra, chapter 12).

For Ogbu, an anthropologist and Nigerian immigrant to the United States, knowledge of his own society provided the insight that explanations for low African American school achievement popular in the 1970s—poverty and low parental education—could not be true. He knew that, in Africa in his generation, almost all school children were much poorer than African Americans and had parents who had never even been to school. Yet these economically disadvantaged children of unschooled parents achieved in school perfectly well; African universities were full of such students. For Ogbu, these facts required a new theory of minority school achievement. His resulting explanation of low African-American achievement was the following: The United States possesses a caste-like system that makes formal education worth much less in terms of societal rewards for African Americans than for Euro-Americans (Ogbu, 1978). No U.S. social scientist had ever come up with the notion of caste-like minorities. I believe that it was Ogbu's perspective, both as a Nigerian and as a deeply knowledgeable outsider living in the United States, that enabled him to develop this theoretical model.

Furthermore, his perspective as a Nigerian led him to realize that the same minority group will behave very differently depending on whether its origin in a particular country is voluntary or involuntary. Hence, the children of a Nigerian immigrant will act like voluntary immigrants in the United States; they will act like involuntary immigrants (with corresponding problems in school achievement) in Great Britain where their presence stems from British colonization of their homeland. Ogbu's knowledge of Nigeria, which sends immigrants to both the United States and Britain, provided a perspective from which to recognize such a difference.

Ogbu's insight makes an extremely important theoretical point: **The same historical culture has quite different consequences for socialization and development, depending on the history of intergroup relations in its current societal context** (cf. Cocking, chapter 19, this volume). Culture not only *is* context; it *has* context as well.

From Introspectionism to Multiple Perspectives

In psychology, introspectionism was rejected many years ago because there was no way of knowing if what was introspected was "true." However, it is now possible to see that the introspective viewpoint is simply the insider's perspective. In postmodern thinking, we have reached the point where we see that there is not a single privileged viewpoint, either the objective or the subjective, the outsider or the insider. There are simply different perspectives, each one with its own psychological reality. The postmodern condition of cultural mixture and fragmentation has led to a recognition in various fields that what has been reified as **the** viewpoint is but one of multiple potential perspectives.

A complete picture of socialization and development must describe, relate, and synthesize these different viewpoints. Therefore, it is of theoretical importance that, in this volume, both insiders' and outsiders' perspectives are brought to bear on all of the groups whose development and socialization we consider.

At the point where we recognize the psychological reality and scientific validity of multiple perspectives, we also have a theoretically inspired rationale for eliminating a colonialistic science of development in which a dominant perspective defines normative development (Cocking, chapter 19, this volume) in all cultures and all countries. We have a principled theoretical reason for replacing a single monolithic scientific view with a multiperspectival, multicultural view of development and its socialization. **Multiple perspectives do not signal the end of science, a popular view of the cultural criticism school (e.g., Gergen, 1982). They simply signal the beginning of a new scientific paradigm in which the perspectives of researchers and subjects are specified and studied, not assumed.**

IMPLICATIONS FOR THEORY AND PRACTICE

Toward a Model of Minority Child Development

We hope that further understanding of the cross-cultural roots of minority child development will help society and research move (a) away from a deficit model of minority child development, in which differences are seen as deficiencies (Cole & Bruner, 1971); and (b) beyond a coping model of minority child development, in which differences are seen simply as adaptations to unfavorable conditions in the dominant society (McLoyd, 1990; Ogbu, chapter 18, this volume). Even more fundamental is a diversity model (Cole & Bruner, 1971; Rogoff & Morelli, 1989), in which learning differences are viewed as rooted in historic cultural values that need not be assimilated out of existence but, instead, can make an important contribution to a diverse society.

Implications for Research on Minority Child Development

The juxtaposition of development in ethnic groups in the United States and in their regions of origin suggests a new strategy for studying development and socialization in minority groups: Begin with knowledge of values and cognitive socialization in the cultures of origin. The chapters that follow suggest many specific hypotheses to which this strategy can be applied. It is hoped that an important function of these investigations will be to stimulate further research, including longitudinal studies of immigration in both country of origin and country of destination. An example of such research is the current project of Luis Laosa, in which he follows Puerto Rican immigrants, longitudinally, back and forth from Puerto Rico to the New York metropolitan area.

The further hope is that research carried out in the perspective developed in this chapter and this book will be a force for social change in the relations between majority and minority groups. If a more accurate picture of cultural roots succeeds in changing the way members of culturally dominant majorities view members of less powerful minority groups, at the same time modifying the way that members of both majority and minority groups view themselves, then we will also have changed the evaluation and definition of each group's worth in the dominant society.

Implications for Education

An understanding of the positive sources of learning and cognitive development fostered by diverse cultural groups can help schools to appreciate, utilize, and adapt to the strengths that children from various groups bring with them to their educations. New knowledge of cultural roots will enable members of the dominant society to understand and appreciate the distinctive styles of cognitive socialization and learning in minority groups, and vice versa. Finally, the contrasts between the sociocultural roots of different minority groups in the United States should offer insight into the different cognitive and learning adaptations they have made to the majority culture in the United States.

Mental Health Implications

Ethnic Identity and Cross-Cultural Respect.   From the perspective of mental health, an understanding of positive cultural sources of learning and cognitive styles has the potential to improve self-esteem. In more general terms, an understanding of cultural roots creates pride in oneself and one's group. Indeed, this is the import of Jesse Jackson's suggestion that the term *Black* be replaced by *African American*, a term that emphasizes the relevance of the African roots (Njeri, 1989).

The oppositional identity of involuntary minorities articulated by Ogbu (chapter 18, this volume) cries out for a change in society that would allow members of these groups to develop positive ethnic identities. Suina and Smolkin (chapter 6, this volume) and Joe (chapter 5, this volume) make a case for the value of bicultural identities for Native-American children and adults. Harrison, Wilson, Pine, Chan, and Buriel (1990) found that parents of successful African American children emphasized ethnic pride in their socialization practices.

Increased knowledge of their cultural roots on the part of both members of the minorities and members of the dominant society is a possible way out of the impasse of an oppositional identity and a step toward the recognition of positive bicultural identities. It is hoped that the exploration of cultural roots in the countries of ancestral origin contained in this volume will support involuntary minorities in developing sources of underlying cultural identity that can ultimately replace the oppositional identities that currently hold so much power.

For voluntary minorities, it is also important to mental health to maintain pride in the culture of origin, rather than erasing ethnic identity in an assimilation or accommodation process (depending on your perspective), as Kim and Choi (chapter 11, this volume) demonstrate for Korean Americans and Korean Canadians.

It is equally important that the exploration of cultural roots of minority development lead to increased respect for minority cultures and peoples and increased awareness of their own cultures by dominant majorities. This exploration of cultural roots should also help researchers build positive models of cultural factors in minority child development, factors that are protective even when development takes place in an unfavorable or hostile milieu of the dominant majority.

Mental Health, Culture Conflict, and Biculturalism.   On a more pragmatic level, continuity with the ancestral orientation toward interdependence can be experienced as conflict with the dominant culture. For example, I have seen Asian American psychology students at the University of California-Los Angeles (UCLA) who are very confused by their parents' desire to choose a field of study for them based on the economic needs of the whole family. To bring up a child to contribute economically to the whole family is a normal developmental goal in a culture oriented around an interdependence developmental script. However, the home culture of these students is surrounded by a dominant society with a strong independence script. In line with this independence script, they witness their Euro-American peers struggling to choose a field of study that will bring out their own individual potential and fulfill their own unique desires. As one UCLA undergraduate exposed to an interdependence script at home observed, "individualism is a lot easier." It is also socially dominant in the United States. Hence, there is a real internal conflict, the sources of which are not always well understood by the person experiencing such conflict.

For example, Asian students often feel selfish for desiring to choose a field of study. They do not realize that what is labeled **selfishness** in their subculture is valued as **self-actualization** in the dominant society. In other words, they do not realize that they are caught in a conflict between two value systems. The "culture-free" psychology that they have studied has certainly not helped make them aware of value conflicts.

Sometimes such value conflicts occur because a value that is adaptive for socialization under one set of societal conditions becomes maladaptive under another. Kim's comparative study of Korean parental strictness in its society of origin (i.e., Korea) versus two societies of immigration (i.e., the United States and Canada) provides just such an example (Kim & Choi, chapter 11, this volume). Kim's findings show that a collectivistic childrearing practice such as strictness can become maladaptive under new societal conditions. Because of altered family conditions (the lesser involvement of working mothers) and altered societal context (the individualistic value of independence), parental control, a positive feature of the parent–child relationship in Korea, turns into a negative for the adolescent children of Korean immigrants to the United States and Canada.

Sometimes the trick, as Takanishi (chapter 17, this volume) points out, seems to be to embody old values in new practices that are better adapted to current societal conditions; Takanishi draws on examples of a high degree of "togetherness" in Japanese-American family activities (Schneider, Hieshima, Lee, & Plank, chapter 16, this volume) to illustrate her point.

Sometimes the interdependence script from the ancestral culture works better in the context of immigration than do individualistic ones. Takanishi (chapter 17, this volume) points out that Asian-American parents provide the monitoring and support into adolescence that Euro-American early adolescents report that they would like. Correlated with this guidance are fewer adolescent problems. Tapia Uribe, LeVine, and Levine (chapter 2, this volume) note the network of familial and community support that is so important to the survival and success of many Mexican immigrants.

As Suina and Smolkin (chapter 6, this volume), Joe (chapter 5, this volume), and Kim and Choi (chapter 11, this volume) conclude in their chapters on Pueblo, Navajo, and Korean–American/Canadian samples, respectively, neither the giving up of ancestral cultures through complete accommodation to the dominant culture nor the preservation of the ancestral culture through isolation and rejection of the dominant culture leads to good mental health outcomes. Therefore, all of these authors advocate a bicultural adjustment for minorities. Successful biculturalism implies that ancestral values are retained, often embodied in new practices, as new values and practices are learned and incorporated into life in general and socialization in particular. With respect to Native Americans, Joe (chapter 5, this volume) advocates mastering the technology and social means of Euro-American lifeways, while retaining Native American values. As an ultimate ideal, Ho (chapter 14, this volume) sees a biculturalism in which both cultures are equal as a mode for the future. The relationship of English and French culture in Canada might be considered such a model.

When pressure from an individualistic surround leads to the loss of a way of living and raising children based on interdependence, what is the psychological price? This is a question that has received very little attention because almost all research is done from the perspective of the dominant society. It is an issue that begs for future research.

Implications for Developmental Theory

By and large, the theoretical implications revolve around a single major theme: The need to recognize that patterns and norms of development previously thought to be universal are often specific to Euro-American culture, the culture of most developmental scientists. The sections that follow list and discuss a number of conceptual steps that will begin to remove this ethnocentric bias. To do so, there must first be scientific recognition that different cultures value different developmental trajectories and that different trajectories arise as adaptations to different ecological niches (cf. Super & Harkness, 1986). Development cannot be understood apart from developmental history.

Independence and Formal Education Are Culture-Specific Goals of Development. We have forgotten fundamental underlying variables in our developmental theories precisely because one pole of the dimension became like the fish's water: assumed but not recognized. Therefore, we have failed to realize that there was another pole, mistaking a variable for a constant. Thus independence and school-based cognitive development have been assumed to be universal goals of development. Our developmental theories have not really considered the opposite poles of interdependence and subsistence skills. This situation has led to developmental theories that purported to be universal, but were really culture specific.

Most devastating to developmental theory, value judgments concerning the superiority of the independent individual became reified in supposedly value-free science. For example, respect for elders and the socialization practices that support it have been given a negative evaluation in developmental psychology as lack of initiative and authoritarian childrearing (cf. Baumrind, 1980). They have not been considered as simply derivatives of a contrasting value system—an interdependence developmental script.

LeVine (1991) pointed out that our cultural script of the independent individual has led to serious scientific misconceptions: Many researchers have assumed that certain kinds of autonomy must be achieved at certain age levels by all humans when the standards actually derive from their own culture.

> We are beginning to realize that a lot of these things which are supposed to be universal are actually culture specific, and without pathological consequences if they deviate from the contemporary American norms. . . . We are faced with a very serious . . . scientific problem . . . of trying to disentangle . . . what comes to us from . . . the folk culture of intellectuals in our present culture in America from what is a property of some general psychological or social process. (LeVine, 1991, pp. 88–89)

As an example of this problem, LeVine (1991) went on to point out the cultural bias in the psychological concepts of field independence and field dependence. On the perceptual level, field independent people are more able to extract information from an embedding context than are field dependent people. On the social level, field independent people have greater autonomy than field dependent people, who are more interpersonally dependent or sensitive (Pascual-Leone, 1989). Instead of being recognized as two equal but different cognitive styles, field independence is evaluated positively, whereas field dependence is evaluated negatively. This judgment is not based on a universal principle, nor is it objective. Instead, it is based on the cultural script of the independent individual. It has been suggested that the culture-specific negative connotations of field dependence could be avoided by relabeling that pole of the dimension *field sensitivity*.

Tharp (chapter 4, this volume) does something like this when he conceptualizes a similar dimension as wholism versus analyticity. Navajo culture evinces a preference for learning that starts with the whole and moves to the parts of any particular phenomenon; Euro-American culture evinces the reverse preference. Separation of parts is precisely what defines the field independent cognitive style. However, unlike the field independence/dependence concept, wholism/analyticity is not imbued with a culturally biased preference for one end of the dimension over the other.

When our developmental research assumes the developmental goal of an independent individual, it has implications in the topics we select for study and those we neglect. For example, the developmental goal of an independent individual is manifest when we study the development of self-regulation rather than other regulation, of independence training rather than interdependence training, when we study the child's acquisition of information from books rather than from people, or when we concentrate our study of communicative development on a dyad in which the mother focuses exclusively on the child (cf. Ochs & Schieffelin, 1984) rather than placing the child in a communication network that includes a third party (cf. Rabain-Jamin, chapter 8, this volume). In other words, the developmental goal of an independent individual permeates the very definition of research problems, suffusing our supposedly value-neutral science.

Cultural Values Are Internalized, Such That They Travel with People into New or Changed Societal Contexts.   For example, Mexican immigrants bring the value of respect with them from Mexico (Delgado-Gaitan, chapter 3, this volume). Native Americans have maintained this value centuries after their conquest (Joe, chapter 5, this volume). Immigrants from China, Japan, and Korea bring an orientation toward interdependence and a high value on schooling with them to the United States (Kim & Choi, chapter 11, this volume; Schneider, Hieshima, Lee, & Plank, chapter 16, this volume). Comparative reading of the chapters that follow provides many more examples of the continuity of cultural values in new ecological environments.

The Same Cultural Value Can Be Expressed by Different Means in a Different Ecological Context.   Oloko (chapter 10, this volume) notes that, in present-day urban Nigeria, familialism—a system of unlimited mutual obligation among family members—takes on new forms. For example, a professional woman may be called "mother" or "auntie" by workers at the office. The family is the model for nonfamilial professional relations in an urban environment in which many everyday relations are with nonkin.

The Same Cultural Values Have Different Developmental Outcomes in Different Societal Contexts.   Another take-home message is that cultural factors have different socialization effects depending on the societal context in which they appear. Korean adolescents associate parental strictness with parental warmth in Korea, whereas they associate it with parental coldness in the United States and Canada. The different outcomes have to do with the different ecological conditions and cultural scripts that surround and influence Korean life in the United States and Canada. **In our developmental research and theory, we must remember that culture not only is a context, but that it has one as well.** Takanishi (chapter 17, this volume) suggests the value of studying the adaptation of the same cultural group as immigrants to different countries (e.g., Japanese in Hawaii, the U.S. mainland, Peru, Brazil, Canada, and Southeast Asia). Ho (1989) has done this for ethnic Chinese around the world, and it was this strategy that led to Ogbu's insights into voluntary and involuntary minorities.

Adaptation from the Point of View of the Dominant Majority Consists of Both Assimilation and Accommodation.   Generally, *adaptation* to the dominant society is considered exclusively from the point of view of the majority. Consequently, *assimilation* refers to the process by which the dominant society takes in the minority and makes it just like itself. Developmental psychologists recognize this as Piaget's concept of assimilation, applied to the level of cultural groups rather than individuals.

However, for Piaget, assimilation was but one half of the process of adaptation. Accommodation was the other half. From the point of view of the dominant society, there are accommodations to minority cultures as well. In the United States, one can look around and see numerous accommodations to voluntary and involuntary immigrants on the cultural level: the foods we eat, the form of congratulations on the basketball court, our music and dance, Spanish street names in southwestern states, Boy Scouts and Girl Scouts. These accommodations go unacknowledged in our teaching of history as they do in our consideration of socialization and development.

What effects have minority groups in the United States and other countries had on patterns of socialization and development in the dominant majority? What are the accommodations to minority cultures that are going on in socialization patterns right now? For example, there were generations of Euro-American children whose first caregivers were African Americans. Currently, there are innumerable Euro-American children whose first caregivers are from Mexico or Central America. Other Euro-American children are cared for by European caregivers who come to the United Status *au pair*. In developmental psychology, we know absolutely nothing of the accommodations in socialization patterns that these intercultural contacts produce. Research in this area would produce findings of both theoretical and empirical interest.

It Is Necessary to Consider Cultural Adaptation from the Point of View of Minority Groups; Adaptation from This Perspective Also Consists of Both Assimilation and Accommodation. Assimilation from the perspective of the majority (and note that the everyday usage of the term *assimilation* has taken the perspective of the majority) is accommodation from the point of view of the minority group. Important examples of cultural accommodation in socialization include school attendance by Native-American children (Suina & Smolkin, chapter 6, this volume; Tharp, chapter 4, this volume) and the elicitation of preschool children's opinions by Mexican-American mothers (Delgado-Gaitan, chapter 3, this volume).

Assimilation from the point of view of minorities involves changes that they make in dominant cultural features as they adapt to them. Suina and Smolkin (chapter 6, this volume) provide numerous examples. For example, the extreme reticence of Pueblo children when asked to introduce themselves individually to an adult visitor to their classroom constitutes an assimilation of schooling to the respectful collectivism of Pueblo culture. Similarly, in Delgado-Gaitan's chapter (chapter 3, this volume) we learn that Mexican-American immigrants restrict adult elicitation of children's verbal opinions to the school-related situation of book reading. In this way, they assimilate the independent opinions required for school progress to the Mexican value of respect for elders. Perhaps most striking is the assimilation of the independence script of formal education to an interdependence value orientation when family or group improvement is seen as the primary goal of schooling.

Cultural History Must Be Part of Any Serious Theory of Development. Finally, the insight that a study of cultural origins provided into minority child development suggests that cultural history must be part of any serious theory of development. The elimination of the historical perspective can lead to a reification of the ethnographic present, as has been realized in social anthropology. For example, the value of formal education is assumed in East-Asian cultures in chapters by (a) Schneider, Hieshima, Lee, & Plank; (b) Azuma; (c) Stevenson; and (d) Ho. Yet Lebra (1991) pointed out that formal schooling in Japan was originally an unwelcome import from the West, a stimulus for peasant revolts. In this light, we can see the goal of education to enhance the standing of the Japanese family as the product of a past assimilation of an individualistic import by a society oriented around interdependence.

Every Cultural Group Contains Diverse Individuals Within It. Kim and Choi (chapter 11, this volume) highlight individual differences in strategies of acculturation to a new country for Korean Americans and Korean Canadians. Suina and Smolkin (chapter 6, this volume), and Joe (chapter 5, this volume) make the same point for Native Americans. Ho (chapter 14, this volume) emphasizes individual differences in adherence to Confucian values in East-Asian parents. An important take-home lesson is that we must not let group characterizations, even positive ones, make us forget that individual differences are as great in minority groups and their societies of origin as they are in members of the dominant groups in North America or Europe. Although this chapter and this book focus on shared culture, the avoidance of limiting stereotypes (L. M. Ward, personal communication, 1993) requires that we not lose sight of the fact that every culture, minority and majority, is possessed by people with differing personalities and aptitudes.

ACKNOWLEDGMENTS

I would like to thank Rod Cocking, Ira Blake, and Jennifer Jacobs for their helpful comments on this chapter. An important source of material was the discussion at the Workshop on Continuities and Discontinuities in the Cognitive Socialization of Minority Children organized by Greenfield and Cocking and supported by the National Institute of Mental Health (USA), the International Society for the Study of Behavioral Development, the Grant Foundation, and UCLA, and sponsored by the International Committee of Division 7 (Developmental Psychology) of the American Psychological Association. I owe a debt of gratitude to Blanca Quiroz for much of my insight into the interdependence developmental script.

REFERENCES

Azuma, H. (1991, June/July). Discussion. In P. M. Greenfield & R. R. Cocking (Chairs), *Continuities and discontinuities in the cognitive socialization of minority children.* Proceedings of a workshop, Department of Health and Human Services, Public Health Service, Alcohol, Drug Abuse and Mental Health Administration, Washington, DC.

Barry, H. III, Child, I. L., & Bacon, M. K. (1959). Relations of child training to subsistence economy. *American Anthropologist, 61,* 51–63.

Baumrind, D. (1980). New directions in socialization research. *American Psychologist, 35,* 639–652.

Berry, J. W. (1967). Independence and conformity in subsistence-level societies. *Journal of Personality and Social Psychology, 7,* 415–418.

Berry, J. W. (1968). Ecology, perceptual development and the Müller-Lyer illusion. *British Journal of Psychology, 59,* 205–210.

Berry, J. W. (1971). Ecological and cultural factors in spatial perceptual development. *Canadian Journal of Behavioural Science, 3,* 324–336.

Berry, J. W. (1987, August). *Ecological analyses for acculturation research.* Paper presented to the International Association for Cross-Cultural Psychology, Newcastle, Australia.

Berry, J. W. (in press). An ecological perspective on cultural and ethnic psychology. In E. Trickett, R. Watts, & D. Birman (Eds.), *Human diversity: Perspectives on people in context.* San Francisco: Jossey-Bass.

Chodorow, N. (1978). *The reproduction of mothering.* Berkeley: University of California Press.

Choi, S.-H. (1992, July). *The inter-subjective selfhood of Korean children: A communicative analysis.* Paper presented to the International Association for Cross-Cultural Psychology, Liege, Belgium.

Cole, M., & Bruner, J. S. (1971). Cultural differences and inferences about psychological processes. *American Psychologist, 26*, 867–876.

Dasen, P. R. (1984). The cross-cultural study of intelligence: Piaget and the Baoulé. In P. S. Fry (Ed.), *Changing conceptions of intelligence and intellectual functioning: Current theory and research* (pp. 107–134). New York: North-Holland.

Dozon, J. P. (1986). En Afrique, la famille à la croisée des chemins [In Africa, family at the crossroads]. In A. Burguière, C. Klapisch-Zuber, M. Segalen, & F. Zonabend (Eds.), *Histoire de la famille* (pp. 301–337). Paris: A. Colin.

Draper, P., & Cashdan, E. (1988). Technological change and child behavior among the !Kung. *Ethnology, 27*, 339–365.

Gergen, K. J. (1982). *Toward transformation in social knowledge*. New York: Springer-Verlag.

Gilligan, C. (1982). *In a different voice: Psychological theory and women's development*. Cambridge, MA: Harvard University Press.

Greenfield, P. M. (1966). *Culture, concepts, and conservation: A comparative study of cognitive development in Senegal*. Unpublished PhD dissertation, Harvard University, Cambridge, MA.

Harrison, A. O., Wilson, M. N., Pine, C. J., Chan, S. Q., & Buriel, R. (1990). Family ecologies of ethnic minority children. *Child Development, 61*, 347–362.

Ho, D. Y. F. (1989). Continuity and variation in Chinese patterns of socialization. *Journal of Marriage and the Family, 51*, 149–163.

Ho, D. Y. F. (1991, June/July). Discussion. In P. M. Greenfield & R. R. Cocking (Chairs), *Continuities and discontinuities in the cognitive socialization of minority children*. Proceedings of a workshop, Department of Health and Human Services, Public Health Service, Alcohol, Drug Abuse and Mental Health Administration, Washington, DC.

Hofstede, G. (1980). *Culture's consequences*. Beverly Hills, CA: Sage.

Horton, R. (1967). African traditional thought and Western science: Part I: From tradition to science. *Africa, 37*, 50–71.

Ito, K. L. (1985). Affective bonds: Hawaiian interrelationships of self. In G. M. White & J. Kirkpatrick (Eds.), *Person, self, and experience: Exploring Pacific ethnopsychologies* (pp. 301–311). Berkeley: University of California Press.

Joe, J. R. (1991, June/July). Discussion. In P. M. Greenfield & R. R. Cocking (Chairs), *Continuities and discontinuities in the cognitive socialization of minority children*. Proceedings of a workshop, Department of Health and Human Services, Public Health Service, Alcohol, Drug Abuse, and Mental Health Administration, Washington, DC.

Kagitçibasi, Ç. (1985). Culture of separateness—Culture of relatedness. *1984: Vision and Reality. Papers in Comparative Studies, 4*, 91–99.

Kagitçibasi, Ç. (1987). Individual and group loyalties: Are they compatible? In C. Kagitcibasi (Ed.), *Growth and progress in cross-cultural psychology* (pp. 94–104). Lisse: Swets & Zeitlinger.

Kesteloof, L. (1962). *Aimé Césaire*. Paris: Editions Pierre Seghers.

Kim, U. (1987, July). *The parent-child relationship: The core of Korean collectivism*. Paper presented to the International Association for Cross-Cultural Psychology, Newcastle, Australia.

Kim, U. (1991, June/July). Discussion. In P. M. Greenfield & R. R. Cocking (Chairs), *Continuities and discontinuities in the cognitive socialization of minority children*. Proceedings of a workshop, Department of Health and Human Services, Public Health Service, Alcohol, Drug Abuse and Mental Health Administration, Washington, DC.

Kitayama, S., & Markus, H. R. (1992, May). *Construal of the self as cultural frame: Implications for internationalizing psychology*. Paper prepared for symposium on Internationalization and Higher Education, University of Michigan, Ann Arbor.

Lambert, W. E., Hammers, J. F., & Frasure-Smith, N. (1979). *Child-rearing values: A cross national study*. New York: Praeger.

Lave, J., & Wenger, E. (1991). *Situated learning: Legitimate peripheral participation*. Cambridge, England: Cambridge University Press.

Lebra, T. S. (1991, June/July). Discussion. In P. M. Greenfield & R. R. Cocking (Chairs), *Continuities and discontinuities in the cognitive socialization of minority children.* Proceedings of a workshop, Department of Health and Human Services, Public Health Service, Alcohol, Drug Abuse, and Mental Health Administration, Washington, DC.

LeVine, R. A. (1987). Women's schooling, patterns of fertility, and child survival. *Educational Researcher, 16,* 21–27.

LeVine, R. A. (1991, June/July). Discussion. In P. M. Greenfield & R. R. Cocking (Chairs), *Continuities and discontinuities in the cognitive socialization of minority children.* Proceedings of a workshop, Department of Health and Human Services, Public Health Service, Alcohol, Drug Abuse and Mental Health Administration, Washington, DC.

Lewis, D. K. (1975). The black family: Socialization and sex roles. *Phylon, 36,* 221–237.

Lykes, M. B. (1985). Gender and individualistic vs. collectivist bases for notions about the self. *Journal of Personality, 53,* 356–383.

Marin, G., & Triandis, H. C. (1985). Allocentrism as an important characteristic of the behavior of Latin Americans and Hispanics. In R. Diaz-Guerrero (Ed.), *Cross-cultural and national studies in social psychology* (pp. 69–80). Amsterdam: North-Holland.

Markus, H. R., & Kitayama, S. (1991). Culture and the self: Implications for cognition, emotion, and motivation. *Psychological Review, 98,* 224–253.

McLoyd, V. C. (1990). The impact of economic hardship on black families and children: Psychological distress, parenting, and socioemotional development. *Child Development, 61,* 311–346.

Merrill-Mirsky, C. (1991, June/July). *Eeeny meeny pepsadeeny: Ethnicity and gender in children's musical play.* Presentation in P. M. Greenfield & R. R. Cocking (Chairs), Workshop on continuities and discontinuities in the cognitive socialization of minority children, Washington, DC.

Miller, J. B. (1976). *Toward a new psychology of women.* Boston: Beacon Press.

Morelli, G. A., Rogoff, B., Oppenheim, D., & Goldsmith, D. (1992). Cultural variation in infants' sleeping arrangements: Questions of independence. *Developmental Psychology, 28,* 604–613.

Mundy-Castle, A. C. (1968, December). . . . _ _ _ . . . . Paper presented at a workshop in social psychology, the Makerere Institute of Social Research and Syracuse University, New York.

Mundy-Castle, A. C. (1974). Social and technological intelligence in Western and non-Western cultures. *Universitas, 4,* 46–52.

Mundy-Castle, A. C. (1991, June/July). Commentary and discussion. In P. M. Greenfield & R. R. Cocking (Chairs), *Continuities and discontinuities in the cognitive socialization of minority children.* Proceedings of a workshop, Department of Health and Human Services, Public Health Service, Alcohol, Drug Abuse and Mental Health Administration, Washington, DC.

Njeri, I. (1989, January 29). What's in a name? African-American is the accurate ethnic label of the past and the future, Black leaders say. *Los Angeles Times,* p. VI-1.

Noddings, N. (1984). *Caring: A feminine approach to ethics and moral education.* Berkeley: University of California Press.

Nsamenang, A. B. (1991, June/July). Discussion. In P. M. Greenfield & R. R. Cocking (Chairs), *Continuities and discontinuities in the cognitive socialization of minority children.* Proceedings of a workshop, Department of Health and Human Services, Public Health Service, Alcohol, Drug Abuse and Mental Health Administration, Washington, DC.

Ochs, E., & Schieffelin, B. (1984). Language acquisition and socialization: Three developmental stories and their implications. In R. Shweder & R. LeVine (Eds.), *Culture theory* (pp. 276–320). Cambridge, MA: Cambridge University Press.

Ogbu, J. U. (1978). *Minority education and caste: The American system in cross-cultural perspective.* New York: Academic Press.

Pascual-Leone, J. (1989). An organismic process model of Witkin's field-dependence—independence. In T. Globerson & T. Zelniker (Eds.), *Cognitive style and cognitive development* (pp. 36–70). Norwood, NJ: Ablex.

Rabain, J. (1979). *L'enfant du lignage. Du sevrage à la classe d'âge chez les Wolof du Sénégal* [Child of the lineage. From weaning to the age-graded peer group among the Wolof of Senegal]. Paris: Payot.

Rabain-Jamin, J. (1991, June/July). Discussion. In P. M. Greenfield & R. R. Cocking (Chairs), *Continuities and discontinuities in the cognitive socialization of minority children*. Proceedings of a workshop, Department of Health and Human Services, Public Health Service, Alcohol, Drug Abuse and Mental Health Administration, Washington, DC.

Richman, A. L., LeVine, R. A., New, R. S., Howrigan, G. A., Welles-Nystrom, B., & LeVine, S. E. (1988). Maternal behavior to infants in five cultures. In R. A. LeVine, P. M. Miller, & M. M. West (Eds.), *Parental behavior in diverse societies* (pp. 82–97). San Francisco: Jossey-Bass.

Rogoff, B., & Morelli, G. (1989). Perspectives on children's development from cultural psychology. *American Psychologist, 44*, 343–348.

Sampson, E. E. (1988). The debate on individualism: Indigenous psychologies of the individual and their role in personal and societal functioning. *American Psychologist, 43*, 15–22.

Scribner, S. (1984). Studying working intelligence. In B. Rogoff & J. Lave (Eds.), *Everyday cognition: Its development in social context* (pp. 9–40). Cambridge, MA: Harvard University Press.

Scribner, S. (1985). Vygotsky's uses of history. In J. Wertsch (Ed.), *Culture, communication, and cognition: Vygotskian perspectives*. New York: Cambridge University Press.

Serpell, R. (1993). *The significance of schooling: Life journeys in an African society*. Cambridge, England: Cambridge University Press.

Shweder, R. A. (1982). Beyond self-constructed knowledge: The study of culture and morality. *Merrill-Palmer Quarterly, 28*, 41–69.

Shweder, R. A., & Bourne, E. J. (1982). Does the concept of person vary cross-culturally? In A. J. Marsella & G. M. White (Eds.), *Cultural conceptions of mental health and therapy* (pp. 97–137). Boston: Reidel.

Sudarkasa, N. (1988). Interpreting the African heritage in Afro-American family organization. In H. P. McAdoo (Ed.), *Black families* (2nd ed., pp. 27–43). Newbury Park, CA: Sage.

Suina, J. H. (1991, June/July). Discussion. In P. M. Greenfield & R. R. Cocking (Eds.), *Continuities and discontinuities in the cognitive socialization of minority children*. Proceedings of a workshop, Department of Health and Human Services, Public Health Service, Alcohol, Drug Abuse and Mental Health Administration, Washington, DC.

Super, C., & Harkness, S. (1986). The developmental niche: A conceptualization at the interface of society and the individual. *International Journal of Behavioral Development, 9*(4), 545–570.

Tapia Uribe, F. M. (1991, June/July). Discussion. In P. M. Greenfield & R. R. Cocking (Eds.), *Continuities and discontinuities in the cognitive socialization of minority children*. Proceedings of a workshop, Department of Health and Human Services, Public Health Service, Alcohol, Drug Abuse and Mental Health Administration, Washington, DC.

Triandis, H. C. (1989). Cross-cultural studies of individualism and collectivism. *Nebraska Symposium on Motivation, 37*, 41–133.

Triandis, H. C., Leung, K., Villareal, M., & Clack, F. L. (1985). Allocentric vs. idiocentric tendencies: Convergent and discriminant validation. *Journal of Research in Personality, 19*, 395–415.

Turiel, E. (1994). Morality, authoritarianism, and personal agency in cultural contexts. In R. J. Sternberg & P. Ruzgis (Eds.), *Intelligence and personality* (pp. 271–299). Cambridge, England: Cambridge University Press.

Wober, J. M. (1967). Individualism, home life, and work efficiency among a group of Nigerian workers. *Journal of Occupational Psychology, 41*, 183–192.

Wober, J. M. (1974). Towards an understanding of the Kiganda concept of intelligence. In J. W. Berry & P. R. Dasen (Eds.), *Culture and cognition* (pp. 261–280). London: Methuen.

Under the guidance of her teacher, Marta explores and communicates her cross-cultural roots. Bellagio Road Newcomers School, Los Angeles, California, USA, 1993.
Photograph by Lauren Greenfield

AMERICAN ROOTS

Immigrant parents visit their children's school. They spend the day learning what their children study, California, USA, 1993 (see chapter 3).
Photograph by Lauren Greenfield

2

MATERNAL BEHAVIOR IN A MEXICAN COMMUNITY: THE CHANGING ENVIRONMENTS OF CHILDREN

F. Medardo Tapia Uribe
Centro Regional de Investigaciones Multidisciplinarias
UNAM, Cuernavaca, Morelos, Mexico

Robert A. LeVine
Sarah E. LeVine
Harvard Graduate School of Education

This chapter describes how socioeconomic change has affected the contexts in which children are reared in a Mexican town from which migration to Los Angeles and Chicago is frequent. Its central point is that the Mexican communities generating migrants to the United States have been changing as environments for child development, particularly in their conditions of health, fertility, parental education, and media exposure, as well as in their family attitudes, childrearing practices, and differentiation by socioeconomic status (SES).

As Mexico's institutions have changed in the last few decades, so has its population. Research into the psychological development of Mexican immigrants in the United States should take account not only of their distinctive cultural background as Mexicans, but of changes that have taken place and are continuing in the communities and families from which they come. This chapter provides information on processes of social change affecting Mexican parents and children who move to the United States.

Study Site

Tilzapotla, where the study was conducted, is a rural town of about 4,500 inhabitants in the state of Morelos, located 80 miles south of Mexico City and thus some 800 miles from the Texas border. Despite the great distances and international borders, migration to Los Angeles and Chicago is a major fact of life for many of the families in Tilzapotla. Cars with Illinois and California license plates can be seen there, and new houses built with the earnings of migrants are noticeable in the center of town. Weddings in East Los Angeles are videotaped for showing on the VCRs back home, as the couple returns for a second wedding in the Tilzapotla church. Older residents talk about their grandchildren attending schools in Chicago. These signs of migration back and forth and continued contact between members of the same family living in the two countries are not unique to Tilzapotla but are found in many towns and villages in central Mexico. Thus, Tilzapotla residents participate in the large-scale process of Mexico–U.S. migration; and although they cannot be claimed to be representative in any exact sense, they share many characteristics with other recent migrants.

Collectivism

One of these common characteristics is the development of family relationships from childhood onward that are in continuity with the collectivistic cultural values of mutual aid and support among kin long found in Mexican agrarian communities. Taking care of others within the family is a paramount value that is expressed in a variety of contemporary situations, from the care of young children by their older siblings to family strategies for emigration to the United States. Emigrants help others to emigrate, and they provide assistance to those family members who must be left behind, either temporarily—in the case of the emigrant's siblings or wife and children—or permanently, as in the case of his parents. This powerful tendency to maintain kin ties and use them for mutual adaptation represents a clear continuity with Mexican traditions.

Changes in Parenting Values

Discontinuities in development, strongly influenced by the recent expansion of formal education, appear in new models of parenthood and child care that enhance children's cognitive development and survival under modern conditions: reduced fertility and greater investment of maternal attention in the preschool child. Fundamental psychosocial changes like new attitudes with respect to family size, contraception, reproductive decision making in the husband–wife relationship, and mother–infant interaction are indications of these shifts.

MEXICO: CHANGING PARAMETERS
OF PARENTHOOD AND CHILD CARE

Mexican society has been transformed since 1940 by industrialization, urbanization, population growth, and the expansion of health, education, and other social services. By 1982, when its current economic crisis began, Mexico had become a "middle-income developing country" according to the World Bank classification (i.e., one of the most affluent and developed countries of the Third World except for the small-population oil producers of the Middle East). On a variety of socioeconomic indicators such as gross national product (GNP) per capita and rates of child mortality, fertility, and literacy, Mexico now falls between the Third World as a whole and the industrial countries of North America, Europe, and East Asia. Socioeconomic progress was rapid between 1940 and 1980, and (apart from GNP per capita, which declined) the process continued, although at a slower rate, during the economic paralysis of the past decade.

Although income, education, and health improved dramatically for the country as a whole over the last half century, the national population quadrupled and the gap between city and countryside widened on all of these dimensions, motivating an exodus from the rural areas in pursuit of a better life. Hence, Mexico City and all other cities and towns throughout the country grew abundantly as Mexico was transformed from a predominantly rural to a predominantly urban society. The inability of the Mexican economy to absorb all of its rapidly growing labor force created a widespread economic incentive in favor of migrating to the United States.

Some of the ways in which these macrosocial processes affected the environments of children is suggested by demographic indicators: The mortality rate of children under 5 years of age dropped from 140 per 1,000 live births in 1960 to 51 per 1,000 in 1989, and the total fertility rate (roughly equivalent to the number of children an average woman bears in her lifetime) declined from 6.8 to 3.4 over the same time period. Although in both cases the 1989 figures are much higher than those of the United States in that year (under 5 mortality rate = 12; total fertility rate = 1.8), the historical trend indicates a demographic transition of major proportions (UNICEF, 1991).

School expansion outpaced massive population growth during the same years, permitting an increasing proportion of each birth cohort to attend and go further in school. For example, in the decade 1960–1970, the proportion of those 15–19 who have attended middle school increased from 10.8% to 30.2% (Alba, 1982). The proportion of adults (ages 15 years or older) who had never attended school declined from 31.6% in 1970 to 15.3% in 1987, and even these were concentrated in the older ages (only 5.1% of those 15–29 years old were unschooled). These adults were also concentrated in the rural areas: In towns with between 2,500 and 19,999 inhabitants, like Tilzapotla, 26.5% of the adults over age 15 in 1987 had never been to school, whereas in metropolitan areas like Mexico City only 6.6% were unschooled.

Women as well as men attended school in unprecedented numbers: By 1987, 88.5% of Mexican women in their childbearing years (ages 15–49) had been to school and 62.4% had at least completed primary school (Direccion General de Planificacion Familiar, 1988). Thus, during the 1980s, especially in the cities, Mexican children had a better chance of survival and were more likely to be members of smaller families with more educated parents than their counterparts only 20 years earlier.

Migration has been one of the major means by which Mexican parents have obtained better conditions for their children. Because the rural villages lacked the economic opportunities, health services, and schools that were rapidly emerging in the cities, parents moved to towns to give their children these advantages. This resulted not only in large-scale urbanization but also a movement of population to the northern region of the country where there was more industrial development. Although migration to the United States, both temporary and permanent, was always part of this larger pattern, the economic crisis since 1982 has made it particularly attractive.

It must be emphasized that parents moved for jobs and income as well as for access to schools and health services that were absent in their rural communities. Many families moved when their children reached school age or when their eldest completed the village primary school, relocating to an urban center where higher schooling was available. Furthermore, living in the city meant better access to clinics and hospitals for medical treatment as well as healthier conditions in terms of piped water, sanitation, and other facilities. These amenities helped to stem the spread of childhood disease. On the whole, then, moving to the city represented the striving of parents to improve the welfare of their children.

In the transformation of Mexican society since 1960, maternal schooling has proved to be a key factor relevant to child development. Survey research has shown that a mother's years of school attendance is consistently associated with reduced child mortality and fertility and effective use of health and contraceptive services, even when other socioeconomic factors (rural or urban residence, income, husband's education) are statistically controlled (LeVine et al., 1991). No other household-level factor is as robustly related to these health and reproductive outcomes in national surveys conducted during the 1970s and 1980s. Our research, conducted first in the Morelos capital of Cuernavaca (population of 280,000) and subsequently in the rural town of Tilzapotla (population of 4,500) 30 miles to the south, was designed to shed light on the processes intervening between female schooling and the changing conditions of child care.

TILZAPOTLA AS AN ENVIRONMENT
FOR WOMEN AND CHILDREN

Economy

In the late 19th century, rural Morelos was one of the major sugar cane producing areas in the world. Cane was grown on large *haciendas* (estates) owned
by absentee landlords. The mestizo village of Tilzapotla in southern Morelos, whose founders had come from the neighboring state of Guerrero, was
inhabited by *peones* (field hands) on the nearby *hacienda* of San Gabriel. This
area, the home of Emiliano Zapata, was the scene of military conflict during
the Mexican Revolution (1910–1920), as the *haciendas* were destroyed, eventually to be replaced by communal landholdings (*ejidos*). Tilzapotla was burned
down in 1913, and its people fled to the mountains of Guerrero and surrounding towns. They returned in 1920 to rebuild the village on an adjacent site.
A 1922 census recorded 140 households with a population of 860. By 1927,
the local land that had belonged to the *hacienda* was assigned to the village
as an *ejido*.

Many changes occurred in the following 60 years. The *ejido* land is now
used for the rain-fed cultivation of maize (for home consumption and local
sale) and sorghum (sold in Mexico City), and the raising of dairy cattle for
locally marketed milk and cheese. It also contains a limestone quarry that
supplies the raw material for the production of plaster in 22 local workshops.
Several other privately owned quarries on the outskirts of town provide raw
material from which mortar is made in two small factories there.

This small-scale industrial development has attracted migrants to Tilzapotla,
largely from adjacent parts of Guerrero. By 1990, the population had
grown to about 4,500. Furthermore, the area to the west of Tilzapotla has
become a weekend tourist resort for Mexico City residents, and 4 miles from
the town is a national resort center owned by one of the government social
security systems.

Despite this local economic development, migration to the United States
also became established as an economic strategy to raise capital for family
businesses, house-building, and household property. Although only 4% of the
177 mothers surveyed in 1987 said their husbands were currently working
in the United States and 34% said that their husbands had done so in the
past, the survey did not cover men who were not yet married or those whose
wives were with them.

A large proportion of young men currently go to work in the United States
to raise money for marriage; some meet women from Tilzapotla there and
marry them. Others go to work in Mexico City and Cuernavaca, often as construction workers. Thus, the community, although still basically rural, has

a local industry, and its residents participate as producers and consumers in the regional, national, and international economies.

Socioeconomic Characteristics of the Sample. In Tilzapotla, mothers of families basically do not work outside the home. A relevant statistic is that 95% of the women who had access to social security services in two of the neighborhoods had it through their husbands' work. When women do work, it usually takes the form of activities such as washing for other families or street vending, sometimes for lack of a husband, rather than a formal job or career. For this reason, the economic character of the community in general and of our sample in particular can best be seen in the distribution of husbands' occupations in the sample. About 82% of the husbands are manual workers; of them, almost 90% are peasants, construction workers, or limestone mine workers (quarriers and haulers). Nonetheless, there is a considerable range of occupations, which reflects the range of the town as a whole.

Education

Tilzapotla has a history of commitment to schooling. It began in 1926, when the first primary school was built by the community, which also provided the teacher's salary. When federal funding for the school had been secured, the town financed two of its young residents for the training in Mexico City that would qualify them to serve as its principals. A second primary school opened in 1970, a middle school (*secundaria*, Grades 7–9) in 1971, and a high school (*preparatoria*, Grades 10–12) in 1978. In all cases, the labor and raw materials for the buildings were supplied by the people of the community.

Although it is said that the priest used to advise parents against sending their daughters to school, it has long been conventional to do so and it is considered traditional among the older residents of the town. In fact, it is the relatively large proportion of mothers with complete primary or higher schooling that induced us to conduct our rural study of maternal schooling in Tilzapotla. There are other such rural towns in southern Morelos, but they are rare elsewhere in rural Mexico.

Social Stratification

Tilzapotla is socially stratified. The families of the original settlers (i.e., the *ejidatarios*) live in the center of town, own the land and benefit from what it produces, more frequently have houses with piped water and sanitation, and have gone farther in school than the others. Their lifestyles show the influence of urban sophistication on their tastes and preferences, which their relative affluence enables them to gratify. The poorer people have recently moved to Tilzapotla from small villages in Guerrero to work in the quarries and small factories, live on the periphery of the town in houses lacking facilities, have little or no land of their own, and are more likely to have attended school a few years or not at all.

This pattern of social differentiation replicates in microcosm the social hierarchy of Mexican cities, in which earlier settlers have established themselves as property owners as well as with access to strategic resources for family welfare, including educational advancement, leaving more recent settlers in a marginal social and economic position. The dynamic quality of this process, involving continued migration and the search for new opportunities, makes it perilous to predict how long such local patterns of stratification will endure.

FINDINGS CONCERNING THE EFFECTS OF MATERNAL SCHOOLING

This section summarizes findings from our ongoing analysis of data collected in Tilzapotla from 1987 to 1990 (see LeVine et al., 1991). We begin with the relationships between maternal schooling and reproductive and health behaviors that have been discovered in national surveys in the 1970s and 1980s (e.g., Hobcraft, McDonald, & Rutstein, 1984; United Nations, 1986), which we replicated at the microlevel in low-income neighborhoods of Cuernavaca in 1984–1985, asking whether the same relationships hold in Tilzapotla. Then we move to an analysis of the pathways that mediate the influence of schooling on the maternal behavior involved in demographic change.

Health and Reproductive Behavior

Our 1987 survey of 177 mothers of children under 48 months of age in Tilzapotla showed that maternal and child health care was strongly related to the mothers' years of school attendance. For example, the proportion of pregnancies with prenatal care varied from a mean of .40 among the unschooled women to .98 among those with 7–9 years of formal education. The correlation of maternal schooling with prenatal care was .46 ($p < .001$); the partial r with SES controlled was .39 ($p < .001$), indicating that the relationship is not due simply to family economic resources or other access variables. This highly significant effect of maternal schooling independent of socioeconomic status is particularly interesting, given, as might be expected, that maternal schooling and SES are significantly related in this sample (LeVine et al., 1991). In Tilzapotla, as in urban Cuernavaca and other Latin American communities, then, maternal schooling is independently related to the utilization of medical services affecting maternal and child health.

The impact of maternal schooling on reproductive behavior is equally evident. For example, the percentage of mothers who reported using contraception varied from a mean of 17.5 among the unschooled to 57.4 among those
who had attended school 7–9 years. Thus, contraceptive use among the most
educated women of Tilzapotla is still far lower than the 90% of low-income
mothers with 1–9 years of schooling who reported contraceptive use in urban Cuernavaca, indicating the familiar rural–urban differential in fertility
behavior. However, it suggests that the same educational process may be
working in both places. That contraceptive use is related to women's fertility goals in this sample was indicated by the fact that, on the average, the
unschooled mothers reported wanting about one child more than those in
the highest education category (unschooled = 3.7; 7–9 years of school = 2.8).

A regression analysis of the number of children actually born to these 177
mothers showed that, when maternal age (M = 25 years old) is controlled,
husband's schooling but no other aspect of SES (apart from maternal schooling) is significantly related to fertility. When age, husband's schooling, and
SES are controlled, a mother's schooling remains strongly related to the number of children she bears.

Based on this regression model, a predicted mean number of children ever
born was generated for mothers at each of four levels of school attainment,
with age, husband's schooling, and SES controlled as follows:

No school	3.83
2 years	3.56
6 years	3.02
9 years	2.62

Thus, women with no schooling have about 1.2 more children on average
than women with 9 years of schooling, when mothers' ages and husbands'
education have been controlled (LeVine et al., 1991). Therefore, this finding
points to a different conception of childrearing among those who have attended school longer, and suggests that school experience has reshaped their
preferences toward the bearing of fewer children.

In many ways, this finding signifies more fundamental psychosocial change
than the mere use of maternal and child health services. For a woman to
use modern health services effectively requires the adoption of new means
for old ends (viz. child survival). But birth limitation through contraception
requires the adoption not only of new means but for a new end (viz. limitation of family size). Until the 1970s, large families with many children were
almost universally wanted in Mexico, and this attitude has been slower to
change in rural communities. Furthermore, Mexican men often want more
children than their wives and tend to dominate in reproductive decision

making. Against this cultural background, the effect of women's schooling on childbearing in Tilzapotla is indicative of a major shift in attitude.

Sources of Maternal Schooling Effects

The sources of this shift are far from obvious because the schools do not teach sex education or birth control, and the impact of schooling on maternal health and reproductive practices operates consistently across levels of schooling at which the curriculum varies. Keeping a daughter in school longer may be indicative of parental characteristics such as family resources and a positive attitude toward women's careers, but the evidence to date suggests that such prior characteristics account for only a small part of the school effect on child health and fertility. Our current explanatory model concerns features of the school as an institutional learning environment in which girls from agrarian communities are resocialized, acquiring new motives, identities, skills, and models for interpersonal behavior.

In this view, the school is first of all embedded in an academic–occupational hierarchy that the child experiences as a ladder of ranked statuses stretching above her and which she is invited to ascend through academic performance. The longer she attends school, the longer the woman desires advancement through learning and considers herself a different kind of person as the result of her place on that ladder.

Her conception of learning is formed by the nature of the classroom, an institutional setting uniquely dedicated to the transmission of skills and knowledge through verbal interaction between experts and pupils, as opposed to the apprenticeship model of graduated participation that prevails in agrarian learning environments outside of school (e.g., Childs & Greenfield, 1980; Greenfield, 1984; Greenfield & Lave, 1982).

Thus, the woman who has attended school is not only inclined to learn more in the verbal mode (e.g., from the media, health clinics, public health campaigns) but, when she becomes a mother, to teach more in that mode as well. She reinterprets the task of child care in pedagogical terms and engages her child in verbal interaction from the start, before the infant is capable of speech. Zukow (1984) found a dramatic change toward a more didactic language socialization style as a function of higher levels of schooling in Mexican mothers observed interacting with their toddlers at home. This pedagogical model commits the mother to a more interactive relationship with the preschool child, with a greater investment of maternal attention during early childhood, increasingly elicited by the child. A greater investment of maternal attention contributes to the increasing labor intensity of child care, making it too expensive in terms of maternal energy to repeat more than a few times. School fees above the primary level add to the investment on an economic level for an educationally oriented mother.

This model, revised in the course of our urban study in Cuernavaca, is consistent with the findings from the home observations and maternal interviews conducted there from 1983 to 1985. For example, they showed that mothers with more schooling were more verbally responsive to their babies at 5, 10, and 15 months but held their babies less at 15 months of age (LeVine et al., 1991).

This pattern represents a change in survival strategies that is responsive to new societal conditions. A few decades earlier, medical facilities were rare even in the cities. As in rural areas now, mothers relied on close physical contact with their babies and frequent nursing to maximize the chances of survival (LeVine, 1977) in the absence of medical services and a source of clean drinking water.

Under such conditions, the parental strategy we have identified with maternal schooling would have failed miserably as a strategy for offspring survival. Clean water and medical services have, of course, increased the potential for infant survival way beyond that secured by continuous bodily contact and frequent nursing.

Changes in maternal strategy stimulated by mothers' schooling are key to utilizing this potential. In terms of maternal interaction, in infancy the change is from proximal (holding) to distal (looking, talking) interaction; in early childhood, the primary change is from less to more verbal participation by the child (Laosa, 1978, 1982; LeVine et al., 1991).

Maternal Behavior in Tilzapotla

The Tilzapotla findings provide the possibility of further tests for the model. In the 1987 survey, maternal schooling was correlated with a test of decontextualized language skill ($r = .47$) and a composite media exposure index ($r = .40$); these correlations are significant at the .001 level and remain highly significant with SES controlled. Preliminary analysis of the home observations conducted during 1989–1990 shows level of maternal schooling to be positively correlated with the proportion of maternal behavior to the infant that is verbal, with SES controlled ($r = .50$, $p = .008$).

Decontextualized language is language that has been divorced from a known social and pragmatic situation. Decontextualized language provides a means for communicating with those who do not share a common contextual background. This skill, transmitted in the classroom, has been shown to predict academic performance in other settings (Snow, 1990). It is generally absent from normal conversation in small face-to-face communities where people can safely assume that hearers share their contextual perspective (LeVine et al., 1991).

Decontextualized language skill is the verbal skill not only of the classroom but also of bureaucratic discourse in general, valuable in bureaucratized health services and in understanding health information. Media exposure indicates an avenue of adult learning through radio, television, and print media, all of which include public health messages and are available in Tilzapotla. Media messages, intended for a broad, often national, audience, are decontextualized in their format. The verbal interaction of the mother with her child is an indicator of her conception of child care as a labor-intensive task beyond infancy. Thus, these three variables correlated with maternal schooling suggest that the latter makes its impact through the acquisition of new forms of communicative competence in the classroom, which lead to increased learning from the media years later and to more intensive verbal communication with her child.

Incorporating Individualistic Schooling in a Collectivistic Society

Our findings also indicate that the child's acquisition of new forms of communicative competence in school influences parent–child interaction at home during the school years and after. This is not always viewed favorably by parents whose authority is challenged by the child's verbal complaints. Some parents consider this and the economic burden of schooling as important problems and even reasons for *not* sending children to school. One of our informants at the bottom of the socioeconomic ladder, with only 1 year of schooling, exemplifies this attitude:

> Children who keep attending school particularly after primary school don't want to do anything. Besides, they become *rezongones* (complainers). School also demands too many books and materials. It is better that he (a son who is completing primary school this year) start working.

Under conditions of economic scarcity and insecurity, the parents of Tilzapotla seek to retain for their children the advantages of their Indian and Mestizo (Indian-Spanish and Indian-African) agrarian heritage (i.e., social security through the reciprocal ties of kinship) by socializing them for mutual dependence, as suggested for other Mexican communities by Lomnitz (1977) and Arizpe (1989).

At the same time, they want their children to take advantage of the opportunities presented by schooling, which leads them to place emphasis on individualism and academic competence. Given their relative poverty, their strategy is to raise children who will gain from new forms of social participation while not giving up the old ones.

CONCLUSIONS

Seen through the lens of a single rural town in southern Morelos, it is evident that maternal behavior in Mexico has changed and continues to change in ways that have demographic and psychosocial consequences. Formal education is a dominant influence in this process, and the direction of this influence is similar to what has been identified earlier in the United States by Laosa (1978, 1982) and other investigators. Our investigation differs from many others that link maternal education to demographic variables in Third-World countries (e.g., Bongaarts, 1978; Cleland, 1990; Mosley & Chen, 1984) in identifying intervening processes and pathways by which maternal schooling achieves its effects.

Although the cognitive socialization of Mexican children was not the topic of our research, we believe that mothers who have attended school longer and who are more verbally responsive to their infants are initiating a process of cognitive socialization that prepares children for participation in schools.

In this respect, the statistically average Mexican mother, even in a rural place like Tilzapotla, differs from her counterpart of 20 or 30 years ago. The women migrating to the United States from Tilzapotla have usually attended middle school, and some have gone much farther. They are more sophisticated about the process of schooling for their children (i.e., about classrooms and homework and reading) than earlier migrants with less formal education. Studies of cognitive socialization among recent Mexican migrants should take this into account.

The social and cultural context of childrearing in Mexican families differs from that of White middle-class Euro-Americans in ways that have become familiar in the literature: The Mexicans show more hierarchy by age and gender, more emphasis on respect and obedience, less emphasis on independence and separation during childhood, less social distance between the generation of adults in the family, and greater maintenance of kinship ties throughout the life course. When Mexicans move to the United States, these more interdependence-oriented or collectivistic cultural traditions are thrown into relief as migrants feel the pressure to change. Because close family and kinship ties serve migrants well—indeed, their migration is often part of a family strategy involving extended kin—there is also resistance to change.

But it would be no more accurate to assume that these traditions are unchanging than it would be to assume that the Mexican birthrate is not declining because Mexican Americans are known to have a higher birthrate than other American ethnic groups. In Mexico, urbanization and the expansion of schooling are changing the cultural values affecting family life, as we observed in Cuernavaca. Maternal schooling in the city affects women's attitudes toward husband–wife and parent–child relationships in a generally egalitarian direction. This tendency may be less pronounced in rural settings, but it occurs there too. Thus, the culture that migrants bring with them is one that is being contested, not only in their new home, but in their country of origin.

In general, because of their higher education level, recent immigrants arrive in the United States culturally better equipped than their predecessors to face totally foreign environments. The reconceptualization by Mexican women (and men) of (a) familial relations, (b) the number of children they want to have, (c) the forms of childrearing, and (d) the nature of children's health care has occurred and continues to take place. These new ideas and the changed practices that accompany them are important in the context of U.S. immigration: They permit greater social participation and increase the possibilities for Mexican immigrants to contribute to the societies into which they enter. The dominant culture of the United States probably will find, in new generations of better educated immigrants, Mexican Americans who are more active critics and participants in their new country.

This chapter has shown briefly the predicament of parents in a rural town of central Mexico: They are increasingly educated and look to formal education to improve the life chances of their children; but they are also poor and cannot relinquish the mutual dependence of kinship ties that has provided security to their forebears. In the United States, where they go in increasing numbers, they bring these continuities and discontinuities with them in their roles as the parents of North American schoolchildren.

REFERENCES

Alba, F. (1982). *The population of Mexico: Trends, issues and policies.* New Brunswick, NJ: Transaction Books.

Arizpe, L. (1989). *La mujer en el desarrollo de México y de America Latina* [Women in Mexico and Latin American Development]. Mexico City: CRIM, UNAM.

Bongaarts, J. (1978). A framework for analyzing the proximate determinants of fertility. *Population and Development Review, 4,* 105–132.

Childs, C. P., & Greenfield, P. M. (1980). Informal modes of learning and teaching: The case of Zinacanteco weaving. In N. Warren (Ed.), *Studies in cross-cultural psychology* (Vol. 2, pp. 269–316). London: Academic Press.

Cleland, J. (1990). Maternal education and child survival: Further evidence and explanations. In J. Caldwell, S. Findley, P. Caldwell, G. Santow, W. Cosford, J. Braid, D. Broers-Freeman (Eds.), *What we know about health transition: The cultural, social and behavioural determinants of health* (Vol. 1, pp. 400–419). Canberra: Australian National University Press.

Direccion General de Planificacion Familiar, Secretaria de Salud, Mexico. (1988). *Encuesta nacional sobre fecundidad y salud, 1987* [Fertility and Health National Survey]. Mexico City: Direccion General de Planificacion Familiar, Secretaria de Salud.

Greenfield, P. M. (1984). A theory of the teacher in the learning activities of everyday life. In B. Rogoff & J. Lave (Eds.), *Everyday cognition: Its development in social context* (pp. 117–138). Cambridge, MA: Harvard University Press.

Greenfield, P. M., & Lave, J. (1982). Cognitive aspects of informal education. In D. Wagner & H. Stevenson (Eds.), *Cultural perspectives on child development* (pp. 181–207). San Francisco: Freeman.

Hobcraft, J. N., McDonald, J. W., & Rutstein, S. O. (1984). Socio-economic factors in infant and child mortality: A cross-national comparison. *Population Studies, 38,* 193–223.

Laosa, L. (1978). Maternal teaching strategies in Chicano families of varied educational and socioeconomic levels. *Child Development, 49,* 1129–1135.

Laosa, L. (1982). School, occupation, culture and the family: The impact of parental schooling on the parent child relationship. *Journal of Educational Psychology, 74,* 791–827.

LeVine, R. A. (1977). Child rearing as cultural adaptation. In P. H. Leiderman, S. R. Tulkin, & A. Rosenfeld (Eds.), *Culture and infancy: Variations in the human experience* (pp. 15–27). New York: Academic Press.

LeVine, R. A., LeVine, S. E., Richman, A., Tapia Uribe, F. M., Correa, C. S., & Miller, P. M. (1991). Women's schooling and child care in demographic transition: A Mexican case study. *Population and Development Review, 17,* 459–496.

Lomnitz, L. A. (1977). *Networks and marginality: Life in a Mexican Shantytown.* New York: Academic Press.

Mosley, W. H., & Chen, L. C. (1984). An analytical framework for the study of child survival in developing countries. *Population and Development Review, 10,* 25–45.

Snow, C. E. (1990). The development of definitional skill. *Journal of Child Language, 17,* 697–710.

UNICEF. (1991). *State of the world's children 1991.* New York: Oxford University Press.

United Nations. (1986). *Education and fertility: Selected findings from the World Fertility Survey Data* (United Nations Population Division Working Paper ESA/P/WP/96). New York: Author.

Zukow, P. G. (1984). Folk theories of comprehension and caregiver practices in a rural-born population in Central Mexico. *The Quarterly Newsletter of the Laboratory of Comparative Human Cognition, 6,* 62–67.

3

SOCIALIZING YOUNG CHILDREN IN MEXICAN-AMERICAN FAMILIES: AN INTERGENERATIONAL PERSPECTIVE

Concha Delgado-Gaitan
University of California, Davis

This chapter is a case study of family socialization observed in households of two different generations: first-generation Mexican-American families and Mexican-immigrant families in Carpinteria, California. It presents a three-tier analysis of parent–child socialization in: (a) first-generation parents who attended Carpinteria schools when they were segregated; (b) immigrant parents, educated in Mexico, whose children attended the same Carpinteria schools after special programs to address education of Latinos were implemented but prior to any community organization; and (c) the same immigrant families after the formation of a community–school organization. The two cohorts represent three important educational experiences in this particular community—experiences that are reflected in parent–child interaction and, ultimately, in child development.

Cultural continuity and discontinuity theories have explained sociocultural adjustment of Mexican-American families in the United States (Delgado-Gaitan, 1987; Ogbu, 1982; Suarez-Orozco, 1989; Williams, 1990). How Mexican Americans have achieved and advanced in employment, school, and political life within the larger society has a great deal to do with the way in which home life and daily cultural practices are valued and maintained within the group. That is, the continuity and discontinuity of cultural systems between Mexican-American families and the institutions in which they participate has varied on aspects of language, values of interpersonal communication, and goals and aspirations, such that it has affected access of opportunity for Mexican-American families.

Mexican family life in the United States has generally been depicted by researchers as deficient and incapable of providing children with the necessary environment to promote successful adjustment to the larger society in general, and to school in particular. The myth that Euro-American (termed *Anglo* by Mexican Americans) culture is superior to other cultures including Mexican American is reflected in the literature of a generation ago (Bereiter & Engleman, 1966; Deutsch, 1967; Dunn, 1987; Heller, 1966; Hess & Shipman, 1965; Holtzman, Diaz-Guerrero & Swartz, 1975; Zintz, 1969). Proponents of this cultural deficit theory claim that persistent poverty creates cognitive deprivation, ignorance, and low aspirations.

Although poverty, per se, creates isolation and diminishes access to mainstream resources and rewards, it does not necessarily disable parents' or children's mental and social capacities (Achor & Morales, 1990; Cromwell & Ruiz, 1978; Laosa, 1978). The crucial issue is the way effective childrearing in different cultures is defined. LeVine (1974) hypothesized that parenting is both universal and highly variable—a specific framework with chronological parameters in which people care, protect, and nurture their young. Common goals shared by parents everywhere include children's physical survival, economic self-maintenance, and realization of cultural values, including the shaping of behavior.

The nature of socialization and culturally variable parenting is strongly influenced by socioeconomic conditions and other ecological forces (Bronfenbrenner, 1982; Garbarino, 1982; LeVine, 1974; Ogbu, 1982, 1990; Steward, 1955). Whiting and Edwards (1988) described the power of cultural forces in the way they interact with parental pressures, behaviors, and developmental process that program the daily lives of children in different cultural communities. Cultural differences such as religion, moral values, recreation, and education are also reflected in childrearing practices, whereas the age, gender, and social behavior of children have influenced the process of socialization (Pence, 1988; Spindler, 1974, 1987; Whiting & Edwards, 1988).

In Carpinteria, a community in California that is the focus of this chapter, parents in first-generation Mexican-American and Mexican-immigrant families share a common set of values, such as respect for elders and concern for collectivity, which promote interdependence and family unity. These values vary in the degree to which they motivate practice because they are influenced, to a large extent, by external macrostructures. Thus, it is hypothesized that childrearing practices and socialization of children will vary between families who are recent immigrants and Mexican-American families who have been in the United States for a long time. Differences in socializing children between the two cohorts can be attributed to their historical experience with the dominant groups in the United States on issues such as the value they place on education and schooling. How families view their opportunities in the United States influences the parents' role in inculcating values in their children and their verbal and nonverbal interaction in their homes and community.

LeVine (1982) noted that early learning in the home is shaped by the family social system and influences children in two major ways: (a) through family structure, which determines the nature of the child's earliest interpersonal experience and which in turn is affected by the wider social system within which it is integrated; and (b) through parental mediation (Inkeles, 1955), by which deliberate training of children for successful adaptation to a changing social order occurs. If external forces beyond the family influence this process, we need to better understand how such factors mediate cultural change for immigrant families and for subsequent generations, and how these forces manifest themselves.

Modifications of cultural continuities and discontinuities between generations and between home and school culture have emerged through the practice and process of empowerment. Essentially, family empowerment has as a main feature a "critical reflection" process that

> engages people in careful examination of the assumptions that guide self, family and institutional norms, values, policies, and decisions that direct their lives including institutional policies and practices in education and other social services. As a consequence, the group's awareness and consciousness of their shared experience (past and present) becomes the basis for collective action. (Barr, 1989, p. 5)

The immigrants in this study organized to realize their political potential, which helped them in their sociocultural adjustment in their families and in their relationship to the school.

STUDYING THE FAMILY SETTING: METHOD AND BACKGROUND

A great deal can be learned from examining parent–child interaction at close range, and this study attempts to understand child socialization as it occurs in face-to-face exchange. The primary research question guiding the study was: What are the principles by which immigrant and first-generation Mexican families raise their children? The study was designed to observe and analyze verbal and nonverbal interactions ethnographically. The categories discussed in this study are characterized by three selected dimensions of early family socialization: (a) respect/critical thinking, (b) interdependence/independence, and (c) language preference and use. The first two are components of the collectivism/individualism dimension.

This study is part of a larger research project on family, school, and community relationships in which a bilingual preschool program played a signifi-

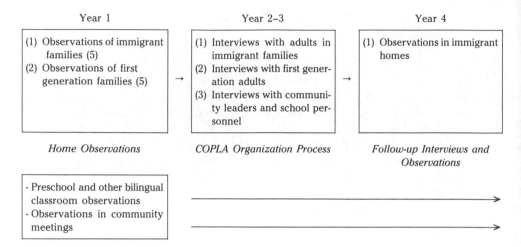

FIG. 3.1. Study design.

cant role. The design of the study is shown in Fig. 3.1. The top row of boxes refers to data sources for the present chapter. Five immigrant and five first-generation families with preschool children were randomly selected from a larger sample of Mexican American families with elementary school children. The only selection criterion was that the family have a preschool age child. All of the families' names used in this chapter are pseudonyms, although the names of the community and organization are real.[1] Each family constituted a case study in itself. All five of the immigrant families were active in the Comité de Padres Latinos (COPLA) when it was organized about a year after observations began. This Latino parent/community organization, COPLA (*C*omité de *P*adres *La*tinos), is a Spanish acronym that means couplet—a united stanza in a poem.

COPLA was organized by Spanish-speaking immigrant families to unite and support families in addressing school-related issues and to break the cycle of isolation that Mexican families had experienced. It was conceived as an instrument of family empowerment. Over the 3 years of COPLA covered in this chapter, the parent/community organization began to achieve its goal and to become instrumental in supporting families as they changed and asserted their voice in the community. Its purpose was the sharing of knowledge about ways to adjust in the community and relate to schools. COPLA stressed maintaining Spanish and Mexican cultural values and establishing a cooperative dialogue with the schools to encourage them to provide effective bilingual programs for their children.

---

[1]It was deemed appropriate to use the real name of the town because approval was received from the school district superintendent; it is also obvious because the actual name is used in newspaper accounts cited in the text.

The study focused on the rearing of children who were between the ages of 2 and 4 at the outset of data collection. By the end of Year 3, when the second year of observation of the immigrant families began, some of the immigrant families had a younger preschool child who then became part of the observations. The main focus of the study was on the balance between change and constancy in socialization practices that both distinguish and unify immigrant and first-generation Mexican-American parents.

The adults in the immigrant cohort were employed, for the most part, in factories and agricultural work. They spoke only Spanish and had attended school in Mexico. Employment for adults in the first-generation cohort was, as might be expected, more variable, ranging from clerical jobs to professional positions as teachers, in medicine, or as a computer analyst (see Table 3.1). All of the parents in the first-generation cohort had attended school in the United States. Seven of the nine had attended public school in Carpinteria; the remaining two had attended Catholic schools in Southern California. As Table 3.1 shows, this group of parents had a higher overall level of education than the immigrant group. Indeed, there was very little overlap between the educational attainment of the two groups. This situation is not surprising, given that school facilities are still in the process of development in Mexico (Tapia-Uribe, LeVine, & LeVine, chapter 2, this volume). Clearly, the acculturation that distinguishes immigrants from first-generation Mexican Americans includes educational and socioeconomic processes.

All of the immigrant families were first observed over a period of 1 year (immediately prior to their involvement in the parent/community organization). The first-generation families were also observed during this same year. Observations took place at least once a month and lasted approximately 1–2 hours each time. During the next 2 years, interviews were conducted with adult members of the 10 families, community leaders, and school personnel. In the fourth year, there was a post-COPLA year of observing the immigrant families, again at least once a month. Throughout the period of study, observations were also carried out in schools and in the community meetings which gave birth to the parent/community organization.

Observations in the households were announced to the families but they were asked to carry out their usual routine and, as much as possible, to try to ignore the observers. This accomplishment was attributed to a high degree of rapport established in prior months.

Family settings are private domains and observations are rarely value-free or totally objective. The challenge to study what Goffman (1959) termed *backstage behavior* deserves the rigor, intensity, and sensitivity afforded any other setting. Ethnographic research in the study of childrearing and early socialization has a well-rooted history in the disciplines of psychology, anthropology, and sociology (Baca-Zinn, 1980; Blood, 1963; Bott, 1957; Childs & Greenfield, 1980; Daniels, 1978; LeVine, 1974, 1982; Stacey, 1990; Watson-

TABLE 3.1
Profile of Immigrant and First-Generation Families

Family Name	Parent Employment	Parent Education	No. of Parents	No. of Children
		Immigrants		
Calvo	M, factory	M, EM	2	4
	F, gardener	F, HM		
Chapa	M, factory	M, EM	2	2
	F, plant nursery	F, EM		
Baca	M, school aide	M, EM	2	2
	F, plant nursery	F, HM		
Suarez	M, school aide	M, HM	2	3
	M, clerk	F, HM		
Mejia	M, unemployed	M, EM	2	2
	F, gardener	F, EM		
		First Generation		
Mendez	M, secretary	M, HS	2	2
	F, teacher	F, Univ		
Chavez	M, cook	M, JrHi	1	2
Ortiz	M, clerk	M, HS	2	3
	F, carpenter	F, HS		
Islas	M, secretary	M, HS	2	2
	F, teacher	F, Univ		
Alva	M, medicine	M, Univ	2	2
	F, computer analyst	F, Univ		

Note. M = mother; F = father; EM = elementary education in Mexico; HM = equivalent of high school in Mexico; JrHi = junior high school; HS = high school in the United States; Univ = university education.

Gegeo & Gegeo, 1992). Ethnographic methods reveal the processes embedded in the day-to-day interaction, which makes important abstract values explicit.

BEING A MEXICAN IN CARPINTERIA

Mexicans who have immigrated to Carpinteria during the past 20 years know a very different community than those who came earlier. Many people of Mexican descent came to Carpinteria in the early 20th century when immigration laws were more relaxed and the economic incentive to seek better opportunities was strong. Descendents of this migration wave constitute a significant part of the present-day Mexican-American family population in Carpinteria. The first-generation cohort share this history. The agricultural industry in Carpinteria was an appropriate "fit" for Mexicans who had the desired skills and motivation. It should be noted that the Chumash Indians had resided in Carpinteria since the 16th century and were hunters and fisherman; this left ample opportunities in agriculture for Mexicans.

The total population of Carpinteria did not exceed 1,000 residents until the mid-1940s (Stockton, 1960). Predictably, employment differentiated ethnic groups, as did geographic boundaries. The Mexicans took different jobs and resided in neighborhoods apart from the non-Latino population. This would be true of most heterogeneous U.S. urban areas.

Lemons and avocados were the principal crops worked by Mexicans in the Carpinteria area. By 1950, the Bracero program had brought in a new migration of Mexicans to work specifically in agriculture. Dutch, Japanese, and a few Mexican Americans owned ranches that employed Mexicans as laborers. This cohort of men did not bring their families because they were obligated to return to Mexico after their contracts terminated. However, many men married local women and raised their families in Carpinteria.

Mexican workers were valued but that did not grant them equal status in the work force, housing, social activities, or the schools (Menchaca & Valencia, 1990). Institutionalized segregation was active in the schools until the early 1970s. Mexicans were treated as a subordinate minority, their treatment historically conditioned by U.S. conquest of Mexican California (cf. Ogbu, chapter 18, this volume). According to a newspaper article from a nearby town, Santa Paula, the Carpinteria school board segregated Mexicans by classifying them as Indians; the state of California had ruled that isolating Indians was lawful:

> School authorities of Carpinteria have caused considerable interest in all parts of the state with their decision in declining to accept the ruling of Attorney General U.S. Webb that they cannot segregate Mexican, Chinese, Japanese and Indian children. . . . The Carpinteria school board takes the ground that children of Mexican born parents are Indians. . . . In Santa Paula the Mexican situation is handled in a tactful manner, school authorities believe. Many of the Mexicans are going to school in the Canyon and Ventura schools situated in their own sections of this city . . . the school situated in their own districts take care of the majority of the Mexican children, and special courses of study have been arranged for them. They are said to be happy in their own schools. (*Santa Paula Chronicle*, 1929, p. b-6; cited in Menchaca & Valencia, 1990, p. 240)

Institutionalized segregation was active in the schools until the early 1970s. By classifying Mexicans as Indians, the schools could legally segregate Mexicans into the Aliso School, which became known as the Mexican School. Children who attended the school at the time it was segregated recount the low expectations of their teachers:

> I remember being in the eighth grade and before that I was in low reading groups; it was a real shock for me because when I was in Catholic school I was

a very good student. Anyway, I did something silly and I turned in a terrible assignment. My teacher, who was the only Chicano teacher in the school said to me, "Jose, this is not like you and I expect a lot more from you." I felt so embarrassed and from that point on I began taking note of what I did and performing better. I guess I felt that I had someone who cared about how I did in school.

Jose was fortunate to have had a teacher who communicated clearly her higher expectations. However, most students faced constant ridicule simply because they were Mexican.

Mexican children were constantly reminded by the Euro-American community that they were inferior in school as well as in community affairs. An incident cited by one of the parents, Mr. Mendez, illustrates this point:

> If you ever brought *tacos de frijoles* to school, kids made fun of you so even though you loved to eat them more than any other food, and so you tried not to bring them. We were mostly Mexican but still it was like people already knew that being Mexican wasn't good enough. Anyway, one Saturday some of my friends and I went to the Tradewinds theater and most of us could not afford the money to buy popcorn and other goodies, so we took our own snack from home. So we were outside the theater waiting to get in and along comes Jesus, this kid riding on his bike. He hit a rock and flipped over and his lunch bag flew open and out come the tortillas and beans. I can still hear the comments ridiculing that kid. All I could think was, "sure glad it wasn't me."

Mexican children who had attended the segregated school and are first-generation parents in this study graduated from the high school by the time efforts were undertaken by the school district to provide equitable education. In fact, the climate for change in the schools was created in part by the same students who had come through the segregated school experience and had gone on to become teachers. Two of those teachers (Mendez and Islas) are part of the first-generation cohort in this study. In the early 1970s, the federal government provided funding for a bilingual program for limited English-speaking students. Carpinteria used these funds to create a bilingual program and preschool. The children who took advantage of these programs had parents who had immigrated more recently. For the most part, they were born in the United States, but their parents were predominantly Spanish speaking.

The current generation that immigrated during the past 15 years (after terminating their education in Mexico) arrived in Carpinteria at a time when the schools and the community had changed its segregationist policies. The bilingual preschool and bilingual program in the Carpinteria schools began to tug at the ethnic and language awareness of the educators. Since the inception of bilingual programs for Spanish-speaking students, educators have become more conscious of the educational needs of these children.

After federal funds were exhausted, the school district was not able or willing to assume financial responsibility for continuing the bilingual programs alone. As a consequence, the direct benefit to students, provision of teacher training, and the resources of teacher assistants were lost. All of these components had supported teachers' effectiveness in working with Spanish-speaking students.

By the mid-1980s, Spanish-speaking students were no longer making the academic gains that had initially characterized the school district's bilingual programs. The one exception to the declining quality of programs that addressed the needs of Spanish-speaking students was the bilingual preschool program. The teacher in charge of this program provided a rich curriculum (in Spanish), and also had created a strong relationship with the Spanish-speaking families and the community.

However, when the children left the preschool, few resources existed to help Spanish-speaking parents to make the connection with the school. As Spanish-speaking children moved up the academic ladder and learned more English, parents were distanced from them and the schooling process (Delgado-Gaitan, 1990). Some parents reported that by the time a child reached junior high school they felt as if they were "living with a stranger."

Parental knowledge about the school system is seen as an essential ingredient to effective socialization, and the impact of this factor in the home provides a powerful link between the family setting and social institutions.

The distance between many of the families and the school created problems for children's schooling.

The research yielded an action outcome: the formation of COPLA, a parent leadership group that taught Latino families to communicate better with the schools and to help their children in the home.

The first phase of the study occurred prior to the organization of the parent group. It functions as a baseline to highlight the changes in family interaction after the family's participation in COPLA.

SOCIALIZING CHILDREN: FAMILIES AT HOME

Family organization between parents and preschool children was constructed around verbal and nonverbal interaction in day-to-day activities. The themes that emerged from the data define the nature of parent–child cultural interaction in the homes.

What parents and children did and talked about varied with each family. At the same time, general patterns of interaction transcended individual differences. As a result, one can speak of a general cultural milieu as well as in-dividual family differences. Families shared common practices because they participated in the same social networks and social institutions.

For example, all of the families in the immigrant cohort knew each other as a result of their involvement with the schools. Teacher parents in the first-generation cohort also knew all of the immigrant parents because they had made contact through school committees. Some parents in the first-generation cohort knew each other because they had gone to school together, as had their children.

All of the families lived within the Carpinteria city limits; some lived in the poorer section of town, and two families lived on the ranches where they were employed as gardeners. Their living conditions and shared experiences made families in both cohorts fairly representative of Mexican Americans in the United States.

CRITICAL THINKING VERSUS RESPECT

Critical thinking is conceived as skills in verbal analysis, verbal questioning, and verbal argumentation. Although the operational definition of critical think-ing is verbal, it is assumed that practice and stimulation in critical speaking will ultimately be internalized as critical thinking processes. In the United States, a Eurocentric perspective defines an argument in terms of a linear model moving from Point A to Point B. The locus of authority in the individual is independent of age. That is, either an adult or a child can establish a posi-tion of power if he or she can formulate the correct logical argument.

Critical thinking can collide headlong with the value of respect brought by immigrants from Mexico (cf. Tapia Uribe, LeVine, & LeVine, chapter 2, this volume). The term *critical thinking* rather than *criticism* is used here be-cause it is not only criticism that would be considered disrespectful; it is any verbal expression of the child's opinion to an adult, especially one that differs from that of an older family member.

In their culture of origin, children are expected to politely greet their elders; they are not supposed to argue with them. In the company of adults, chil-dren are to be good listeners and can participate in a conversation only when solicited. To raise questions is to be rebellious.

Parents in both cohorts adamantly wanted their children to be respectful. Respect was an unquestioned value in these homes, although its actual manifestation varied across the cohorts. In the immigrant homes, children were constantly reminded not to be *malcriados* (naughty, meaning disrespect-ful). Respect was expected to be given to older members of the family, espe-cially adults. Sometimes parents tried to enforce a more respectful behavior between siblings but this was difficult.

Immigrant Families

Immigrant families evidence the value of respect in their daily activities. For example, on arrival at their grandmother's house, children would be instructed by their mother or father to greet their grandparents.

"Saluda a tu abuelita mi hija, ven aquí" [Say hello to your grandmother, my daughter, come here]. Mrs. Baca escorted Rosa toward her grandmother as she tried to run away and join her cousins whom she saw in the back yard. Rosa stood on her toes as if to try and reach her grandmother's face to kiss her cheek. Her grandmother bent down enough for Rosa to reach her and hug her tightly.

Rosa temporarily forgot about her cousins and walked into the kitchen with her mother, grandmother, father, and older brother. Rosa sat at the kitchen table and watched her grandmother approach the stove. *"Quiero de ese"* [I want some of that]. *"A donde apuntas, mi hija?"* [What are you pointing at, my daughter?] asked the grandmother. Rosa caught her mother glancing at her from the corner of her eye and lowered her voice and said, quietly, *"Quiero de esa tortilla con queso"* [I want some of that tortilla and cheese]. Mrs. Baca adds, *"Se dice por favor, Rosa. Pedir así no más es falta de respeto"* [You say "please." To ask just like that is nothing more than a lack of respect]. *"Por favor"* [Please] repeats Rosa. Rosa ate her snack and then lingered at the table nibbling on her tortilla, becoming interested in her mother's conversation with her grandmother on the topic of her older brother. Mrs. Baca began to recount that her son's belligerence had been a real problem during the week and that on one day, he missed the school bus. Rosa decided to enter the conversation, *"Y se tuvo que quedar en la casa leyendo"* [And he had to stay home reading]. Mrs. Baca looked at Rosa sternly and said, *"Usted acabe de comer y vaya a jugar afuera. Estas son platicas de adultos no para niñas. Es falta de respeto estar metiendo su cuchara"* [You finish eating and go outside to play. This is an adult conversation not for children. It's lack of respect for you to be putting in your two cents].

Mrs. Baca's message to Rosa instructed her in more than politeness. It was instruction on how to understand her role in the family system and what that entitles her to do. Children's place in the family did not include being a part of adult conversation.

Respect often meant that how one interacted with another should be guided by a sense of caring that is communicated through politeness. Almost all of the immigrant families (four out of five) addressed their children, especially the younger ones, in the formal *usted*, rather than using *tu*, the informal second-person pronoun. This was perhaps done as a model to teach them to use *usted* because children were expected to address their parents in the *usted* form as an indicator of respect. The formal register is generally expected of all age groups when addressing parents, although some variation may exist.

Immigrant Families After 2 Years
in an Educationally Focused
Parent/Community Organization

In COPLA, parents had been instructed to carry out academic activities, such as reading stories or writing letters and numbers, at home with their children. After participating in COPLA, immigrant parents did such activities and encouraged their children's verbal responses—questioning and negotiating—in the process. For example, Mrs. Mejia had learned from the preschool teacher to read with her children, and in addition had become quite active in the parent/community organization.

> After dinner, Mrs. Mejia sat with her preschool age daughter, Becky, to read her the story about Cinderella, a much requested favorite of Becky's. Mrs. Mejia began to read the story and was quickly interrupted by Becky who had a designated part of the story that she wanted to read herself. "*No leas esa parte, ya la se*" [Don't read that part, I already know it]. "*Esta bien, cual parte quieres que te lea. Yo creo que sabes todo el cuento, es tu favorito.*" [That's fine, which part do you want me to read to you? I think you know all of the story, it's your favorite]. Becky flipped the pages until she found the part where the fairy godmother gave Cinderella a beautiful dress. "*Aqui esta parte*" [Here this part]. Mrs. Mejia began to read the text, which told of the godmother who waved her wand and instantly gave Cinderella a new dress. "*Yo quiero un vestido asi, mami*" [I want a dress like that mommy]. "*Y que quieres que haga yo?*" [And what do you want me to do?] "*Tu eres mi madrina y me lo das asi como ella*" [You be my godmother and give it to me like her]. "*Aquí te va*" [Here you go]. She waved her hand like a wand. "No! *Tu no sabes como hacerlo. Mira no tengo un vestido chulo.*" [No! You don't know how to do it. Look I don't have a handsome dress]. "*Si, mira es color de rosa, que lindo se te ve*" [Yes, look it's pink, how beautiful it looks on you]. "No! *Comprame uno mami!*" [No! Buy me one mommy].

Fantasy here in the midst of a storytelling period allowed Mrs. Mejia to exchange with Becky in a way that permitted Becky to express her desires, both fantasy and real, and, most important, to critically negotiate with her mother.

However, a more authoritarian mode was evident in parent–child exchange at other times; for example, when Becky wanted to watch a television program forbidden by her father.

> One evening, Mrs. Mejia prepared dinner in the kitchen as Mr. Mejia sat in the living room reading the newspaper and turned on the Spanish-language news on television. Becky came in the room and whispered in Mr. Mejia's ear. His response implied that she had requested to change the channel on the TV. "*No mi hija. Horita no*" [No my daughter, not right now]. Becky sat next to her father

and said, "*Si, si! Yo quiero ver los Care Bears*" [Yes, yes. I want to see the Care Bears]. Mom from the kitchen called out. "*No sea malcriada, mi hija. Vayase a jugar con su hermano*" [Don't be spoiled, my daughter. Go play with your brother]. Mr. Mejia then called out. "Adrian, *llevate a tu hermana*" [Adrian, take away your sister].

There appeared to be a conscious separation between school-related activities and what Becky was allowed to do at home in interactions involving more routine activities. There were two sets of values operating here: one originating in the school environment, and the other originating in the family.

When children raise questions during family routines, it is considered rebellious by the parents. Yet when similar questions are raised in reference to school matters, parents accept and encourage interaction. In this situation, the children's behavior is viewed as necessary to academic progress and not as resistant to parental authority.

Role of Maternal Education

According to Laosa (1978, 1983), maternal education should be more important to interactions encouraging critical thinking than immigrant status per se. Variability within the immigrant cohort supports this view (see also Tapia-Uribe, LeVine, & LeVine, chapter 2, this volume). The only immigrant mother who attended high school in Mexico, Mrs. Suarez, always responded positively when her children asked questions, and she usually extended their questions.

> While looking at a family photograph album, Mario, the 4-year-old son asks, "*¿Quien es esa señora?*" [Who is that lady?]. Mrs. Suarez responds, "*Es mi tía, pero ustedes no la conocen*" [It's my aunt, but you don't know her]. "*Y por que se ve tan chistosa, mira como tiene el brazo?*" [Why does she look so funny, look at how she has her arm?] Mrs. Suarez responds, "*Pues, asi se paro, mi hijo. No es que tiene mal su brazo, es que asi estaba parada cuando tomaron la foto*" [Well, that's the way she stood up, my son. It's not that she has a bad arm, that's the way she was standing when they took the picture].

First-Generation Families

The formal register was not a part of the address between parents and children in any of the first-generation families. However, respect was a value that all parents in this cohort expressed as a top priority in early childrearing. For the most part, these adults had been raised by immigrant parents who expected respect, just as those in the immigrant cohort described here did.

First-generation parents wanted their children to be respectful to them, to grandparents, to other elders, and to their peers. Stressing respect was a conscious part of their interaction with their children; yet negotiation had also entered that discourse, as illustrated in an observation of the Mendez family.

It was after dinner; most of the family was watching TV. Four-year-old Paul called from his bedroom, "I don't want put on my pajamas yet Mom and Steve [older brother] says that I have to." "Well, you don't have to go to bed yet, dear, but I want you to start getting ready. Maybe I'll read you a story," responded his mother. Mr. Mendez then called to him also, "*Mi hijo*, [my son] do as your mother says, come on be a good boy." "But, how come Steve doesn't have to put on his pajamas right now? You pick on me cause I'm just a kid." "Paul, just put on your pajamas and stop whining." "I'm not whining or whatever you said I'm doing. That's not fair. Okay, if I put my pajamas right now can I come out there and watch TV?" "Okay, *mi hijo*, just for a few minutes," agreed his mother.

Paul and his parents showed us a style of negotiation that was not as prevalent in the immigrant families. Recognizing his position in the family, Paul tested the limits of his older brother's and parents' authority to obtain more freedom.

Such an exchange between children and parents was evident in other more structured scenarios such as in reading a story. Parents posed questions to their children about the story but children also asked questions. Mrs. Chavez reported reading to her 3-year-old daughter, Nancy. Mrs. Chavez read often to Nancy. Although she read some stories in English, she did speak Spanish to her children because her aunt from Mexico lived with them, and she did not speak English.

After dinner one evening, Nancy and her mother read one of her favorite books, *Minnie and Mickey's Picnic*, which was neatly placed in a space on the shelf in her room dedicated especially for books. With her mother at her side, Nancy began to leaf through the book and then her mother turned to the beginning of the book and began to read aloud. She read about two pages as Nancy listened. "It think Mickey and Minnie like picnics, don't you honey?" asked her mother. "Yeah, I like taking hamburgers to the park. Mom, they should pay attention to the television to see if it's going to rain; that way they wouldn't get wet." "Yes, dear that's a good suggestion. What would you do if you got caught in the rain during a picnic?" asked her mother. "I don't know. Probably run to the car. Mom, can we go on a picnic?" "Yes, maybe one of these weekends," responded her mother.

This brief excerpt from the Chavez' family reading activity shows the conversational nature of parent–child interaction congruent with that stressed by the teachers in school—a style that immigrant parents who participated in a community organization were attempting to learn.

All but one of the first-generation parents completed at least high school, and all persistently emphasized education for their children. Even before their children had begun preschool, parents actively helped them recognize numbers and colors, and they read to them frequently. The parents who were teachers seemed to almost always talk to their children as they did to their students. Their discourse often resembled teacher–student interaction as they read to their children or when they played a game or sang with them (cf. Tapia Uribe, LeVine, & LeVine, chapter 2, this volume). Spouses were also conscious of the need to have children express their thoughts and to pose analytical questions, but they were less strict about structuring their children's practice in writing and reading.

In comparison with the immigrant generation, first-generation parents invited more of their children's opinions and thoughts than did the immigrant families. In this generation, critical thinking had attained a broader scope of application, whereas respect had attained a narrower one.

INTERDEPENDENCE AND INDEPENDENCE

Interdependence as a practice and value in Carpinteria families refers to a person's role as an active, sharing family member. It does not necessarily mean dependent on others in a way that renders the person incapable of being responsible. In fact, interdependence in older children and adults is characterized by an expectation of performing household duties and supporting others. There is a collective character to the concept of interdependence that allows individuals to give and receive support. Collectivity is manifested by children with friends and other members of the family in tasks or play. Particularly in immigrant families, preschool children are not expected to perform household tasks. Interdependence in these families means expecting and accepting help when you are very young, then learning to give help as you get older.

In opposition to interdependence, independence, as shown by children taking action individually without instruction, often elicited help where needed from adults. In contrast to groups emphasizing the value of independence, autonomous behavior can be manifest to the extent that it does not cause inconvenience to self or others.

For example, a young girl wants to tie her *rebozo* but has difficulty so that it slows down her walking. Her mother notices this and walks back to ask her if she is having problems tying her *rebozo*. The child does not answer her, yet her mother proceeds to tie it, holding the ends and tying it as the daughter watches her mother's hands (Bertely Busquets, 1990).

In the first-generation families, verbal interaction plays a role as parents begin to teach independence. Yet, as we observe, independence takes the form of self-reliance with an underlying emphasis on collectivity.

Immigrant Families

Young children in immigrant families are not excluded from household tasks but their participation is not obligatory. Communication in this area is essentially nonverbal. Their closeness to other family members enables them to participate and learn not necessarily the technical task, but the social organization that embraces it.

Young children find themselves accompanying adults to (a) the grocery store, (b) the laundromat, (c) the post office, (d) the garden, and (e) the kitchen to wash dishes, as well as other places to perform daily chores. Apprenticeship (Lave, 1982) is not the goal in households; however, there is an aspect of learning that occurs in these contexts. That is, by the time children are old enough to be responsible for specific chores in the family, they have already become familiar with the task by being included as other family members do the chores.

Children in working-class immigrant families are expected to assume a great deal of responsibility by the time they are 7 years old, as observed in a northern California community (Delgado-Gaitan & Trueba, 1991). This is not necessarily a shift to independence. Rather, it is the other side of interdependence—responsibility for others, the distinction being autonomy (doing things for oneself) and interdependence (dependence on others and responsibility for others).

Often, parents cannot afford child care beyond the preschool hours, and thus rely on siblings and other family members to assist them in caring for young children. Perhaps because sibling and extended-family caregiving is a tradition in Mexican culture, something more than expediency is conveyed to children during the time they spend with others. Their older siblings and cousins become models for future socially responsible behaviors.

Relying on others for help was acceptable behaviors for young children, who sometimes requested assistance in dressing, eating, finding their playthings, carrying objects from their house to the car, and going to bed at night. At other times, they were provided help without requesting it. Immigrant parents believed that young children were naturally dependent on others. At the same time, young children were cared for by older members of the family, who assumed this responsibility. Children were not coached and coaxed to develop self-care skills. The nonverbal language of interdependence was subtle and almost went unnoticed compared with verbal interaction concerning independence in first-generation families in similar circumstances.

Did Participation in the Parent/Community Organization Increase the Socialization of Independence?

Immigrant parents involved in the parent/community organization applied many strategies in relating to their children, which they had learned from each other. However, teaching their children independence was not as readily adapted as critical thinking skills. Nonetheless, after COPLA, the language of independence ("You need to learn how to do it yourself") began to be used occasionally by immigrant parents.

First-Generation Families

When children reach 4 years of age in first-generation families, they have had a great deal of instruction about the need to be independent learners. Independence is stressed even though the child is still involved in family activities that emphasized interdependence. In other words, children may help their mothers do the wash at home while at the same time receiving explicit messages of independence.

For example, the Ortizes wanted Saul to learn how to play cooperatively with peers and to learn how to work cooperatively with family members. However, the verbal messages to Saul showed that independence was valued as well.

> One Saturday, Saul accompanied his father to the hardware store. His mother saw him run out without his jacket. "Come back here and put on your jacket, dear." Saul returned and walked into his room. "I can't find it," claimed Saul. "Where did you leave it?" called his mother from the living room. "I don't know," he responded. "Then look for it," suggested Mrs. Ortiz. Just then she caught sight of a sleeve of his jacket hanging behind the observer on the smaller couch. "Look, Saul, it's out here in the living room. Tell Mrs. Delgado-Gaitan 'excuse me' and get your jacket." Saul ran out the door and did not respond to his mother's last instructions, "You be good, and mind your father."

It was common for parents to assist children in everything they needed but to mediate the interaction with instructions to develop independent behavior. Both interdependence and independence were valued behaviors in these families.

A different example was evident in the interaction between Mr. Islas and his daughter.

He and 3-year-old Mimi were in the living room one evening after dinner. Mrs. Islas had returned from the corner store with two small bags of groceries and asked Mimi to take one of the bags and put it on the table in the kitchen. Mimi lifted the bag and said, "Heavy, mom, heavy." Mrs. Islas just kept walking into the kitchen without saying anything and Mimi dropped and left the bag in the middle of the living room. Mr. Islas offered to help, "Here, dear, I'll take it into the kitchen." Mrs. Islas: "It's not that heavy, she just wants you to carry it." "Well what do you want me to do, just leave it on the floor in the living room?" asked Mr. Islas. "No, just pretend to help her carry it and have her do it. She can learn how to do some things by herself. That's what the preschool teacher says." Mr. Islas then found the opportunity to have her help. "Mimi, *mi hija*, can you hand me the book from that table?" Mimi shook her head no and her father continued to cajole her until finally she responded and ran to the coffee table and handed him his book.

Parents sometimes differed in the way that they taught their children to be independent. However, the message here was clear: The parents were trying to comply with what the preschool teacher suggested.

The foregoing exchange between Mrs. and Mr. Islas typifies a slight difference in their relationship with the children. Although Mr. Islas had been a teacher in the Carpinteria schools and had more education than his wife, she tended to stay in closer contact with the teachers and followed the school curriculum closely. Mr. Islas spent less time with the children, and, although he cared for them and wanted them to enjoy school, he seemed less attentive to the explicit instructions and specific ways of shaping children's behavior. More often, he grabbed the children, one under his left arm and the second under his other arm, and swung them around, then rubbed their heads and told them to go play outside while he read the newspaper or talked to the research team. The children were left begging for more swinging but he would laugh and promise them more swings later. On occasion, he allowed Mimi to sit on his lap for a while but after a couple of minutes he told her to leave also.

The Islas children attended an English-speaking preschool where mostly Euro-American parents and very few Mexican Americans sent their children. It had a very good reputation in the community and it emphasized a great deal of play, but it also taught strict independence and self-reliance at an early age. Interdependence was apparently highly valued by immigrant families but became modified in subsequent generations.

If we look at interdependence and independence as a continuum, first-generation parents have acculturated and taught their children how to adapt to values such as independence as a response to this norm, which is emphasized by the school and society at large.

FAMILY UNITY AS AN ASPECT
OF INTERDEPENDENCE

Despite the variation of interdependence and independence, family practices
in the two cohorts of Mexican Americans in Carpinteria expressed strong
commitment to family unity. This was evidenced in their social networks with
family members who lived in Carpinteria, in neighboring communities, in
other states, and in Mexico. An advantage of observing families on weekends
was the opportunity to be invited to family social gatherings including first
communions, birthday celebrations, special community awards ceremonies,
weddings, *quinceñeras*,[2] and an occasional special shopping trip for major
items like a car to make a trip to Mexico. Most of these families in both cohorts lived in independent dwellings, with an occasional relative visiting for
an extended period of time. Other relatives lived nearby in Carpinteria and
Santa Barbara.

Immigrant families communicated frequently with other family members
in Carpinteria. However, the nature of their contacts was usually for the purpose of soliciting or providing daily needs such as child care and transportation to the doctor or the store. Sharing food items was also done, especially
when the relative lived across the street or next door. Families who lived
on the ranches where they worked or whose close family members worked
on ranches often had access to large quantities of fruit and vegetables that
were shared.

Communication with family members in Mexico was frequent. Immigrants'
trips to Mexico were far more frequent than those of the first-generation families. Funerals and weddings of close relatives, as well as *quinceñeras* and
baptisms occasioned trips to Mexico, even if only one member of the family
was able to attend. Frequent contact with family members in Mexico occurred
by telephone for more urgent matters such as the exchange of money. Occasionally letters were written by the adults and some of the older children,
who wrote in Spanish to their cousins and grandparents.

First-generation families had more relatives who lived in the Los Angeles
area and in other states but they also had relatives in Mexico and continued
contact with them concerning weddings, funerals, and *quinceñeras*. For fes-
tive events, communication usually occurred through the mail. Invitations
or letters arrived well in advance of the event. Members of the first-generation
families usually did not attend weddings in Mexico but cards or letters were
sent as a formality and out of respect. However, family illnesses and deaths
were announced through telephone, even those of distant relatives in Mexico.

---

[2]*Quinceñera* is the major celebration for 15-year-old Mexican girls. It is a combination of
religious and social event used to introduce the young lady to the community. The young lady
is escorted by a young man and has attendants who also have escorts. They attend a mass, followed by a dinner and a dance.

First-generation adults attended funerals of relatives in Mexico if it was a death of a close relative such as a grandfather or uncle.

Contact between family members in Carpinteria and those a short distance away was frequent. This occurred almost daily, or at least a few times during the week, by phone, especially with the parents (grandparents of the children in the study). Communication revolved around health issues, purchasing new items for the house, or making plans for visiting family members during the weekend. Saturday night dinners and late Sunday afternoon lunches were popular times for celebration, as well as a time for the children to visit grandparents.

Family networks reveal the value of interdependence across the two generations, even though independence is stressed with young children in first-generation families. Family unity persists as a value in the way that families serve as "funds of knowledge" for each other, as anthropologist Velez-Ibañez (1988) argued. He described the concept of "funds of knowledge" with various generations of Mexican Americans in Tucson, Arizona. He made the point that, as Mexican Americans remain in the United States for longer periods of time, and as they move into higher education and the professions, they often lose their language. However, this fact does not necessarily distance them from their culture. They remain close to other aspects of their culture through networks established with other members of the cultural group, trading services (child care, mechanics, restaurants, lawyers, etc.) provided by members of that community.

LANGUAGE PREFERENCE AND LANGUAGE USE

Hernandez-Chavez (1991) pointed out that availability of a full range of interactions is usually necessary for completely normal language acquisition. This is most likely to occur in a monolingual community. Thus, language loss accompanies diminished language use. As the social functions of an ethnic language become more restricted, so do the opportunities for the broad variety of meaningful interactions that are necessary for successful transmission of the language to the next generation.

In Carpinteria, language loss in the first generation and retention of Spanish in the immigrant families has occurred in a historical process.

Immigrant Families

Children in immigrant families grow up learning Spanish in the home. The preschool curriculum was totally in Spanish, therefore children continued its use in school as well as at home.

How and how much parents talked with children was more important than the choice of language. Immigrant parents generally said that they did not talk much with their children before their participation in the parent/community organization. The only exception was the Suarez family, the only immigrant family in which the mother had attained a high school education in Mexico. As mentioned earlier, this exception was very much in line with Laosa's (1978, 1983) conclusions concerning the effect of maternal education on parent–child interaction.

Parents commented that the children of an earlier generation were well nurtured, loved, and cared for. How parents spoke to children was not considered a factor in the children's social and academic development. Mrs. Mejia recalled that when her oldest son, Adrian, was the same age as her preschool daughter, she hardly talked to him except when accompanying him to the store. She was not aware that talking to her child was important until her son's kindergarten teacher told her that he would have to repeat a grade because he had not developed expressive language or sufficient vocabulary necessary for the first grade.

The teacher complained that Adrian did not respond to her when she asked him questions. When she questioned Mrs. Mejia about how much he talked at home, it was discovered that he usually played alone, that he was an only child, and that little if any conversation occurred between him and his parents.

Parents typically included their children in all family functions, although some may have not engaged in deliberate face-to-face conversation with their knee-high children as often as others. Children's play was typically something that children did alone or with other siblings. Parents agreed that although children received facile attention as infants, verbal communication with babies was "silly" because they believed that children could not understand them until later—after they began to talk.

The more-educated Suarez parents were exceptional among the immigrant parents in that they verbally engaged their children very early. They said that they had learned that talking with children in early years was important to develop language skills. Mrs. Suarez explained:

"Para nosotros hablar con nuestro niños es lo más importante. Yo les hablé desde que estaba yo en sinta y les cantaba. En mi familia los niños siempre han tenido mucha atençión de los papas y tios y abuelitos. Todos les hablan a los niños con mucho cariño y asi aprendi hacerlo yo con mis niños desde que estaban muy chiquitos" [For us, talking with our children is the most important thing. I talked to them since they were in the womb and I sang to them. In my family, the children have always received a great deal of attention from their parents, aunts and uncles, and grandparents. Everyone talks to the children with a lot of affection and that's the way I learned how to do it with my own children since they were babies].

Language Development through Participation
in a Parent/Community Organization

In the parent/community organization, parents shared ways to communicate with their children that enhanced their Spanish language development and ultimately helped them in school. Children's educational needs were the focus of the community organization, and as parents learned new skills and ideas they began to apply them at home.

For example, the Calvo parents began to talk more often with 3-year-old Mona than they had previously with their three older children. Mona stayed with a child-care provider (a nonfamily member) during the day because she did not meet the low economic criteria for this state-operated preschool. After work, Mrs. Calvo picked her up and brought her home.

> While Mrs. Calvo prepared dinner, Mona played in the living room. She talked in Spanish to her doll: "*Tu sientate aquí y yo voy a dibujar aquí. Ves tengo un color azul y voy a pintar una muñequita como tu*" [You sit here and I'm going to draw a picture. You see I have a blue color and I'm going to paint a little doll like you].
>
> From the kitchen, her mother called to her and asked her if she wanted juice. "*Mi hija, quieres poquito jugo de naranja?*" [My daughter, do you want a little bit of orange juice?]. Fresh orange juice was squeezed. Oranges were abundant in their household because the father tended the citrus fruit ranch on which they lived. Drawing a picture of her doll, she responded to her mother's question. "*Si, mami*" [Yes, Mommy]. Mrs. Calvo carried a small glass of orange juice into the living room and told Mona, "*Quidado que no se caiga el vaso en el sofa*" [Be careful that the glass does not tip over on the couch]. [Mona makes no response as if she did not hear.] "*Mi hija, No comprendes? Te hablo*" [My daughter, don't you understand? I'm talking to you]. Without responding to her mother's question, Mona looked up and handed her mother her drawing, "*Mira mami, mi muñeca*" [Look mommy, my doll]. She watched her mother as she smiled and commented, "*Ay que bonita la muñeca de mi hija. Como se llama tu muñeca? Eh?*" [How pretty the doll of my daughter! What is your doll's name?].
>
> Mona shrugged her shoulders and said, "*No se*" [I don't know]. Her mother then continued the conversation, "*Pues si no tiene nombre todavia, a ver si le damos uno ahorita. A ver como le llamamos?*" [Well, if she doesn't yet have a name, let's see if we give her a name right away. Let's see what we name her]. Mona quickly called out, "*Muñeca.*" "*Si, mi hija, pues eso es ella pero también puede tener nombre como tu. Eres una niña y te llamas Mona*" [Yes, my daughter, since that is she, but she can also have a name like you. You're a little girl and your name is Mona]. "*Le llamamos Betty*" [Let's call her Betty.] "*Me gusta mucho ese nombre. Yo creo que a tu muñeca le va gustar también*" [I like that name a lot. I think your doll will like it too]. At that point, the mother had returned to the kitchen.

This youngest child in the Calvo family has benefited from her parents' participation in school in a way that their older children did not.

The Calvos said that they had always read to their children including the oldest ones before they became involved in a parent/community organization. However, through their participation they had learned how to ask more precise and critical questions to their children about the stories in the book and to engage their children in conversation about their books and other daily activities. This kind of language use stimulates critical thinking, which was discussed earlier. Significantly, parents learned about the school's expectations and ways that they could help their children, despite their own limited school experiences.

First-Generation Families

Parents who had been schooled in the United States had an experience to share with their children different from that of immigrant parents. Some of them had attended segregated elementary schools in Carpinteria and did not have a university education. Some parents had completed their university education and held professional positions in spite of having attended segregated schools. In all but one case these were two-parent families. Distinct from immigrant families, this cohort spoke English as their primary language with Spanish spoken only on occasion, or with extended family members such as grandparents, who usually spoke only Spanish.

Active verbal engagement between parents and children was evident from the time of infancy. Home activity between parents and children during the child's preschool age usually included conversation. Commands, instructions, explanations, questions, and other conversations were frequent as mothers picked up children from their preschool or child care. Of these, the least common were commands and the most common were verbal instructions and questions. Verbal instruction of preschool children in household tasks tended to replace simply allowing them to observe and "peripherally participate" (Lave & Wenger, 1991), the mode favored by immigrant parents. For example, Mrs. Chavez made it a point to instruct her son, Carlitos, who was 7 years old at the time of the study, to help her do the chores around the house. Her 3-year-old daughter, Nancy, demanded a great deal of her time, and so she taught her son to help her with household chores. *"Carlitos, mi hijito, cuando laves los platos, tienes que limpiar el sink"* [Carlitos, my dear son, when you wash the dishes, you have to clean the sink]. Carlos returned to the sink without a word and wiped off the sink. Different from other first-generation families in the study, Mrs. Chavez occasionally spoke Spanish to her children. Although Mrs. Chavez was instructing Carlos to do something, and that could be considered a command, one could also view this as verbally teaching him how to perform a task.

During dinner, children usually initiated conversations with their parents. For example, Philip Alva often talked about his books and the puppy without addressing anyone in particular. Occasionally, Mr. or Mrs. Alva asked Philip if he liked his dinner.

"Do you like the rice, Lipe [his nickname]?" "Uh Ha, yeah. I want some more juice." "Okay," responds Mr. Alva, and gets up to fill his cup with more apple juice. Philip catches his sister's attention and says, "Hey, cherry cola." Then he bursts out laughing and this starts her laughing till Mrs. Alva tells them to stop being silly: "All right you two, either stop laughing and playing with your food or put your dishes in the sink and go to your rooms."

Mrs. Alva seemed to talk to Philip more than did his father. This difference may simply reflect the fact that, in our sample, mothers had primary responsibility for child care.

Nonetheless, Philip's father included him and his sister, Monica, in Saturday activities. Usually Monica declined and Philip and his father went to run errands together. On their trip, Mr. Alva called Philip's attention to planes or trucks they might see. For example:

Mr. Alva pointed to a plane and said, "Look, Lipe there's a plane." [Philip] "Look at the plane. Look at the plane, daddy." "Yeah, there it goes," responded the father. "Oh, look at the long truck, Lipe." Philip calls out, "Daddy, daddy, the truck, oh look at the truck. What color? It's white," says Philip. Father does not respond and continues driving.

In contrast, Mrs. Alva encouraged perception and differentiation. Philip's interactions with his mother differed from those with his father.

After school, Philip, who was 3 years old, his favorite book on zoo animals tucked under his arm, sat on the floor to "read." "Look Mom, look at the puppy." Mrs. Alva, washing dishes in the kitchen, stopped to look at the picture of the puppy in the book, "Yes, that's a coyote, look at his tail. Is that a short or long tail?" "Yeah, a tail; look Mom; look at the alligator. Oh look, what color is it? Green," he answered himself. "Look, Lipe, where does the alligator live?" asked his mother. Philip: "Water; look, look, look at the water. What color is it? Blue." His answer followed his question. Philip stayed on the kitchen floor and continued leafing through the book, talking to himself when his mother walked out of the room, "A bear, oh a bear. Look, there's a seal, and more seals. How many? One, two, three, four, eleven." In asking himself questions about the book, he has internalized his mother's role as interlocutor.

Initiating interaction between parent and child was mutual between Philip and Monica and their parents. Although parents addressed children, the children addressed their parents and expected responses. Parents responded to the children positively and extended their questions so as to make the children think again about what they were seeing. This type of interaction was more expected in the first generation than in the immigrant families before their participation in the parent/community organization.

Language: Comparing the Two Samples

The dialogue between parents and their preschool-age children in immigrant families that had participated in the parent/community organization differed little from what was found in the first-generation families. Parents verbally interacted with their children in both cohorts; the only difference was the intent. Parents who participated in the organization learned that talking with children in particular ways enhanced the opportunity for academic success.

Prior to participating in the organization, the one immigrant family with the most school experience talked to their children just as much, but they did not consciously do it for the purpose of cooperating with the expectations of the school. The culture of the school became explicit when Spanish-speaking parents organized with other parents and taught each other about the school and ways to prepare their children.

Language shift occurred between and within both cohorts. First-generation families spoke primarily English at home, whereas immigrant families spoke Spanish. Not only had English become the first language in one generation, but Spanish language loss was significant in most cases where its use was restricted to conversation with family elders.

Within the immigrant cohort, changes in language interaction that enhanced children's educational opportunity occurred in Spanish in the same generation as a result of the parents' social interaction with others in the community organization. In this social interaction, immigrant families learned about their position in the community and how it was possible to reshape their social conditions to obtain the resources due them. Just how the parent–child language patterns continue as the children advance in school and learn English needs to be studied.

INTERGENERATIONAL SOCIALIZATION OF CHILDREN: A DISCUSSION

This study focused on a California community in which Mexican Americans have undergone a significant cultural change. This cultural change raises some questions about etiology. In Carpinteria, Mexican-immigrant families were influenced by specific organizational forces that did not affect first-generation Mexican-American families. Change experienced by the immigrant families

studied involved principles that differed from the acculturation patterns experienced by the first-generation families. These principles related to family
strengths and the impact of change on the family delineated by Bronfenbrenner (1979), Cochran (1988), Cochran and Woolever (1983), and Delgado-
Gaitan (1990). They assumed that: (a) all families have strengths (Bronfren-
brenner, 1979; Cochran, 1988; Cochran & Woolever, 1983; Delgado-Gaitan,
1990); (b) different forms of childrearing are legitimate and promote the development of high-achieving students; and (c) parents can marshal resources
to help school their children (Cochran & Woolever, 1983; Delgado-Gaitan,
1990).

As children, parents in the first–generation families faced cultural and linguistic isolation and alienation in the school and community. This exacer-
bated the cultural discontinuities of social knowledge between home and
school. Although most of the parents had lost a great deal of their Spanish
language, their experiences in school and their educational attainment shaped
the learning environment for their children. Mostly, they tried to make it
congruent with the school's values while maintaining a sense of identity with
their own culture.

Immigrant and first-generation Mexican families wanted their children to
adapt successfully. Parents often tried to "remake" their roles as primary socializing agents and to rethink their goals in the face of historical and current community influences. In so doing, the home culture became more
congruent with that of the school and community at large.

The parent/community organization, COPLA, allowed families greater opportunity to participate without rejecting their language and culture. It provided immigrant families a structure, which led to empowerment in the process
of cultural change.

The effect of Spanish-speaking families learning how to improve their children's schooling opportunities was twofold. First, it forced the schools to improve their programs for Spanish speakers (see Delgado-Gaitan, 1992). Second,
families learned from each other how to build learning environments in their
homes that would correspond to the school's expectations (e.g., about expressive language).

That parents decided on their agendas for change in the community organization raised their experience of cultural change to a level of empowerment beyond that of school-mediated interventions. That is, families reflected
on their cultural values and their position in the community and used this
knowledge to determine their own direction for change.

Immigrant families involved in the parent/community organization recognized their strengths and built on them. They wanted their children to learn
to become respectful and cooperative people as they learned how to participate in U.S. society. Within the framework of these goals, they learned how
to extend their language patterns to include those learned in school. Like

the first-generation parents, immigrant parents used their newly acquired competencies to enhance their children's learning environments.

In a study of Chicano parents and their 5-year-old children, Laosa (1983) concluded that

the schooling level attained by a Chicano woman is a very strong predictor of the strategy that she, as a mother, will use to teach her own child. In contrast, the measured occupational status, either the woman's or her husband's, is generally unrelated to the woman's choice of maternal teaching strategies. (p. 85)

This study makes a strong case for the kind of education that community empowerment-based organizations, such as the parent/community organization illustrated here, can provide for mothers, and the contribution that it makes toward the overall sociocultural adjustment of low socioeconomic families. The study also provides more evidence concerning the impact of maternal schooling on how a mother teaches her own children at home. However, we see that learning and education are available not only through formal schooling but also through various informal means, illustrated by the way in which immigrant parents' participation in COPLA has been a catalyst for cultural change in Carpinteria.

Cultural change in family values as examined here raises the possibility of cultural loss in the areas of respect, interdependence, and language. Essentially, respect is valued more than the maintenance of Spanish in first-generation families. Even when Spanish language is lost, parents insist on children being respectful of themselves and others.

But what happens as new behaviors, such as inquiry skills, are acquired? When a child is expected to question or challenge, does he or she lose respect? For immigrant families who participated in the parent/community organization, respect and critical thinking were accommodated in dual contexts. Respect, in its culturally specific definition, seems to mean being highly considerate of others and is displayed in allowing the other person to hold authority. But what happens to such consideration when the expectation is for the child to question or challenge? What seems to be happening in immigrant families is that such challenging behaviors are relegated to school-related contexts and become appropriate in those contexts and those contexts only.

On the other hand, first-generation parents have integrated both behaviors in a way that still holds respect as an esteemed value when addressing persons of authority (e.g., parent, relatives, teachers) but consider children's inquiry skill a necessary competency for success in the world outside of the family. Possibly the parents' own acculturation experiences have made them incorporate a sense of reality and the need to accommodate *both* values in a way that allows them to fit in both worlds: family and society. This reality is what is transmitted to their children. The tacit expectation on the part of the parents is that both can and should coexist and do not necessarily detract from one another.

To say that parents do not get concerned about changing family values would be to ignore a real tension that haunts immigrant parents in particular. During the preschool-age years, parents are able to exert a strong influence on their children. As children get older, parents fear that they will become too Americanized and forget their language and culture (Delgado-Gaitan & Trueba, 1991). They watch their children lose their language as they move up the academic ladder; they feel that they have to supervise their children carefully to protect them from negative peer influence. They often feel inadequate to guide them in their academic and occupational decisions.

An active parent in the parent/community organization, Mrs. Aranda, shone a different light on the concerns of Mexican families. She often began her talks with the Spanish-speaking parents by stating that one of the important roles of this type of organization was to reinforce the bonding that Mexican families had and the continuation of traditional cultural values. She reminded them that they shared a common language, religion, and set of cultural values that raised the importance of family and children above all else. She increased their sense of pride by adding that it was these shared interests that would support them in their new direction to obtain the resources they needed for their children. This sense of community that parents participating in the organization were attempting to build legitimized their language and other cultural values as the core of their dialogue with the schools and the larger community.

Cultural change considered in this context is reminiscent of Freire's (1973, 1985) work. Through the collective process, people who have historically been oppressed discover their strengths and make a conscious choice to transform the condition that has traditionally isolated them. The goal of such educational movements must be to use collective means to adapt to the demands of the school for critical thinking and individual achievement.

CONTINUITY AND DISCONTINUITY

Continuities and discontinuities exist not only between Mexican-American and Euro-American mainstream populations but also between the first-generation and the immigrant group. On the macrolevel, both of these groups experience discontinuities from the mainstream society primarily on issues pertaining to historical discrimination from Euro-American society. On a more microlevel, both groups experience discontinuity with schools and other institutions because they have been excluded from full participation in the schools. What parents most often lack is cultural knowledge on how to deal with the schools, creating continual discontinuity between home and school.

Although first-generation families lose Spanish language proficiency, they become more continuous with mainstream culture in English language communication, as well as competitiveness (Kagan & Madsen, 1972) and individuality. However, their continuity with Mexican family values reveals loyalty and unity, allowing them to participate in multiple communities.

Economic and historical developments both constrain and permit access to opportunities accorded the dominant cultural groups, and they played a role in shaping the day-to-day lives of Mexican families in Carpinteria. Both groups of Mexican families have been isolated in that they have historically and in present times faced differential treatment as a result of skin color, language, and social class.

Although values and practices such as respect, interdependence, and the Spanish language provide part of a common thread, that same thread frays at different points because of historical changes in the conditions of immigration. When their parents immigrated to the United States, the first-generation group in Carpinteria faced discriminatory social policies and practices that relegated the adults to low-paying jobs in agriculture and separated the families socially, geographically, and educationally by punishing the children for using Spanish. Segregating Mexican children and banning use of Spanish in school denied them use of their language and access to good schools, and pushed them into social isolation. Children growing up under these conditions adapted by ignoring Spanish and preferring English so as to prevent them from facing further prejudice. Thus, English became the dominant language of the first-generation parents and the vehicle used to raise the second generation.

In contrast, immigrant families in this study came into Carpinteria during an entirely different political climate, which provided their children with educational programs that allowed the use of Spanish and where ethnic, cultural, and racial differences were tolerated more than in previous years. Their children were expected to maintain the use of Spanish and to learn English as well. Parents were cultural mediators between the old and new. Community organizations like COPLA in Carpinteria facilitate a better transition for immigrant families into a new culture, because cultural values and traditions of the particular group are recognized as strengths and are used to build the necessary links between parents and children, as well as between families and schools.

ACKNOWLEDGMENTS

I would like to thank Patricia Greenfield, Rod Cocking, Emmy Werner, Karen Watson-Gegeo, and Marcia Goodman for their insightful feedback on earlier drafts of this chapter. Earlier versions were presented in a workshop of

the National Institute of Mental Health on continuities and discontinuities in
the cognitive socialization of minority children in Washington, DC, June 1991,
organized by Patricia M. Greenfield and Rodney R. Cocking.

REFERENCES

Achor, S., & Morales, A. (1990). Chicanas holding doctoral degrees: Social reproduction and cul-
tural ecological approaches. *Anthropology & Education Quarterly, 21,* 269–287.
Baca-Zinn, M. (1980). Employment and education of Mexican American women: The interplay
of modernity and ethnicity in eight families. *Harvard Educational Review, 50* (February), 47–62.
Barr, D. (1989). *Power and empowerment* (Final Report for the Ford Foundation, Grant #875-0719).
Ithaca, NY: Cornell University, College of Human Ecology.
Bereiter, C., & Engleman, S. (1966). *Teaching disadvantaged children in preschool.* Englewood
Cliffs, NJ: Prentice-Hall.
Bertely Busquets, M. (1990). *Procesos de adaptacion escolar y docente en una comunidad maza-
hua del estado de Mexico.* Mexico: Departamento de Investigaciones Educativas de Centro
de Investigacion y de Estudios Avanzados del Instituto politecnico Nacional.
Blood, R. O. (1963). New approaches in family research: Observational methods. In M. B. Suss-
man (Ed.), *Sourcebook in marriage and the family* (pp. 538–543). Boston: Houghton Mifflin.
Bott, E. (1957). *Family and social network.* New York: The Free Press.
Bronfenbrenner, U. (1979). *The ecology of human development: Experiments by nature and de-
sign.* Cambridge, MA: Harvard University Press.
Bronfenbrenner, U. (1982). *The ecology of human development.* Cambridge, MA: Harvard Univer-
sity Press.
Childs, C. P., & Greenfield, P. M. (1980). Informal modes of learning and teaching: The case of
Zinacanteco weaving. In N. Warren (Ed.), *Studies in cross-cultural psychology* (Vol. 2, pp.
269–316). London: Academic Press.
Cochran, M. (1988). Between cause and effect: The ecology of program impacts. In A. R. Pence
(Ed.), *Ecological research with children and families* (pp. 143–160). New York: Teachers Col-
lege Press.
Cochran, M., & Woolever, F. (1983). Beyond the deficit model: The empowerment of parents
with information and informal supports. In I. E. Sigel & L. P. Laosa (Eds.), *Changing families*
(pp. 225–245). New York: Plenum.
Cromwell, R., & Ruiz, R. E. (1978). The myth of macho dominance in decision making within
Mexican and Chicano families. *Hispanic Journal of Behavioral Sciences, 1,* 355–373.
Daniels, A. K. (1978). Women's worlds. *Society, 15,* 44–46.
Delgado-Gaitan, C. (1987). Traditions and transitions in the learning process of Mexican chil-
dren: An ethnographic view. In G. Spindler & L. Spindler (Eds.), *Interpretive ethnography
of education at home and abroad* (pp. 333–362). Hillsdale, NJ: Lawrence Erlbaum Associates.
Delgado-Gaitan, C. (1990). *Literacy for empowerment: The role of parents in children's educa-
tion.* London: Falmer.
Delgado-Gaitan, C. (1992). School matters in the Mexican-American home: Socializing children
to education. *American Educational Research Journal, 29,* 495–513.
Delgado-Gaitan, C., & Trueba, H. (1991). *Crossing cultural borders: The education of immigrant
families in America.* London: Falmer.
Deutsch, M. (1967). *The disadvantaged child: Selected papers of Martin Deutsch and associates.*
New York: Holt, Rinehart & Winston.
Dunn, L. (1987). *Bilingual Hispanic children on the U.S. Mainland: A review of research on their
cognitive, linguistic and scholastic development* (Research monograph). Circle Pines, MN: Ameri-
can Guidance Service.

Freire, P. (1973). *Education for critical consciousness.* New York: Continuum.

Freire, P. (1985). *The politics of education: Culture, power and liberation.* South Hadley, MA: Bergin & Garvey.

Garbarino, J. (1982). *Children and families in the social environment.* New York: Aldine.

Goffman, E. (1959). *The presentation of self in everyday life.* New York: Doubleday.

Heller, C. (1966). *Mexican American youth: Forgotten youth at the crossroads.* New York: Random House.

Hernandez-Chavez, E. (1991). *Native language loss and its implications for revitalization of Spanish in Chicano communities.* Unpublished manuscript, University of New Mexico, Albuquerque.

Hess, R. D., & Shipman, V. C. (1965). Early experience and the socialization of cognitive modes in children. *Child Development, 36,* 869–885.

Holtzman, W., Diaz-Guerrero, R., & Swartz, J. (1975). *Personality development in two cultures—A cross-cultural longitudinal study of school children in Mexico and the United States.* Austin: University of Texas Press.

Inkeles, A. (1955). Social change and social character: The role of parental mediation. *Journal of Social Issues, 11,* 12–23.

Kagan, S., & Madsen, M. C. (1972). Rivalry in Anglo-American and Mexican children of two ages. *Journal of Personality and Social Psychology, 24,* 214–220.

Laosa, L. M. (1978). Maternal teaching strategies in Chicano families of varied educational and socioeconomic levels. *Child Development, 49,* 1129–1135.

Laosa, L. M. (1983). School, occupation, culture, and family: The impact of parental schooling on the parent–child relationship. In I. E. Sigel & L. M. Laosa (Eds.), *Changing families* (pp. 79–136). New York: Plenum.

Lave, J. (1982). A comparative approach to educational forms and learning processes. *Anthropology and Educational Quarterly, 13,* 181–188.

Lave, J., & Wenger, E. (1991). *Situated learning: Legitimate peripheral participation.* Cambridge, England: Cambridge University Press.

LeVine, R. (1974). Parental goals: A cross-cultural view. *Teachers College Record, 76*(2), 326–331.

LeVine, R. (1982). *Culture, behavior and personality: An introduction to the comparative study of psychosocial adaptation.* New York: Aldine.

Menchaca, M., & Valencia, R. (1990). Anglo-Saxon ideologies in the 1920's–1930's: Their impact on the segregation of Mexican students in California. *Anthropology and Education Quarterly, 21,* 222–249.

Ogbu, J. (1982). Cultural discontinuity and schooling. *Anthropology and Education Quarterly, 13*(4), 290–307.

Ogbu, J. (1990). Cultural mode, identity and literacy. In J. W. Stigler, R. A. Shweder, & G. Herdt (Eds.), *Cultural psychology: Essays on comparative human development* (pp. 520–542). New York: Cambridge University Press.

Pence, A. R. (1988). *Ecological research with children and families: From concepts to methodology.* New York: Teachers College Press.

Spindler, G. (1974). The transmission of culture. In G. Spindler (Ed.), *Education and cultural process: Toward an anthropology of education* (pp. 279–310). New York: Holt, Rinehart & Winston.

Spindler, G. (Ed.). (1987). *Education and cultural process: Anthropological approaches* (2nd ed.). Prospect Heights, IL: Waveland.

Stacey, J. (1990). *Brave new families.* New York: Basic Books.

Steward, R. A. (1955). *Theory of culture change.* Urbana, IL: University of Illinois Press.

Stockton, G. (1960). *La Carpinteria.* Carpinteria, CA: The Carpinteria Valley Historical Society.

Suarez-Orozco, M. (1989). *Central American refugees and U.S. high schools: A psychological study of motivation and achievement.* Stanford, CA: Stanford University Press.

Velez-Ibañez, C. (1988). Networks of exchange among Mexicans in the U.S. and Mexico: Local level mediating responses to national and international transformation. *Urban Anthropology and Studies of Cultural Systems and World Economic Development, 17*(1), 27–51.

Watson-Gegeo, K., & Gegeo, D. W. (1992). Schooling, knowledge, and power: Social transformation in the Solomon Islands. *Anthropology and Education Quarterly, 23*(1), 10–29.

Whiting, B. B., & Edwards, C. P. (1988). *Children of different worlds: The formation of social behavior.* Cambridge, MA: Harvard University Press.

Williams, N. (1990). *The Mexican American family: Tradition and change.* Dix Hills, NY: General Hall.

Zintz, M. V. (1969). *Education across cultures* (2nd ed.). Dubuque, IA: Wm. C Brown.

4

INTERGROUP DIFFERENCES AMONG NATIVE AMERICANS IN SOCIALIZATION AND CHILD COGNITION: AN ETHNOGENETIC ANALYSIS

Roland G. Tharp
University of California at Santa Cruz

As one examines continuities and discontinuities between societies of origin and societies of contemporary minority status, and the consequences for cognitive functioning and socialization, a consideration of Native-American Hawaiians and Native-American Navajos offers a comparison of some interest. Both groups have been incorporated into the United States by conquest, and they are highly similar in a socialization for survival typical of traditional peoples. However, they are sharply different in the dimension of socialization for individualism versus collectivism. For Hawaiians, the island ecological system produced a collective productive economy, and a socialization system that produced cognitive operations of a collective style. The nomadic, and later pastoral, eco-productive system of the Athabascan peoples (of which the Navajo are the currently most salient group) produced a much more individualistic orientation, both in production and cognition. Although the patterns of individualism are still collectivistic in comparison with Euro-American tradition, Navajo child cognition contrasts clearly in important dimensions in Hawaiian child thinking—in ways that correspond to surviving socialization practices in the two cultures.

In this discussion, I draw on observations made largely in schools because that has been my domain of activity for some years. Although the domain is limited, it has the advantage of revealing cognitive processes while fully engaged and in action. These data, often ethnographic or entirely informal, nevertheless are often more illuminating than the results of abstracted and decontextualized measurements of different cognitive abilities. This issue was clearly phrased by Minick (1985):

> [T]he key to understanding the relationship between the social and the psycho-logical lies not in comparing the cognitive capacities that characterize the think-ing of middle class white Americans and traditional Navajos, but in comparing the thinking of the Western trained physician and the Navajo herbal specialist. It is in studies of the mind in social action. . . . Inherent in an activity oriented approach to this problem is a movement away from the kinds of dichotomous modes of characterizing cultural differences in thinking that have . . . dominat-ed discussions of mind and society throughout the history of anthropology. Also inherent in this approach is a movement away from the equally dichotomous modes of characterizing cultural differences in thinking that are typical of much of contemporary cross-cultural psychology (e.g., those reflected in such con-trasts as between field dependent and field independent or the presence and absence of formal operations). (pp. 361–362)

The first section of this chapter is a brief review of the theoretical frame-work for developmental processes that informs this work. I then describe a particular cognitive dimension (wholistic vs. analytic), on which the chap-ter focuses, and then describe how this dimension appears to operate in the two groups of children in schools, Hawaiian and Navajo, offering a brief description of the relevant dimensions of the cultures that appears to under-grid the cognitive organizations.

LEVELS OF CAUSATION

As I consider the sociocultural roots of cognitive functioning and develop-ment, my explicit concern with continuities and discontinuities acknowledges that I presume causative influences both proximal and distal, both historical and contemporary. Of course, it is known that all human events are "over-determined" (i.e., they cannot be understood by any simple causal attribu-tion). For example, the phylogenetic and ontogenetic levels of explanation are not contradictory but mutually enriching. I suggest that the forces acting on any one developmental event can be understood as operating through a funnel of four levels, in which each level is simultaneously potent.

Thus, the phylogenetic level of causation operates through processes that I term *evolutionary*, and typically in spans of time between aeons and millen-nia. The ontogenetic level of causation operates through processes that I describe as *biographical* and in time spans roughly between centuries and decades. The microgenetic causative level operates through acquisitional processes (of learning, imitation, etc.) and in time periods that vary from dec-ades to moments.

Seldom considered, however, is the level of causation that operates in processes that I call *historical* and in time periods between millennia and centuries. In Fig. 4.1, that level is labeled *ethnogenetic*, meaning by this term the process whereby a people (i.e., an ethnic group) comes into and modifies the terms of its existence.

This "funnel and filter" conception is the latest revision (see, e.g., Tharp & Burns, 1989) of my efforts to schematize this layering of genetic levels. The concept derives from L. S. Vygotsky, and many of his interpreters have made similar efforts (e.g., Engestrom, n.d.; Cole, 1992). This conception is now beginning to impact American academic developmental psychology but ethnogenesis as an explanatory level has been historically and peculiarly absent in major theoretical systems of Western psychology. This is despite the obvious: Conditions of human life, present in every significant transaction, flow from historical processes—processes that have matured for hundreds of years and that operate causatively in present time.

In this chapter, I propose to exemplify this model of analysis by considering cognitive and educational problems and solutions at the ethnogenetic level (i.e., by taking into account the historical processes of culture of origin but considering them as they are filtered by events and forces in individual life history, learning experiences, and current conditions). Ethnogenetic analysis does not per se discount more contemporary and individualized development events; to consider less than the entire layered funnel of developmental processes would result in stereotypy and deny the richness of the individual differences in accommodation characteristic of the members of each ethnic group.

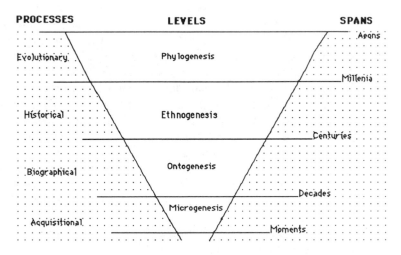

FIG. 4.1. The funnel and filters of development.

WHOLISTIC VERSUS ANALYTIC THOUGHT

The particular cognitive dimension that is the focus of this chapter is that of wholistic versus analytic thinking. If there is one descriptive feature common to descriptions of Native-American cognition it is that of "wholistic." Indeed, the Native American can be regarded as the anchor example for wholism. The principal position of this chapter is that although Native Hawaiians tend toward wholistic thinking as compared with Euro-Americans, Native Indians are far more wholistic in cognition than either. Later in the chapter these differences in cognitive style are linked to socialization processes emerging from econiche differences, and these in turn are examined for implications for educational processes in public schools.

In wholistic thought, the pieces derive their meaning from the pattern of the whole; in analytic thought, the whole is revealed through the unfolding of the sections. Wholism and analyticism operate in perception, problem solving, interpretation, and action. In the light of available evidence, it is conservative to say that Native Americans are more likely to operate wholistically, whereas Euro-Americans are more likely to operate analytically.

Two examples are illustrative. R. Scollon (personal communication, 1988) told the story of involving Yukon Native elders in constructing a lesson plan unit for the school that would teach a traditional craft, making moccasins of caribou skin. The elders' 16-week unit began with preparations for the hunt; moccasins per se did not appear until the 15th week.

To the elders' way of thinking, it is not possible to understand the moccasin outside the context of the leather, which is not understandable outside the spiritual relationship of the caribou to the land. Contrast this with the analytic way of proceeding, in which we probably would have given the children the pattern to start cutting out the leather in the first 15 minutes.

A Chilcotin Indian informant told me the story of her learning to prepare salmon. She was allowed to watch her mother and gradually take on portions of the task. She was also allowed to ask questions if they were important; once she told her mother that she did not understand how to do the backbone part. In response, her mother took another entire fish and repeated the process. It is not possible to understand the backbone except in the context of the whole fish; it is not possible to understand the moccasins except in the context of the relationship of band to the caribou.

In usual scientific discourse, we attempt to understand wholistic thinking by writing about it in an analytic, linear, sequential way. Here, I reverse the process and attempt to explain this central difference by wholistic, visual representations.

Figure 4.2 may be taken as representing a "Thing To Be Understood." It is an abstract representation—a sign for any "Thing."

Figure 4.3 represents the action of an analytic thinker attempting to un-

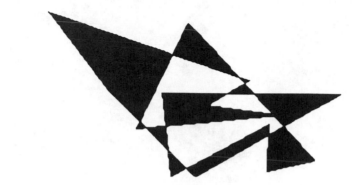

FIG. 4.2. The Thing to be understood.

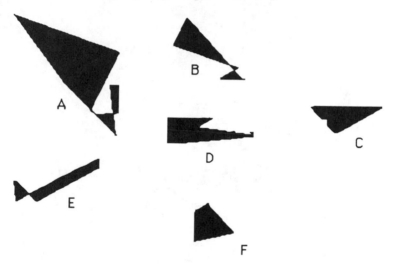

FIG. 4.3. The Thing disassembled.

derstand this Thing. It is dissassembled, each of its parts are inspected, and their relationships to one another and to the whole are considered.

A next, more intense effort to understand the Thing is represented by Fig. 4.4, in which the parts are considered as separate things. Thus, A, B, C . . . n are rotated and inspected, and hypotheses about other possible relationships and dynamics are considered.

As the final act of understanding in this analytic mode, the Thing is reassembled (return to Fig. 4.2). At that point, the linear thinker can say that the Thing is understood.

Wholistic thinking approaches understanding in an entirely different way. Figure 4.5 indicates this process: For wholistic thinking to say that the Thing is understood, the context must be discovered. In Fig. 4.5, an examination

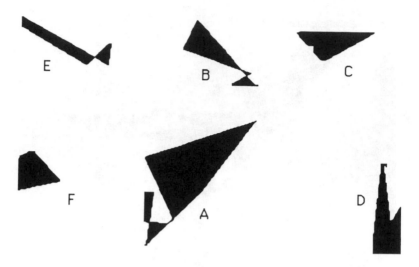

FIG. 4.4.   The parts of the Thing inspected.

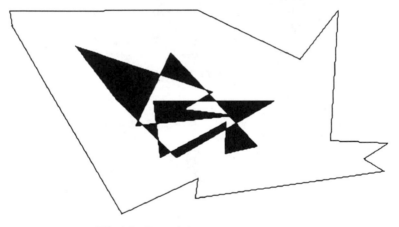

FIG. 4.5.   Finding the context of the Thing.

of the context of the Thing reveals a larger white field in which the Thing is located. The discovery of that field allows us to understand the Thing more deeply. For example, we can perceive that the white inner portions of the Thing are of the same material as the white surround. We then understand that the black is not only an enclosure but is enclosed.

A second, more intense effort to understand the Thing wholistically is represented by Fig. 4.6, in which the context of the context is discovered. The black field that surrounds the white context reveals that the black portions of the Thing are related to the larger whole; then we may understand why the thing is black, and we perceive that the Thing exists in a

FIG. 4.6. The context of the context of the Thing.

pattern of deep rhythm—beats of which lie both within and beyond our perception.

When the widest possible context has been discovered, wholistic thought is satisfied and the thing may be said to be understood. The backbone is placed in the fish, and the moccasins are understood in the context of band and caribou.

As we shall see, when children are taught to "understand," these two understandings of understanding produce different classroom transactions.

AN ETHNOGENETIC ANALYSIS OF WHOLISTIC THINKING

How does this pattern of thinking come about? The wholistic pattern of thought exists as a historically generated complex, that can be seen in many intersupportive aspects: (a) Perceptual, (b) problem-solving, (c) semiotic, (d) neurological, (e) representational, (f) sociological, and (g) interpersonal dimensions are each aspects of a unified whole. Different writers have emphasized on or more of these dimensions. My purpose here is to emphasize their unity and mutual interdependence.

A fundamental aspect of this complex is observational learning. Cazden and John (1971) discussed this preference for "learning by looking more than learning through language" (p. 256)—an aspect of Indian children's superior visual abilities. Longstreet (1978), Werner and Begishe (1968), and Deyhle (1983) all discussed that, among Native-American peoples, there is a learning system of private, imagined practice that allows "learning without public failure." Cazden and John (1971) discussed this as "competence before performance."

This complex necessarily includes a sociological dimension: For a society to rely on observational learning as the major mode for child socialization, adult behaviors and role performances must be available for prolonged and careful scrutiny by children; the culture must be "within the direct reach of the sensory organs" of the child (Pettit, 1946). This means that children are incorporated into the activity settings of the society. Technological cultures often require verbal explanation before children can understand adult activities. In the "observational learning complex," the adult behaviors can be understood with only occasional verbal explanation.

The process was put succinctly by Tafoya (1983), doyen of American-Indian potters, herself both daughter and mother in a family of distinguished artists in clay:

> My girls, I didn't teach them . . . they watched and learned by trying. I was taught to stay with the traditional clay designs, because that was the way it was handed down to my mother and me. I am thankful for my mother teaching me to make the large pieces (which require special skill and understanding). I watched her and tried to do like she did. And, I did.

The complex has a dimension of semiotics. Wyatt (1978–1979) and Phillips (1983) reported that the Mt. Currie and the Warm Springs Indian children are expected to listen quietly to the long telling of stories. John-Steiner and Osterrich (1975) discussed this same phenomenon among Pueblo children and provided a link from this interpersonal event to a cognitive style:

> Children listening to the many legends of their people learn to represent these visually . . . because they are not allowed to ask questions or verbally reflect on what they hear. They are to say only *aeh hae* to acknowledge auditory attention. As a result, while the verbal representations of some of these legends are fairly simple nursery tales, the inner representations of the same legends, for older children and adults, are replete with highly abstract visual and symbolic articulations of cultural values. (p. 192)

Is there a neurological dimension? The wholistic versus analytic cognitive pattern has been reified into a typology by the recent popular work on cerebral hemispheric specialization, with the wholistic described as a "right-brain" function and the linear sequential pattern a "left-brain" location. Cerebral hemispheric specialization has generated a proliferation of theories and some solid experimental evidence (e.g., Allen, 1983) and considerable discussion of the educational implications of right- versus left-hemispheric specialization (e.g., Bogen, 1975). This issue is relevant here because many writers have leaped an evidential chasm; they have concluded that, because Native Americans demonstrate patterns of abilities and proclivities that sound rather like what the neurocognitive literature describes as "right-brain" patterns, therefore American Indian are characteristically, and presumably genetically, right-brain rather than left-brain dominant (e.g., Browne, 1984). In a recent review of this position, Chrisjohn and Peters (1986) concluded that the "right-brained Indian" has to be considered a myth rather than a scientifically valid fact.

Regardless of how cognition is organized neurologically, there are clear patterns of perception and problem-solving abilities that are associated with the wholistic complex. For example, Browne's (1984) own study presented a set of factored intellectual abilities data, demonstrating an American-Indian pattern clearly different from that of the (predominantly) non-Indian standardization sample. In WAIS tests, for Native Americans, the four highest ranking subtests were Mazes, Object Assembly, Picture Completion, and Block Design, with a significant overall Performance over Verbal subscale difference—a frequently reported pattern. McShane and Plas' (1982) results of comparative testing again demonstrated that Native Americans' cognitive patterns include spatial abilities that are better developed than sequencing skills, and that are superior to conceptual and acquired knowledge performances.

Speidel (1981) emphasized that Native Hawaiians also perform consistently better in tests involving visual structures than those involving verbal structures. Indeed, performance scores are superior to verbal scores in virtually every reported Hawaiian sample, and the visual/spatial/performance versus verbal/conceptual/analytic differences in Hawaiian children has been linked to experimental studies of maternal socialization practices. Hawaiian mothers offered less verbal assistance in teaching tasks than did Euro-American mothers. In another study, the children of mothers who interacted more in maternal teaching tasks did not tend to show the performance/verbal test discrepancy, whereas the children of those who interacted less tended to score higher on visual/spatial/performance than on verbal tests (Speidel, Farran, & Jordan, 1989). Thus, the pattern of problem-solving abilities appears to be linked to the observational learning complex.

These studies of intellectual abilities also seem to implicate a representational dimension, in that a feature of this complex appears to be a visual, as opposed to a verbal, proclivity in perception as well as in abilities. This generalization is consistent with virtually all relevant published work. For example, in the Lombardi (1970) study, the Papago scored above the standardization norms of the Illinois Test of Psycholinguistic Abilities (ITPA) only on "visual sequential memory" (1969 version of the ITPA). Collier (1967) found that the Navajo excelled at identifying and interpreting details in photographs, some of which were not even visible to the investigator. A recent review of the literature (Kaulback, 1984) reported near total consistency in available research: Indian children are most successful at processing visual information. Berry (1976) consistently found a relatively high visuo-spatial functioning ability in American Indians, which he attributed to a functional adaptation to the demands of an environment in which perceptual-motor skills are highly useful. This visual rather than verbal proclivity maps easily onto the wholistic versus analytic patterns because visual perception presents itself wholistically, whereas language (both oral and written) presents itself sequentially in a linear pattern of emerging parts.

There is a problem with this analysis, however. Many, if not most, traditional American-Indian cultures socialize their children by the teaching story and through oral history—surely an auditory, linear, and linguistic modality. So the emphasis on observed, whole, and visual fields of learning and perception would appear to be weakened. However, it seems likely that the result of this auditory learning is a cognitive-visual representation. Recall Wyatt's (1978–1979), Phillips' (1983), and John-Steiner and Osterrich's (1975) discussions of children listening and imagining the stories as they hear them, and not representing them verbally (because they must be silent) but transforming them into visual imaginings and symbolizations of great richness.

In any event, the wholistic pattern of cognition is associated with an entire "observation-learning" complex. Perceptual, cognitive, (possibly) neurological, semiotic, sociological, and interpersonal dimensions are each aspects of a unified whole, as inseparable and interacting aspects of the same unity. Perhaps a recognition of this unity will illuminate the wrenching that the Native-American child experiences in conventional education, in which the entire world of being is violated by another equally powerful but alien complex—the technological, verbal, sequential, left-hemispheric, segmented, publicly performing society where all day long children are isolated from all adults except the teacher of the school.

The observation-learning complex is characteristic of many, if not most, American-Indian groups, as well as many other traditional peoples. However, it is by no means ubiquitous. If the proposed correlation between the complex and a preference for wholistic thinking is correct, one would expect wholistic thinking to be associated with the observation-learning complex, not with traditionality per se. This corresponds to observed differences between Navajo and Hawaiian socialization patterns and thinking styles. The wholistic cognitive style of the Navajo is not so salient in the Hawaiian. The observation-learning complex as described earlier was drawn largely from Native-American examples; Native-Hawaiian children are socialized in some crucially different ways.

SOCIALIZATION OF HAWAIIAN CHILDREN

Contemporary Hawaiian culture is only a few generations away from its traditional heritage, and features of the traditional social organization persist. Cultural features similar to those throughout Polynesia, and thus presumably more traditional, tend to be present more often in lower income families. Higher income and more educated families tend to be more acculturated into mainstream U.S. patterns. Thus, contemporary Hawaiian culture is a continuum. The description given here is more characteristic of rural (and lower income, urban) families.[1]

Families are started early, grow to be large, and extend beyond the nuclear family. Young women often remain in the parental household after their first child is born; older couples frequently live with a son or daughter and family; cousins and other kin come to stay for longer or shorter periods, and there is a high rate of formal and informal adoption, especially between related households. The child's life is peopled by a wide variety of both real and fictive kin.

Children are not socialized to leave the family. Rather, they are socialized to be responsible and competent within the family, and to adhere to the values of interdependence, responsibility for others, sharing of work and resources, cooperation, and obedience and respect toward parents. Child care is shared by parents and older siblings, who are often the primary caregivers. By the age of 2 or 3, children operate as part of the sibling group and turn to siblings for help with routine problems and needs. Children learn to make requests of elders indirectly and accept their decisions without arguing; they do not intrude on adult activity or approach adults for assistance unless the adult signals receptivity. Direct confrontation or negotiation between children and adults of acknowledged authority is rare. Adult supervision is usually mediated through older siblings. Families are organized in a "shared-function" system that involves role flexibility and joint responsibility for family tasks and obligations. Thus, children have considerable independence, felt autonomy, and competence.

"Rascality" is one aspect of the assertiveness that all children (especially male) are expected to show, particularly with peers. This is part of the quality that children admire as "toughness." Among boys, toughness is associated with companion bands—male neighborhood same-age groups, which usually have a leader, the "bull." Members engage in dominance contests but are also nurturant to one another.

It is in the social interactions within the sibling and companion groups that a great deal of children's learning takes place. Children learn skills for household, child-care, and self-care tasks by participating in those tasks with and, initially, under the supervision of older children. Consequently, they soon develop repertoires for teaching and learning from other children. Still, much knowledge filters from adults, although through older children. Children participate as part of the sibling or companion group in many activities along-

---

[1]The description here is modified from Tharp et al. (1984), where the primary sources are liberally cited.

side adults. There they have opportunities to observe full, correct performances, and to have errors corrected. Children are often unobtrusively present at adult activities.

Thus, in the Hawaiian home, emphasis is on learning from models, shared functioning, and on direct correction of errors. Learning occurs in activity, as the learner is engaged in performing the skill or task. Emphasis is not on "I'll tell you how to do it," but on "watch," "listen," "participate," and "try." Hawaiian children are eager to attempt new skills, and trial and error (with frequent feedback and often intrusive assistance by others) is typical and expected. Hawaiian adults continue to learn new skills in this way.

As can be gathered from this description, some aspects of the observational learning complex are present in Hawaiian socialization, and others are attenuated or absent. For example, a Hawaiian child does observe adult activities and learn from them but leaps into activities whenever allowed, expecting correction from adults and peers. The Hawaiian child's characteristic activity setting is small-group work of cleaning house or yard, cooking, or laundry while awash in instructions and verbal play with siblings and friends.

Although Navajo children are also socialized partially through sibling caregiving, Navajos live in widely dispersed dwellings. Ordinarily, a child would have close access only to siblings—a more restricted social environment than the companion bands (i.e., large same-age play and work groups) that are such a prevalent feature of traditional and contemporary Hawaiian life. This does not occur among Navajo, and children in traditional home settings have little occasion to engage in activity settings made up of same-age mates. The Navajo child in the traditional community, to be discussed next, has a characteristic early socialization activity of sheepherding, which, from the age of 5 or 6, may be done alone—surely a setting to encourage visual perception, visual imagination, and wholistic problem solving in silence.

In Hawaii, the age-graded society allows vigorous verbal activity among age mates, and the long listening to adult discourse is infrequent. One would not expect them to develop the long interior musings and visual representations of the American-Indian child, who observes in patient silence.

WHOLISTIC ISSUES IN SCHOOLS

In the ordinary educational processes characteristic of North America for 150 years (Tharp & Gallimore, 1989), both Navajo and Native-Hawaiian children do not prosper and are among the most alienated and frustrated of students. Can education of minority children be more effective if they are taught in a process that is compatible with their natal culture? Educators of Native children have proposed this argument for at least two decades. Among Pueblo-Indian children, "In those classrooms where these (cognitive and learning style) patterns were recognized as strengths and were built upon, other, more traditional 'school-learning,' including verbal growth, was also successful" (John-Steiner & Osterreich, 1975, p. 192). In Honolulu, the Kamehameha Early Education Program (KEEP), developed a language arts program of demonstrated effectiveness for children of Native-Hawaiian ancestry, and attributed the program's success to compatibilities of instructional practices with natal-culture elements (Tharp et al., 1984).

To test this hypothesis of effectiveness due to cultural adaptations, we installed a similar program in a Navajo reservation school in Rough Rock, Arizona, and observed the adaptations necessary to make the program effective for Navajo children. Among those adaptations was a necessity to accommodate to more wholistic, visually represented thinking in the Navajo school as compared with the Hawaiian one.

THE ROUGH ROCK NAVAJO SCHOOL
AND COMMUNITY

Located deep in the Navajo reservation where sheepherding and ranching remain more prominent than mining, Rough Rock School lies in the shadow of Black Mesa, whose residents take pride in being undefeated still. Many of their ancestors took refuge in Black Mesa's recesses, and thus escaped Kit Carson's drive of the Navajo people into the Basque Redondo relocation camp. Rough Rock, like most "communities" on the Navajo reservation, consists of a trading post, a mission, a small health clinic, a fire station and a school, along with a housing compound in which about a third of the staff of the school or health clinic live at least part of the time. Most of the pupils of Rough Rock come from traditional Navajo families living within a 20-mile radius of the school. About one third of the children are boarding students either because they live far from the school or because the roads to their homes are mere tracks in the desert, often impassable in wet weather. Despite these conditions, many boarding students manage to get home every weekend.

THE KEEP LANGUAGE ARTS
INSTRUCTIONAL PROGRAM

One crucial feature of the KEEP reading lesson, developed on and for Hawaiian children, is that instruction in comprehension generally follows a pattern of repeated thematic routines labeled "E-T-R sequences" (see Au, 1979, 1981, for a full description). The teacher introduces content drawn from the children's experiences (E), followed by text (T) material, followed by establishing relationships (R) between the two. A typical lesson begins with E questions that bring into active awareness ideas and knowledge of the children that may relate to the story to be read. Once reading begins, teachers often return to E questions to build additional experiential background, as new ideas and unexpected lines of discussion emerge. T questions guide processing of text so that processing occurs at various levels of comprehension, from literal details to higher order inferences. R questions assist children in relating to existing knowledge and experiences (E) to new ideas and information (T). The E–T–R protocol does not prescribe specific questions to be asked; the teacher is expected to be responsive to the rapid verbal interchanges in the group discussion. The E–T–R sequences may last from a few sentences up to several minutes. Typically the teacher divides the text story into sections; after silent reading, the teacher will begin an E–T–R sequence over that section.

HAWAIIAN-NAVAJO DIFFERENCES
IN INSTRUCTIONAL PREFERENCES

A notable similarity between Hawaiian and Navajo classrooms is the effectiveness of this general strategy of relating text to experiences. The E–T–R prescription engaged the interest and participation of Navajo children as reliably as it did the Hawaiian children. This is congruent with the "integrated" teaching methods advocated by Wyatt (1978–1979) for the Mt. Currie band's children: "drawing on personal, community-based experiences . . . of students and native instructors . . . as the foundation for developing school skills" (p. 25). However, the more wholistic orientation of the Navajo called for an overall E–T–R sequence, rather than shorter E–T–R bursts. A general preparatory E segment at the beginning of the lesson, followed by the entire text and then an R-based discussion, appeared to be desirable.

This was not a subtle difference. The Navajo children objected frequently and vigorously to stopping the story to talk about a piece of it. They insisted that they could not intelligently talk about a part until they had heard the whole thing. In the context of the whole, they were interested and competent in discussing segments and incidents but they clearly took offense at being asked to make foolish inferences about events whose context was being withheld.

Navajo children and teachers exhibited a preference for wholeness in many ways. A Navajo teacher was offered the segmented training in the KEEP program that has been successful with scores of Asian-American and Euro-American teachers in Hawaii. She firmly declined this method, preferring to sit close by the experienced teacher, observing her for many weeks so that she could "see the whole thing working." When she felt ready, she assumed the instruction of the entire system virtually all at once. The Navajo teacher explained that she could not profit from piecemeal instruction because only in the observation and comprehension of the whole could she understand the purpose and meaning of the sections.

Subsequent to achieving full competence, the Navajo teacher and the Euro-American teacher continued to share the teaching duties of the class to some extent so that each could have some research and planning time. Research conducted on their respective teaching styles, with students and subject matter held constant, indicated that the Navajo teacher asked more contextual and inclusive questions of the children than did the Euro-American teacher, who asked more questions pertaining to detail and sequence of events (White, Tharp, Jordan, & Vogt, 1989).

Wholeness is the subject of inner representations. The whole has been symbolized, across cultures and centuries, by the circle. The circle is central in the symbology of American Indians, and its repeated appearance in the Navajo classroom is another manifestation of wholism in cognitive style. An entry from Vogt's journal (Vogt, Jordan, & Tharp, 1987) illustrates:

> On a long drive across the Reservation, Afton (the Navajo teacher) alluded to the Navajo preference for the circle in all parts of their environment. She challenged me to try to think of a common story plot as being represented by circular patterning, as opposed to the linear and sequential way I usually diagrammed the plots on the blackboard.
>
> Later, after nearly an hour and a half of discussion, . . . I managed to represent the events from one rather complex story in an arrangement somewhat like a flower, with petals around the circle of a central problem. The next day I struggled to explain the story in terms of this complex symbol to the students. One of them finally seemed to understand what I was attempting—and suggested that the structure could be represented as a *spiral*, coming up from the center.

Consideration of an entire text allows visual representation of the story's structural form. This preference by the Navajo children allows text analysis on a high level indeed; many instructors would be pleased to have this response from college sophomores.

The ability of even third graders to think in terms of wholistic form, and their proclivities for circular symbols, was repeatedly demonstrated. For example, the blackboard representations of word associations, called "webbing," is preferred by Navajo teachers and children when it is represented by a circular design—like the sun, with "rays" of words. The same teaching device in Hawaii is preferred in free-form, ad-hoc "webs."

CONCEPTUAL IMPLICATIONS
OF HAWAIIAN–NAVAJO COMPARISONS

Hawaiian and Navajo peoples have many similarities in conditions known to affect cognitive patterning and socialization. Both are minorities by conquest. The traditional socialization patterns have been for subsistence survival rather than for school. Although both are collectivistic rather than individualistic, by contrast with Euro-American groups, there are sharp differences that favor a stronger group orientation for the island-dwelling Hawaiian than for the widely dispersed, pastoralist Navajo. I have suggested that cognitive differences in wholistic versus analytic thinking derive more directly from the observation-learning complex, which appears to operate independently of any of the other dimensions.

Future research is needed to investigate the wholistic–analytic dimension for Native Pueblo-Indian children in order to clarify the relationship among wholism, individualism/collectivism, and subsistence/school socialization goals. The Pueblos' town/agricultural ecosystem should produce a collective orientation similar to the Hawaiians', as Suina and Smolkin (chapter 6, this volume) have found. However, the observation-learning complex, highly similar to that of the Navajo, may be expected to produce a strong wholistic cognition.

When teaching and learning activities are congruent with the cognitive elements of natal culture, the strengths of the observation-learning complex can be harnessed to the verbal and arithmetic skill goals of the school. More (1985) observed that when reading programs are congruent with the "simultaneous" (wholistic) style of Indian children, as opposed to the "successive" style of non-Natives, these programs can result in strengthening "successive" or linear abilities. Cognitive abilities are not fixed forever by either the phylogenetic or the ethnogenetic levels. Krywaniuk and Das (1976) reported significant improvement in sequential memory tasks as a result of effective instructional programs for Indian children.

Presumably the reverse would also be true; that is, majority culture members could also be brought to greater facility with wholistic, simultaneous thought processes if they are brought to it by engaging their verbal, linear, successive skills. Both strategies, adopted in a crossover pattern, should be a goal of public education in America, so that all children can benefit from the dual repertoire.

CONCLUSIONS

I have attempted here to explicate some differences in cognitive style between two culturally distinct groups, and to relate those differences in prevalence to ethnogenetic processes. The emphasis on differences in cultural groups does not imply that analytic and wholistic thought belong exclusively to any cultural group, nor that wholistic and analytic intelligences cannot exist in the same culture and indeed in the same individual. John-Steiner (1991) proposed the term *cognitive pluralism* to describe the reality of existing complexities in ways of thinking:

> In proposing a pluralistic approach to thinking, I have argued that while an individual may have a dominant mode of representation (or internal code), there is no single universal language of thought. As human beings, we each embody a subset of human possibilities. There are wide variations among individuals in the extent to which their internal, symbolic codes are based on verbal language, abstract visual schemata, musical representations, or kinesthetic images . . . the coordinated use of two differing codes can assist a thinker in successfully solving a demanding task. (p. 73)

So, too, with cultures. Individuals within cultures also vary. Ethnogenesis does not supercede ontogenesis, rather it sets the conditions in which individual differences are expressed.

Ethnogenesis is a concept that also helps to account for continuities in cultural practices and peoples, even though there are enormous discontinuities in an econiche. Hawaiian people, now virtually absorbed into an urban cash economy, still exhibit continuities of social organization, socialization practices, and strong vestiges of cognitive style that appear to have originated in an island agricultural econiche of millenia past. Even more, the Navajo, in a more continuous relationship with their pastoral roots, continue to show a pedominance of wholistic thought.

The enlightened goal of education should be to produce a cognitive pluralism that will allow, within each society and each individual, the coordinated use of differing processes to solve the demanding task of coping with contemporary pluralistic society.

REFERENCES

Allen, M. (1983). Models of hemispheric specialization. *Psychological Bulletin, 93*, 173–194.

Au, K. H. (1979). Using the experience-text-relationship method with minority children. *The Reading Teacher, 32*(6), 677–679.

Au, K. H. (1981). The comprehension-oriented reading lesson: Relationships to proximal indices of achievement. *Educational Perspectives, 20*, 13–15.

Berry, J. W. (1976). *Human ecology and cognitive style*. New York: Sage-Halsted.

Bogen, J. E. (1975). Some educational aspects of hemisphere specialization. *UCLA Educator, 17*, 24–32.

Browne, D. A. (1984). WISC-R scoring patterns among Native Americans of the northern plains. *White Cloud Journal, 3*, 3–16.

Cazden, C. B., & John, V. P. (1971). Learning in American Indian children. In M. L. Wax, S. Diamond, & F. O. Gearing (Eds.), *Anthropological perspectives on education*. New York: Basic Books.

Chrisjohn, R. D., & Peters, M. (1986). The right-brained Indian: Fact or fiction? *Canadian Journal of Native Education, 13*, 62–71.

Cole, M. (1992). Context, modularity, and the cultural constitution of development. In L. T. Winegar & J. Valsiner (Eds.), *Children's development within social context* (Vol. 2, pp. 5–32). Hillsdale, NJ: Lawrence Erlbaum Associates.

Collier, J. (1967). *Visual anthropology: Photography as a research method*. New York: Holt, Rinehart & Winston.

Deyhle, D. (1983). Measuring success and failure in the classroom: Teacher communication about tests and the understandings of young Navajo students. *Peabody Journal of Education, 61*, 67–85.

Engestrom, Y. (n.d.). *Learning, working and imagining*. Unpublished manuscript, University of California Laboratory of Comparative Human Cognition, San Diego.

John-Steiner, V. (1991). Cognitive pluralism: A Whorfian analysis. In B. Spolsky & R. Cooper (Eds.), *Language, society and thought: Essays in honor of Joshua A. Fishman's 65th birthday* (pp. 65–77). Berlin: Mouton-Gruyere.

John-Steiner, V. P., & Osterreich, H. (1975). *Learning styles among Pueblo children: Final report to National Institute of Education*. Albuquerque: University of New Mexico Press.

Kaulback, B. (1984). Styles of learning among Native children: A review of the research. *Canadian Journal of Native Education, 11*, 27–37.

Krywaniuk, L. W., & Das, J. P. (1976). Cognitive strategies in native children: Analysis and intervention. *Alberta Journal of Educational Research, 22*, 271–280.

Lombardi, T. P. (1970). Psycholinguistic abilities of Papago Indian school children. *Exceptional Children, 36*, 485–493.

Longstreet, E. (1978). *Aspects of ethnicity*. New York: Teachers College Press.

McShane, D. A., & Plas, J. M. (1982). Wechsler Scale performance patterns of American Indian children. *Psychology in the Schools, 19*, 8–17.

Minick, N. J. (1985). *L. S. Vygotsky and Soviet activity theory: New perspectives on the relationship between mind and society*. Unpublished doctoral dissertation, Northwestern University, Evanston, IL.

More, A. J. (1985, November). *Indian students and their learning styles: Research results and classroom applications*. Paper presented at the meeting of the National Indian Education Association, Spokane, WA.

Pettit, G. A. (1946). Primitive education in North America. *University of California Publications in American archaeology and Ethnology, 43*(Whole no. 1).

Phillips, S. U. (1983). *The invisible culture: Communication in classroom and community on the Warm Springs Indian Reservation*. New York: Longman.

Speidel, G. E. (1981). *The relationship between psycholinguistic abilities and reading achievement in dialect-speaking children*. (Tech. Rep. No. 91). Honolulu, HI: The Kamehameha Early Education Program.

Speidel, G. E., Farran, D. C., & Jordan, C. (1989). On the learning and thinking styles of Hawaiian children. In D. Topping, V. Kobayashi, & D. C. Crowell (Eds.), *Thinking across cultures: The Third International Conference on Thinking* (pp. 55–77). Hillsdale, NJ: Lawrence Erlbaum Associates.

Tafoya, M. (1983). *The red & the black: Santa Clara pottery*. Posterboard, Wheelwright Museum of the American Indian, Santa Fe.

Tharp, R. G., & Burns, C. E. B. (1989). Phylogenetic processes in verbal language imitation. In G. E. Speidel & K. Nelson (Eds.), *The many faces of imitation in language learning* (pp. 231–250). New York: Springer-Verlag.

Tharp, R. G., & Gallimore, R. (1989). *Rousing minds to life: Teaching and learning in social context*. New York: Cambridge University Press.

Tharp, R. G., Jordan, C., Speidel, G. E., Au, K. H., Klein, T. W., Calkins, R. P., Sloat, K. C. M., & Gallimore, R. (1984). Product and process in applied developmental research: Education and the children of a minority. In M. E. Lamb, A. L. Brown, & B. Rogoff (Eds.), *Advances in developmental psychology* (Vol. 3, pp. 91–141). Hillsdale, NJ: Lawrence Erlbaum Associates.

Vogt, L. A., Jordan, C., & Tharp, R. G. (1987). Explaining school failure, producing school success: Two cases. *Anthropology & Education Quarterly, 18*, 276–286.

Werner, O., & Begishe, K. (1968, August). *Styles of learning: The evidence from Navajo.* Paper presented at the Conference on Styles of Learning in American Indian Children, Stanford University, Stanford, CA.

White, S., Tharp, R. G., Jordan, C., & Vogt, L. (1989). Cultural patterns of cognition reflected in the questioning styles of Anglo and Navajo teachers. In D. Topping, V. Kobayashi, & D. C. Crowell (Eds.), *Thinking across cultures: The Third International Conference on Thinking* (pp. 79–91). Hillsdale, NJ: Lawrence Erlbaum Associates.

Wyatt, J. D. (1978–1979). Native involvement in curriculum development: The native teacher as cultural broker. *Interchange, 9*, 17–28.

5

REVALUING NATIVE-AMERICAN CONCEPTS OF DEVELOPMENT AND EDUCATION

Jennie R. Joe
University of Arizona

The literature on Native-American culture abounds with descriptions by social scientists of how various Indian cultures differ from mainstream American culture (Chisholm, 1983; Kluckhohn & Strodtbeck, 1961; Pelletier, 1969). These differences range from superficial and generalized value-laden characterizations that are obviously ethnocentric, such as the view that Indians are "... permissive and indulgent ..." (Granzberg, 1973), to detailed characterizations of particular cultures by participant observers. Characterizations of differences between Indian and non-Indian ways on the part of Indians themselves are rare but are needed to balance the generally stereotyped and ethnocentric views. Not only is there a need for the "insider's" views, but also there is a need for the use of culturally relevant paradigms such as the wholistic model described by Tharp (chapter 4, this volume). Such models enrich our understanding and give us an opportunity to state or re-state many of our research questions differently.

RESEARCH APPROACHES

Although the linear research approach has given us valuable information on certain aspects of minority child development, the single vision focus has left us with many unanswered questions as well as generalizations that fed into a variety of negative stereotyping. With minority populations, this is relatively easy to do because it is often the problems and not the strengths of the minority population that are under investigation. For example, much of what we know about Native-American children or youth is related to "problem investigation" and not to normal development or the positive aspects of their development or behavior. For example, Havighurst (1957) conjectured that, among Indians, their ". . . cultural status and experience cause them [Indian children] to score lower on tests . . . especially in high school subjects" (p. 105). Havighurst further speculated that an Indian "tribal philosophy of sharing and cooperation" stands contrary to the competitive, individualistic motivation used in the mainstream U.S. education program. The lack of non-Indian experience coupled with cultural conflict is then seen as one of the key reasons why Indian children do so poorly in school. Similarly, Saslow and Harrover (1968) noted that "between the fourth and seventh grades, a decline in achievement begins and the typical Indian student falls behind his White counterpart" (p. 224). Saslow and Harrover attributed this phenomenon to "a failure in psycho-social development of Indian youth during the latency and early pubertal years, which contributes heavily to the reported incidences of problem behavior and differences between Indian and non-Indian youth" (p. 224). Mason (1969), who tested junior high school children, reported that the Indian students in that study tended to be passive, socially inept, and had lower self-esteem than the other students.

As a subject of many studies, Native Americans have been examined and reexamined by a variety of researchers. As the life and behavior of Native Americans are held under the microscope, there is often an implicit or explicit assumption that traditionalism or strong adherence to the tribal culture is a strong negative force that prevents Native Americans from being "normal" and/or like other members of mainstream society. Therefore, traditionalism is blamed for poor outcomes. For example, Miller and Caulkins (1964) noted that Indian youth from less acculturated families in the city tend to drop out of school due to the pressure of the discontinuity of values. In this and other studies, other causalities such as "cultural marginality" appear as themes in helping to explain differences or "maladjustments" of Native Americans. Rarely are those maladjusted or dysfunctional members of the Native-American communities compared with the "norms" of Native Americans. They are compared only with majority culture's identification of "norms."

However, "norms" are culturally derived rules (i.e., how an individual should think, speak, and act in every prescribed situation). For example, in many Indian tribes, "a good Indian child" is defined as one who shows respect to persons older than him or herself. Respect is also a concept defined differently in every culture, but the social rules of respect constitute "taken-for-granted" behavioral prescriptions held by the members of every culture. However, when individuals are members of one culture, and this culture is affected by a second, more powerful culture, those "taken-for-granted" norms may become the source of conflict, and are therefore subject to radical change and interpretation. In the area of childrearing, the culturally based norms and expectations of children's behavior held by a child's parents may become confused, inappropriate, and behaviorally destructive for both the parent and child. Unfortunately, the long-range impact of these varying destructive forces has not been well documented for Native-American childrearing practices.

SOME RESEARCH GAPS:
THE PROBLEM OF ASSIMILATION

Besides having research that is basically one sided, there are also gaps in the research. For example, we need to trace the effects of intergenerational transmission of cultural and social alienation on the contemporary generation of Native Americans. On the other hand, there is ample documentation of the (a) poor social conditions, (b) cultural disintegration of core values and institutions, and (c) hazardous and precarious position of the American-Indian family. But there are only a few systematic studies (Metcalf, 1976) that attempt to relate, for example, the Indian mother's degree of acculturation to the maternal experience and to the norms and expectations held for the child's development in a bicultural world.

Some of these shortcomings are being examined, and new approaches are being proposed. For example, in the comparison between the socialization and cognitive development between Native Hawaiians and Navajo children, Tharp (chapter 4, this volume) delineates a useful model that might replace the single and narrow vision field of the social scientist's microscope with a new culturally sensitive "wide-lens." In the process of presenting his observations, Tharp explains *and* demonstrates with vivid examples the sociocultural factors that contribute to or reinforce the learning style or cognitive orientation of Navajo and Native-Hawaiian children. The observations presented of the two groups also illustrate the salient points concerning inter- and intragroup differences.

Native-Hawaiian and Navajo families are under social pressure to become "assimilated," but many strive instead to become acculturated (i.e., able to master the technological and social means of non-Indian lifeways while retaining their cultural values). Note that this is a specific meaning of *acculturation*, more restricted than the definition used by Kim and Choi (chapter 11, this volume). The distinction between assimilation and acculturation is important in understanding the forces at work in the development of Indian children. Values may be in conflict between the two worlds, but an acculturated Indian person may accept the means, tools, technology, and skills used in the non-Indian world while still retaining the Indian values. On the other hand, an assimilated native American accepts non-Native values and tools, and therefore becomes the same as a non-Native in act, word, and deed (i.e., he or she has abandoned the vestiges of his or her traditional culture or traditions). Because there are intra- as well as intertribal differences, it is important to note whether the group in question is either highly traditional, acculturated, bicultural, and/or assimilated.

Researchers often do not explain where on the assimilated–nonassimilated cultural continuum their samples most likely appear. For example, too many studies just identify the study group as Navajo, Sioux, and so on. However, the in-culture researcher is interested in knowing from where the sample is drawn. For example, it is helpful that Tharp (chapter 4, this volume) explains how acculturated or nonacculturated the children were in his study. By knowing that the sample of Navajo children were from Rough Rock community, the knowledgeable researcher has an immediate expectation that most of these children will come from homes that are less acculturated than other communities on the Navajo reservation, such as Window Rock, Arizona.

THE CULTURAL MEANINGS OF KNOWLEDGE

Just as there are different levels of acculturation, so also are there different understandings of what learning means. For example, despite culture change and the introduction of mandatory education, it is generally understood that learning encompasses three different arenas in the traditional Navajo world. One is the learning that lasts throughout one's lifetime, which originates at birth and helps mold the individual into a respected and useful member of Navajo society. The learning methods in this instance are generally informal, and teaching may come from many sources. Within this context are the learning of language, kinship, religion, customs, values, beliefs, and the purpose of life.

This molding or learning process also introduces occupation and/or ways to make a living, which is the second arena of learning. Because this learning often requires an apprenticeship, the process may take a Navajo person into a slightly different or more restrictive educational arena, where he or she has a chance to match his or her interest and talent with skills for making a living (e.g., as a farmer, a sheep herder, a weaver, a hunter, etc.).

The third educational arena is usually most restrictive because this is the arena reserved for those who are interested in becoming healers or religious leaders. These specialists are expected to make lifetime commitments, in addition to having other means of livelihood, to training and serving as healers or religious leaders.

When formal schooling was introduced to the Navajos, most families resisted and many refused to send their children to government schools. This form of education was foreign to the Navajos. Also, most Navajos misunderstood what formal schooling meant; many equated this type of learning with specialized learning—learning that a promising young Navajo adult might undertake to become a religious leader. Therefore, children were too young to take up such serious training and, because their spirits were still weak, the learning itself was thought to bring them harm. It was also wrong in the eyes of many Navajos to force children to go to school because most Navajos value individual autonomy and do not like to impose their will on someone else. The Navajo term *nila*, which translates into the equivalent of "it is up to you," is often used to state the unwillingness of one to make a decision for someone else.

In addition to these ideas about schooling, there were other barriers, some less verbalized, such as the fear of sending Navajo children to institutions controlled by non-Navajos, especially by those who were counted among the enemies of the Navajos. Although the situation has changed and almost every Navajo child now attends school, the role of the educational institution is still not well understood by some Navajo families. For example, social and behavioral problems among youth are often blamed on the failure of the schools to teach students to have respect for their culture and/or to uphold certain moral standards. Many Navajo families are not aware that religious teachings are not part of most educational curricula. In their view, they assume that learning in the schools encompasses all aspects of preparation for life, including the spiritual.

Conditioned by years of the federal government's policy of preventing parental or community involvement with education, many Navajo families are still reluctant to question and/or visit their children's schools. Moreover, because the government schools took Navajo children and mandated that they be placed in boarding schools, most Navajo parents unfamiliar with formal schooling assumed that once their children finished school, they would be prepared for a job as well as ready to start and support families of their own.

With the schools dismissing the role of the parents or family in the education of the children, most families did not participate in the schooling of their children. Sometimes distance alone discouraged families from visiting their children in school. In some instances, Indian children were purposefully placed in boarding schools far removed from their parents and tribes. School officials often justified this practice so that Indian children could be isolated from the "uncivilized" or "heathen" influences of their family or tribal members.

With this type of experience, it is not difficult to understand why formal schooling and learning remains "outside" the Navajo family circle. This is not to say that learning is not valued in the Navajo culture. It is. It used to be (before most Navajo babies were born in hospitals) that most Navajo newborns were symbolically "shaped" or groomed so they would develop healthy minds and bodies. These prayers were said as each child was examined, stretched, and massaged by a medicine person or an elder. Later on, special abilities for the child might also be requested, and a special ceremony took place to bless the young child with the spirit or characteristics of certain animals. For example, the spirit of the deer might be called on to bless the new child with agility and speed.

Even the cradle board on which a newborn was placed was selected and blessed with a series of songs and prayers, not only to keep the child from harm's way, but also to ensure the child's mental and physical development (Leighton & Kluckhohn, 1947). Each part of the child's cradle board symbolically represented the wholistic environment of the Navajo: mother earth, the sky with its rainbow, rain with its moisture and lightning, and the sunbeams of the sun. The child's place in the fabric of the Navajo universe was further assured when the child's umbilical cord was returned to Mother Earth. For a girl, the umbilical cord might be "planted" under a rug loom so that she might grow up to be a great weaver. Similarly, a boy's umbilical cord might be "planted" in the corral so that he might grow up to be a good shepherd, blessed with many horses, sheep, or other livestock. With the umbilical cord "anchored" to Mother Earth, it was also believed that a Navajo child would never wander or be homeless but could always return to the place where his or her umbilical cord was planted.

The developmental milestones for the Navajos also differed. The child's first laugh, for instance, was celebrated as was the ceremony marking puberty. Although the focus of some of the more acculturated Navajo parents follow the typical developmental milestones of the majority culture (i.e., they celebrate birthdays and leave money for the "tooth fairy"), there are still a significant number of Navajo families who retain the developmental milestones observed by their ancestors. For example, these mothers generally do not remember when their children said their first words, took their first steps, or were weaned. A researcher who is interviewing and expecting detailed information on the developmental timetable from these families will most likely have to be satisfied with incomplete data.

CONCLUSIONS

If there is a message in the new approaches being proposed, it is this point. Casting the research net wider and/or looking through the research microscope with a deeper cultural sensitivity and awareness is very important. It is important because the cultures of many non-Western societies are changing very rapidly, and what seemed relevant in the way we perceive the social cognitive development of minority children a few years ago may not be relevant today.

The histories of American Indians and Native Hawaiians have been impacted by a series of political, economic, social, and cultural forces emerging from within as well as from without. Many tribes, for example, have questioned and/or resisted the dominant society's value on the temporal rather than spiritual, individual rather than community, change rather than stability, and what seems like chaos instead of harmony. Because they have been slow to embrace some of these values, the cultures of native peoples have been viewed as stagnant, inefficient, and hampered by communal values. On the other hand, many native peoples also have not been able to harness the resources necessary to protect their traditional ways of life. Thus, they have continually experienced cultural discontinuities. Survival has required change, adaptation, and/or blending the old with the new.

REFERENCES

Chisholm, J. S. (1983). *Navajo infancy: An ethnological study of child development*. Albuquerque: University of New Mexico Press.

Granzberg, G. (1973). The psychological integration of culture: A cross-cultural study of Hopi type initiation rites. *Journal of Social Psychology, 90*, 3–7.

Havighurst, R. J. (1957). Education among American Indians: Individual and cultural aspects. *Annals of the American Academy of Political and Social Science, 311*, 105–115.

Kluckhohn, F. R., & Strodtbeck, F. L. (1961). *Variation in value orientations*. New York: Row, Peterson.

Leighton, D., & Kluckhohn, C. (1947). *Children of the people*. New York: Octagon Books.

Mason, E. P. (1969). Cross-validation study of personality characteristics of junior high students from American Indian, Mexican, and Caucasian ethnic background. *Journal of Social Psychology, 77*, 15–24.

Metcalf, A. (1976). From schoolgirl to mother: The effects of education on Navajo women. *Social Problems, 23*(5), 534–544.

Miller, F. C., & Caulkins, D. D. (1964). Chippewa adolescents: A changing generation. *Human Organization, 23*, 150–159.

Pelletier, W. (1969). Childhood in an Indian village. *This Magazine Is About Schools, 3*, 6–22.

Saslow, H. L., & Harrover, M. J. (1968). Research on psychosocial adjustment of Indian youth. *The American Journal of Psychiatry, 125*, 224–231.

6

FROM NATAL CULTURE TO SCHOOL CULTURE TO DOMINANT SOCIETY CULTURE: SUPPORTING TRANSITIONS FOR PUEBLO INDIAN STUDENTS

Joseph H. Suina
Laura B. Smolkin
University of New Mexico

*If you paint
a foreign language
on my skin
my innermost soul
cannot breathe*

*The glow of my feelings
will not get through
the blocked pores.*

*There will be
a burning fever
rising in me
looking for a way
to express itself.*

—Leporanta-Morley (1988)

For educational researchers who explore the needs of nonmainstream students, unblocking the pores so that students' innermost souls will breathe freely in classroom settings is a most pressing issue. In her review of the research on responding to the needs of nonmainstream students in terms of literacy instruction, Farr (1991) noted that information from ethnographic studies has been utilized to enhance classroom practice in two distinctive ways. The first addresses "local ways of using language," and may be seen as a concern with process. Notable in this line of research have been the efforts of the Kamehameha Early Education Project (Au & Jordan, 1981), which modified classroom reading instruction, aligning it more closely with a Hawaiian speech event known as "talk story," thereby minimizing the discontinuities between native culture and schooling. The second use of information from ethnographic studies has been to design appropriate content. Farr cited the works of Heath (1983) and Diaz, Moll, and Mehan (1986); both used information from the local community as content to increase student participation.

The notion of basing reading instruction on culturally appropriate materials is a frequently advocated position. Reyhner and Garcia (1989) stated: "To counter cultural discontinuity in reading materials that are dissonant with the student's home and language background, materials reflective of the student's background and culture are needed" (p. 86). In their article, they cited a program in Los Lunas, New Mexico, and the Rock Point Bilingual Program on the Navajo reservation in Arizona as exemplary situations for overcoming the school–home discontinuity problem because each uses materials derived from local culture as the basis for reading instruction.

This chapter contributes to the literature an examination of the continuities and discontinuities between the orientations of Pueblo natal culture and the stances taken by classroom teachers as they attempt to make their literacy instruction culturally compatible. The first part of this chapter, based on a study completed by the first author (Suina, 1988), speaks to the enculturation and socialization of Pueblo children within their native world. The second part of this chapter presents data from an ongoing ethnographic study of literacy instruction. The third part of this chapter addresses the implications of the data presented in terms of content and process.

ENCULTURATION AND SOCIALIZATION OF PUEBLO CHILDREN WITHIN THEIR NATIVE WORLD

Among the Indian tribes in the United States, the Pueblos of the southwest are considered the group least changed by encounters with Europeans; their languages, governments, social patterns, and cultural components remain uniquely Pueblo. These 20 or more closely knit villages in New Mexico and Arizona are autonomous and independent of one another. Like their Anasazi ancestors of prehistoric times, their lives revolve around the observance of ceremonial activities reflective of an agricultural society. Pueblo dances, songs, legends, and prayers reflect the seasonal concerns of planting, growing, and harvesting.

Certain Pueblos cling more closely to traditions than others. Those Pueblos who have had significant contact with the outside world, either through employment by the railroad and mining industries or due to considerable tourist industry in the Pueblo, have adopted many values and behaviors of the dominant Euro-American society.

Teaching and Learning

Teaching and learning in the more traditional Pueblos remain in the hands of all Pueblo members, in contrast to formalized American schooling where education is the province of "experts." Corrections for inappropriate behaviors may be supplied at any time, in any place within the village, and for any type of unsuitable action. Similarly, any member of the Pueblo who witnesses exemplary appropriate behavior is expected to praise and/or encourage the individual. Although the intent is primarily for elders to teach youth, a youth is said to have as much authority, if not more, to correct a misguided elder. Such a reprimand of an elder by a youth would represent one of the greatest indignities of Pueblo life. Elders who neglect their teaching responsibility to youth are subject to the censure of tribal elders and the village at large. An example from the personal experiences of the first author demonstrates the strength of this stance.

> My cousin and I were hunting rabbits. Unable to locate the desired game, we began shooting at tin cans and other assorted targets. One of those happened to be a pig. The injured pig drew attention to the situation, causing the two of us to be summoned before the tribal council for corrective measures. During the hearing, a council member disclosed that he had witnessed our reckless shooting. An older council member inquired what the man had done about the situation. "Nothing," replied the first. He couldn't, he elaborated, because it was about to rain, and then proceeded to remind the other council members of the dire consequences of neglecting a hay crop when a rain threatened. The negligent member was quickly reminded of what happens to the villages' children when they are neglected. For neglecting his duty, the derelict council member was required to pay half the price of the pig; we were required to pay the remainder, our punishment in addition to a whipping by the village governor.

Like many collective societies, the community carefully monitors the behavior of all members, whether young or old.

Models. Pueblo children learn through listening, watching, and doing. Although considerable information is imparted orally, children, who attend most of Pueblo life's activities, have continual access to adult models. The few adult-only activities still permit children's presence as onlookers, and even in these settings children learn a great deal about appropriate behaviors. Learning by example is central to traditional Pueblo education.

Private Practice.   Learning by doing is another important aspect of traditional Pueblo life. Children try out, through enactments, thinking, and feeling, that which is seen or heard in order to make the knowledge or the skill their own. Imitation through role playing and practicing (e.g., being an artist, a hunter, or a buffalo dancer) is a natural part of growing up in Pueblo society. These ordinary activities of children's play are eventually permitted expression before adults and in some cases, such as children's dances, before the entire community. An example from the first author's childhood shows the progression of private practice.

> My brother and I worked privately to master the Buffalo Dance. We substituted jackets for the actual buffalo skin, placing them over our heads, so we might better imagine the feelings of the dancers as we perfected the appropriate steps. For one of our practice sessions, we even attached cardboard horns to the jackets, to make them more authentic. When we reached a certain stage of readiness, we had our father supply the singing to accompany our ever-improving performance. Finally, the dance was deemed sufficiently ready to share with relatives when they came to visit.

Clearly, behaviors such as dancing, which are prized and rewarded by adult attention, are given considerable study as Pueblo children strive for perfection and seek to excel. Excelling in the Pueblo world differs considerably from the competitive stance found in the larger Euro-American society. To shine as an individual in the Pueblo world is to have done so on behalf of the extended family and community; such excellence brings pride and cohesion to the group.

Appropriate Contexts.   For the Pueblo learner, all knowledge is to be acquired in its appropriate wholistic context. This is the case whether the learner is an adult or a child. Again, an example from the life of the first author serves as illustration.

> There was going to be a ceremony performed in our village that had not occurred in 40 years, and I wanted to participate. When I questioned one of the tribal elders, seeking permission to come late because of my teaching responsibilities, he said that would be acceptable, but that I should speak with my father concerning the ceremony itself, so that I could be prepared. I arose early the following morning to visit my father, wanting to know what I needed to do in the ceremony, but conscious mostly of my need to be elsewhere. My father greeted me, but sensing my hurry, my distraction, told me to relax, to sit down. He wanted, I think, to extract me from the very segmented modern society where I had found my profession, to restore me to a sense of integrated wholeness. My father began to speak, but not about the ceremony. Instead, he spoke of the time when the ceremony had been performed last—the tribal members

who had been present, who was alive, who was in office, how the hunt was that year, how the harvest had been that year—what was happening in the world the last time the ceremony was performed. "Do you remember your grandfather?" he asked me. "No," I replied, "I don't remember him. He must have died when I was very young." "Well," my father continued, "he used to carry you on his shoulders when you were young and he sang songs for you. It's no wonder you have a good feel for songs." The time when the ceremony was last performed had been just the beginning of World War II, when so many young men were leaving the village, and perhaps that was what had precipitated its need. The effect my father's speech had on me was the same sense that I get when I look at mountains and boulders, a sense of eternity, a sense of connection between generations, events. I felt connected with people, with long chains of events, and intensely felt that I was just a small piece in all of this. And I knew that the small piece was not what was important, but rather, what was absolutely crucial was the whole picture. After about 2 hours of recollections, my father finally wended his way to the purpose of the dance, to some of the symbols that were involved. And after a while longer, he spoke of what I would need for that evening in terms of clothing and other paraphernalia. Finally, my father told me how I was to act, and what words I was to use. When it was over and done with, I no longer felt anxious; it no longer seemed crucial to me to worry about the details of my teaching on this one day. I could see myself again as just one little piece in a much larger picture.

For Pueblo people, proper contextualization of knowledge is an essential aspect of learning.

Three Generations: Literacy as an Unraveler of Tradition

For the first author, on the day of the ceremony described in the previous passage, the distinction between Euro-American ways of accessing information and Pueblo ways of distributing knowledge became powerfully obvious. In the Euro-American world, when one wishes to know about an event a simple visit to a library and a copying machine makes the knowledge portable and accessible to any who wish it. In the Pueblo world, many forms of knowledge are restricted; they are imparted only to those who are deemed ready, only to those who will have need for the information. As the first author's recollection demonstrates, the knowledge was transmitted orally *and* intergenerationally. The tribal elder would not impart the needed information; instead, it was to come from a father who had, in turn, also received it orally from his own father.

In the Euro-American world, the first author would be seen as a man who possesses a doctorate; he is a "man of letters." His father would be seen as possessing only a third-grade education, at most considered a functional literate. In the Pueblo world, the roles would be exactly reversed—the first author with only minimal knowledge, his father a man of considerable wisdom, a repository of information.

The Pueblo world contrasts with the Euro-American world in the roles that the generations play for one another. In the dominant society, elders, for a variety of reasons, are frequently absent from the lives and education of their grandchildren. Whether due to mobility, distance, and disconnectedness of the modern family or to dominant society's images of the elderly as doddering, grandparents interact with grandchildren during infrequent visits. In the Pueblo world, grandparents, living only a few feet from their grandchildren, often even residing in the same household, are esteemed for their considerable knowledge of the proper ways of approaching life's many occasions. Whether it be the prescribed way to participate in various ceremonies and dances, or the more mundane concerns of a proper herb to treat a grandchild's stomachache, children and their parents almost continually seek grandparents' advice.

When a society conceives of itself as having developed appropriate orientations to living, the maintenance of tradition becomes paramount. For the continued development of the Pueblo people, in the end grandchildren are expected to be very much like their grandparents.

Secrecy in Pueblo Religion

As noted, the nature of knowledge in the Pueblo world differs significantly from erudition in Euro-American society: Knowledge is not to be asked for, but is a gift bestowed at relevant moments in appropriate contexts. Certain types of knowledge, particularly those concerning the Native religion, can be transmitted only when an individual has committed him or herself to use that information in the service of the Pueblo people. Elders may opt to bestow other information only when an individual is deemed mature or trustworthy— responsible to act for the good of others. Still other types of information can be procured on the basis of gender alone.

Teachers and others from the dominant society who provide services to the various Pueblos may experience frustration as they deal with the Pueblo orientation that knowledge cannot be gained by the simple asking of questions. Many interpret this stance as a form of exclusion, which some attribute to racial discrimination, designed to keep "outsiders" in their place. Other outsiders, wishing to avoid offense, determine that they will abstain from all mention of Native religious ceremonies. Still other outsiders, often teachers who lack a desire to deal with the unfamiliar, choose to charge Pueblo secrecy as their reason for deleting cultural considerations from the functions they perform. In truth, *who* may possess *what* knowledge lies at the core of the conundrum.

Partnerships: The Key to Productive Living

One of the key phrases that every Pueblo person hears is "help each other so the burden won't be so heavy." In work situations, the notion of partnering is omnipresent. For the Pueblo person, *work* is defined as any effort that will result in the attainment of security for the group. In prior times, and even today, this would include activities such as procuring food, constructing shelters, and baking bread together. School work is seen as constituting work because, although it may not result in an immediate product, the belief is that the work will eventually allow the individuals, and therefore the group, to acquire the essentials for living.

For example, a tribal official such as a war chief never serves by himself; there is always a partner, a "brother," who will assist him. Although war chief is the more primary position, the "brother" supports him in the duties and responsibilities in his office.

This can be seen in more informal situations also, as in a deer hunt. Rarely if ever does one go hunting by oneself. So much of expected behavior in the Pueblo world is partnering that there are prescribed rules for dividing the kill among not only two partners, but even for a third or fourth member of the party.

Exceptions to the notion of partnering are found in certain creative activities and in competitive games. In terms of artistic creations, composition of songs, paintings, pottery, or jewelry design is seen as appropriately pursued by the individual alone. In the case of games or competitive sports, the individual is expected to surpass his or her peers—to fulfill his or her potential.

Group Consensus

The notions of assistance extend beyond simple partnering into group decision making. When questions or concerns surface at meetings, there is a group response but, unlike Euro-American culture, accord is not achieved through voting. If there is no controversy after an individual has stated the issue, all men present at the gathering will voice their reactions simultaneously. The simultaneous, cacophonous nature of the response makes it impossible to distinguish a single individual's reaction from the 40 or 50 voices that may answer but such information would be of no importance. What is deemed crucial is the consensus of the group. If the topic that the individual raises is one that generates debate, a council meeting may last throughout the night until each man present has had the opportunity to be heard. No one is to leave the meeting without some sense of satisfaction, even if the basic issue has not been resolved as each individual would have wished.

It is important to note that consensus in these settings is a male activity. Within the Pueblo world, there are clear distinctions as to what are appropriate behaviors for both male and female tribal members.

EXPLORING CULTURAL COMPATIBILITY IN LITERACY INSTRUCTION

The data presented in this section of the chapter have been selected from a longitudinal ethnographic study of literacy instruction in Pueblo students' classrooms. It has long been known (Parmee, 1968; Peters, 1963; Zintz, 1960) that academic achievement of Native-American students declines through-out their elementary school careers; it is the goal of this work to alleviate that decline, which becomes particularly pronounced after third grade. The research is guided by the "least change" principle, advanced by Jordan (1985), to assist in designing literacy instruction for the upper elementary grades. The notion of least change advocates improving classroom instruction by selecting from existing practices, rather than imposing newly invented ones.

Three male and three female Euro-American teachers of third-grade students agreed to participate in the study. Four of the six teachers had experience with Navajo children prior to teaching in their current school. The number of years that the participants had been teaching ranged from a low of 2 years to a high of 20 years.

The data presented in the sections that follow have been collected through field notes, videotapes, and interviews during systematic observations over a 2-month period in those six third-grade classrooms. In the first section, teachers' self-reports of efforts to make literacy instruction culturally compatible are explored. The second section presents teacher-initiated events that represent discontinuities with cultural patterns. The third section presents teacher-initiated events that represent continuities with cultural patterns.

Teachers' Efforts to Create Culturally Appropriate Instruction

Each of the six teachers was interviewed at the end of the 1991 school year. During the interviews, each was asked to answer the question "In what ways are you adapting your instruction for this cultural group?" Six different categories of adaptations were mentioned by the teachers; three dealt with content, two with local Native orientations, and one with Native language.

Selecting Content from the Community: The Secular World.   As noted in the introduction, teachers have been advised by researchers to select content from the community as part of the curriculum, and this approach was addressed by all six teachers. Two of the male teachers, Ed and Nate, spoke of "trying to give children the opportunity to explore their physical environment." Each had done projects during the year that stressed the geology of the area—the mesas, buttes, and canyons. Daniel had sent his children out to do interviews, which were later compiled into a class book. In her social studies class, Nancy had enhanced the study of state and federal government by an inclusion of tribal government. Katherine had incorporated aspects of daily life into the story problems her children did during math lessons. "We try to make a conscious effort just to weave it into the curriculum," she explained.

Selecting Content from the Community: The Religious World. Religious events, as might be suspected from the issue of secrecy discussed earlier, represented a source of conflict for teachers in their efforts to make literacy instruction culturally compatible. In discussing the Ha-nahti celebration, Evelyn reflected this quandary: "Like at Ha-nahti time, we always write a book about the activities. . . . This year we collaborated on the stories, and they had to write about the various activities that the men and women do. *We don't touch on the religious things,* [italics added] but all the cooking and the building and everything else that takes place." The fact that only one other teacher even mentioned religious events indicates the level of discomfort the teachers experienced with the acknowledgment of the Native religion.

Selecting Content from Other Cultures. Daniel and Katherine, the most veteran of the six teachers, both mentioned their use of other cultural groups as part of their instructional orientations. Katherine spoke about the ties she had created for the children.

This was right before the war, right when the war was breaking out and we felt like we just wanted something that would speak to the unifying aspect of humankind. And we, we had the children list all the people of another culture that they knew. And then we asked them to come and interact with the kids, and it really blossomed. But one of the things we did was have a Pueblo culture specialist, language specialist come and show the children words in Pueblo that had relatives in Spanish and English, and maybe some other languages too.

Both of these more experienced teachers envisioned culturally appropriate instruction as extending beyond the local culture.

Perspectives. Daniel noted that he had "a lot of parents working in the classroom" who contributed a Native perspective and brought an awareness to the children "that we're not always separate from the family." Katherine reflected on a similar point: "What we really want to stress is your life every

day, just how, the way you do things, or the way you are. That's valued."
Katherine's 13 years of teaching Navajo students, combined with her 5 years
at the Pueblo elementary school, had advanced her to a stage of ethnosensi-
tivity that permitted her to value, and incorporate, "the way you do things."

Awareness of the Collective Nature of Pueblo Life. Speaking of the collaborative nature of many of the activities in his classroom, Daniel commented
on one of the unique orientations of the elementary school: "I guess that's
the way our school allows them to operate as, to maintain . . . what they
already know as Pueblo kids. Of working together, of being cooperative, of
seeing a common goal with each other. Even though they might be independent thinkers, they still know that they have to get together on a lot of
things."

Nancy also spoke of the collective aspect of the culture: "I want the kids
to have a strong sense of pride in who they are. And in the Pueblo, the Pueblos are not just themselves, their own individuals, because that's kind of counter to the way the culture is." In Nancy's classroom, as in four of the others,
children were provided many opportunities to work collaboratively.

Language. Four of the six teachers spoke of their incorporation of the
Native language as part of their literacy programs. In particular, Ed had done
projects based on the integration of art and Native language labeling. He spoke
of the children's reaction to seeing their spoken language in its written form
under the animals that they had drawn.

> Each kid did about two, and then the Pueblo name for the animal under it.
> And the thing that really is amazing to me is that when I first showed them
> these words, the Pueblo words, some of the kids said, "What's this word?" and
> they expected me to read it. They thought it was English. It was written, and
> . . . that really was surprising to me, they were not aware that their language
> could be written. And that it's a word, it's written, so Ed knows it. That was
> their attitude. "Nuh uh, I don't know it." I said, "Well, what is it?" You know,
> some of the animal names they knew and some they didn't. "Well, what is the
> word for this in Pueblo?" And they knew it and they could say it.

Ed had moved from this initial labeling activity to the study of local geology
mentioned earlier. After the creation of papier-mâché models of land forms,
the children attached labeling flags written in their Native language.

A Native-American aide worked in both Katherine's and Nancy's classrooms. The woman was quite proficient with Native literacy; both teachers
made use of her abilities. In a unit on Native-American literature, Nancy requested the aide to conduct reading lessons of simple Native language texts
that were present in the school.

Evelyn spoke of her use of the Native language as a method of enhancing student understanding of concepts covered in class.

> Whenever possible, we use Pueblo language, if that's a better way of doing it. I'm limited but I have no problem with somebody else using the language, and a lot of times, the kids translate for each other. And if they have difficulty saying something in English, they'll say it in Pueblo, and somebody will come up with it, and it works out. Or if they're not understanding something, someone will chime in in Pueblo, and if that works, then you go for it. There's no reason not to use it. It's their language.

Hence, teachers saw the Native language as content to be studied but also, for some, as a tool for explanation.

Discontinuities with Cultural Patterns

In this section, we recount two incidents that occurred during our visits, only one of which was literacy related. However, both serve to demonstrate a discontinuity between Pueblo mores and those of the dominant culture.

> It is our first visit to Ed's room, and we have just finished introducing ourselves to the children. Ed turns to the class and tells them to introduce themselves to us. No one speaks. Ed calls on one of the children to begin. The boy is almost inaudible; we lean forward to hear better. The next child is the same. None of the children makes eye contact with us, although they are glancing at one another. Finally, the last child has finished. Ed, sensing the same discomfort that we have, addresses the children. "Gee, maybe next time I should have you introduce each other. Maybe that would work better."

As has been discussed earlier, Pueblo children learn that to be singled out is appropriate only on certain occasions, such as when playing games or when engaged in an artistic endeavor. Clearly, introducing oneself is an instance of rising out of the group; the children were embarrassed because the behavior falls within neither of the acceptable situations. A perfectly acceptable request in Euro-American classrooms, Ed's solicitation of personal introductions causes conflict and discomfort for these Pueblo third graders. The awareness that Ed, a novice teacher of only 2 years, displays of having violated the children's sense of appropriateness is commendable.

Also established earlier is the importance of consensus in decision making in the Pueblo world. As noted before, voting to achieve a majority position is a notion that is foreign to the Pueblo world; such a procedure would deny each Pueblo person the right to express his or her sense of what should happen. The following incident is taken from the field notes of the second author.

As a thank-you present for the teachers, I have brought three new children's books, all photo essays of modern-day Native-American children, and have indicated that each of the teachers can select whichever they would like. Evelyn has asked me to describe the books for the children so that they can vote on which of the three they would like her to have as a present. I share the books with the children, explaining that *Pueblo Boy* (Keegan, 1991) is about a child in San Ildefonso Pueblo, that *Pueblo Storyteller* (Hoyt-Goldsmith, 1991) describes the life of a little girl from Cochiti Pueblo, and that *Totem Pole* (Hoyt-Goldsmith, 1990) is about a little boy from the Tsimshian tribe in Washington State. Evelyn indicates that it is time to vote. "How many for *Pueblo Boy*?" she asks. The children glance at each other, then slowly, hesitantly, still looking about, six children raise their hands. "How many for *Pueblo Storyteller*?" asks Evelyn. Again, the children hesitate. It seems there are seven hands raised this time, more girls, I think, but I also see some hands that have been raised before. Evelyn is unhappy with the children's reluctance. "You are supposed to have your own opinions," she remonstrates. "You have your own ideas, and you should express them." She asks how many children want *Totem Pole*. Again, there is hesitation; only a few children raise their hands. "Oh," I say to Evelyn, "I'm sorry. I lost count. Could we do this over?" We begin again. "How many for *Pueblo Boy*?" Evelyn queries. With a minimal amount of eye contact exchange, 13 children raise their hands. For *Pueblo Storyteller*, only two girls raise their hands. This time, for *Totem Pole* no hands are raised.

Once again, the behavior requested by the classroom teacher is not only acceptable in Euro-American classrooms but represents a procedure that is very much accepted as part of being a "good American." The selection of a book that will become part of the class collection is an important decision, and such decisions that will affect the future of the group, the Pueblo children know, are made in a very specific fashion—through consensus. Evelyn has not allowed time for the children to express their personal opinions on each book; pressed for time at the end of the day, she simply asks them to vote for their favorite. When the children exhibit reluctance to perform in the fashion deemed appropriate in the dominant society, Evelyn responds with frustration.

Continuities with Cultural Patterns

In this section of the data, we share two teacher-initiated events taken from our field notes that appear, in content, to be quite foreign to the Pueblo children who are involved. However, each event shares behavioral pattern structures with the natal culture that permit successful instructional moments. The first is an exercise in editing:

The children and Daniel, assembled at the front of the class near the blackboard, have just finished sharing articles and personal writings they have prepared about ongoing world events. Informing the children that they haven't had editing practice in a long time, Daniel selects two students to begin the editing process. The boy and girl walk to the board, and begin correcting the errors that appear in a story that Daniel has written earlier. As the children correct the errors in the writing, Daniel announces the changes to the class. Other children come to the board. Daniel acknowledges a girl's insertion of quotation marks, and then reads from the story, "One village women." One of the children exclaims, "We need to say 'woman.'" Daniel suggests that they change the *e* to an *a*. Another child has gone to edit at the board. He is unable to find the word *point*. One of the children sitting close to the board kneels, touching the spot in the story where the word appears, aiding the current "editor." Neither Daniel nor the other students comment on the assistance. Daniel selects a child to read the edited version of the story. The child reads until he encounters a difficult word. Daniel addresses the group, "Who can help us with that word?" After another child supplies the pronunciation of the troublesome word, the reader continues. When the child finishes, Daniel compliments the reader. Finished with the editing, the children approach the blackboard, holding their hands before their faces, saying, "click, click, click," as they "take photographic images" for their brains.

Daniel, whether operating out of an awareness of the importance of partnering in the Pueblo world or out of a more Euro-American version of collaboration, has created an environment in which the process of approaching the task very closely resembles the Pueblo notion of "helping to carry the load." From his initial selection of two children to begin the editing exercise, to his unspoken permission for an "unrecognized" child to aid the current editor at the board, to his appeal to a group member to "help us with that word," Daniel creates an instructional environment that is completely congruent with Pueblo behavior.

The second of the two events, preparing a group presentation on March weather, is perhaps the more significant because of the interweaving of behaviors of the natal culture and the dominant culture.

Katherine assembles the group of third- and fourth-grade students who are working as "teachers" in a first-grade classroom. She initiates a discussion of their upcoming presentation on the study they have done of the weather in March. Katherine queries, "If they didn't understand what temperature means, what could you show them? Specifically, what were our criteria for a lion day?" As the children start to explain, she redirects. "Be specific. Tell some numbers." Katherine says that they will need a recorder to list the topics that will be presented to the first graders. One girl leaves the group, and brings paper from her personal supply drawer. After the children have suggested various statements that they can make about how the study was conducted, Katherine proposes to the recorder that she might simply write "Ellen thermometer." "That would be a short way to write it," continues Katherine. One of the children extends the idea of abbreviated writing, "She can write it *therm*." Katherine continues to guide their construction of the presentation, "Who can tell us about the cri-ter-i-a, what it means? And don't do it like in that Buster story, who was reading that with me? He went the long way around, didn't he?" The child who had read the story with Katherine recounts the tale for the others. Katherine returns to the issue at hand, "What's the criteria for 'lamb day'?" One of the children responds, "Sunny." "But say it in a sentence," presses Katherine. The child restates, "This is what makes a lamb day," and finishes supplying the criteria. "Really explicit," compliments Katherine. One of the children asks, "May I take this home to practice?" "Yes," replies Katherine, "I agree you do need time." She suggests that they practice, like they did for the science fair, and the children move into the hall to prepare by themselves. On their return to the classroom, Katherine and two students role play being first graders. Throughout the presentation, Katherine makes various suggestions. As they finish, Katherine prompts, "Okay, one thing at the end of presentations, what is it good to do?" A girl in the group smiles and inquires, "Are there any questions?" "Yes," responds Katherine, "I have a question. What did you mean the lions won by 13 and the lambs by 7?" One of the presenters rejoins, "I thought you were a little kid." "I'm very advanced," retorts Katherine as she smiles. Once again, the children rehearse in the hall, and return. Their presentation has integrated Katherine's question about lion days winning. Katherine commends one of the girls, "I really like the way you took that suggestion from before."

Close examination of this event reveals three distinct themes: natal culture behavior, dominant culture content, and dominant culture behavior. Katherine, a master teacher, weaves these themes effortlessly, creating a superior instructional moment for her Pueblo students. Like Daniel, Katherine adapts patterns of behavior from the natal culture. When the child asks if she might take the paper home to practice, Katherine seizes the suggestion to allow the entire group a period of time for "private practice." Just as the two brothers in the coat-and-cardboard-antlers Buffalo Dance described earlier practiced alone, so do Katherine's children work by themselves to perfect a performance. Just as the two brothers brought their evolving efforts to share with their parents, so the children in Katherine's class share their developing performance expertise with their significant adult.

As with Daniel, Katherine's incorporation of Pueblo structures allows children comfort with content that is very much part of the dominant culture: criteria, recorders, abbreviations of written forms, and concern for temperature. However, Katherine propels her pupils beyond the mere grasping of curricular content into the domain of dominant world expertise. When the child responds to Katherine's question on the criteria for a lamb day with the single word *sunny*, Katherine urges her student into the "elaborated" speech patterns deemed most acceptable in the dominant society. Her push toward standard English form is evident again when, in her role playing of a first grader, she questions the form of the child's statement "the lions won by 13 and the lambs by 7."

The warp that Katherine stretches on her students' mental looms boasts more than a simple threading of standard English forms. What glistens in the fabric of her teaching is the access she provides beyond the syntactic to the discourse level structures of the dominant world. "At the end of presentations," she quizzes her pupils, "what is it good to do?" That her students are internalizing this dominant world discourse structure is evident in the child's smile and immediate response: "Are there any questions?" Katherine captures a key component of the natal culture, "private practice," braids it through the content, through the culture of schools, and discloses a pattern of considerable importance in the culture of the dominant world.

IMPLICATIONS OF THE STUDY

Sensitivity to Cultural Patterns of Appropriate Behavior

What, then, can be said to those who seek a way to allow "the glow" of students' feelings to penetrate a paint that public education pours over the souls of children from nonmainstream cultures? Minimally, as Baugh (1981) suggested, teachers need to be ethnosensitive. For the teacher who understands the place of competition in the Pueblo world, the place of work in the Pueblo world, and the place of consensus in the Pueblo world, there will be considerably less mystification and considerably less frustration when students fail to behave in ways that are commonplace for dominant-culture students.

For the teacher who is aware of the ways that teaching and learning occur within a nondominant culture, the possibility of adaptation such as is demonstrated in Daniel and Katherine's teaching is greatly enhanced. However, McLean (1990) made the point that teachers range in reflections on culture from those at a "surface curriculum" level (which may have an "aborigines" unit of study) to those at a level of "committed reflectors." Only those teachers in touch with their innermost feelings, in touch with their personal sense of self, and who have addressed the disparity between their own belief systems and those of the cultural groups in which they teach will be able to capture that which is key to the natal culture and adapt it for the culture of schools.

Issues of Content, Process, and Access

In considering the frequently promoted advice that teachers should devise content from natal culture (cf. Reyhner & Garcia, 1989), a very basic question of purpose in schooling must be addressed. If teachers believe that schools are to serve as bridges, opening access to the avenues of the dominant society for those students who wish to walk those paths, then the design of culturally compatible instruction should highlight culturally appropriate processes, beginning with those of the natal culture but never dismissing those of the dominant culture. From natal culture to school culture to dominant-world culture, the master teacher supports, propels, and magnifies the vistas of students, allowing innermost souls to breathe freely.

REFERENCES

Au, K., & Jordan, C. (1981). Teaching reading to Hawaiian children: Finding a culturally appropriate solution. In H. Trueba, G. Guthrie, & K. Au (Eds.), *Culture and the bilingual classroom* (pp. 139–152). Rowley, MA: Newbury House.

Baugh, J. (1981). Design and implementation of writing instruction for speakers of non-standard English: Perspectives for a national neighborhood literacy program. In B. Cronnell (Ed.), *The writing needs of linguistically different students* (pp. 17–43). Los Alamitos, CA: SWRL Research and Development.

Diaz, S., Moll, L., & Mehan, H. (1986). Sociocultural resources in instruction: A context-specific approach. In Bilingual Education Office, California State Dept. of Education (Ed.), *Beyond language: Social and cultural factors in schooling language minority students*. Los Angeles: Evaluation, Dissemination and Assessment Center, California State University.

Farr, M. (1991). Dialects, culture and teaching the English language arts. In J. Flood, J. M. Jensen, D. Lapp, & J. R. Squire (Eds.), *Handbook of research on teaching the English language arts* (pp. 365–371). New York: Macmillan.

Heath, S. B. (1983). *Ways with words: Language, life and work in communities and classrooms*. Cambridge, England: Cambridge University Press.

Hoyt-Goldsmith, D. (1990). *Totem pole*. New York: Holiday House.

Hoyt-Goldsmith, D. (1991). *Pueblo storyteller*. New York: Holiday House.

Jordan, C. (1985). Translating culture: From ethnographic information to educational program. *Anthropology and Education Quarterly, 16*, 105–123.

Keegan, M. (1991). *Pueblo boy: Growing up in two worlds*. New York: Cobblehill Books.

Leporanta-Morley, P. (1988). My language is my home. In T. Skutnabb-Kangas & J. Cummins (Eds.), *Minority education: From shame to struggle* (pp. 172–173). Clevedon, England: Multilingual Matters LTD.

McLean, S. V. (1990). Early childhood teachers in multicultural settings. *The Educational Forum, 54*(2), 197–204.

Parmee, E. A. (1968). *Formal education and culture change: A modern Apache Indian community and government education program*. Tucson: University of Arizona Press.

Peters, H. D. (1963). Performance of Hopi children on four intelligence tests. *Journal of American Indian Education, 2*(2), 27–31.

Reyhner, J., & Garcia, R. L. (1989). Helping minorities read better: Problems and promises. *Reading Research and Instruction, 28*(3), 84–91.

Suina, J. H. (1988). *The early years*. Princeton, NJ: Carnegie Foundation.

Zintz, M. V. (1960). *The Indian research study: The adjustment of Indian and non-Indian children in the public schools of New Mexico*. Unpublished manuscript, University of New Mexico, Albuquerque.

AFRICAN ROOTS

West Africans from Mali celebrate a wedding at home in Paris, France. Entire families from infancy to adulthood are expected to attend.
Photograph by Darryl Evans

7

SOCIALIZATION OF NSO CHILDREN IN THE BAMENDA GRASSFIELDS OF NORTHWEST CAMEROON

A. Bame Nsamenang
Ecole Normale Superieure, Cameroon

Michael E. Lamb
National Institute of Child Health and Human Development

In this chapter, we explore the ideas and values that give directive focus to the socialization of children—especially Nso children—in the Bamenda Grassfields of Cameroon, shaping their affective, social, and cognitive development. We highlight the continuity across generations in the face of discontinuities introduced by such factors as formal schooling, urbanization, and the economic necessity for parents, especially mothers, to relinquish their traditional roles and participate instead in the labor force. Familial values foreshadow the content and mode of cultural transmission and, eventually, the pattern of intelligence children acquire and cherish. In other words, children in every culture are socialized to acquire the intelligence that already exists in their own culture (Ogbu, chapter 18, this volume). Thus, by studying socialization values in any culture, we can gain insight into the ideas or notions that give directive force (D'Andrade, 1984) to the process of socialization in that culture.

Today, the Bamenda Grassfields roughly comprise the Northwest Province, one of Cameroon's 10 Provinces. It is composed of several centralized fondoms (ethnic kingdoms) whose demographic history reveals population movements, the adjustment of cultural patterns, and the adaptation of customary traditions to accommodate the savanna (grassland) ecology (Nkwi, 1983). Nso is the largest of the Bamenda Grassfields fondoms. Nso people cluster around patrilineal heads in compounds organized in villages that vary in size, population, and importance. The bulk of the population lives in Nsoland, but some migrants have settled outside the ancestral land, especially in Bamenda, a city 65 miles (about 108 km) to the south.

We begin the chapter by providing a conceptual framework for the understanding of Nso enculturation, drawing on both behavioral ecology and recent work on the central role played by language in the acquisition of sociocultural knowledge. Next, we describe the values and beliefs of parents from the Bamenda Grassfields, emphasizing the high value placed on community spirit, social intelligence, and the demarcation of life stages by social criteria. Third, we describe the processes of socialization, showing how parents and other members of society directly and indirectly influence the acquisition of socioaffective and cognitive skills by young children. The findings are placed in context in the final section.

CONCEPTUAL FRAMEWORK

Human development always occurs in a specific ecoculture, defined by geography, history, climate, and the sociocultural system. Physical and social environments provide culturally meaningful experiences for their occupants. In addition, the sociocultural system offers the agents, institutions, and scripts that permit and facilitate the humanization of offspring and their social integration and enculturation (Nsamenang, 1992a). Whereas some—especially Western—cultures emphasize academic, technological, or cognitive modes of social integration, other—especially African—cultures place primacy on socioaffective socialization (cf. Mundy-Castle, 1968, 1974). Both social and technological intelligence (Mundy-Castle, 1968, 1974) are embedded in the ecocultural imperatives that focus and channel individuals to acquire the right moral posture, the appropriate social graces, and the technical skills required for acceptable, functional membership in the culture. The school system is a cultural artifact of external colonial origin that, like other societal institutions, "provides practice in the use of specific tools and technologies for solving particular problems" (Rogoff, 1990, p. 191).

In virtually every culture, there are three major sources of parenting values: folk knowledge, ontogenetic experience, and literature or expert advice (Harkness, Super, & Keefer, 1992). The directive force of each of these sources of knowledge varies across individuals and societies, depending on an array of such background factors as world view, social history, education, religion, place of residence, and so on. Institutions and the values they engender vary considerably across cultures. Values and skills also differ considerably with respect to the emphasis they place on individuality as opposed to collectivism and on social responsibility as opposed to instrumental or technological progress.

Language and the Acquisition of Culture

Of course "children are not born with an understanding of their cultural identity . . ." (Harkness et al., 1992, p. 1); they acquire it during ontogeny. Language, both verbal and nonverbal, is central to the acquisition of cultural forms of thought and behavior. In fact, "the unique qualities of human behavior are due to language which make 'culture' possible" (Segall, Dasen, Berry, & Poortinga, 1990, p. 9); language is a medium or tool for the acquisition of culture (Harkness, 1989; Schwartz, 1981). As articulated in the Sapir-Whorf hypothesis, "language predisposes or predetermines its speakers to certain modes of observation and interpretation of the environment" (Hoosain, 1986, p. 507). Therefore, as a socializing tool, "language and discourse become the most critical tool for the child's construction of the social world, because it is through language that social action is generated" (Corsaro, 1985, p. 74). Children acquire sociocultural knowledge through exposure to and coparticipation in everyday verbal exchanges (Rogoff, 1990; Schieffelin & Ochs, 1986).

Verbal fluency or literacy alone do not ensure the centrality of language in the acquisition of culture; nonverbal language is equally critical, especially in nonliterate cultures. For example, in the Bamenda Grassfields, as in much of West Africa, sign or symbolic language and terse proverbs are more widely used and perhaps far more effective than extensive verbal instructions. In addition, affect is an important component of sociocultural knowledge. Because "concepts of feeling are bound to concepts of person in all societies" (Ochs, 1988, p. 146), children everywhere are expected to acquire an understanding of the affective orientation of verbal as well as nonverbal cues. Emotions are a subcategory of feeling both emotion, and feeling entails awareness (Levy, 1984). The study of emotion as discourse then permits researchers to explore how local views are encoded in language (Abu-Lughod & Lutz, 1990). "Through the use of affect-marked speech, [for example,] Samoan caregivers socialize young children into local expectations concerning appropriate social behavior" (Ochs, 1988, p. 168), as do their West-African counterparts.

Although academics generally distinguish between the socialization of affect and cognitive socialization (Schwartz, 1975), both are facets of one and the same process (Jahoda & Lewis, 1988). The cognitive and affective features of development are intimately interwoven. For instance, "as part of becoming socially and linguistically competent members of particular social groups, children must learn how to appropriately convey their feelings to others as well as to recognize the moods and emotions that others display" (Schieffelin & Ochs, 1986, p. 178). Furthermore, affective competence involves learning how to evaluate the relationship between self (as speaker) and audience, and bringing to bear this relationship knowledge on the interpretation of verbal or nonverbal behavior (Ochs, 1988). In this way, children develop an understanding of the affective meanings of both verbal and non-verbal cues with respect to such communicative relationships.

VALUES AND NORMS

Collectivism

A frame of reference that focuses on the individual does not come to the West African readily. To use the terminology of Triandis (1985, 1989), West Africans differ from Europeans and North Americans in their perspective, which is collectivistic rather than individualistic. In the West-African world view, "man is not man on his own; the individual gains significance from and through his relationships with others" (Ellis, 1978, p. 6). The nature of the self is interdependent more than independent (Kitayama & Markus, 1992; Markus & Kitayama, 1991).

Traditional life fosters a sense of community that supports individuals and families; it accords them a deep and comforting sense of tradition and community, thus promoting collective responsibility and rendering individual and collective miseries more bearable (Nsamenang, 1992a). This kind of social ecology certainly enriches some but undoubtedly stifles other aspects of development. For instance, losses in individuality and personal freedom are as inevitable as gains in the security that may accrue from active membership in an extensive supportive social network (Nsamenang, 1989b).

Obiechina (1975) vividly portrayed the relationship between the individual and the community by remarking how

> The West African novel tends to show the individual characters not through their private psychological experiences, but through community and social life and activities of collective and general nature with individual sentiments and actions deriving force and logic from those of the community. (p. 35)

Nsamenang (1987a) amplified this tendency by pointing out that persons who assert individual rights and interests over those of the community "do so at the expense of their peace of mind and at great risk of losing the psychological comfort of a feeling of belonging" (p. 279). Esen (1972) even equated the lack of a feeling of not belonging to one's kingroup to some kind of death. West Africans rationalize their subordination of individual interests to those of the group by reasoning that "individuals come and go but the group persists" (Nsamenang, 1987a, p. 279). It is thus clear that the West African "exists in and for the community" (Atado, 1988, p. 7).

Social Intelligence and Social Stages

West Africans clearly distinguish between illiterate intelligence and print (literate) intelligence, as well as between social and technological intelligence. For example, the Baoulé of the Ivory Coast, like other West Africans, hold that "One may know how to read and write but be quite dumb" because one "may know much of Baoulé intelligence without knowing much on paper" (Dasen, 1984, p. 427). Thus, the common feeling is that academic or technological intelligence must be integrated with social intelligence because a person's abilities are useless unless they are applied for the good and well-being of the social group (Dasen, 1984).

For West Africans, the infant is a "project-in-progress" (Nsamenang, 1992a), and stages of social integration are demarcated using social rather than biological signposts. In other words, children are progressively assigned different roles at different life stages, depending on their perceived level of social competence rather than on their biological maturation. This emphasis reflects the fear that some persons who are mature in chronological terms may behave irresponsibly. Thus, the notion of social intelligence changes according to ontogenetic status, as children are systematically incorporated into different roles at different stages of life. Without functional integration into "this" or "that" social stratum, individuals are considered mere "danglers" to whom the designation of *person* does not appropriately and fully apply. Therefore, human offspring need other humans to attain full selfhood: A sense of self cannot be attained without reference to the broader community.

However alien it may appear to those whose world view promotes individualism and freedom of choice, students of West Africa must understand the significance of deference and obedience to elders and superiors, including older siblings. Such orientations are the product of a socialization pattern in which emphasis is placed on notions of authority, with a fear that children will be "spoiled" if they do not serve or perform some duties.

In summary, Nso parents have a particular ethnotheory of development (Kagitçibasi & Berry, 1989; Super & Harkness, 1986). Socialization in the Bamenda Grassfields exposes children to a social reality and a set of experiences that channel their development with different purposes and in different directions than children in Western cultures. Socialization is not organized to train children for academic pursuits or to become individuals outside the ancestral culture. Rather, it is organized to teach social competence and shared responsibility within the family system and ethnic community. As Kagitcibasi (1982, 1985, 1988) noted, this pattern of socialization is typical of traditional, rural agricultural groups with large, close-knit family systems. Nevertheless, many children who have ventured outside their ethnic niches have adapted remarkably well and have excelled in alien contexts. For instance, in 1988, Penn Sama, a 6-year-old "fresh" immigrant from Bamenda (Cameroon) became a "math champ" in his class in a New Orleans (Louisiana) school (Martyn Sama, personal communication, December 1989).

Contemporary Forces and Changes

Currently, however, the social system is in total flux. For instance, children are frequently more knowledgeable in matters of contemporary life than their (illiterate) parents. This reverses traditional roles and makes it difficult for parents to be role models or to teach their children "the correct ways of the world." Unfortunately, little is known of the extent to which traditional values are being renounced in the process. To address the question, we have attempted to explore ideas and attitudes of parents of diverse ages, backgrounds, and economic stations. In this research, we are comparing the ideas and values of parents and grandparents, from rural and urban areas, both to give life and voice to the Nso people, as well as to quantify the extent to which there is a generational change in belief systems. Interestingly, although we sought largely to describe popular beliefs, many respondents claimed that our interview was the first time they had ever verbalized their parenting attitudes and practices.

An Empirical Study.   Our study involved 211 men and 178 women who were either parents (persons who had at least one child 10 years of age or younger) or grandparents (persons with at least one grandchild). Nearly 25% (95) claimed adherence to African theodicy, 58% (226) were Christian, and 18% (68) were Moslem. Two thirds (263) lived in Nso villages, whereas the remainder (126) lived in Bamenda town.

One parent in each of the 389 families volunteered to participate in the study. Data were collected using the Lamnso (Nso language) version of the open-ended Parent Interview Guide (PIG), developed by Nsamenang and Lamb (1988). During its development, an English version of the PIG was progressively "refined" after extensive discussions with colleagues and several trial interviews before being translated into Lamnso, field tested with Nso parents in Bamenda, and finalized. Interviews were audiotaped. On the basis of the first author's knowledge of Nso culture, supplemented by a content analysis of the pilot interviews, coding categories were developed. The coding scheme was later revised to accommodate responses that could not be coded reliably using the preliminary scheme.

The interviews yielded a large body of data on parental beliefs and values about childhood, parenthood, and socialization, which we are only now beginning to evaluate and synthesize. When asked why Nso people might want children, respondents tended to give answers that conveyed a very traditional view of the value of children. Thus, 56% mentioned the performance of domestic chores, another 30% mentioned running errands, and 36% mentioned respect for and obedience to parents. However, when asked about their expectations of children, only 27% mentioned filial service. Instead, half mentioned good progress in school, and 45% "success in life," although less than a fifth of them mentioned either vocational or social competence specifically. Of the mothers and fathers, 40% felt that boys and girls should be raised differently, although they were not very articulate about the specific ways in which they should be treated differently.

There was considerable agreement between parents and grandparents in the perceptions of desirable and undesirable characteristics. "Good children" were expected to display (a) obedience and respect (90%), (b) filial service (89%), (c) hard work (91%), (d) helpfulness (90.5%), (e) honesty (100%), and (f) intelligence (100%). In contrast, the following characteristics were deemed undesirable: (a) disobedience and disrespect (92.5%), (b) laziness (96.7%), (c) fighting (95.4%), (d) greed (99%), (e) playfulness (99%), (f) fearfulness (100%), and (g) inquisitiveness (100%). These preferences were especially prominent in the responses of the rural parents, who endorsed slightly more traditional views than did the urban respondents.

In previous analyses, we found that modern values and beliefs (e.g., concerning childbirth, early childcare, and early development) are rapidly replacing traditional values (Nsamenang & Lamb, 1991). In these areas, young urban women represent the vanguard of change, whereas older rural men cling to the most traditional beliefs. Similar patterns were clearly not evident where parental values and expectations were concerned. For the most part, traditional values were widely endorsed.

Ellis (1978) noted that all African cultures have been exposed to extremely powerful external cultural influences. This fact notwithstanding, Nso socialization values seem to be of indigenous origin, reflecting "the influence of a well-defined cultural background that has strong roots" (Palacios, 1990, p. 150), rather than of alien world views and cultural values. For example, parental concern with school progress, although not strictly an indigenous motive, derives from a cultural belief in social competence. It also derives from the realization that, because education and farming are incompatible (Ohuche & Otaala, 1982), contemporary realities demand that raising children be guided by what provides the basic requirements for functional and meaningful citizenship. A plausible explanation for the tenacity of Nso socialization values in face of potent modifying forces is Uka's (1966) claim that childrearing beliefs "are never amenable to easy changes because beliefs about the origin of life are not held on a rational basis" (p. 29).

Disagreements, of course, do arise when the values of individuals change at different rates. Nsamenang (1987b) reported that mothers in the Bamenda Grassfields accused fathers of not performing their traditional roles in the family production line, whereas fathers and mothers also quarreled about how the proceeds of women's economic activities should be used. Social change is often manifested in a clash between traditionalism and "modernism"—a clash that produces dilemmas and incompatible role demands that confuse both parents and children. Where this occurs, it gives rise to parental bitterness as well as an increasing incidence of psychological disturbances in children.

SOCIALIZATION AND SOCIAL INTERACTION

As explained earlier, the socialization values of the Nso primarily stress social competence and social intelligence. However, "children's cognitive development is inseparable from the social milieu in that what children learn is a cultural curriculum: from the earliest days, they build on the skills and perspectives of their society with the aid of other people" (Rogoff, 1990, p. 190). Parents in the Bamenda Grassfields are oriented toward this pattern of cognitive socialization. The ecoculture is represented to children by the people who instruct, explain, or act as models; "but even more pervasively by those with whom the child cooperates in shared functioning" (Tharp et al., 1984, p. 93)—hence the significance of the ubiquitous peer group in West-African communities.

How then do children learn from adults? Adults construct the social context formed by adults with whom children interact, shaping the behavioral settings that provide opportunities for children to learn and develop. In general, "much knowledge filters from adults through older children" (Tharp et al., 1984, p. 100) who are co-participants, alongside adults, in the routine tasks and activities of teaching younger ones. For example, among the Wolof of Senegal, some of the basic social norms of the culture begin to be systematically and, in the main, painlessly instilled into the children almost immediately after weaning through the powerful agency of the sibling group in this process (Rabain, 1979; Zempleni-Rabain, 1973).

In the Bamenda Grassfields, as elsewhere in West Africa, social and cognitive stimulation literally begin at birth. Although Ellis (1978) suggested that West Africans do not talk to babies because they believe that babies do not "hear" baby talk, West Africans freely tell babies whom they resemble, what their names should be, what they signify, and what sort of adults they are expected to become.

Nso children learn culturally appropriate forms of behavior and thought systems primarily through "hands-on" socialization (Harkness et al., 1992; Whiting & Whiting, 1975), more under the mentorship of older siblings and peers than of parents or other adults. Regularities or continuities in the ecoculture and the expectable social roles and culturally defined life stations "provide material from which the child abstracts the social, affective, and cognitive rules of the culture, much as the regularities of grammar are abstracted from the speech environment" (Super & Harkness, 1986, p. 552).

The reported parental values encourage "an active apprenticeship experience for children" (Weisner, 1987, p. 238). Typically completed by adolescence, this apprenticeship usually proceeds while the individual learns to perform the domestic tasks essential for family and community survival. By encouraging children to take part in different tasks of social life, to observe seniors, and to listen to and later join in discussions, the Grassfields adolescent acquires a sense of solidarity and responsibility as he or she completes his or her physical, intellectual, and practical education (*L'encyclopedie de la Republic unie du Cameroun*, 1981).

The fact that parents endorse the assignment of responsibilities to children underscores their assumption that children are capable and socially responsible (Nsamenang, 1989a). It also connotes an awareness of developmental milestones. The pattern of socialization is such that children are systematically "graduated" from one role position to another until they assume adult roles. By permitting children to learn to speak and act within "pivot roles," the Grassfields caregiving milieu facilitates this kind of socialization.

Children in the Bamenda Grassfields acquire cultural competence primarily by way of (a) observation and imitation, (b) attention to the themes of prototypic stories, and (c) co-participation in major activities, especially within the peer culture (peer mentoring). Socialization practices depend on watching and learning from adults, siblings, and peers in role rehearsal or reenactment when error occurs.

Children are expected to observe the performance of tasks and to imitate or rehearse them, especially while playing with peers, with little if any instruction. Consequently, it is common to find toddlers playing mother or father, typically under the corrective surveillance and mentorship of elder siblings or peers, rather than that of parents and other adults. Strangers are often surprised at the extent to which children spontaneously respond to sign or symbolic (hidden) language.

As in Hawaii, learning occurs in a mode of "enterprise engagements," whereby the child actually performs or attempts to practice the skill or task that he or she is learning. The emphasis is not on "I'll tell you how to do it," but on "watch," "listen," "participate," and "try" (Tharp et al., 1984, p. 101).

Shared functioning of this sort eases the passage from play to productive activities (Bekombo, 1981). For example, because it is not a West-African tradition to provide children with commercial toys, they are usually encouraged to create their own playthings or to make miniature replicas of common objects. The immediate recognition of such "creations" as "products" certainly enhances the creator's self-image. "The process of making these toys teaches the children how to plan work, organize tools and materials, to make measurements, and to conceive of objects in three-dimensional space . . ." (Segall et al., 1990, p. 123). The genesis of the rich tradition of African sculpture, embroidery, leather works, and pottery is rooted in this pattern of socialization.

Traditionally, an adult is responsible for a particular task or service and is usually assisted by children and younger persons of the same gender (Oppong, 1983) who are expected to observe and rehearse the roles, especially during play. At moments in a typical scenario, the child must defer to older persons, especially parents, older siblings, and peer mentors. Later, the child becomes the primary enactor of the same role, "assuming responsibility and utilizing decision-making skills" (Weisner, 1987, p. 248), particularly in sibling care and collective performance of chores.

This implies that the child's behavior varies depending on whether older, more senior members of the social niche are present. When older persons are available, the child's direct responsibility and activities are limited and stereotyped because of "the child's low status rank in that setting at that point in time. A later point in the day may find the child to be relatively senior in rank and in charge, directing other children and displaying" more responsible behaviors (Weisner, 1987, p. 248).

Nso children experience the intimacies and conflicts engendered in social interactions within extended families and peer groups from an early age. The "free" climate and absence of overt adult control within the peer culture breed conflicts as well as compromises. They permit and facilitate peer mentoring and perspective-taking (Dunn & Kendrick, 1982), encouraging children to notice and even anticipate the feelings and needs of younger children. This mode of informal education offers opportunities to learn performance skills, particularly during play, as well as social skills such as learning to (a) collaborate or disagree, (b) lead and follow others, (c) cooperate in collective responsibility, and (d) disagree about diverse tasks and issues (Nsamenang, 1989b). It also provides opportunities for children to discover their abilities and limitations and to learn adult roles. "Children learn skills for household, child-care, and self-care tasks by participating in those tasks with and, initially, under the supervision of, older children" (Tharp et al., 1984, p. 100). "When these children are not involved in tasks and chores, they are usually engaged in friendly sociability" (Weisner, 1987, p. 253). Thus, it is clear that the extent of child-to-child socialization of skills, affect, and cognition is substantial—perhaps far more extensive and developmentally more critical than direct parental socialization (Nsamenang, 1992b).

Many lessons are also taught with proverbs and folktales that contain moral themes and describe virtuous acts for children to emulate. Other tales are suffused with myth to give a sense of the strange and fearful, and thus deter children from wrongdoing (Nsamenang, 1992c). Failure to learn to behave appropriately is admonished, usually with a terse proverb or verbal abuse, and sometimes punished by the withdrawal of privileges. In general, children accept punishment without rancor and accept that parents have the "right to deal with them" as they think fit (Jahoda, 1982, p. 110). Parents rationalize the strictness of their behavior by referring to such folk maxims as: "If a person is trained strictly then that person becomes a good person" (Ellis, 1978, p. 156); "to beat a child is not to hate it" (Jahoda, 1982, p. 111). Children accept parental punishment because "my father punishes me to correct my behavior; my mother rebukes me because I am wrong" (Ellis, 1968, p. 156).

The authority of elder siblings over youngsters is derived from parental authority over children. With such authority, older siblings are usually charged with the care and supervision of younger brothers and sisters whom they can reprimand and correct. A distinctive feature of socialization in much of West Africa is that parents do not retain the sole responsibility for fostering socioaffective and cognitive development in children; children themselves are co-participants in other children's socialization. Thus, socialization is a shared responsibility among members of the social network. In fact, a daily routine that keeps both parents away from the home at work, the marketplace, or other activities, and a heavy work load for adult women in particular, encourages sibling care (Weisner, 1987).

Child caregiving generally involves multiage, multigender groups with charges ranging in age from 20 months to 6 or 7 years under the supervision and guidance of one or two children (usually girls) ages 8 to 10 years (Nsamenang, 1992b). After they have been weaned, infants spend most of their time in such peer and sibling groups, and most socialization takes place in this context (Nsamenang, 1992b). Although children spend a considerable amount of time in child-to-child interactions and engage in creative activities by themselves, they are still constrained by adult norms because "a mechanism of self-regulation exists in the fraternal group, due to the power inherent in the word of the adult, whose direct intervention is no longer needed" (Zempleni-Rabain, 1973, p. 233).

Because Bamenda Grassfields children spend far more time in direct interaction with one another than with adults, they, like their Kokwet counterparts, learn to talk more from each other than from their parents (Super & Harkness, 1986). Children also consolidate the social graces, moral imperatives, and skilled activities of their culture through shared functioning within the peer culture.

Child caregiving is but one form of children's roles. Child "work" is an indigenous mechanism for social integration—a strategy that keeps children in contact with existential realities and the activities of daily life. It represents the participatory component of social integration, an essential preparation for economic and civic participation in societies where the school system has distanced itself from the realities and basic skills needed for agrarian economies (Serpell, 1992). In summary, children in the Bamenda Grassfields are integrated into a dense social network characterized by norms of sharing and exchange. Unfortunately, many aspects of this traditional system of education and socialization are under siege, disrupted by the competing demands of the "modern" nation–state.

SUMMARY AND CONCLUSION

The central idea in this chapter is that children's affective and cognitive development is dependent on and shaped by their sociocultural milieu. Social, affective, and cognitive skills are closely linked to the familiar tasks and interpersonal encounters in which children and adults engage. They are embedded in the social contexts and cultural institutions in which the skills are demanded and enacted. Communication, both verbal and nonverbal, is central to the acquisition of cultural forms of behavior and thought. Cultural differences in social orientation, affective posture, and cognition emerge primarily from varying ecocultural imperatives, the socialization values that direct how children progress toward adult cultural forms, and the extent to which cultural repertoires of skills and competencies are encoded in the language. Within shared-function social niches characterized by deference and hierarchy, Nso children, in collaboration with their families, are active participants in their own socialization. The emphasis in socialization is on obedience and social responsibility, rather than on proficiency in verbal expression and individuality. Despite obvious Westernization, Nso socialization values are still deeply rooted in their ancestral traditions. Nevertheless, compared with the parents of previous generations, contemporary parents may be less certain about their socialization values and the changing world for which their children are being prepared.

REFERENCES

Abu-Lughod, L., & Lutz, C. A. (1990). Introduction: Emotion, discourse, and the politics of everyday life. In C. A. Lutz & L. Abu-Lughod (Eds.), *Language and the politics of emotion*. New York: Cambridge University Press.

Atado, J. C. (1988). *African marriage customs and church law*. Kano, Nigeria: Modern Printers.

Bekombo, M. (1981). The child in Africa: Socialization, education and work. In G. Rodgers & G. Standing (Eds.), *Child work, poverty, and underdevelopment*. Geneva: World Health Organization.

Corsaro, W. (1985). *Friendship and peer culture in the early years*. Norwood, NJ: Ablex.

D'Andrade, R. (1984). Cultural meaning systems. In R. A. Shweder & R. A. LeVine (Eds.), *Culture theory: Essays on mind, self, and emotion*. New York: Cambridge University Press.

Dasen, P. R. (1984). The cross-cultural study of intelligence: Piaget and the Baoule. *International Journal of Psychology, 19*, 407–434.

Dunn, J., & Kendrick, C. (1982). The speech of two- and three-year-olds to infant siblings. *Journal of Child Language, 9,* 579–595.

Encyclopedie de la Republique unie du Cameroun [Encyclopedia of the United Republic of Cameroon]. (1981). Douala, Cameroon: Eddy Ness.

Ellis, J. (1968). *Child-rearing in Ghana, with particular reference to the Ga tribe.* Unpublished master's thesis, University of Ghana, West Africa.

Ellis, J. (1978). The child in West African society. In J. Ellis (Ed.), *West African families in Britain.* London: Routledge & Kegan Paul.

Esen, A. (1972). A view of guidance from Africa. *Personnel and Guidance Journal, 50,* 792–798.

Harkness, S. (1989). A cultural model for the acquisition of language: Implications for the innateness debate. *Developmental Psychobiology, 23,* 727–740.

Harkness, S., Super, C. M., & Keefer, C. H. (1992). Learning to be an American parent: How cultural models gain directive force. In R. G. D'Andrade & C. Strauss (Eds.), *Cultural models and motivation.* New York: Cambridge University Press.

Hoosain, R. (1986). Language, orthography and cognitive processes: Chinese perspectives for the Sapir-Whorf hypothesis. *International Journal of Behavioral Development, 9,* 507–525.

Jahoda, G. (1982). *Psychology and anthropology.* London: Academic Press.

Jahoda, G., & Lewis, I. M. (1988). Introduction: Child development in psychology and anthropology. In G. Jahoda & I. M. Lewis (Eds.), *Acquiring culture: Cross-cultural studies in child development.* London: Croom Helm.

Kagitçibasi, Ç. (1982). *The changing value of children in Turkey.* Honolulu, HI: East–West Population Institute.

Kagitçibasi, Ç. (1985). Culture of separateness—culture of relatedness. In *1984: Vision and reality.* Columbus: Ohio State University Press.

Kagitçibasi, Ç. (1988). Diversity of socialization and social change. In P. R. Dasen, J. W. Berry, & N. Sartorius (Eds.), *Health and cross-cultural psychology: Toward applications* (pp. 25–47). Newbury Park, CA: Sage.

Kagitçibasi, Ç., & Berry, J. W. (1989). Cross-cultural psychology: Current research and trends. *Annual Review of Psychology, 40,* 493–531.

Kitayama, S., & Markus, H. R. (1992, May). *Construal of the self as cultural frame: Implications for internationalizing psychology.* Paper prepared for symposium on Internationalization and Higher Education, University of Michigan, Ann Arbor.

Levy, R. (1984). Emotion, knowing, and culture. In R. Shweder & R. LeVine (Eds.), *Culture theory: Essays on mind, self and emotion.* New York: Cambridge University Press.

Markus, H., & Kitayama, S. (1991). Culture and the self: Implications for cognition, emotion, and motivation. *Psychological Review, 98,* 224–253.

Mundy-Castle, A. C. (1968, December). . . . _____ . . . . Paper presented at a workshop in social psychology organized by the Makerere Institute of Social Research and Syracuse University, New York.

Mundy-Castle, A. C. (1974). Social and technological intelligence in Western and non-Western cultures. *Universitas, 4,* 46–52.

Nkwi, P. N. (1983). Traditional diplomacy, trade and warfare in the nineteenth century Western Grassfields. *Science and Technology Review, 1,* 3–4.

Nsamenang, A. B. (1987a). A West African perspective. In M. E. Lamb (Ed.), *The father's role: Cross-cultural perspectives* (pp. 273–293). Hillsdale, NJ: Lawrence Erlbaum Associates.

Nsamenang, A. B. (1987b). *Parental education and socialization of children in the Bamenda Grassfields: A research report.* Unpublished manuscript, Institute of Human Sciences, Bamenda, Cameroon.

Nsamenang, A. B. (1989a, May). *Another style of socialization: The caregiving child.* Poster presented to the Conference of the Iowa International Network on Personal Relationships, Iowa City, IA.

Nsamenang, A. B. (1989b, July). *The social ecology of Cameroonian childhood.* Poster presented to the International Society for the Study of Behavioral Development, Jyvaskyla, Finland.

Nsamenang, A. B. (1992a). *Human development in cultural context: A third-world perspective.* Beverly Hills, CA: Sage.

Nsamenang, A. B. (1992b). Early childhood care and education in Cameroon. In M. E. Lamb, K. J. Sternberg, C. P. Hwang, & A. G. Broberg (Eds.), *Child care in context: Cross-cultural perspectives* (pp. 419–439). Hillsdale, NJ: Lawrence Erlbaum Associates.

Nsamenang, A. B. (1992c). Perceptions of parenting among the Nso of Cameroon. In B. S. Hewlett (Ed.), *Father–child relationships: Anthropological perspectives* (pp. 321–343). Hawthorne, NY: Aldine.

Nsamenang, A. B., & Lamb, M. E. (1988). *Parent interview guide* (Unpublished interview schedule). Bethesda, MD: National Institute of Child Health and Human Development.

Nsamenang, A. B., & Lamb, M. E. (1991). *Attitudes and beliefs regarding childbirth and perinatal care among the Nso of Northwest Cameroon.* Unpublished manuscript.

Obiechina, E. N. (1975). *Culture, tradition and society in the West African novel.* Cambridge, England: Cambridge University Press.

Ochs, E. (1988). *Culture and language development: Language acquisition and language socialization in a Samoan village.* New York: Cambridge University Press.

Ohuche, R. O., & Otaala, B. (1982). *The African child in his environment.* Oxford, England: Pergamon.

Oppong, C. (Ed.). (1983). *Female and male in West Africa.* London: Allen & Unwin.

Palacios, J. (1990). Parents' ideas about the development and education of their children: Answers to some questions. *International Journal of Behavioral Development, 13,* 137–155.

Rabain, J. (1979). *L'Enfant du lignage: Du sevrage a la classe d'age* [Child of the lineage: From weaning to age-graded peer group]. Paris: Payot.

Rogoff, B. (1990). *Apprenticeship in thinking: Cognitive development in social context.* New York: Oxford University Press.

Schieffelin, B. B., & Ochs, E. (1986). Language socialization. *Annual Review of Anthropology, 15,* 163–191.

Schwartz, T. (Ed.). (1975). *Socialization as cultural communication.* Berkeley, CA: University of California Press.

Schwartz, T. (1981). The acquisition of culture. *Ethos, 9,* 4–17.

Segall, M. H., Dasen, P. R., Berry, J. W., & Poortinga, Y. H. (1990). *Human behavior in global perspective.* New York: Pergamon.

Serpell, R. (1992). African dimensions of child care and nurturance. In M. E. Lamb, K. J. Sternberg, C. P. Hwang, & C. P. Broberg (Eds.), *Child care in context: Cross-cultural perspectives* (pp. 463–476). Hillsdale, NJ: Lawrence Erlbaum Associates.

Super, C. M., & Harkness, S. (1986). The developmental niche: A conceptualization at the interface of child and culture. *International Journal of Behavioral Development, 9,* 545–569.

Tharp, R. G., Jordan, C., Speidel, G. E., Au, K. H-P., Klein, T. W., Calkins, R. P., Sloat, K. C. M., & Gallimore, R. (1984). Product and process in applied developmental research: Education and the children of a minority. In M. E. Lamb, A. L. Brown, & B. Rogoff (Eds.), *Advances in developmental psychology* (Vol. 3, pp. 91–141). Hillsdale, NJ: Lawrence Erlbaum Associates.

Triandis, H. C. (1985). Collectivism vs. individualism: A conceptualization of a basic concept in cross-cultural social psychology. In C. Bagley & G. K. Verma (Eds.), *Personality, cognition and values.* London: MacMillan.

Triandis, H. C. (1989). Cross-cultural studies of individualism and collectivism. In *Nebraska Symposium on Motivation.* Lincoln: University of Nebraska Press.

Uka, N. (1966). *Growing up in Nigerian culture.* Ibadan, Nigeria: Ibadan University Press.

Weisner, T. S. (1987). Socialization for parenthood in sibling caretaking societies. In J. B. Lancaster, J. Altman, A. S. Rossi, & L. R. Sherrod (Eds.), *Parenting across the lifespan: Biosocial dimensions* (pp. 237–270). Hawthorne, NY: Aldine de Gruyter.

Whiting, B. B., & Whiting, J. W. M. (1975). *Children of six cultures: A psycho-cultural analysis.* Cambridge, MA: Harvard University Press.

Zempleni-Rabain, J. (1973). Food and the strategy involved in learning fraternal exchange among Wolof children. In P. Alexandre (Ed.), *French perspectives in African studies* (pp. 221–233). Oxford, England: Oxford University Press.

8

LANGUAGE AND SOCIALIZATION OF THE CHILD IN AFRICAN FAMILIES LIVING IN FRANCE

Jacqueline Rabain Jamin
Université René Descartes

THE NOTION OF CULTURAL CONTEXT

Certain forms of communicative, perceptive, postural, and cognitive activities of the young child have universal structural features, as do the parental elicitations of these activities. In contrast, other forms vary with social context and social environment. Observed regularities can be due to cognitive constraints or the presence of communicative universals, whereas observed differences can be attributed, from the standpoint of cultural ecology (Berry, 1976; Dasen & Heron, 1981; LeVine, 1977), to specific cultural emphasis.

For example, in the extensively researched area of African children's motor development, in native African settings (Bril & Sabatier, 1986), as in emigrant environments (Hopkins, 1976; Rabain-Jamin & Wornham, 1990), it has been shown that postural manipulations that infants are exposed to through handling constrain infants to make posturomotor adjustments with the maternal caregiver. This can explain African children's motor precocity in the first year of life.

In the area of the acquisition of cognitive skills, Dasen and Heron (1981) demonstrated that concepts that are mastered earlier by children from a given culture (e.g., the concept of space in Inuit children [Canada] and the concept of quantity in Baoulé children [Ivory Coast]) are linked to domains that are highly valued in these cultures.

According to Berry (1976), ecology and mode of production are the determinants of a set of sociocultural factors, in particular, modes of socialization, which promote the development of skills and knowhow in those areas where there is a real need (Dasen, 1988). LeVine (1977) posited that educational practices are adaptive response strategies to environmental constraints. Parents' primary concern is the survival of the child, and only when this is ensured do they turn to the acquisition of culturally valued skills. However, the anthropologist Sahlins (1976) argued that it is culture that determines the way in which ecological and technological constraints are defined or appropriated by society. As Benedict (1935) stressed, cultural activity is selective, and there are many possible solutions to problems raised by ecological constraints.

The notion of "developmental niche" put forward by Super and Harkness (1986) assigns key roles (alongside environmental constraints) to customs concerning care and educational practices, as well as to the representations that caregivers have of child development. Systems of representations are integral parts of contextual variables.

Referring to the notion of symbolic culture focuses on the fact that other factors aside from milieu, environment, and ecology introduce contextual differences: Factors such as conceptual frame, beliefs, and value systems shared by individuals in a given culture also enter into contextual differences. These value systems cannot be equated with purely ecological or adaptive variables. Rather, they can modulate fundamental interactive processes, orient parental behavior in one direction or another, and confer a specific style to communicative exchanges and communication in general.

THE SOCIAL CONTEXT OF LANGUAGE USE IN IMMIGRANT SETTINGS

Parent–child verbal interactions in different cultural contexts—in both native countries or in immigration situations—have not been studied widely. However, verbal exchanges are one of the key ways in which the socialization process takes place. There are specific uses and special registers across cultures that develop from the basis of universal possibilities. There are discourse universals related to the linguistic bases of communication (e.g., the existence of fundamental rules of conversation, turn taking), but verbal exchanges are also indicative of a social context of language use (e.g., Rabain-Jamin & Sabeau-Jouannet, 1989)—a specific articulation of the verbal and nonverbal.

In traditional African cultures, modes of speech adhere to a system of relations that strictly defines the position (the status) of each individual in relation to others. Speech is a status attribute. The rank of elder legitimates taking the speaker's role. These hierarchies affect the community as a whole.

Recourse to mediation or spokesmen are part of indirect request strategies or negotiation. Felicitous use of speech also calls for mentioning commentaries in the third person or maxims referring to tradition or custom.

Stating a belief in the first person is seen as indecorous or practically meaningless. Custom founded on ancestor worship is something that is inherited. Living in accordance with ancestors' customs is accepting the efficiency of certain practices (Ortigues, 1979). The fact that shared knowledge is fairly stable may lead to making verbal exchanges less explicit than what is required in Western societies, or may be conducive to the development of argumentation in one area rather than another (e.g., in the area of relations and behavioral rules, which are often the topic of debate and negotiation).

Learning conversational roles in specific semantic contexts takes place in childhood and merits investigation in itself. Verbal exchanges convey values and are accompanied by emotional involvement. Each individual gives special value to the forms of expression and representation that are transmitted to him or her in the home community and that serve in evaluating and experiencing situations and events. Individuals differ in their degree of possible involvement in different forms of communication, and tend to prefer those forms they were familiarized with in their native cultures; these carry greater emotional significance for them. The impact of these first involvements go far beyond language itself.

The studies to be presented were designed to compare differences in communicative interactive styles between mothers and children in African families that immigrated to Paris less than 15 years ago with styles in French families. These observations are compared with findings obtained in an African society—the Wolof of Senegal (Rabain, 1979; Zempleni-Rabain, 1973).

The Soninke and their neighbors, the Toucouleur, who compose the sample that was studied in the 20th district of Paris are natives of regions bordering on Senegal, Mali, and Mauritania. Men were the first to emigrate as unskilled workers. Up to 1974, when immigration laws became stricter, these men, whether they were married or unmarried in Africa, set up a migration chain between men already in France and members of their family still in Africa (Barou, 1991). The younger brother replaced the older brother on his job in France while the older brother returned to Africa. The cutback on immigration put an end to this system and prompted a rise in family immigration. The Soninke and Toucouleur women in this sample were Muslim, for the most part illiterate, from rural backgrounds, and did not work. A small number were city born and could speak French when they arrived. Some were living in polygamy, a situation that was at times concealed from the French authorities because of the legal problems that it created.

On many counts, during the first years of immigration changes took place slowly. These African immigrants in Paris maintained close ties with their native environments because immigration was recent and they had contacts with their families in Africa. The models of authority, the systems of representations, and the values of the native cultures, although integrating new elements, continued to guide behavior and to give it meaning. In a study on caregiving of these immigrant African women, I have shown that the rapid switch to Western forms of health care did not fundamentally change the traditional system of interpretation of illness, which is viewed as a disorder affecting the family as a whole (Rabain-Jamin & Wornham, 1990). Language, seen here as a linguistic tool *and* a symbolic device that is used to name objects and events and to establish meaningful connections, reflects changes or preservation of these reference models beyond apparent changes in behavior.

A first approach to the study of the social uses of language in early mother–infant relationships consists of examining verbal interactions as they are related to other modes of relationship. I look at the results of a study concerning the role played by verbal exchanges about objects compared with verbal exchanges about social communicative acts.

MOTHER–CHILD INTERACTIVE STYLES
IN AFRICAN CULTURES

The few existing studies on cultures other than the ones I investigated here have shown that the distribution of modes of mother–infant interaction is culturally dependent. Some of these modes are prominent, whereas others are less frequent. Richman et al. (1988) conducted a comparative study on mother–infant interactive styles at 3–4 months and at 9–10 months in five different cultures. Their findings indicate that, in contrast to mothers in the United States or Europe, Gusii (Kenya) mothers tend to prefer holding and physical contact and have low rates of visual and verbal interaction. These differences become more pronounced at 9–10 months. The preference for physical contact in the Gusii is not dependent on the motor development of the infant. The importance assigned to verbal exchanges in African mother–infant relations appears to be minimized compared with other forms of sensory, rhythmic, and postural communication. Western mothers tend to show a much more marked scaffolding of verbal exchanges. The situation is the reverse as regards postural communication.

A study on Wolof children (Senegal) showed that vocal and verbal exchanges between mother and infant take place chiefly via onomatopoeia, and partially coded vocalizations, at times by short rhythmic phrases associated with chanting of the child's name and rocking (Rabain, 1979). Proper names are part of a category system and hence enter into a system of differences (Derrida, 1966). In nursery rhymes, a girl child's name is linked with the names of her brothers and the boy's name with those of his sisters. The child's name is linked with his or her namesake (i.e., the person for whom the child was named). For example, the mother murmurs to Karjata (6 months): "Karjata . . . Where is Malik's sister? . . . Here is Umar's sister? . . . Where is Bokar's mother? . . . Where is Demba's mother? . . . One mustn't hurt someone's mother!" (Malik and Umar are Karjata's brothers. Bokar and Demba are the sons of another Karjata, her namesake. Therefore, Karjata is named their "mother.") Thus, the child is situated in the network of kinship and social relations. The caregiver places the infant within a social fabric before teaching him or her to make requests. What linguistic or cultural function is the adult trying to share with the child? This is one question worth asking.

THE NOTION OF FORMS OF MATERNAL "RESPONSIVENESS"

Other field studies in Africa provide a complementary picture. They show that across different cultures, the value placed on maternal adjustment ("responsiveness") to the child can vary greatly as a function of area of activity: activity at a distance with objects, proximal postural activity, or communicative vocal activity (Bakeman, Adamson, Konner, & Barr, 1990; Dasen, Inhelder, Lavallée, & Retschitzki, 1978; Rabain, 1979). In addition, responsiveness can be oriented toward verbal or nonverbal responses.

Recall that the notion of responsiveness (Bornstein, 1989; Pêcheux, 1990), defined as the ability of the mother to change her behavior as a function of the infant's behavior in order to give the infant an appropriate response (a response that has a certain degree of stability over time), has been used in a number of studies. The concept of responsiveness points to the crucial role played by contingency and regulation of parental responses in young children's acquisition of a feeling of their own effectiveness ("self-efficacy"; Lamb, 1981) and their development of exploratory activities (Riksen-Walraven, 1978). Through the "responsiveness" of the caregiver, the baby becomes able to see him or herself as an individual having a certain amount of control over his or her environment, and comes to trust familiar people and anticipate some of their actions (Pêcheux, 1990). However, responsiveness is not a unitary feature, and there are probably many forms of responsiveness.

This notion of responsiveness has been studied in European and U.S. contexts in which objects are the major elements in adult–child interaction scenarios. However, in a reassessment of the Konner survey data on !Kung children (Botswana) from the ages of 1–22 months with their caregivers, Bakeman et al. (1990) showed that in that culture children are not encouraged to take an interest in objects through comments or stimulation from the people around them. In contrast, caregivers consistently respond when the children engage in social communicative acts (e.g., vocalizations, laughs, smiles) in situations other than actions with objects. The only exception to this general pattern concerns offers of objects that are embedded in communicative social exchanges and where certain ritual forms of exchange are encouraged early in children. Bakeman et al. concluded that in !Kung culture communication is more centered on interpersonal than on referential communication.

Similar conclusions were reached in a study on young Wolof children in Senegal (Rabain, 1979). Exploratory activities and handling involving objects and tools in the daily environment do not elicit the tight fabric of exchanges, negotiations, and functional and instrumental explanations that are found in middle-class European and U.S. mothers, who operate in a physical and social environment where objects are specialized and adult and child spaces are separate. Wolof mother–child interactions tend to emphasize learning of the social grammar of exchanges with parents and relatives. The acquisition of technical skills is seen as implicit and parallel to social acquisitions.

Interactive games place the child in the role of social actor. Infant–mother exchanges take place in the form of rocking, which can be equated to a social spectacle of dancing; or with 3-year-old children through question–answer routines with familiar adults. The mother and the people around the child at different stages of development provide the child with a highly consistent set of exchange settings, but these settings are partially specified by the culture.

What is the impact for a baby to have perceived regularities in one domain rather than in another? I cannot immediately conclude that parental behavior that highlights one form of behavior in the child (at the expense of others) will shape the mode of cognition. There may be an impact on the social level. This is what Mundy-Castle (1974) stressed when he emphasized the importance of integration between what he termed *technological intelligence* and *social intelligence*. Technological intelligence has expanded in Western societies at the expense of social intelligence. Its growth is linked to the development of writing systems, object handling, and control over the physical environment. Non-Western societies or dominated groups tend to value more socially oriented skills. Mundy-Castle stressed that education in traditional African cultures "includes learning in the context of meaningful social action." The remainder of this chapter is devoted to presenting several empirical findings and observational data that illustrate these differences, with an emphasis on immigrant settings.

OBJECT PLAY IN AFRICAN AND FRENCH FAMILIES LIVING IN PARIS

I conducted a comparative study, published in part elsewhere (Rabain-Jamin, 1989), on the interactive styles of French mothers and African mothers living in Paris in an object-play situation with their 10- to 15-month-olds. The aim was to show how differences in verbal and nonverbal interactive routines in these two groups of mothers draw on cultural specificities, involving both the status of objects and the language situations that are valued in the two cultural contexts.

Forty mother–child dyads (composed of two groups of children ages 10 and 15 months with 10 dyads per cultural group at each age) took part in the experiment. The group of African mothers came from West-African countries (Senegal, Mali, Mauritania). Mothers were Soninke (16) or Toucouleur (4), had received no formal education in Africa, and had all lived in Paris for less than 10 years. Their husbands were blue-collar workers. The French families were either middle class, working class, or upper middle class.

The 10-minute observation sessions were conducted in the mothers' homes. A set of objects provided by the observer were placed on the floor. The set included a (a) cup and spoon, (b) comb and brush, (c) pink panther, (d) cardboard tubes, and (e) rods. Because of the reticence of the African mothers to be filmed, partially motivated by the political context, verbal exchanges were audiotaped. The mothers' gestures were coded according to a preestablished grid in a sequential manner that differentiated the type of action concerning objects and the presence or absence of concurrent verbalizations. The children's behaviors toward objects were differentiated from socially oriented behaviors (e.g., smiles, vocalizations, extended gaze toward mothers or third party) as well as their postural motor behavior. The mothers' reactions and responses to these different initatives on the part of the children were scored. All sessions took place in each mother's maternal language.

Preliminary data analysis consisted of defining four mutually exclusive categories characterizing the mothers' behaviors in the object-play situation. These categories were: (a) nonverbal behavior (defined as object-related gestures or actions that were not produced in conjunction with verbal exchanges); (b) joint verbal and nonverbal behavior; (c) verbal object-related behavior (e.g., the mother describes an object and comments on the child's actions without participating herself); and (d) verbal nonobject-related behavior (maternal speech on a topic other than the objects; i.e., concerning the postural motor or social activity of the child).

The proportion of nonverbal exchanges was significantly higher in African mothers in both the 10-month-old group and the 15-month-old group. In contrast, French mothers made proportionally more joint nonverbal and verbal utterances than the African mothers at both ages (Rabain-Jamin, 1989). In their verbal exchanges with their children, the French mothers (like U.S. mothers; see Murphy & Messer, 1977) tended to employ descriptive utterances involving object labels, descriptions of their properties, and comments. Comments and descriptive utterances were rare in African mothers, and when they did occur they were listener rather than object oriented. In other words, the child was the subject, and topic focus was the listener rather than the object (e.g., "You're tired"). African mothers made proportionally more direct requests for action than did French mothers (Rabain-Jamin, 1989).

Furthermore, each child's object-related initiatives were differentiated from other types of behaviors (e.g., glances toward a third party, changes in posture, vocalizations, crying, etc.). An analysis of variance showed that French mothers responded to a significantly higher percentage of initiatives on the part of the child as regards objects at 10 months [$F(1,18) = 4.94, p < .05$] and at 15 months [$F(1,18) = 6.02, p < .05$] than did African mothers (see Table 8.1). In both groups, the mothers tended to respond proportionately more when the child was older [15 months; $F(1,36) = 3.66, p < .10$]. When the mothers' responses to object initiatives were contrasted with responses to the child's other interests and initiatives, the trends were reversed. With a 10-month-old child, African mothers responded to a significantly higher percentage of messages that were unrelated to objects than did French mothers [$F(1,18) = 10.71, p < .01$] (see Table 8.1).

African mothers tend to be less responsive to their child's initiatives concerning objects than French mothers, and to be more responsive to their child's glances toward a third party, vocalizations, and changes in posture. One plausible interpretation is that they perceive a communicative intent in their child's visual and vocal behavior, which they feel calls for a response—a behavior that they do not perceive to the same extent in their child's object-centered activities. In everyday situations, mother–child sharing of object-centered activity takes place in the way described by Dixon, LeVine, Richman, and Brazelton (1984): There is more visual than verbal guidance of activity.

TABLE 8.1
Initiatives by Child Followed by Maternal Responses

		Object versus Social Initiatives			
		Mother Responds to Child-Initiated Object Activity		Mother Responds to Child-Initiated Social or Postural-Motor Activity (Glances, Vocalizations, Postural Changes)	
Age		French	African	French	African
10 months	m	60.2*	40.0	62.9**	89.4
	SD	17.7	22.4	20.2	15.4
15 months	m	71.3*	51.9	65.5	75.8
	SD	17.1	18.2	38.9	19.0

Note. Responses could be verbal and/or nonverbal. m = mean percentage. SD = standard deviation.
*, F significant at .05 level.
**, F significant at .01 level.

Regardless of culture, achieving joint attention, sharing the same focus of attention, begins by being a goal between the adult and infant. When a child is 2–3 months of age, there are universal periods of face-to-face interaction between mother and infant (Dixon, Tronick, Keefer, & Brazelton, 1981; Super & Harkness, 1982). The need to go beyond the dyad is reached when the child is about 4 months old (Trevarthen & Hubley, 1978). At this age, African mothers often use social objects to structure interaction around external topics, whereas European or American mothers more often use inanimate objects that the child can handle or explore.

Unstructured observation of three Soninke and Toucouleur families in Paris gives an indication of the culturally different role of the object in interactions during the first year of life. The data in Table 8.2 show an evolution in duration of object handling over the 2-hour observation sessions from the ages of 6 to 10 months and the respective amounts of object activity initiated by mother and baby.

At 6 months, the babies have low object-handling times (roughly 7% of the observation time). At this age, the physical contact time with adults is extremely high. A study by Findji (1993) showed that at 5 months French babies, in sharp contrast, spend on the average of 34% of their time focusing their attention on objects (i.e., looking and handling). At 8 months, the percentage rises to 50%. The African babies at 10 months tend to have comparable percentage of object-handling time (52.1%).

As mentioned, African mothers tend not to verbalize in conjunction with object exploration. If the object-mediated relationship is oriented toward simple management of the infant's attention, the verbal and nonverbal registers can have equal weight. If the communicative aim is information on the object and its properties, verbal exchange becomes a necessity. Although the African sample is very small, what emerges from these observations is that the differences in interactive styles between French and African mothers can

TABLE 8.2
Activities with Objects at 6 and 10 Months in
Three Toucouleur/Soninke Infants in Paris

| Activities | Age | *Three Toucouleur/Soninke Infants* | | | |
		Soro	*Fatoumata*	*Aminata*	*Mean*
Object activity initiated by child	6 mos	1.7	4.2	2.7	2.9
or independent activity	10 mos	38.8	47.0	39.4	41.7
Object activity initiated by	6 mos	5.0	1.7	5.4	4.0
Mother and/or intervention	10 mos	10.6	9.9	10.6	10.4
Physical contact with adult, no	6 mos	93.3	94.1	91.8	93.1
object contact	10 mos	50.6	43.1	50.0	47.9

Note. Figures refer to percentage of time.

mainly be defined on the level of verbal and didactic scaffolding of object activities. Exploration in the African child seems to be simply shifted in time compared with exploration in the French child. This suggests that it is the socialization of the child's cognitive activity, rather than the cognitive activity itself, that is structured differently across the two contexts.

Every culture has a different perspective on what is appropriate and relevant to put into words and what is better left unsaid. Immigrant African mothers do not usually talk to their children during child care or diapering, which, in contrast, are rich exchange periods for French or American mothers. In Soninke mother–infant exchanges, words are not used to explain object use and function or action schemes. Rather, as is the case of !Kung mothers, language serves to stress the social actions that can be carried out with the object. If language is cast in terms of two poles (i.e., the logical pole oriented toward the referent and the social pole oriented toward exchange), African mothers' utterances tend predominantly toward the exchange pole and relationships with others.

African cultures do not endow words with the educational function of planning, as an organizer of ongoing activity. Rather, they place value on the definition and construction of social relations. In traditional cultures where an individual's actions are expected to correspond to his or her social status, exchange is not necessarily governed by the value of things exchanged, as is the case in technologically developed cultures where efficiency of action and exchange predominate. Often in jokes and playful exchanges in African compounds, promised as well as real objects can be exchanged as a means of defining status. For example, "I brought you some Kola nuts but there was a hole in my pocket and they fell out" (Pradelles de Latour, 1991, p. 15). The most highly valued social gesture is gift giving, which places the giver in a valued position. In terms of status, the winner is always the giver, who moves up in status by making the receiver indebted to him or her (Rabain, 1979; Zempleni-Rabain, 1973).

Gifts of food and clothing are characteristic of traditional cultures. Children are also expected to share food and objects. There are few restrictions on young children's exploratory activities. Only really dangerous objects are kept out of children's reach. In immigrant settings, this behavior is only partially modified. This attitude is based on fundamental social values. A mother of a 15-month-old boy lets him carry off the family transistor that he just dropped. The mother explains by saying

> The French are very careful about things. We let children touch things so that they can have their share of what is in the house. Everyone is entitled to his share. A person who wants to keep things without giving others their share frightens us, we say that this type of person doesn't like others.

Refusal of object circulation is a prime antisocial act that is equated to refusal to share food.

A number of researchers have stressed the role of naive conceptions of child development in adult behavior (Keller, Miranda, & Gauda, 1984; Ninio, 1979) and the way in which these conceptions define the childrearing timetable. The mother of this same 15-month-old stated,

> You shouldn't tire a child out with toys. We give them toys to play with. You give them toys to learn something, for the future. Some toys are so hard. The child gets tired but doesn't want to let go of the toy. The mother or the elder sister gets him, cleans him up, she holds him against her and two seconds later the baby is asleep.

This mother's statement appears to follow the hierarchy of parental concerns defined by LeVine (1977). However, other forms of childrearing are also said to put the child to sleep quickly, such as "body techniques" like bouncing or massage, which also play a role in the acquisition of postural and emotional control (Rabain-Jamin & Wornham, 1990).

By criticizing the "tiring" toy, these African mothers, for whom, relative to Africa, Paris is a socially deprived context that makes the expression of fundamental social values more difficult to achieve, may be formulating a concern over the loss of communication that can be caused by solitary play where cognitive problems are thought to dominate, placing the child in a separate world. The child can be perceived as being absorbed in an imaginary world that contrasts with the world of symbolic games, in which social reality can be represented with its rules and enactments. A U.S. or European mother might express this same type of fear regarding video games. It is clear that a culture that values the mastery of objects is more conducive to isolation.

African cultures are concerned about transmitting the notion of social utility of learning to their children. All acquisitions are perceived as goal oriented and destined toward consolidating social bonds. At the current time, when there is controversy over the academic performance of immigrant children, family attitudes toward the goal of schooling may enter into the picture. In some cases, schoolwork can be seen as not having immediate outcomes. Naturally, immigrant workers hope that, through the school, their children will gain some upward mobility and be better integrated in the community. But to many of these immigrants, school fails to meet expectations because it is not a guarantee for finding a job and moving up in society. School may not promote the transfer of the family's economic responsibilities from parents to children, whereas in traditional societies children are part of the family work force from a very early age (see Oloko, chapter 10, this volume).

In addition, school and the acculturation connected to it can be seen as a source of challenge to the authority of the elders and religious traditions, cutting off the child from the family and the ethnic or religious community. In immigrant settings, the Soninke, in particular, place more value on their Moslem identity than their ethnic identity, which is perceived negatively, and tend to crystallize their demands for recognition of identity on religion (Timera, 1989).

GROUP ORIENTATION AND COMMUNICATIVE EXCHANGE ROUTINES

In immigrant African families, very young children are expected to be social actors in their relations with third parties. Snow (1977) showed that in the first mother–infant exchanges, the relational, conversational framework is more important than the conversational content. But when an African mother says to her 3-month-old, "Go answer Wendy," orienting the baby in the visitor's direction, the mother is providing the baby with a linguistic form that accompanies a social action. This is less a pedagogy of words than a simulation of the position the child is to occupy. This position implies that a child is placed early in exchange situations with several partners. This chapter now turns to data that show the role assigned to a third party in mothers' speech to their infants.

MOTHER OR FAMILIAR ADULT SPEECH TO BABIES: THE MEDIATION OF THE DIRECT MOTHER–CHILD RELATIONSHIP

Ochs and Schieffelin (1984) described how Kaluli children (Papua-New Guinea) very early on learn to take part in triadic (and not dyadic) interactions involving several partners. Kaluli mothers do not attribute the same degree of importance and meaning to dyadic exchanges as do Euro-American mothers. Kaluli mothers give their babies practice in triadic exchanges by simulating the infant's role as speaker, or through modeling of utterances for the child to repeat to a third party (e.g., "Whose is it? Say like that").

Observation of infant-oriented utterances in Wolof immigrant mothers is similar on some counts to the Kaluli data. The importance of mediation of the direct mother–infant relationship through real or fictitious reference to a third person emerges as a decisive factor. Here is one illustration.

Five corpora of early exchanges between Wolof (Senegal) immigrant mothers living in Paris and their 3-month-olds were compared with five corpora of French mother–infant early exchanges. The family settings were comparable regarding the number of siblings (three or more). The Wolof immigrant mothers had attended school. They were part of another larger sample of African immigrant women encountered while conducting a study on behavioral changes in mothering and caregiving in immigrant settings (Rabain-Jamin & Wornham, 1990). These educated Wolof mothers spoke readily to their children, almost as much as French mothers, but their styles of address differed on several counts. Mothers' speech directed to their children was broken down into semantic categories as a function of whether the mother interpreted or elicited child behavior (Rabain-Jamin & Sabeau-Jouannet, 1989).

Preliminary data reveal great similarities, but some differences in emphasis in the use of different semantic categories (Rabain-Jamin & Sabeau-Jouannet, 1993). Maternal speech dealing with the emotional and physiological state of the baby is important and comparable across the two cultures. In contrast, the most notable difference between the two groups relates to metalanguage (talking about talking), which is more frequent among the French mothers. On the other hand, reference to performance activities (e.g., jump, dance) has a tendency to be slightly more frequent among the African mothers.

African mothers produce more utterances concerning volition (want) addressed to their 3-month-olds than did French mothers, and these are primarily in the socioemotional domain. This emphasis is also found in the communication of African-American mothers studied by Blake (chapter 9, this volume). African mothers' expressions of intent deal chiefly with expressive body action (e.g., want to jump, to dance) or mood. For these mothers, intent is conveyed basically through gestures and body language. If I focus now on mothers' speech referring to verbal activities (semantic categories: say, tell, ask, answer, discuss, protest, insult), the percentage of metalinguistic utterances is almost four times as high in the French mothers as in the African mothers. African mothers emphasize the motor and physical expressivity of the baby and give expressivity a social and communicative value. They place lesser emphasis on purely verbal communication.

The percentage of mothers' utterances referring to verbal activity and directed to the baby were scored as follows: (a) percentage referring to the baby's utterances ("What are you saying to your Mommy?" "Is that all you've got to say?" "Go answer Jacqueline"); (b) percentage of utterances referring to the mother's own utterances ("I told you it's nap time"); and (c) the percentage of utterances referring to real or fictitious utterances of third parties (present or absent; "Grandma said to go to Africa," "Your brothers told you to come play") or referring to utterances having an indeterminate source ("Nobody told you to sing").

The mean percentages for these three categories are shown in Table 8.3 for the African mothers and for the French mothers. French mothers usually made the baby the speaker and constructed dyadic exchanges (81% of their metalinguistic utterances refer to the infant's utterances; 72.6% of these

TABLE 8.3
Metalinguistic Activity Categories in French and African
Mothers' Speech to Their 3-Month-Olds

Metalinguistic Activity		Dyad	Triad	Total
Reference to the	French	72.6	8.5	81.1
child's speech	African	38.3	8.3	46.6
		Dyad		Total
Reference to the	French	9.1		9.1
mother's speech	African	12.9		12.9
		Specified	Indeterminate	Total
Reference to a third	French	8.3	1.5	9.8
party's speech	African	20.8	19.6	40.4

Note. Figures refer to mean percentages.

concern the dyad; only 8.5% concern the baby's utterances to a third party). African mothers also encouraged their babies to be speakers (46.6% of their metalinguistic utterances concerned the baby's messages), but much less frequently than French mothers. Above all, they gave equal weight to metalinguistic utterances in which the baby was the addressee of messages from real, fictitious, or indeterminate third parties (40.4% of their utterances). This was rare in French mothers (9.8% of the utterances in this semantic category).

At 3 months, the African infant is conceived more as a receiver than a speaker. Characteristically, infant communication can be jokingly deprecated by African mothers (e.g., "There is nothing good at all in what you are saying," said to the child). This is another way of treating communication—a playful way that often involves three partners.

Thus, African mothers try to enlarge the dyadic relationship and connect the baby to other potential conversational partners. These partners are sometimes present, but often absent (brothers and sisters at school, the grandmother in Africa), and are made present through evocation. The mothers transmit requests from these third parties (to come, to answer); these are orders in a playful register that encourage the baby to take part in communicative activity or pretend play where he or she has an assigned status role. The insertion of the child in a series of triadic relations implies a different way of thinking about and developing the individual—a theme to be taken up and expanded in my conclusion.

Potential conversational partners can also be indeterminate third parties ("Who spoke?" when hearing a noise outside; "Nobody told you to sing"). Reference to the speech of indeterminate partners points to the importance of maxims or proverbs that refer to general knowledge—a known cultural context.

TRIADIC EXCHANGE MODEL
AND SIMULATION GAMES

Statements made by others that are repeated to the baby can be real and recurrent or often simulated. Making a statement about the utterances of others is the equivalent of making an indirect request for action to the child by suggesting appropriate forms of response to other people. The use of impersonal negations ("Nobody told you to take the chair") is an indirect form of order or prohibition. This shift has playful overtones. Use of the indeterminate form attenuates the force of a direct order.

The stress on infant participation in exchanges with third parties who are often not named also emerges in mother's speech concerning the infant's emotional states. The mention of (fictitious) actions of an unnamed third party ("Who made fun of my baby? Who hit Kajja?") helps manage the infant's moods. These are actions with relational significance (e.g., hit, shove, bother, irritate, tease, etc.) that are thought to have an effect on the baby's mood. In the earlier example, the mother replaces a direct order by encouraging the infant to situate him or herself in relation to a third party. In these examples, she relates the baby's emotional state to a (virtual) action performed by a third party. Discomfort should leave the body and enter into a social relationship. The appeal to a third party serves as a shift, as a means of reframing. The mother directs the infant's attention toward others and reinforces the social bond.

The seeking out of mediation by a third party, of social consensus, is more developed and more striking in mother–infant dialogues in African than in French families. This register of social conventions is approached in a playful way, in pretend play: simulations of something said by third parties to the child ("Grandma told you," "Your brothers told you," etc.) and simulation of the baby's communicative competence in relationships with third parties ("Tell him"). The mother develops an example-driven pedagogy and encourages learning through modeling. Social relations, rather than language itself, is modeled but interactions convey linguistic modeling as well.

Another striking feature of pretend-play episodes is that the introduction of a category of pretend play can take place within everyday relationships solely through verbal means: "Where is Tiamel? Tell Tiamel to give you some couscous, bring it here," said a Toucouleur mother to her toddler, 2 years, 8 months, in Paris (Tiamel is the paternal grandmother who lives in Africa). Elicitation of a fictitious action is set up by the adult without any additional frame, using the situational context as a background. The activity in the pretend play is shifted (in time and place) from current activities. Dialogue about people is extended to situations that are distant in time and that are brought into being through simulation. The only real support is the use of the proper name. The context that makes the utterance meaningful is the existence of a repetitive naming routine of third parties, which lightens the cognitive load of labeling. This can be seen as a means of alleviating constraints of reference for the child in general. In most families, there is a stable naming routine of absent family members whose photos are on the wall.

In addition, the role of the child as a communicator is mimed or played by the adult rather than really taken on by the child. The dialogues are short and do not place cognitive pressure on the child. They are a form of teaching through role play and role modeling, and the actions the child needs to perform to take on his or her role as a social actor are cited without explaining their practical features. The child is taught to assume his or her role as a social actor in a tightly knit framework that is predefined by adults.

COMMUNICATIVE SITUATIONS IN AFRICAN AND IMMIGRANT SETTINGS

The communicative situations in which young children are engaged in traditional African cultures emerge as more numerous and more distinctive than in Western societies. They instigate and provide models of verbal exchange where the status of speaker and hearer are more highly defined. The range of people who are involved in child care provides an equally wide range of communicative situations for the young child. The child who is just starting to talk is "the one who knows nothing." He or she is not a serious rival, and is the butt of playful questioning and directives. At times equated to an ancestor, the young child in the preverbal period and at the start of the verbal period is set apart—he or she is not in any defined category.

For older children, the type of behavior required differs greatly depending on whether he or she is talking to his or her parents, grandparents, or paternal and maternal uncles and aunts. The relationship between parent and child that calls for respect and restraint, which does not preclude affection, is contrasted with the "joking relationship" that bonds, for example, grandson and grandmother, or child, mother, and the father's younger brother, allowing for flexible games for expressing aggression. In the case of mother and father's brother, the uncle jokes about the baby but his remarks are also aimed at the mother. As another example, grandson and grandfather are permitted a more affectionate relationship than are father and son, according to the principle of alternating generations. This variety of registers of address helps balance social relations.

The interactive modes of immigrant families reflect both a discontinuity and continuity with the reference models of the native cultures. When partners are absent, children and adults try to reestablish substitute relationships, often outside of the family group. In an article on Soninke families in Paris, Barou (1991) reported that in certain families living in relative isolation some children only have a fear relationship with their father and mother, and have no opportunities to have more positive emotional or playful relationships with other relatives. These children develop attitudes that can range from virtually permanent mutism to excessive aggressivity. Although mother–infant relationships are generally playful, the presence of familiar visitors gives the older child a greater range of possibilities for contacts and dialogues, mirroring to a greater or lesser extent the playful exchanges with several partners that are found in an African compound.

Some researchers such as Vermès (1990), who have examined sociolinguistic minority children's difficulties in learning to read and write, have asked whether these children's exposure to a wide range of language forms in their interactions with adults (through repetitions, reformulations, language games) may foster cognitive analysis of the combinatorial units and equivalences among the languages they know (Vermès, 1990). The children of African immigrants often allow a passive (comprehension only) competence to come about in their parents' native language and, at school age, answer their parents in French as soon as the parents master some elements of the language. Thus, the issue of the variety of interactive types and communicative situations (child–adult, child–child) in immigrant settings is far from being resolved, as is the question of whether this context is conducive to the development of metacommunicative and metalinguistic awareness.

CONCLUSION

Certain types of interactions rather than others are more highly valued in early exchanges. Centering on people rather than on objects may have a social rather than a cognitive impact in the long term, but we need longitudinal studies to prove it. For example, at adulthood, it may make it more difficult for the adult to mobilize other forms of thought that are socially valued in the academic or occupational settings with which immigrants must come to terms.

Beyond the people/object difference, which in the final analysis really only reflects a difference in emphasis, a different prism on the world, the native African cultures, as well as the immigrant cultures, attempt to construct the social status of the child. In a lineage system, each individual is expected to behave according to his or her status. This establishes community membership ties that unite individuals. These status norms are the basis for ethical values, which are accompanied by feelings of pride or shame.

The French anthropologist Mauss (1938) stressed the universality of the sense of individuality. In traditional cultures, divination sets the individual apart. Even though the diviner does not address him or herself directly to the seeker, he or she announces his or her specific destiny (Ortigues, 1974).

Mauss contrasted this notion of the individual to the notion of "person," and showed that it is a specific construction based on the specific values of a given social structure. In the Tallensi of Ghana, studied by Fortes (1987), kinship and lineage status are the chief determinants of the full status of a person.

In industrial societies, performance enables individuals to modify their status and reflects another conception of the person and personal autonomy. Rules are not justified by reference to origins, but rather to an impersonal social law (Ortigues, 1988).

In urban African communities, there has been a change in hierarchies and the organization of status. Attending school almost always implies a break with tradition and develops aspirations to be released from the duties of lineage (Dozon, 1986). In African-immigrant communities in France, social and economic ties have been maintained with the home community in Africa, but the social and educational fabric has been severed and exchanges have been impoverished. It appears critical for the social group to evolve at the same time as the individual—to be able to change so that community ties can be preserved through the transformations engendered by emigration.

In traditional cultures, emotional life is primarily expressed on a collective level. The values governing the different domains of social, economic, and technological activity are fairly similar. These values diverge in complex societies and become conflictual. Although the development of critical reasoning and personal autonomy are enhanced, the emergence of a full-fledged emotional life may be hampered or impeded.

REFERENCES

Bakeman, R., Adamson, L. B., Konner, M., & Barr, R. G. (1990). !Kung infancy: The social context of object exploration. *Child Development, 61*, 794–809.

Barou, J. (1991). Familles africaines en France: De la parenté mutilée à la parenté reconstituée [African families in France: From mutilated kinship to reestablished kinship]. In M. Segalen (Ed.), *Jeux de familles* (pp. 157–171). Paris: Presses du CNRS.

Benedict, R. (1935). *Patterns of culture*. Boston: Houghton Mifflin.

Berry, J. W. (1976). *Human ecology and cognitive style*. New York: Sage/Halsted/Wiley.

Bornstein, M. H. (Ed.). (1989). *Maternal responsiveness: Characteristics and consequences. New directions for child development*. San Francisco: Jossey-Bass.

Bril, B., & Sabatier, C. (1986). The cultural context of motor development: Postural manipulations in the daily life of Bambara babies (Mali). *International Journal of Behavioral Development, 9*, 439–453.

Dasen, P. R. (1988). Cultures et dévelopement cognitif: La recherche et ses applications [Cultures and cognitive development: The research and its applications]. In R. Bureau & D. de Saivre (Eds.), *Apprentissages et cultures: Les manières d'apprendre* (pp. 123–141). Paris: Karthala.

Dasen, P. R., & Heron, A. (1981). Cross-cultural tests of Piaget's theory. In H. C. Triandis & A. Heron (Eds.), *Handbook of cross-cultural psychology: Vol. 4. Developmental psychology* (pp. 295–342). Boston: Allyn & Bacon.

Dasen, P. R., Inhelder, B., Lavallée, M., & Retschitzki, J. (1978). *Naissance de l'intelligence chez l'enfant baoulé de Côte d'Ivoire* [Birth of intelligence in the Baoulé child of Ivory Coast]. Berne: Hans Huber.

Derrida, J. (1966). Nature, culture, écriture (De Levi-Strauss à Rousseau) [Nature, culture, and writing (From Levi-Strauss to Rousseau)]. *Les Cahiers pour L'Analyse, X*(4), 1–45.

Dixon, S. D., LeVine, R. A., Richman, A., & Brazelton, T. B. (1984). Mother-child interaction around a teaching task: An African-American comparison. *Child Development, 55,* 1252–1264.

Dixon, S. D., Tronick, E., Keefer, C., & Brazelton, T. B. (1981). Mother-infant interaction among the Gusii of Kenya. In T. M. Field, A. M. Sostek, P. Vietze, & P. H. Leiderman (Eds.), *Culture and early interaction* (pp. 149–168). Hillsdale, NJ: Lawrence Erlbaum Associates.

Dozon, J. P. (1986). En Afrique, la famille à la croisée des chemins [In Africa, the family at the crossroads]. In A. Burguière, C. Klapisch-Zuber, M. Segalen, & F. Zonabend (Eds.), *Histoire de la famille* (pp. 301–337). Paris: A. Colin.

Findji, F. (1993). Attentional abilities and maternal scaffolding in the first year of life. *International Journal of Psychology, 28.*

Fortes, M. (1987). *Religion, morality and the person. Essays on Tallensi religion.* Cambridge, England: Cambridge University Press.

Hopkins, B. (1976). Culturally determined patterns of handling the human infant. *Journal of Human Movement Studies, 2,* 1–27.

Keller, H., Miranda, D., & Gauda, G. (1984). The naive theory of the infant and some maternal attitudes. A two country study. *Journal of Cross-Cultural Psychology, 15*(2), 165–179.

Lamb, M. E. (1981). Developing trust and perceived effectance in infancy. In L. P. Lipsitt (Ed.), *Advances in infancy research* (Vol. 1, pp. 101–127). Norwood, NJ: Ablex.

LeVine, R. A. (1977). Child rearing as cultural adaptation. In P. H. Leiderman, S. R. Tulkin, & A. Rosenfeld (Eds.), *Culture and infancy: Variations in the human experience* (pp. 15–27). New York: Academic Press.

Mauss, M. (1938). Une catégorie de l'esprit humain: La notion de personne, celle de moi [A category of the human spirit: The concept of person, of self]. *Journal of the Royal Anthropological Institute, 68,* 263–282.

Mundy-Castle, A. C. (1974). Social and technological intelligence in Western and non-Western cultures. *Universitas, 4*(1), 46–52.

Murphy, C. M., & Messer, D. J. (1977). Mothers, infants and pointing: A study of a gesture. In H. R. Schaffer (Ed.), *Studies in mother-infant interaction* (pp. 325–354). New York: Academic Press.

Ninio, A. (1979). The naive theory of the infant and other maternal attitudes in two subgroups in Israël. *Child Development, 50,* 976–980.

Ochs, E., & Schieffelin, B. (1984). Language acquisition and socialization: Three developmental stories and their implication. In R. A. Shweder & R. A. LeVine (Eds.), *Culture theory: Essays on mind, self, and emotion* (pp. 276–320). Cambridge, England: Cambridge University Press.

Ortigues, E. (1974). Préface. In M. Fortes (Ed.), *Oedipe et Job dans les religions ouest-africaines* (pp. 7–32). Tours, France: Mame.

Ortigues, E. (1979). Préface. In J. Rabain, *L'enfant du lignage: Du sevrage à la classe d'âge chez les Wolof du Sénégal* (pp. 9–21). Paris: Payot.

Ortigues, E. (1988, May). La personne et l'émergence de la loi [The person and the development of the law]. Actes du Colloque de l'association *Sauvegarde de l'Enfance et de l'Adolescence* sur "L'adolescent et la loi," Lille, France.

Pêcheux, M. G. (1990). L'ajustement parental: Un concept à la fois utile et flou [Parental responsiveness: A concept both useful and fuzzy]. *L'Année Psychologique, 90,* 567–583.

Pradelles de Latour, C. H. (1991). *Ethnopsychanalyse en pays bamiléké* [Ethnopsychoanalysis in Bamileke country]. Paris: E. P. E. L.

Rabain, J. (1979). *L'enfant du lignage. Du sevrage à la classe d'âge chez les Wolof du Sénégal* [Child of the lineage. From weaning to age-graded peer group among the Wolof of Senegal]. Paris: Payot.

Rabain-Jamin, J. (1989). Culture and early social interactions. The example of mother-infant object play in African and native French families. *European Journal of Psychology of Education*, *4*(2), 295–305.

Rabain-Jamin, J., & Sabeau-Jouannet, E. (1989). Playing with pronouns in French maternal speech to prelingual infants. *Journal of Child Language, 16*, 217–238.

Rabain-Jamin, J., & Sabeau-Jouannet, E. (1993, July). *Representation of the child and construction of person deixis in French and Wolof: Early mother–infant dialogues.* Sixth International Congress for the Study of Child Language, Trieste, Italy.

Rabain-Jamin, J., & Wornham, W. L. (1990). Transformations des conduites de maternage et des pratiques de soin chez les femmes migrantes originaires d'Afrique de l'Ouest [Changes in maternal behavior and care practices among West African immigrant women]. *Psychiatrie de l'Enfant, 23*, 287–319.

Richman, A. L., LeVine, R. A., Staples New, R., Howrigan, G. A., Welles-Nystrom, B., & LeVine, S. E. (1988). Maternal behavior to infants in five cultures. In R. A. LeVine, P. M. Miller, & M. Maxwell West (Eds.), *Parental behavior in diverse societies* (pp. 81–98). San Francisco: Jossey-Bass.

Riksen-Walraven, J. R. (1978). Effects of caregiver behavior on habituation rate and self-efficacy in infants. *International Journal of Behavioral Development, 1*, 105–130.

Sahlins, M. D. (1976). *Culture and practical reason.* Chicago: The University of Chicago Press.

Snow, C. E. (1977). The development of conversations between mothers and babies. *Journal of Child Language, 4*, 1–22.

Super, C. M., & Harkness, S. (1982). The development of affect in infancy and early childhood. In D. A. Wagner & H. W. Stevenson (Eds.), *Cultural perspectives on child development* (pp. 1–19). San Francisco: Freeman.

Super, C. M., & Harkness, S. (1986). The developmental niche: A conceptualization at the interface of child and culture. *International Journal of Behavioral Development, 9*, 545–569.

Timera, M. (1989). Identité communautaire et projet éducatif chez les immigrés soninke en France [Community identity and educational design among Soninke immigrants in France]. *Migrants-Formation, X*(76), 19–23.

Trevarthen, C., & Hubley, P. (1978). Secondary intersubjectivity: Confidence, confiding and acts of meaning in the first year. In A. Lock (Ed.), *Action, gesture and symbol* (pp. 183–229). London: Academic Press.

Vermès, G. (1990). L'entrée dans l'écrit des enfants des minorités socio-linguistiques [Beginning writing for sociolinguistic minority children]. *Migrants-Formation, X*(83), 54–64.

Zempleni-Rabain, J. (1973). Food and the strategy involved in learning fraternal exchange among Wolof children. In P. Alexandre (Ed.), *French perspectives in African studies* (pp. 221–233). London: Oxford University Press.

9

LANGUAGE DEVELOPMENT AND SOCIALIZATION IN YOUNG AFRICAN-AMERICAN CHILDREN

Ira Kincade Blake
Teachers College, Columbia University

The role of language in the performance of African-American children has been of concern in the social sciences for several decades. However, the bulk of the research has been concerned with form-related aspects (e.g., Bereiter & Engelmann, 1966; Blank & Solomon, 1968; see Baratz, 1973), rather than more recent issues in child language, which focus on how children acquire and learn to use forms in culturally appropriate ways (e.g., Heath, 1983; Miller, 1982; Miller & Garvey, 1984; Schieffelin & Ochs, 1986). Even though language-socialization research is cataloging some distinctive relationships between language components and specific cultural experiences, the persistently poor performance of African-American children in school settings continues to stimulate studies that use a Black–White comparative, experimental model (McLoyd, 1990; Myers, Rana, & Harris, 1979; Washington & McLoyd, 1982). This research seeks to identify those areas where the language behavior of African-American children is structurally different from that of mainstream Euro-American children. As in the past, current research continues to approach the language skills of minority children from a restricted use or a production-deficiency perspective (see Feagans & Farran, 1982; McLoyd, 1990; Tizard & Hughes, 1984). The deficiency is purported to arise directly from language due to limited forms and structures present in the speech of adult models (e.g., Hart, 1982; Tough, 1982), or indirectly because of an inadequate knowledge base resulting from limited experiences with the world (e.g., Snow, 1982). Accordingly, the implications support the need for remedial intervention that provides African-American children with experiences that imitate those of mainstream Euro-American children.

This kind of research does not address larger issues of developmental psychology, nor does it add to our understanding of why the observed differences in the language behavior of African-American and Euro-American children exist. Moreover, such research does not address the interactive role of language and cultural experience of the groups. Rather, the research history has been one with a narrow view of the language of minority children that sets up mainstream children's experiences as the evaluative standard against which all others are judged. What is lost through such a research approach is the recognition that language is learned within a cultural context, and that its most useful, and hence valuable, form and manner of use are those most effective within that cultural context (Feagans & Farran, 1982).

Although this study acknowledges the importance of uncovering the differences in language behavior for African-American and Euro-American children, it also recognizes the need for descriptive information regarding the role of language within the cultural experiences of African-American children and the nature of its development. The important differences between the language of African-American and mainstream American children cannot be understood or reconciled for improving performance in the mainstream if we cannot describe and explain the importance of those differences to the behavior of each group. Consequently, in behavioral science it is important to understand mechanisms of learning and development as well as the mechanisms by which behaviors are maintained. In particular, the present study addresses the questions of how and why language behaviors develop and persist. The documentation of the natural language skills of African-American children and the maintenance mechanism by which those skills are supported is integral to an understanding of their language-related difficulties in school settings (Ogbu, 1982; Tizard & Hughes, 1984).

This study aimed to: (a) describe the language development of three African-American children through the essential components of form, content, and use; (b) compare their semantic–syntactic development with that of Euro-American children; (c) characterize their patterns of language use; and (d) describe the mothers' use of language as a model for their children's patterns. Thus, my intentions are to provide information about the language development of African-American children as the process of acquiring both the forms and meanings necessary for becoming linguistically competent, and the uses of those forms and meanings for becoming linguistically competent in culturally appropriate ways. For the theme of continuities and discontinuities, this chapter explores how language preserves the affective relationships that grow out of early mother–infant interactions.

METHOD

The subjects were three urban, working-class African-American mother–child pairs. The mothers were the primary caregivers, and all three children were firstborn. The mothers' ages ranged from 18 to 30 years; the children's ages ranged from 19 to 27 months during the course of the study. The children were two boys and one girl, given the pseudonyms of Ben, Martin, and Jane.

Prior to the study, each mother–child pair visited the playroom and was visited in their home on several occasions. Informal visits to the children's homes and to the researcher's home continued throughout the study. Because of these visits, natural, relaxed relationships developed, which allowed for spontaneity of mother–child interactions within the research setting (Blake, 1984).

Each mother–child pair was videotaped for 1 hour in a low-structure playroom setting once a month for a minimum of 9 months. A snack was always present at the beginning of each session and was under the control of mother and child. Also present at the onset was a core set of toys, to which additional sets of toys were added at 10-minute intervals (see Blake, 1984, for a description). Each mother–child pair interacted naturally and freely within the setting.

Data for the analyses were taken from the transcriptions of the first session and every other session for each child, for a total of 12 sessions. The multiword corpus for Ben's first session consisted of only 10 tokens, was considered spurious, and consequently was excluded from all analyses except mean length of utterance (MLU). Transcriptions of the speech and non-verbal behaviors of mother–child pairs from 11 sessions (4 each for Martin and Jane, 3 for Ben) served as the database. The ages of the children during these observation sessions are shown in Table 9.1.

The first objective was to document the language development of African-American children in a manner similar to that done in the mainstream, particularly by Bloom, Lightbown, and Hood (1975) for middle-class Euro-American children and by Miller (1982) for working-class Euro-American children.

TABLE 9.1
Ages of Children (in Months and Days) During Observations

	Time 1	Time 2	Time 3	Time 4
Ben	21, 24	23, 25	25, 27	
Martin	21, 5	23, 15	25, 10	27, 9
Jane	19, 23	21, 21	23, 25	25, 26

RESULTS

Mean Length of Utterances

As a general descriptor, the MLU was calculated for each child speech sample. These calculations were based on the first 100 wholly intelligible utterances after the first page of written transcription. Following guidelines of Bloom et al. (1975), immediate self-repetitions, imitations, songs, and rhymes were not counted in the calculation. This calculation was done on all spontaneous, intelligible single-word and multiword utterances and is represented in Fig. 9.1. As can be seen, the average length of utterance for all children increased over time. The range of MLU was 1.26 (Ben at Time 1: 19, 15) to 2.55 (Jane at Time 4: 25, 26). In general, these children initially were producing utterances that averaged a little more than one word at a time; by the last session, they were producing utterances more than two words in length. Thus, the change in MLU indicated general language growth. Similar patterns of MLU increase are reported in the literature for Euro-American children (see Bloom & Lahey, 1978; Brown, 1973; Miller & Chapman, 1981).

Semantic–Syntactic Relations

The children produced 2,228 uninterrupted, spontaneous, intelligible multiword utterances. These multiword utterances served as the database for the remaining analyses.

   Similarities. The objective of the next analysis was to describe the basic kinds of meanings the children were learning to express through language. Basic meanings are viewed as indicators of the kinds of organizational, cognitive processes the child imposes on everyday experience. This analysis was based on 20 categories of semantic–syntactic relation identified in the speech of middle-class (MC) Euro-American children in the work of Bloom et al. (1975) and used in a study of the language development of working-class (WC) Euro-American children by Miller (1982). All 20 categories are presented in Table 9.2. However, the relations are discussed in terms of similarities and differences between the African-American children and the two Euro-American groups. It is important to note that the relations were distinguished as *major* relations and *minor* relations in Miller's study. Major relations were those that occurred most frequently in the original Bloom et al. study, and minor relations included those that occurred infrequently or did not manifest developmental change.

   The comparative proportions of major semantic–syntactic relations for

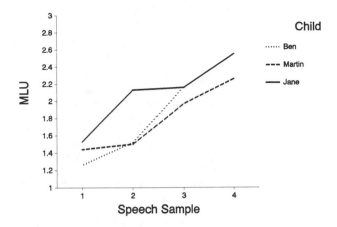

FIG. 9.1. Growth in mean length of utterance.

Bloom's children, Miller's children, and the present African-American children are presented in Fig. 9.2. Comparisons were based on data beginning with the first speech samples with comparable MLUs for all three child groups. Based on 100 utterances, intercoder agreement was .88 for the African-American group. The average proportion of utterances accounted for by those categories for the mainstream Euro-American children was 77%, the working-class Euro-American children was 75%, and for these children the average was 73%. As seen in Fig. 9.2, the proportions of major semantic–syntactic relations are virtually identical for the three groups. Findings revealed that the distribution of the major semantic–syntactic relations over time was similar for the three groups, indicating that development within and across the relations was also similar. Within the major relations, the verb relations (*Action, Locative Action, Locative State, Stative, Notice*, and *Intention*) generally accounted for the greater proportion of relations present in multiword types. Verb relations ranged from 45% to 66% and averaged 56% of all observations. These relations were more frequent than the function relations (*Existence, Negation*, and *Recurrence*), which accounted for an average of 16% of all relations, and the other major relations of *Possession* and *Attribution*, which accounted for an average of 3%. Thus, similar to Bloom's children and Miller's children, these children expressed ideas about actions involving persons and objects, and the physical conditions of persons and objects, more frequently than other ideas.

These findings raise questions about the significance of Black–White (and middle-class vs. working-class) group differences in frequencies for word counts and structural categories (i.e., sentence types) reported in the literature (Hart, 1982; Tough, 1977a).

The significance of this finding is the documentation of similar early

TABLE 9.2
Definitions of Semantic–Syntactic Relations

Major Relations	Definitions
Action	Referred to movement of an actor or an object by an agent where the goal of the movement was not a change in location of the actor or object.
Locative action	Referred to movement of an actor or an object by an agent where the goal of the movement was a change in location of the actor or object.
Locative state	Referred to the location of a person or object with no reference to the movement to that location.
Stative	Referred to internal states of animate beings, temporary states of ownership, and external states of affairs.
Notice	Referred to attention to a person, object, or event.
Intention	Referred to impending action using matrix and main-verb construction.
Existence	Referred to a label for an object or pointed out an object.
Negation	Referred to the nonexistence, disappearance, or rejection of persons, objects, or events.
Recurrence	Referred to another instance of an object or event.
Possession	Referred to the ownership of an object.
Attribution	Referred to counting or identifying features of objects.

Minor Relations	
Wh question	Referred to inquiries about persons, objects, and events using *who, what, why, where,* and *how.*
Inverted question	Referred to inquiries about persons, objects, and events.
Place	Referred to location.
Action + place	Referred to location of an action event.
Notice + place	Referred to location of a notice event.
Dative	Referred to the recipient of an action that also involved an affected object.
Instrument	Referred to the inanimate object that was used in an action to affect another object.
Quantity	Referred to the number of instances of an object or event.
Other	Included the following categories grouped by Bloom et al. (1975) as "either not productive or did not manifest systematic developmental change": *vocative, social expression, stereotype, routine, time, affirmative, mood, manner, conjunctive, epistemic,* and *causality.*
Different form	Included meanings expressed through dialect features and nonconventional forms not found in Bloom et al. categories.
Undetermined	Included utterances for which meanings could not be determined.

Note. From "Structure and Variation in Child Language" by L. Bloom, P. Lightbown, and L. Hood, 1975, *SRCD Monograph, 40*, pp. 10–13. Copyright 1975 by Society for Research in Child Development, Inc.; and from "Amy, Wendy, and Beth: Learning Language in South Baltimore" by P. J. Miller, 1982, pp. 79–82. Copyright 1982 by the University of Texas Press. Adapted by permission.

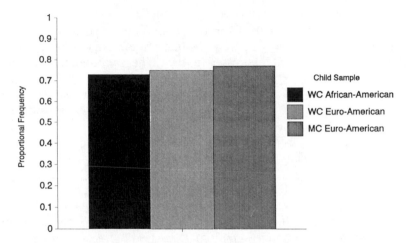

FIG. 9.2. Comparison of group proportions expressing major semantic–syntactic relations.

semantic–syntactic development for African-American and Euro-American children, using a mainstream language paradigm for comparison. Despite the experiences within different sociocultural environments, these African-American children are learning to express the same kinds of basic meanings through word forms that Euro-American children express, and they proceed through development in a comparable manner. This finding challenges the claim that the knowledge base about objects, persons, and events in the world is less developed for African-American children (Snow, 1982). Moreover, this is further evidence for the hypothesis that African-American children develop similar cognitive skills to mainstream children (see Ginsburg, 1986).

Differences. The overall distributions of semantic–syntactic relations demonstrate the similarities in language development for these groups of children, who differ by race, culture, and/or socioeconomic status. This evidence, in conjunction with the work of Stockman and Vaughn-Cooke (1981, 1982a, 1982b), documents similar abilities for the expression of meaning through language forms for the distinctive groups. Such findings have been argued in the literature (see Tizard & Hughes, 1984) as necessary evidence to support the position that test scores underestimate working-class children's language abilities. However, occurring with these similarities are two striking differences: the distributions of the major relation of *Stative* and the minor category of *Other*.

The *Stative* relation was used to express internal states (e.g., "want more coke"; Jane at 21 months, 21 days) and possession (e.g., "I got that fish food"; Ben at 25 months, 27 days). All three groups of children expressed all these ideas. However, unlike the Euro-American children, for whom *Stative* was a relatively late development, all three African-American children expressed the *Stative* relation productively from the first session. (An utterance was considered productive if it was expressed in three different utterance types within a speech sample.)

The difference in relative frequencies for expressing the *Stative* relation are presented in Fig. 9.3. The African-American children expressed *Stative* (10%) in their utterances three times as often as the mainstream Euro-American children (3%) and twice as often as the working-class Euro-American children (5%). An examination of utterances expressing *Stative* revealed that most of the utterances expressed internal states. *Stative* verbs occurring in the speech of these African-American children were *want, need, sleep, like, scared, know*, and *to be*. The verb *want* was the most frequent. As with the Euro-American children, *want* signaled need and desire for these children. Thus, these African-American children expressed more of their needs and desires earlier and continued to express them over time.

The *Other* category included 10 different kinds of meaning relations in the original Bloom et al. (1975) mainstream Euro-American and the African-American studies. The *Other* relations included *Vocative, Social Expression, Stereotype, Routine, Time, Affirmative, Mood, Manner, Conjunctive, Epistemic,* and *Causality*. However, Miller (1982) listed some of the Bloom et al. relations (*Other, Vocative, Stereotype,* and *Rhyme/Routine*) as separate minor relations. To compare the three groups, the requisite Miller relations were combined to create a comparable *Other* category for the working-class Euro-American children. The resulting comparison is informative because it points to the need for a clear separation of ethnicity and class in comparative studies

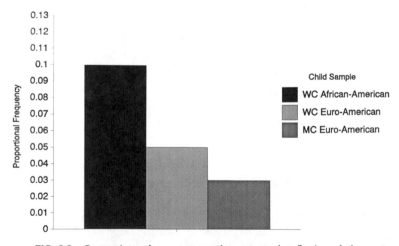

FIG. 9.3. Comparison of group proportions expressing *Stative* relations.

to further our understanding of the relative contributions of each variable to development and learning.

For middle-class Euro-American children, the *Other* category was a minor relation because the children did not express the meanings frequently enough to be productive, and they were not seen as developmental. This was not the case for working-class children, either African American or Euro-American. For both working-class African-American and Euro-American groups, the expression of meanings within the *Other* category occurred more than twice as frequently as they did for the middle-class Euro-American children (16% vs. 14% vs. 7%, respectively). These differences in relative proportions are illustrated in Fig. 9.4.

An examination of the utterances revealed that three *Other* relations were expressed most frequently within multiword constructions. They were: (a) *Vocative*—"Jane" and "Hey"; (b) *Stereotype*—"oh, mmhmm," and "gee whiz"; and (c) *Social Expression*—"thank you" and "I sorry." Although Bloom et al. (1975) reported a collapsed proportional frequency for all relations included in the *Other* category, Miller (1982) listed *Vocative* and *Stereotype* separately as minor relations. In comparison, the relative frequency for *Vocative* averaged 8% for the African-American group and 3% for the working-class Euro-American group. An examination of Miller's definitions and examples for *Stereotype* revealed that she included *Social Expression* in that relation. Therefore, for the purpose of comparison, these two relations were combined and averaged for the African-American children. The combined average was 5% for the African-American children, compared with a 3% average for the working-class Euro-American children. This result indicates a greater use of *Social Expression* and *Stereotype* by African-American children than by Euro-American children matched for social class.

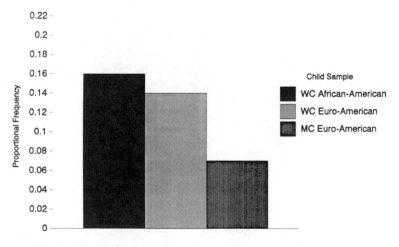

FIG. 9.4. Comparison of group proportions expressing *Other* relations.

Social Organizational Relations

The frequent occurrence of *Vocative, Stereotype, Social Expression*, and *Stative* relations in the speech of the African-American children suggests that some relations serve a different use than previously indicated in the literature. Although the major semantic–syntactic relations are viewed as indicators of how children conceptualize the objects and events in their world, the use of these minor relations can be viewed as helping to organize behavior on a social and emotional plane.

Children construct reality as they learn language. That reality includes a social system, and language is a part of it (Halliday, 1975). Through language, children learn the meanings of the social system—they learn a culture of values, expectations, roles, and rules. All of this learning takes place through other persons within contexts (Heath, 1980, 1983; Miller, 1982; Schieffelin & Eisenberg, 1984). Consequently, the speech and behavior of language-learning children, at any point in learning, is a manifestation of their developing conception of their fit within their culture.

The productive and frequent occurrence of *Stative* and *Other* relations suggests that socioemotional reality for these African-American children is somewhat different from that of Euro-American children. How does the greater occurrence of these relations mark differences between those realities? Is the content of these relations a reflection of different functional orientations for language use?

Language Functions

Children not only learn to express their ideas about persons, objects, and events when learning language; they also learn how their group uses that knowledge to meet personal and cultural objectives. Thus, language learning can be described as the "social contextualization of acquisition" (Grimshaw, 1977), where children learn a language, the social use of that language, and are socialized to assume a particular identity and roles as members of their group (Boykin & Toms, 1989; Schieffelin & Ochs, 1986). Mother–child verbal interaction is one of many ways that cultural values and behaviors are conveyed and learned (Heath, 1983; Miller, 1982; Schieffelin & Ochs, 1986; Ward, 1971). Mothers present a model for the role of language within their cultural experience, and children learn through varied interactions that certain ways of using language are more valued.

Child Language Functions.   To determine how these children were learning to use language, their multiword utterances were examined for the kinds of purpose they served. Unlike the semantic–syntactic relations that were taken from previous studies of mainstream children, the language functions were derived from the speech of these African-American children. Consequently, no comparison with the Euro-American children is possible. The children are their own comparison, as the relative usage of the language functions relied on for expressive communication is examined. Even so, the differences in semantic–syntactic relations suggest a different emphasis in language use for the child groups.

Eight main purposes were identified in the speech of the children. (Based on a sample of 100 utterances, percent agreement between coders was .83.) Definitions and examples are presented in Table 9.3. All eight functions were present in the speech of the children from the first session. Proportional frequencies were calculated for each function and the averages for each child are presented in Fig. 9.5. In general, for all three children an interpersonal function was the most frequent—*Interpersonal Expressive* or *Effective*. (Although in the figure, the overall averages for Martin's *Effective* and *Objective* functions were virtually the same, the *Effective* function was, in fact, predominant for three of his four sessions.) These proportions averaged 21% to 26% of all child functions, and indicated that the children were using language to manage their relations with others. However, the form of management was different under each function. The *Effective* function was used to get things done as in "off mommy" (for aid in getting down from slide) and "wan cookie" (when requesting a potato chip). On the other hand, the *Interpersonal Expressive* function reflected language used to manage the relationship of one person to another. In addition to establishing and maintaining interpersonal contact ("hey"; "mommy"; "mmhmm"), *Interpersonal Expressive* was used to (a) establish roles for persons ("that the daddy"); (b) establish social guidelines ("mommy, suppose play with this?"); (c) influence the behavior of others ("be careful"); (d) participate in social routines ("I'm fine"); and (e) express global affect about persons, objects, and actions ("Oh shoot"; "Wow!"). Thus, *Interpersonal Expressive* was indicative of a socioemotional function. These kinds of language use averaged 40% of all language functions for the children, as shown in Fig. 9.5.

Strengthening the *Interpersonal Expressive* finding is the average proportion (9%) of *Self-Expressive Social* functions for the three children. The relative proportions for *Self-Expressive Social* across speech samples is also presented in Fig. 9.5. The *Self-Expressive Social* function included utterances that expressed to a listener the child's feelings and opinions about involvement with self, objects, actions, and others. Some examples are "like that TV," "I try that," and "I'm scared." Although *Self-Expressive Social* did not serve to manage social relationships explicitly, it did provide the listener with specific information about the internal state of the speaker. Such information would most likely affect social relations. Therefore, *Self-Expressive Social* also was viewed as serving a socioemotional function. When added to the frequencies

TABLE 9.3
Definitions and Examples for Language Functions

Language Functions	Examples
Interpersonal Expressive	
me vs. you function—establishes, describes, and manages relationships and influences the quality of behavior	*that mines* (Jane 19, 23) (pretend dispute with M over baby doll) *Loyce said, "Bye now"* (Jane 25, 26) *baby gotta make kakee* (Ben 25, 27) *Hi Carol* (Martin 21, 5)
Effective	
gimme/get function—results in material gain and direct changes in behavior	*you can help you* (Martin 23, 15) (wants help opening cookie bag) *I wan french fry* (Jane 21, 21) (requesting one of M's french fries)
Objective	
you do/you are function—identifies and describes persons, objects, and actions	*train fell down* (Ben 25, 27) ("train" falls over) *baby pants* (Jane 23, 25) (examining clothes on doll)
Directive	
I do function—describes and guides actions of self	*gon put this one in* (Jane 19, 23) (standing doll on truck) *take cookie* (Jane 19, 23) (after taking chip from M's hand)
Self-Expressive Social	
I feel function—expresses social customs and reports feelings, attitudes, and opinions about objects, actions, others, and self to an intended listener	*me sleepy* (Martin 21, 5) (lays down on floor and looks at M) *hurt foot* (Martin 21, 5) (bumps foot on slide) *I don't want play ball* (Jane 25, 26) (Ch is already playing with toys; M asks if wants to play catch)
Self-Expressive Nonsocial	
I feel function—expresses social customs and reports feelings, attitudes, and opinions about objects, events, and self not directed to a listener	*wan train* (Ben 23, 25) (walking around room looking at toys) *that's nice truck* (Martin 27, 9) (sitting atop pretend truck)
Attentive	
I see/you see function—focuses listener on an object or action	*mommy look at that baby* (Martin 25, 10) *watch this/watch this/* (Ben 25, 27) (nesting blocks)
Participative	
let's do function—involves listener in actions of speaker	*under chin chin chin* (Jane 23, 25) (M & J playing open, shut them)

Note. Influenced by Halliday (1975) and Dore (1977).

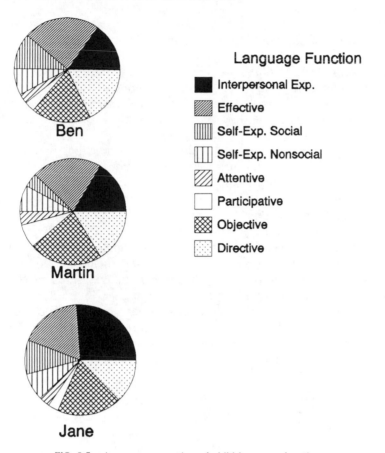

Language Function

■ Interpersonal Exp.

▨ Effective

░ Self-Exp. Social

░ Self-Exp. Nonsocial

▨ Attentive

☐ Participative

▩ Objective

░ Directive

FIG. 9.5. Average proportion of child language functions.

for *Interpersonal Expressive* and *Effective*, the average proportion of utterances serving a socioemotional function for the children was almost half of the total functions. When the role of language in the children's acquisition of knowledge about the objective world and the number and range of possible uses of language are considered, this percentage represents an impressive amount of language use for interpersonal and emotional regulation.

Mother Language Functions. The distribution of child language functions (Fig. 9.5) suggest a socioemotional orientation in language use for these African-American children. Such orientations in language use are conveyed through the "language habits" (Sapir, 1949) of mature language models. It has been suggested (Mitchell, 1980) that information about the rules and customs of the larger community (i.e., social reality) can be derived from the "microculture" of mothers and their children. Mothers convey to their children basic cultural information—often unconsciously—through daily activities, across a range of situations. This information includes both preferred language patterns and modes of interaction among group members. Therefore, just as children learning language distill the essence of form and meaning from the rich language they hear, they must also discover the cultural basics for negotiating their social realities.

The last analysis was the examination of the functions served by the mothers' utterances to determine whether they constituted a model of language use for the socioemotional orientation that the children were learning. To obtain a profile of the mothers' language functions, the first and last speech samples for each mother were analyzed using the same categories of language functions used in the children's analysis. This analysis was performed for all maternal utterances because both single and multiword utterances reveal to the child how language is used socioculturally. Like the children, a substantial proportion of the mothers' functions was *Interpersonal Expressive*; in fact, the proportions were even higher. Proportional distributions for the first and last speech sessions for each mother are presented in Fig. 9.6. On average, Ben's mother used the *Interpersonal Expressive* function in 31% of the total functions served by her utterances; Martin's mother used it in 41% of the total functions in her speech; and Jane's mother used

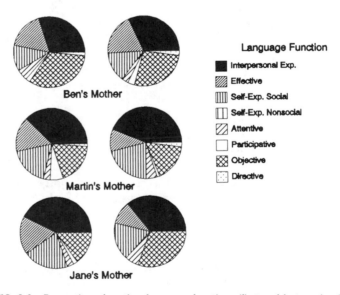

FIG. 9.6. Proportion of mother language functions (first and last sessions).

it in 38% of the total functions in her speech. An examination of the utterances serving this function revealed frequent use of vocatives in conjunction with comments on (a) appropriate behavior ("Martin, don't throw the car like that, okay?"), (b) internal states ("Jane, are you hot?"; "wanna see-saw, Ben?"), and (c) instructions ("You suppose to throw it to me, Ben"). In addition to single-word vocatives and vocatives occurring in multiword utterances, utterances functioning as *Interpersonal Expressive* encoded information about (a) appropriate behavioral rules ("We sit down and drink, right?"; "Mommy said, 'Don't play with those things,' right?") and (b) manners/politeness ("Tell Ira, you're sorry"; "You haven't told Carol thank you once"; "Say, 'Excuse me' "; "Tell Ira that was not nice," when Ira spoke too loudly). Thus, *Interpersonal Expressive* functions frequently occurred when actions or activities could be linked with personal and interpersonal dimensions. At these times, all mothers created or made the most of such opportunities.

It is important to note that Fig. 9.6 illustrates both consistency and change in the mothers' relative use of language functions. Both findings are reasonable in light of developmental expectations; children *and* parents recognize and extend learning opportunities across cognitive, physical, social, and linguistic domains. For example, consider a child's frequent use of requests for information or verification of labels and actions for objects. In terms of relative distributions, there could be an increase in the use of the *Objective* function by either child or mother, thereby influencing the percentage of *Interpersonal Expressive*. The point is that, even when an orientation for language use is apparent in the mother's speech and there is evidence that her child is acquiring it, adjustments to situational demands and the child's learning needs naturally do occur. At the same time, however, the mother's communicative orientation provides the child with the larger cultural frame for interpreting and mastering the world.

The *Self-Expressive Social* function served by the mothers' utterances also did not vary much for the first and last speech samples, as shown in Fig. 9.6. The relative proportions averaged 13% for Ben's mother, 20% for Martin's mother, and 18% for Jane's mother. In many instances, the mothers used variants of the verb *want* to acknowledge, attribute, inquire, and teach about the children's feelings or attitudes about objects and actions, as the following example of maternal teaching illustrates:

(Jane at 19 months, 23 days is having juice, sees mother's potato chips on table, moves toward them)

(Mother puts hands over chips)

Mother	Jane	Language Function[1]
No/No		Effective
	[whispers] [eh-eh]	
Those are mine/		Interpersonal Expressive
	let see/	Effective
Let see what?/		Interpersonal Expressive
What you wanna see?		Self-Expressive Social
	[mmh]/	
	please/	
[smiles & giggles]		
What you want?/		Self-Expressive Social
	(touches Mother's hand)	
(pulling hand away)		
What you want?/		Self-Expressive Social
	[whispering] cookie/	
(lowering head)		
What?/		Interpersonal Expressive
	(pulling at Mother's hand)	
	cookie/	
(lifting hand out of Jane's reach)		
What is this?/		Objective
	[whispering] cookie/	
(lowering hand slightly)		
I can't hear you/		Effective
	let see/	Effective
	(waves hand near Mother,	
	leaning forward on Mother's lap)	
	let see/	Effective
What?/		Interpersonal Expressive
(opens hand)		
	(takes chip & steps back)	
	take cookie/	Directive
Thank you/		Interpersonal Expressive
	thank you/=[2]	

[1]Children's single-word utterances were used only in calculating MLU; they were not used in any of the other analyses. Multiple functions within an utterance and multiple codings of the same function within an utterance are included.

[2]= indicates an imitated utterance.

The mothers also used the *Self-Expressive Social* function to inquire frequently about the children's feelings and desires, again often taking advantage of opportunities or creating them in the midst of object-related activities ("You had it with the truck, huh?"). The following example illustrates how information regarding internal states was interjected within object-related activities:

(Ben at 21 months, 24 days, and mother are playing with and talking about truck and wooden disks as Ben eats cookies)

Mother	Ben	Language Functions
Cookies good?/		Self-Expressive Social
Is it good?/		Self-Expressive Social
Ben, it's good/		Interpersonal Expressive & Self-Expressive Social
Good?/		Self-Expressive Social
Good, Ben?/		Self-Expressive Social & Interpersonal Expressive
	(Gets another cookie, puts in mouth)	
	(Returns to play with truck)	
Car, yeah/		Objective & Interpersonal Expressive

When combined, *Interpersonal Expressive* and *Self-Expressive Social* accounted for an average of 44% of all language functions for Ben's mother, 61% for Martin's mother, and 56% for Jane's mother. Moreover, if the proportions for the *Interpersonal Expressive* (37%) and *Self-Expressive Social* (17%) functions for the mothers are averaged and combined, socioemotional functions accounted for 54% of all functions in language use. Thus, the pattern of the mothers' functions reflected a socioemotional orientation in language use.

The mothers often restructured, repeated, and interjected utterances with content about interpersonal roles, appropriate behavior, and the children's internal states. Baby-doll play presented one of the richest opportunities for the mothers to use socioemotional functions, and all three mothers did exactly that. Because the doll-related activities were generally prolonged, the following example is an abridged version of Martin's mother's speech (Martin's MLU was 1.44) to illustrate the extensiveness of socioemotional content:

Mother	Martin	Language Functions
Let's go see if the baby's crying/	(turns around toward toys)	Participative/Self-Expressive Social
Oh, see/		Participative
(taking Martin's hand from handle)		
Let's go see/	(walks with M toward toys)	Participative
Come on/		Effective
(walking toward toys; picks up baby; holding in front of Martin)		
Is the baby crying?/		Self-Expressive Social
You gonna give the baby a kiss?/		Interpersonal Expressive
	(takes doll; kisses head)	
Give the baby a kiss/		Interpersonal Expressive
That's a nice boy/		Self-Expressive Social
(moves away from Martin)	(touches doll's movable eyes)	
Baby have eyes?/		
		Objective

(Continued)

Mother	Martin	Language Functions
	have eyes/ =	
Yes/Have nose/	*(examining doll's face)*	*Interpersonal Expressive/*
		Objective
You gonna show me the nose?/		*Attentive*
	(walks toward M, stepping on toys; looks down at toys)	
(sitting on floor)		
Okay, show me the—/	*(drops doll as squats near toys; picks up silverware tray as sits down; removes fork)*	
You gonna feed the baby?/		*Objective*
	(touching fork to carpet)	
	no/	
Oh/		*Interpersonal Expressive*
	(feeding doll)	
Oh/		*Interpersonal Expressive[3]*
Baby's eatin' good?/		*Self-Expressive Social*
	no/	
	(holding fork to mouth)	
No/ =		
	(raises doll to chest; looks around as tosses fork into silverware tray)	
Is the baby wet?/		*Interpersonal Expressive*
	(lowers doll)	
	wet/ =	
	(turns over, examines dress)	
Is the baby wet?/		*Interpersonal Expressive*
	(holds doll's head as pulls down on dress)	
Let's try to—/		
(moving toward Martin)		
Wait a minute/Wait a minute/	*(still trying to pull off dress)*	*Interpersonal Expressive/*
		Interpersonal Expressive
Not that way/		*Effective*
(reaching for dress, lifting above doll's head)		
Let's—/No, we can't—/		
Hold—/Let's pull the pant/		*Participative*
(holding dress above doll's head so Martin can see panties)	*(reaching for panties)*	
See/		*Attentive*
	this/	
Let's pull it up/		*Participative*
See?/		*Attentive*
Let's pull it up/		*Participative*
And pull the pants down/	*(pulls panties down but they snap back)*	*Participative*

[3]Although this utterance token is coded here, it was not included in the proportional frequencies for language functions because they were based on types, not tokens, of utterances expressing each function.

Mother	Martin	Language Functions
That's it/		*Interpersonal Expressive*
Is the baby wet?/	*(looking at doll)*	*Interpersonal Expressive*
	no/	
Oh/Okay/	*(pulls panties down)*	*Interpersonal Expressive/*
		Interpersonal Expressive
Then we don't have to put a clean pamper on, right?/		*Interpersonal Expressive*
	no/	*& Interpersonal Expressive*
	(pulls up on doll's dress & down on panties)	
Okay, well let's pull the pants back up then/		*Interpersonal Expressive & Effective*
	the baby/	*Objective*
	(removing one leg from panties)	
Yeah, the baby/		*Interpersonal Expressive & Objective*
Let's put the—/	*(pulls on dress; doll slips to floor)*	
(moving toward Martin, hand extended)		
Let's put the clothes back on the baby, okay?/		*Interpersonal Expressive & Interpersonal Expressive*
(looking at Martin, hand still	*(releasing doll's dress from right extended hand)*	
Can mommy help you?/	*baby/=*	*Interpersonal Expressive*
	(re-grasps with left hand; holding doll up to M)	
	help you/=	
(taking doll from Martin)		
Help you/= Okay/		*Effective/*
		Interpersonal Expressive
(removes panties from other leg)	*baby/=*	
(straightening panties)		
Baby/=		*Objective*
(puts one foot through)		
(putting second foot through)	*baby/=*	
Baby/=		*Objective*
(pushing down baby's dress)		
Okay/		*Interpersonal Expressive*
You gon give the baby a kiss and put it to sleep, okay?/		*Interpersonal Expressive*
		& Interpersonal Expressive
		& Interpersonal Expressive
(kisses doll then holds out to Martin)		

(Continued)

Mother	Martin	Language Functions
	(takes doll onto lap)	
You gon give the baby a kiss?/		Interpersonal Expressive
And put him to sleep/		Interpersonal Expressive
	(touches doll's eyes)	
Baby have eyes?/		Objective
Huh?/		Interpersonal Expressive
Is the baby sleep?/		Objective

Although instructional activities around multipart manipulatives (e.g., puzzles and nuts and bolts) were occasionally lengthy, the length was generally the result of the number of directions and elaborations required to help the child accomplish the object-related task. Interjected within these activities were maternal comments regarding the child's personal state and inquiries about maternal help ("Can I help you?"; "You want me to help?"). The latter were distinguished, based on surrounding context, from maternal utterances that were requests for actions ("Let me help you" when child's shoe needs tying). However, for the doll-related activities, all three mothers prolonged interaction around the interpersonal and personal value of the baby doll by initiating new topics or elaborating on existing ones. In other words, very few instructional activities produced the kind of commenting and joint focus that the interpersonal/personal activities produced.

The Influence of Setting

One half of the children's and more than half of the mothers' language functions produced in the playroom setting served a socioemotional function. However, the playroom setting can be described as geared to objective exploration. Toys were brought in every 10 minutes and placed on the floor near the children. The setting was also "child friendly." The table and chairs were child sized; the snack of cookies and juice was present on the table, readily accessible to the child; and finally the children had their mothers' "undivided attention"; they were the primary interactors. As such, the setting appeared to support functions that served to explore objects and actions through language. Proportional averages ranging from 12% to 24% for the children's *Objective* function and 12% to 22% for the children's *Directive* function reflect such a language use. Similarly, the mothers' averages for the *Objective* function ranged from 18% to 30% for the first and last sessions. However, the combined proportions of *Interpersonal Expressive* and *Self-Expressive Social* and *Effective* indicated that a considerable amount of language use was committed to the management of interpersonal involvement.

It appears that a socioemotional orientation was imposed on the setting, and opportunities to use the requisite language functions were created through mother–child interactions.

DISCUSSION

The similarities in the early form and content of language development for these working-class African-American children and mainstream and working-class Euro-American children are striking. Importantly, these findings provide further documentation of a limited amount of evidence in the literature. Although their cultural environments differ, these African-American children and Euro-American children are learning to talk about their perceptions of, manipulations on, and interactions with their respective environments in similar ways. These findings demonstrate that both the language skills and the related knowledge base were comparable for the three groups of children. Thus, all groups of children acquired a set of basic meanings for language expression and used them in similar ways.

Nonetheless, there were notable dissimilarities in the expression of meanings, as revealed by consistent differences in the frequency of certain meaning relations for the groups. Moreover, the differences related to membership in ethnic/racial group as much as in social class for the African-American children. Whereas group differences in proportion of *Stative* relations seemed to be more a matter of ethnicity than social class (Fig. 9.3), the group differences in proportion of *Other* relations (mainly *Social, Vocative*, and *Stereotyped Expressions*) seemed to be more a matter of social class than ethnicity (Fig. 9.4). However, both ethnicity and social class may have contributed in varying degrees to both categories of relation: Note that in each case working-class Euro-American children occupied a position intermediate between working-class African-American and middle-class Euro-American children (Figs. 9.3 and 9.4). The findings suggest a need to reconsider notions that argue that poverty is the sole cause of performance differences between children of different ethnic groups. Accordingly, the separation of class and ethnicity in future studies is warranted. In addition, the cultural content underlying the notion of learning for various groups requires study.

In general, these African-American children expressed the social and emotional meanings of *Stative* and *Other* relations earlier, productively, and more frequently than both groups of Euro-American children. Through these relations, these African-American children talked about needs, wants, and interpersonal involvement more frequently than did Euro-American children. Tizard and Hughes (1984) proposed that such differences in frequency (as opposed to kind) of "categories of talk" are representative of language style and are related to a difference in underlying values and attitudes. Summarizing her research on language use in advantaged and poor children, Tough (1982) argued that differences in language use (e.g., greater use of language to talk about needs and wants by poor children) reflected an orientation shaped by "differences in children's experiences of the purposes for which language is used" (p. 11). Furthermore, she proposed that the orientation toward language use of poor children is the cause of their poor performance in school: "The main problem in educating children from disadvantaged sections of the community is not that they generally lack language but that their expectations about using language do not support learning" (Tough, 1982, p. 13). The findings of this study indicate that social class and ethnicity must be considered separately.

In their expression of *Statives*, working-class Euro-American children resembled middle-class Euro-American children more in their talk about the world than working-class African-American children. A similar finding was reported by Potts, Carlson, Cocking, and Copple (1979) in a comparative investigation of the structural development of language in (a) middle-class White, (b) working-class White, and (c) working-class Black preschoolers. Although both working-class White and working-class Black children developed grammatical structures later than middle-class White children, the pattern of development for working-class White children paralleled that of middle-class White children. Potts et al. also found structural evidence for a relationship between adult dialects and the variety of language being learned by young children. Specifically, those features with variable rules in Black English appeared to be related to both rate of acquisition and usage in working-class Black preschoolers. Second, working-class African-American children used more of their speech to talk about personal and interpersonal knowledge than both working-class and middle-class Euro-American children. Socioemotional topics of conversation are not considered a cultural emphasis among Euro-Americans. Instead, the cultural frame is argued to be a factive, objective orientation.

These African-American mothers used language to teach by (a) identifying objects ("Here's the pig"; "You see a apple, Ben?"), (b) repeating themselves ("You didn't tell me 'Thank you'—You gon tell me 'Thank you'?"), and (c) expanding ("Ben likes cookies, too" to child's [mm] when eating a cookie), just as middle-class Euro-American mothers did (Newport, Gleitman, & Gleitman, 1977). Such semantically contingent speech is believed to aid young children in learning language as well as in learning about aspects of their world. As importantly, these children asked and talked about objects ("What color is that?"; "this dog") and described actions ("I on sit down chair"; "take cookie"), just as Euro-American language learners did. Again, this study shows that these African-American children and Euro-American children are learning about and conceptualizing the world in a similar fashion. The issue, then, is not one of learning per se but of learning focus. As suggested by their socioemotional orientation in mother–child interactions, these African-American mothers highly value social and emotional knowledge and frequently include such information in their speech. This is not to discount the teaching (and learning) of objective knowledge (as indicated, both occurred), but to identify a distinctive focus in mother–child interactions for these mothers.

Conversely, just as these African-American mothers expressed objective knowledge, Euro-American mothers expressed social knowledge in their mother–child interactions. Learning about social roles and manners, especially in mother–baby role play, has been described in the literature for both working-class and middle-class Euro-American children (Miller, 1979/1982; Miller & Garvey, 1984). Consequently, an analysis of Euro-American early child speech (and mother speech) using the language function categories should produce all functions described here. However, different distributions would be expected for these groups. These proposed distributions are not to be confused with shifting styles through "communicative accommodation" (Schieffelin & Ochs, 1986) to situational variables. Moreover, communicative accommodation does not preclude a more pervasive cultural orientation (or style) based on a larger frame of social experience for various cultural groups.

Taken together, these findings suggest a difference in preferences for language use by African-American and Euro-American groups. The semantic–syntactic similarities and differences between these African-American children and Euro-American children, and the distributions of mother and child language functions in African-American mother-child interactions suggest that the distributions of language functions would be somewhat different for the two groups. Furthermore, the differences reflect distinctive cultural orientations through which the groups learn to use language. It appears that although they learn similar form and content during early language development, African-American and Euro-American children learn to use that form and content in distinctive ways that reflect membership in their respective cultural groups.

The Cultural Basis of a Socioemotional Orientation

The traditional cultural emphases of African Americans include interdependence, extended family, and personal expression (Abrahams, 1974; Boyd-Franklin, 1989; Boykin, 1986; Harrison, Wilson, Pine, Chan, & Buriel, 1990; Smitherman, 1977). Hence, the value of a socioemotional orientation in interpersonal interaction would be instrumental in facilitating relations among members. Generally, these values are discussed from the group's perspective, with major regard given to the importance of the collective "us." However, the "us" is only one side of the proverbial coin, the other being what Abrahams (1970) described as "the constant consideration of the importance of the 'me' element" (p. 1) in Black life. In reflections on his ethnographic study of a Black community, Abrahams uncovered the "tremendous importance placed upon friendships, and rivalries, loves and animosities . . ." (p. 1). The "me" is seen as emotional and social. The significance of learning and teaching about the personal (me) and the interpersonal (us) is illustrated through the extended family configuration. Such a unit requires a communicative profile that facilitates expression and understanding of the states and positions of its participants to negotiate any conflicts between group needs and individual needs. Moreover, one needs to know under what circumstances the personal outweighs the interpersonal. Thus, the individual's internal state and assumable social roles must be known to accomplish larger group goals at best, or to attempt reconciliation for continued valuable involvement (e.g., economic or emotional) at least.

The previous explanation of a socioemotional orientation or "personalization of interpersonal relationships" (Ramírez & Casteñeda, 1974) is supported by ethnographic descriptions of African-American speech communities. Ward (1971) found that adults commented most about the quality of children's behavior (e.g., bad, sneaky, or good children), and parents often requested children to show adults their "talents" (e.g., manners, singing, and dancing). Such requests for performance were made by these mothers as well ("You gonna say hi to Ira"; "Jane, you wanna count for Ira?"), and were reported in an earlier study (Blake, 1979). Heath (1983) described how African-American children in a working-class community learned to use a story or word play to entertain an adult so that their misbehavior would be forgotten. Additional evidence for this position is found in the range of speech events (signifying, rapping, shucking, jiving, and playing the dozens) that employ verbal bantering, teasing, storytelling, and emphatic self-reporting in the African-American community (Abrahams, 1974; Kochman, 1972; Labov, 1972; Smitherman, 1977). Finally, in a context of similar use of semantic–syntactic relations by Euro-American and African-American children, the greater emphasis of African-American children on the expression of internal states and social meanings further support their distinctive cultural orientation for interpersonal interactions.

The integration of culture and language are manifested in the communicative profile of these African-American mothers and their children. In addition to instruction in social conventions and roles, the communicative style fosters the expression and understanding of the states and positions of individual members. This communicative pattern may partly comprise the cultural foundation for the negotiation between individual needs and interpersonal needs for these mother–child pairs. The individual's needs and position must be recognized in some manner to accomplish larger interpersonal needs jointly. Moreover, some individual needs also must be met in some fashion for individuals to commit to and value the group. As illustrated in the previous examples, children learn to express their wants and needs as they learn about social conventions and roles within their speech communities.

In conclusion, information about the language abilities of African-American children is far from complete. Although the distribution of form-meaning relations are similar for these children and Euro-American children, there are still differences in the distribution of those relations in their speech. The differences appear to be related to cultural experience as well as to social-class status. Moreover, the differences are believed to reflect and reinforce a distinctive communicative pattern—a socioemotional orientation in language use.

These findings raise the questions of how the described language functions are distributed across ethnic and social-class groups, and if the distributions are linked to school performance. At least two connections to school performance are possible. First, traditional American schooling could be patterned after a communicative orientation that emphasizes something other than the socioemotional, creating discontinuity between the young African-American child's manner of interacting and the requisite school manner (Harrison et al., 1990). Second, traditional mainstream teachers could be more responsive to and supportive of communicative orientations that reflect social realities similar to their own. The suggestion here is not an orientation that is captured in a high frequency of a particular sentence type, but rather a manner of interacting that reflects a general way of approaching one's social reality. As such, a high frequency of a particular form may be but one aspect of a communicative style that represents a broader interactive orientation. Moreover, this orientation may be influenced less than expected by programs that teach minority children to use certain forms more frequently (Hart, 1982; Tough, 1977b, 1982), with the hope of improving the school performance of African-American children.

As a note of caution, these are only a few African-American children observed in one setting. Although the distribution of language functions in both the children's and mothers' speech appear to be substantiated by anthropological and sociological information about African-American culture, cultural expression is influenced by many variables such as geographic location, age, degree of acculturation, religious affiliation, and socioeconomic status (Hines & Boyd-Franklin, 1982).

Even so, anecdotal evidence from the written works of African-American undergraduate and graduate students suggests that language orientation does influence language-related performance. At issue is the emphasis in writing. On several occasions when my colleagues and I expressed concern about the written product of African-American students, it was often because the students stressed personal feelings, opinions, and experiences related to the course material first, with supportive use of literature seemingly of secondary importance. For example, a Euro-American undergraduate professor wrote the following comments on an African-American female's report on the relationship between man and the computer: "You obviously have definite opinions, but you need to get literature to support your ideas. You are too passionate about your opinions." These remarks, reinforced by discussions with other faculty, suggest the continuity of the socioemotional orientation in language use from early African-American mother–child interactions to later interpersonal communication within the African-American community. The remarks also highlight the discontinuity between the African-American student's emphasis in language use and the school's factive, Euro-American orientation.

In conclusion, this research described the similarities and differences in the early language development of (a) working-class African-American, (b) working-class Euro-American, and (c) middle-class Euro-American children. These three groups were learning the same basic meaning relations in their different language environments. However, the relative distributions of those relations were different for the groups. It was concluded that the differences represented distinctive cultural orientations in language use. These orientations were seen as possible sources of the performance difficulties of African-American students in school settings. Further research on the distribution of language functions and the ways in which the semantic–syntactic relations are used by African-American children in a range of settings is needed. Importantly, the resulting information could prove useful in understanding the role that language use plays in the mainstream performance of African-American children.

ACKNOWLEDGMENTS

This chapter is an extension of earlier dissertation work submitted to Columbia University, in partial fulfillment of the requirements for the Ph.D. degree. The research was supported in part by a National Science Foundation Doctoral Dissertation Research Grant and the Institute for Urban and Minority Education. Versions of this research were presented at the Kentucky State University Arts & Sciences Lecture Series in Frankfort, Kentucky, on February 19, 1991, and the National Institute of Mental Health Workshop in Washington, DC, June 29–July 2, 1991. Special thanks to Lois Bloom for her valuable comments at many stages of this research, and appreciation to Patricia Greenfield and her graduate students for their helpful input, and to Rodney Cocking for his constructive editing of the final version.

REFERENCES

Abrahams, R. D. (1970). *Deep down in the jungle: Negro narratives from the streets of Philadelphia* (rev. ed.). Chicago: Aldine.

Abrahams, R. D. (1974). Black talking in the streets. In R. Bauman & J. Sherzer (Eds.), *Exploration in the ethnography of speaking* (pp. 240–262). London: Cambridge University Press.

Baratz, J. S. (1973). Language abilities of black Americans: Review of research: 1966–1970. In K. S. Miller & R. M. Dreger (Eds.), *Comparative studies of Negroes and Whites in the United States* (pp. 125–183). New York: Seminar Press.

Bereiter, C., & Engelmann, S. (1966). *Teaching disadvantaged children in preschool.* Englewood Cliffs, NJ: Prentice-Hall.

Blake, I. K. (1979, March). *Early language use and the black child: A speech act analysis of mother-child inputs and outputs.* Paper presented at the meeting of the Society for Research in Child Development, San Francisco, CA.

Blake, I. K. (1984). *Language development in working-class black children: An examination of form, content, and use.* Unpublished doctoral dissertation, Columbia University, New York.

Blank, M., & Solomon, F. (1968). A tutorial language program to develop abstract thinking in socially disadvantaged preschool children. *Child Development, 39,* 379–389.

Bloom, L., & Lahey, M. (1978). *Language development and language disorders.* New York: Wiley.

Bloom, L., Lightbown, P., & Hood, L. (1975). Structure and variation in child language. *SRCD Monograph, 40*(2, Serial No. 160).

Boyd-Franklin, N. (1989). *Black families in therapy: A multisystems approach.* New York: Guilford.

Boykin, A. W. (1986). The triple quandary and the schooling of Afro-American children. In U. Neisser (Ed.), *The school achievement of minority children: New perspectives* (pp. 57–92). Hillsdale, NJ: Lawrence Erlbaum Associates.

Boykin, A. W., & Toms, F. D. (1989). Black child socialization: A conceptual framework. In H. P. McAdoo & J. L. McAdoo (Eds.), *Black children: Social, educational, and parental environments* (pp. 33–51). Newbury Park, CA: Sage.

Brown, R. (1973). *A first language: The early stages.* Cambridge, MA: Harvard University Press.

Dore, J. (1977). Children's illocutionary acts. In R. Freedle (Ed.), *Discourse: Comprehension and production* (Vol. 1, pp. 227–244). Norwood, NJ: Ablex.

Feagans, L., & Farran, D. C. (Eds.). (1982). *The language of children reared in poverty: Implications for evaluation and intervention.* New York: Academic Press.

Ginsburg, H. P. (1986). The myth of the deprived child: New thoughts on poor children. In U. Neisser (Ed.), *The school achievement of minority children: New perspectives* (pp. 169–189). Hillsdale, NJ: Lawrence Erlbaum Associates.

Grimshaw, A. D. (1977). A sociologist's point of view. In C. E. Snow & C. A. Ferguson (Eds.), *Talking to children: Language input and acquisition* (pp. 319–333). Cambridge, MA: Cambridge University Press.

Halliday, M. A. K. (1975). *Learning how to mean: Explorations in the development of language.* London: Edward Arnold.

Harrison, A. O., Wilson, M. N., Pine, C. J., Chan, S. Q., & Buriel, R. (1990). Family ecologies of ethnic minority children. *Child Development, 61,* 347–362.

Hart, B. (1982). Process in the teaching of pragmatics. In L. Feagans & D. C. Farran (Eds.), *The language of children reared in poverty: Implications for evaluation and intervention* (pp. 199–218). New York: Academic Press.

Heath, S. B. (1980, November). *What no bedtime story means: Narrative skills at home and school.* Paper prepared for the Terman Conference, Stanford University, Stanford, CA.

Heath, S. B. (1983). *Ways with words: Language, life and work in communities and classrooms.* Cambridge, England: Cambridge University Press.

Hines, P. M., & Boyd-Franklin, N. (1982). Black families. In M. McGoldrick, J. K. Pearce, & J. Giordano (Eds.), *Ethnicity and family therapy* (pp. 84–107). New York: Guilford.

Kochman, T. (Ed.). (1972). *Rappin' and stylin' out: Communication in urban black America*. Champaign, IL: University of Illinois Press.

Labov, W. (1972). *Language in the inner city: Studies in the black English vernacular* (Conduct and Communication No. 3). Philadelphia: University of Pennsylvania Press.

McLoyd, V. C. (1990). Minority children: Introduction to the special issue. *Child Development, 61*(2), 263–266.

Miller, J. F., & Chapman, R. S. (1981). Research note: The relations between age and mean length of utterance in morphemes. *Journal of Speech and Hearing Research, 24*(2), 154–161.

Miller, P. J. (1982). *Amy, Wendy, and Beth: Learning language in South Baltimore*. Austin, TX: University of Texas Press.

Miller, P. J., & Garvey, C. (1984). Mother–baby role play: Its origins in social support. In I. Bretherton (Ed.), *Symbolic play: The development of social understanding*. New York: Academic Press.

Mitchell, J. (1980). Hassling in the kitchen: A context for betting and making rules. *The Quarterly Newsletter of the Laboratory of Comparative Human Cognition, 2*(3), 66–70.

Myers, H. F., Rana, R. G., & Harris, M. (1979). *Black child development in America 1972–1977*. Westport, CT: Greenwood.

Newport, E. L., Gleitman, H., & Gleitman, L. R. (1977). Mother, I'd rather do it myself: Some effects and non-effects of maternal speech style. In C. E. Snow & C. A. Ferguson (Eds.), *Talking to children: Language inputs and acquisition* (pp. 109–149). Cambridge, MA: Cambridge University Press.

Ogbu, J. (1982). A cultural ecology of competence among inner-city blacks. In M. B. Spencer, G. K. Brookins, & W. R. Allen (Eds.), *Beginnings: The social and affective development of black children* (pp. 45–73). Hillsdale, NJ: Lawrence Erlbaum Associates.

Potts, M., Carlson, P., Cocking, R., & Copple, C. (1979). *Structure and development in child language*. Ithaca, NY: Cornell University Press.

Ramírez, M. III, & Casteñeda, A. (1974). *Cultural democracy, bicognitive development, and education*. New York: Academic Press.

Sapir, E. (1949). The status of linguistics as a science. In D. G. Mandelbaum (Ed.), *Selected writings of Edward Sapir in language, culture and personality* (pp. 160–166). Berkeley: University of California Press.

Schieffelin, B. B., & Eisenberg, A. R. (1984). Cultural variation in children's conversations. In R. L. Schiefelbusch & J. Pickar (Eds.), *The acquisition of communicative competence* (pp. 377–420). Baltimore, MD: University Park Press.

Schieffelin, B. B., & Ochs, E. (1986). Language socialization. *Annual Review of Anthropology, 15*, 163–191.

Smitherman, G. (1977). *Talkin and testifyin: The language of black America*. Boston: Houghton Mifflin.

Snow, C. E. (1982). Knowledge and the use of language. In L. Feagans & D. C. Farran (Eds.), *The language of children reared in poverty: Implications for evaluation and intervention* (pp. 257–260). New York: Academic Press.

Stockman, I. J., & Vaughn-Cooke, F. B. (1981). *Child language acquisition in Africa and the Diaspora: A neglected linguistic issue*. Paper presented at the First World Congress on Black Communications, Nairobi, Kenya.

Stockman, I. J., & Vaughn-Cooke, F. B. (1982a). Semantic categories in the language of working-class black children. In C. Johnson & C. Thew (Eds.), *Proceedings from the Second International Congress for the Study of Child Language* (Vol. 1, pp. 157–172). Washington, DC: City University Press of America.

Stockman, I. J., & Vaughn-Cooke, F. B. (1982b). A re-examination of research on the language of black children: The need for a new framework. *Journal of Education, 164*, 157–172.

Tizard, B., & Hughes, M. (1984). *Young children learning*. Cambridge, MA: Harvard University Press.

Tough, J. (1977a). *The development of meaning: A study of children's use of language.* New York: Wiley.

Tough, J. (1977b). *Listening to children talking: A guide to the appraisal of children's use of language.* London: Ward Lock Educational and Drake Educational Associates.

Tough, J. (1982). Language, poverty, and disadvantage in school. In L. Feagans & D. C. Farran (Eds.), *The language of children reared in poverty* (pp. 3–18). New York: Academic Press.

Ward, M. C. (1971). *Them children.* New York: Holt, Rinehart & Winston.

Washington, E., & McLoyd, V. C. (1982). The external validity of research involving American minorities. *Human Development, 25*, 324–339.

10

CHILDREN'S STREET WORK IN URBAN NIGERIA: DILEMMA OF MODERNIZING TRADITION

Beatrice Adenike Oloko
University of Lagos, Nigeria

One of the important strategies of child socialization in Nigeria and other West-African countries from which African Americans originate is responsibility training. *Responsibility training* is defined as expectations and encouragement of the participation of children in household maintenance and domestic economy. The expectation that children should contribute to the welfare of their families is adaptive in subsistence and labor-intensive economies, as has been found in cross-cultural studies carried out in the 1950s and 1960s (Barry, Bacon, & Child, 1957; Barry, Child, & Bacon, 1959; Whiting, 1963; Whiting & Whiting, 1975). Subsistence economies necessitate the pooling of all available labor including that of children for agricultural and other kinds of work.

However, in traditional times, the tasks of children were regulated by cultural norms to match the chronological and mental ages of children. Often, there was a division of labor between parents and their same-gender children, such that certain aspects of domestic and occupational tasks were relegated specifically to children and were scarcely performed by adults. Moreover, responsibility training and its associated obedience and compliance training facilitated the inculcation of the value of collectivism, which is one of the central values that undergirded the social structure of village-based and traditional agricultural societies. In West Africa, the particular form of collectivism is oriented around the intergenerational continuity and collective nature of the extended family and is called *familism*.

The components of the value of collectivism or familism were mutual perceptions of members of the community that they were extensions of one another, the acceptance of a variety of obligations for different categories of kins, reciprocity, redistribution, cooperation, solicitude, respect, and hospitality (Oloko, 1985). The basis of the legitimacy of the value of familism or collectivism was first the belief that they were demanded by injunctions of supernatural authorities and dead ancestors and of their living human representatives and media. Second, there were beliefs that the values had existed from time immemorial. Third, their enforcers were believed to have an ethicojural right to demand compliance with the values. Fourth, the values made sense in terms of efficiency in several means–end schemas.

The process of modernization, the essential components of which are structural differentiation, complex division of labor, rapid urbanization, and industrialization, began in the colonial era and became accelerated in the postcolonial period. It has created a crisis of moral values in view of the fact that the value of familism, which undergirded the social structure, is being gradually and unevenly displaced by scientific and technological values inherent in specialized organizations like schools, which have replaced kin-based structures. The values that undergird modern societies, in which schools endogenously emerged, have been described as self-orientation, universalism, achievement, affective neutrality, and specificity. Values that are approximately opposite to the ones just mentioned have been identified as undergirding the social structure of traditional societies. These values are collectivistic orientation, particularism, ascription, affectivity, and diffuseness (Parsons, 1951).

More recently, the contrasting value orientation in developed and developing countries has been termed *technological* versus *social intelligence* (Mundy-Castle, 1968, 1974). Mundy-Castle postulated a predominance of an orientation toward technology and objects in Western societies compared with a people orientation in non-Western societies. The contrasting value orientations in the two kinds of societies have important consequences for the cognitive development of children. The strategy of socialization in technologically developed societies has been portrayed as a maximization of cognitive and other skill development, whereas child socialization in developing countries has been described as survivalist (LeVine, 1977; LeVine et al., 1990).

One of the objectives of the present investigations, some of whose findings are subsequently presented, was to determine (a) the extent to which an aspect of responsibility training—namely children's street-trading activities—typifies a collective orientation, and (b) the extent to which it was consonant with schooling, which largely promotes a self-orientation. It is maintained that street trading had some value compatibility with schooling in the early stages of the modernization process in Nigeria but it has become maladaptive as a result of some unanticipated consequences of urbanization, such as human and vehicular congestion.

I briefly describe street-trading activities of children to acquaint readers who are not familiar with the Nigerian scene with the phenomenon. By street-trading activities of children I mean the exchange of goods and services on the highways, streets, paths, and alleyways in mobile or stationary positions by children up to 15 years of age. The categories of street work identified in the study were predominantly the vending of goods and secondarily, shoe shining, car washing/watching, begging, and headloading of goods in markets for customers who could not or would not carry them. Children who vended goods displayed their goods on a tray that they carried on their heads. As described in a previous study (Oloko, 1989),

> Children street traders constitute a world of their own and their activities have definite patterns, tempo and meaning. Walking alone or in groups, children traverse parts of the towns sometimes announcing sonorously the wares they sell. Although selling in groups may seem to alleviate some of the burden of headloading and trekking by providing company and opportunities for play, it involves much competition which may offset some of its advantages. When a prospective customer is identified, children sometimes charge at him with as much speed as their headload will permit, each trying to outrun the others. On reaching him, all the children unload their goods, and a keen competition ensues in which attention is called to better quality, freshness, or size of goods, as the case may be. Even after a purchase has been made, the children do not let off easily. They appeal to the customers's sense of fairness, so that the un-wary but kind customer may find himself buying more than he intended.
>
> At the motor parks and nodes of transportation, the competition becomes intense due to the presence of more sellers, adults and children. If the vehicle moves off before children have a chance to collect their money, they run along-side the lorry or car until the customer throws the money out of the window. Children then spend time searching for and retrieving the money from the grass. Sometimes dishonest customers delay payment deliberately, knowing that children may not be able to keep pace with the fast moving vehicle. (pp. 19–20)

Often, child vendors clashed with law-enforcing officers. The more government agencies attempted to enforce laws, which made children's vending illegal, the greater the resistance put up by adult and children vendors. Consequently, a second objective of the two major studies carried out in three cities—namely Lagos, Kaduna, and Calabar, which are subsequently described—was to uncover the economic and other components of street vending that impelled participants to resist the law.

SUBJECTS

The first study was carried out in Lagos between 1987 and 1988 and had four different samples. The first sample consisted of 800 street-trading and nonworking children ages 9–14 years who attended 13 schools in four lower socioeconomic status (SES) areas of Lagos—namely Onike-Yaba, Mushin, Ikeja, and Ajegunle. About 80% of the students identified themselves as currently trading on the streets at the time of the study, whereas 20% said they were not engaged in any trading activities. Of the total sample of working and nonworking students, 34% were male and 66% were female. Of the subsample of working children, 35% were male and 65% were female. With respect to the parental background of the students, nonworking children tended to originate from relatively less deprived families than working children as judged by available household room space, mothers' education, and parental occupation.

The second sample consisted of 400 children ages 9–15 years, 45% of whom were male and 55% female. This sample was interviewed on streets in the same lower SES areas of Lagos, from which the students in the first sample were drawn. Only 10% of the children in the second sample had never attended school for various reasons. The remaining 90% had attended schools in the past or were attending at the time of the study.

The third sample consisted of 224 women traders who were interviewed in markets located in the same areas as those in which the previously described subjects in Samples 1 and 2 resided. About 43% of the women, who were in their 30s, 40s, or 50s had never attended school, whereas 57% of them had received formal education. Approximately two thirds of the women had street traded as children, whereas one third of the women reported that they had never street traded in childhood.

The fourth sample consisted of 100 primary and secondary school teachers, 34% male and 66% female, who taught in the schools attended by the children in the first sample.

The second study consisted of three samples of subjects: First, 800 children, 410 from Calabar and 390 from Kaduna, were interviewed on the streets of both towns in December 1989. The street-trading children ages 6–16 years consisted of 60% boys and 40% girls. Of the children interviewed, 108 were clinically examined by doctors, whereas in the control sample, which consisted of nonworking school children, 100 were medically examined.

The third sample in the Kaduna and Calabar study consisted of 117 experts who, in their professional roles, interacted with young street traders. The experts consisted of teachers, doctors, social welfare officers, police officers, and religious leaders. The experts' survey sought information on dimensions of street work that could not be articulated by children. It also attempted to determine the extent of agreement between experts and children on some pertinent issues. Further methodological details can be found in Oloko (1993).

CULTURAL CONTEXT OF STREET TRADING

The various ethnic groups that comprise Nigeria were in the past, and in some sectors in the present, characterized by subsistence economies. One of the characteristics of a subsistence economy is that the survival of families enjoined the economic participation of all members including children. Children worked largely in family enterprises for the benefit of the family as a whole. The positive valuation of children and the desire to have many of them in Nigeria was not unconnected with the fact that children were economic and social assets.

Often there was a division of labor between parents and their same-gender children such that certain aspects of occupational tasks were designated as children's tasks that adults rarely performed. Mobile street trading was one of such exclusive children's tasks in some areas of the country (Nadel, 1961). As Nadel observed, children deputized for their parents among the Nupe; they hawked through the markets and adjoining streets crying out their wares, a forbidden activity for adults who were sedentary traders.

Street trading by adults and children is rooted in tradition and derives from the open, often undifferentiated location of market places. Periodic and night markets particularly take place around roads, streets, and other adjoining spaces that are blocked off by the sheer volume of participation. Even in those markets that have differentiated and enclosed locations on market days, several kilometers of access roads and street are thickly lined by traders who either could find no place within the full market or desire to take advantage of their strategic location near the market to make high profits or dispose of their goods more readily.

In view of the informal nature of the market place, big and small markets spring up like mushrooms in open and available spaces to meet demands. The tradition of spontaneous occurrence of market places has continued into the present day. However, the state perceives the trend as a nuisance and has legislated against it.

The involvement of children in street trading in the traditional past was associated mostly with marketing (i.e., selling products made by parents). In traditional towns and rural areas in the present time, children are still observed selling mostly raw and processed agricultural goods and cooked food, rather than manufactured products. However, in the traditional urban centers in which women specialized in trading as a professional activity (i.e., buying in order to resell), children's involvement in street trading constituted a proper commercial activity, not merely the marketing of goods produced by their parents.

The involvement of children in marketing or proper trading in traditional times was adaptive in several ways. First, the division of labor, which was undergirded by the attributes of age and gender, necessitated the participation of children in the same occupation as their same-gender parent. For men and women petty traders, street-trading activities of their children constituted occupational preparation, during which relevant knowledge, attitudes, and skills that provided children with tools for productive adult lives were learned (Oloko, 1979).

Second, street trading was adaptive because it constituted a relatively quick way of accumulating capital without overhead cost. This was beneficial because there were no easily available credit facilities; the well-known revolving credit associations that most people relied on to accumulate capital depended on the generation of income from the pursuit of an occupation on a regular basis. In the rotating credit association, a fixed sum is contributed by each member at a fixed time and the total amount is paid to each member in rotation. Third, the unavailability of storage facilities, which has continued to irk the agricultural sector, necessitated the use of children as marketing outlets for perishable goods. Fourth, the involvement of children in street trading provided an effective strategy of beating intense atomistic competition. Children search for opportunities for sales, thus, as I show later, improving the turnover that adult traders could have in a particular period.

Fifth, in a cultural context in which women were secluded, as in the Islamic states, children's street-trading activities facilitated the economic participation of women who traded through their daughters and pre-adolescent sons. Several findings indicate that women's economic activities may be adopted or rejected depending on the availability of the assistance of children (Hill, 1969; Pittin, 1976, 1979; Simmons, 1973, 1975).

However, street trading was equally adaptive for participating young girls in areas in which wife seclusion is practiced (Schildkrout, 1981). They were expected to meet their prospective husbands during street trading or *talla*. The proceeds of their trades constituted part of the financial resources that their mothers used to obtain dowry among the Hausa/Fulani ethnic group in which early marriage is practiced. The findings of an independent survey revealed that by the age of 14, 63% of the women interviewed in Kaduna had been married. Of these, 13% were married between ages 9 and 11 (UNICEF, 1989).

STREET TRADING AND SOCIAL CHANGE

Early Phase

Although street-trading activity was adaptive in traditional culture for children from trading backgrounds, to what extent is its adaptive value attenuated for this category of children in situations of social change generated by the modernizing process? In considering an answer to the question, it is necessary to categorize the process of social change into two phases: early and late. It would be impossible within the confines of this chapter to discuss the process of social change that has significantly affected virtually all aspects of the lives of Nigerians who have been exposed to it. Therefore, I focus on formal education, which has been found to have one of the most important influences on individual modernity in Nigeria (Inkeles & Smith, 1974) and which is also perhaps the most relevant institution for the topic of this chapter.

The first phase in the Nigerian educational system as conceptualized in this chapter occurred between 1906–1975; the later phase began in 1976. The singular event that served as a criterion for the foregoing categorization was educational expansion, which began on a national level in 1976. Before 1976, there were attempts at regional levels to foster educational expansion (i.e., in the 1950s and 1960s), but such attempts encountered difficulties in the wake of dire economic problems, which made it difficult to implement the programs.

Although educational expansion had differential effects on different regions in the country, it can be maintained that, across the country and particularly in the educationally backward areas, it altered the motivational component of school attendance. Prior to the establishment of the Universal Primary Education scheme in 1976, in varying extents in different regions and different decades within the relevant period, school attendance at the primary and secondary levels of children whose parents were petty traders was influenced by parental commitment to formal education.

In view of the cost of schooling and foregone alternatives, many petty traders simply did not send their children to school. Although children from trading families were relatively more represented in schools than those of farmers, the former significantly lagged behind children who had clerical and professional backgrounds, even in educationally advanced Yoruba speaking areas (Yoloye, 1971). Those traders who sent their children to school were sufficiently encouraging to promote adequate scholastic performance in them, in spite of the children's economic involvement. The trading role could have competed with the student role, thus acting as an obstacle to scholastic achievement.

Findings obtained from the teacher and expert samples in the Lagos and Kaduna/Calabar studies indicate that some professional men and women who had traded in childhood attributed their ability to combine their student and work roles partly to the encouragement of their parents and partly to incentives provided by their working experience. The specific acts of parental encouragement, mentioned by 24% of teachers and 48% of experts, were manifestations of pride in the schooling experience of their children, visits to schools, provision of money for school meals, and the general recognition that the children were making due contribution to the household economy.

Apart from obtaining parental encouragement, teachers and other experts who had traded in childhood believed that their trading experience inculcated a sense of responsibility and self-reliance in them. The opinions of professionals agreed with the conclusion reached in some studies of household and economic activities of children (Whiting & Whiting, 1975).

The opinion of respondents in this study was that street trading instilled self-reliance. This is plausible, especially considering the home lives of the children. In traditional households in which the adults were raised and which, until recently, consisted mostly of intact extended families, the supervision and surveillance roles of adults were very marked. The situation in the past differs from the modern trend in which all extended family members do not necessarily reside together. Street trading activities provided children with freedom from frequent adult surveillance and control. Adults who traded in childhood in urban centers reported that they engaged in exploratory and play activities that were curtailed by parents and other adult relations in their households. Vehicular traffic in the pre-independence era, in which the adults were reared, was not as voluminous as it is in present-day urban centers. Thus, street trading afforded young participants the opportunity to explore their physical and social environments in a manner that was not available to their counterparts who had not street traded. Apparently, the independence training, which street trading conferred, did not result in individualistic orientation as indicated by a subsequent discussion.

With respect to school attainment, the evidence so far has indicated that trading in the past was associated with adequate to excellent scholastic attainment. This is contrary to the present-day trend, in which street trading is viewed as an obstacle to scholastic achievement. The sheer fact that the professionals interviewed have attained various amount of success in their careers, despite their childhood trading experiences, corroborates their assertions. However, there are no data concerning the proportion of those who street traded in childhood and who, given appropriate opportunities, attained or failed to attain educational progress.

Anecdotal evidence has been provided even by adults who did not work in childhood: For instance, the exemplary scholastic performance of some working children who reportedly missed school frequently because of the necessity to provide their school fees through work. Yet they out achieved most of their nonworking counterparts in scholastic performance.

The educational evaluation method that obtained in the past (i.e., one-shot examinations) facilitated the educational attainment of working children by providing compensatory opportunities for studying, which was relatively neglected due to their involvement in work. In reviewing discussions with some of the identified prodigies and other professionals who had traded in childhood, the writer was reminded of a cross-cultural finding in which a "conscientiousness syndrome" was identified among boys who were exposed to early responsibility training and who manifested achievement in school subjects despite great odds (McClelland, 1961).

Apart from adjusting to their student roles, interviews conducted on adults who traded in childhood revealed that these professionals were well adapted to both their social milieu of orientation and those of their current participation. On the one hand, the teachers, lecturers, lawyers, doctors, and religious leaders who were interviewed subscribed readily to collectivistic values such as educating members of their extended families; providing financial, social, and moral support for activities in their communities of orientation; and spontaneously accommodating extended family members. On the other hand, they recognized that professional commitment was demanding and that achievement required great attention and dedication. However, adults who had traded in childhood, compared with those who had not, more consistently maintained that rewards from professional progress should be utilized in fulfillment of obligations to needy extended relatives, as well as catering to their nuclear families.

The ungrudging attitude of Nigerians who had street traded in childhood to their extended families was different from that of persons who had had 15 or more years of education, given the experience and reasoned tendency for prolonged education to be associated with diminished extended family ties (Inkeles & Smith, 1974; Moore, 1965). The commitment of professionals to their extended families is attributable to either the amount of assistance they received from these relatives during their schooling years, now being reciprocated, or to a sense of altruism inculcated by their working experience. The answer to this question is unknown and requires documentation.

Assuming that the findings are reliable and generalizable, and assuming that the professionals possessed individual modernity, the issue of what constitutes the optimum in individual modernity from the perspective of the community or society is raised. Is an individualistic orientation that concentrates on the rewards of schooling within the nuclear family more adaptive than a collectivistic orientation that distributes rewards and thereby facilitates the process of individual modernity for others who ordinarily would have been excluded? Plausibly, early childhood working experience may be one of the important mechanisms by which the self-orientation, inculcated by prolonged schooling, is reduced.

Later Phase

Transformations have occurred in both the nature and scope of children's work and the environment of trading. Moreover, school assessment procedures tend to attenuate the adaptive value of street work for educational attainment. Continuous assessment has replaced the older system of one-time testing, making it more difficult for traders to compensate scholastically for their trading-induced absences. The changes that have occurred in children's work include the type of people some children work for, involvement in occupations that were carried out by young adults and adolescents in the past, and changes in work regularity and periods. The volume of children participating in street trading has increased, moreover, and the physical and social environments in which the children work has changed dramatically in several ways. Five examples suffice before I assess the adaptive or maladaptive roles of the new trends.

First, in the past, child traders worked for their parents. However, in recent times, some children have worked for employers and distant relations who do not necessarily have a custodial orientation toward them. In the Lagos study, 11% of the 800 children lived with relatives or guardians, whereas the remainder lived with parents or grandparents. In the Kaduna–Calabar study, 77% of Kaduna children lived with parents or grandparents, whereas 23% lived with employers and other relatives. In Calabar, 64.5% of the children lived with their parents and grandparents, whereas the remaining 35.5% lived with relatives and employers.

To some extent, whether children lived with their parents/grandparents or employers/other relatives tended to influence school attendance and the drop-out rate. However, these tendencies were not as significant as the relationship between the mothers' educational attainment and whether her children attended school.

Second, the regularity of work and work during certain periods of the day tended to make children report tiredness and headaches as two of the encountered problems of trading. In the past, as reported by adults who traded in childhood, children's work was limited to morning and evening periods to avoid the heat of the sun; it also tended to occur during weekends and public holidays. These findings indicate that work now constitutes a daily activity for two thirds of the sample in both Kaduna and Calabar. Only one third of the subjects work as a weekly or weekend activity. With respect to periods of day that children worked, current findings confirm the casual observation that children are visible in all urban centers of the country at any time of the day. The subjects worked during seven periods—all day, morning only, afternoon only, evening only, morning and afternoon, morning and evening, afternoon and evening. In the total sample, only 14%, 11% and 6% of children respectively worked either only in the morning, only in the evening or combined morning and evening periods. Only about 31% of subjects in the total sample escaped working in the afternoon when, under tropical conditions, the heat from the sun is at its greatest.

Third, one of the most significant changes that has occurred in children's work is the increase in the volume of participation. In an earlier study carried out in a town in Lagos State in 1974, it was found that only one in five

children street traded (Oloko, 1979). In recent times, the volume of participation of adults and children in street trading has been described as having
"monstrous dimensions" and as constituting a menace (Coker, 1985).

The findings of the 1988 Lagos survey confirms the journalistic impression. In the four areas of Lagos surveyed, it was found that one in two to
three primary and junior secondary school students readily admitted to participation in street trading. The high proportion of children who admitted
that they participated in street trading was significant because, at the time
of the particular study in Lagos, constant raids of street traders were carried
out by law-enforcing officials. This estimate could be considered a conservative one because some children might have refused to identify themselves
as street traders for fear that they might be reported and subsequently
prosecuted.

Fourth, significant changes that have occurred in the physical and social
environments of children's work include increases in motorable roads, which
make children's street-trading activities relatively unsafe. Approximately one
quarter of all children interviewed admitted having an accident, which in
this context meant harsh falls and being knocked down by vehicles. Neither
age, gender, nor work regularity influenced children's reported experience
of accidents. However, work period in Kaduna significantly influenced the
extent to which children claimed to have had accidents involving vehicles.

Fifth, the social environment in which children worked, as indicated by
findings of the two studies, was unsafe compared with the past. It is startling
that slightly more than half the children in the two towns admitted to having
been assaulted at one time or another. Calabar children claimed to have been
assaulted slightly more than their Kaduna counterparts.

ANTECEDENTS OF CHILDREN'S STREET TRADING

Five cultural and economic factors—namely, the division of labor, limited
credit, limited storage facilities, wife seclusion, and early marriage—facilitated
the involvement of children in street trading in the past. Although these five
factors are still relevant to some extent, depending on regional differences
in the present day, adverse economic circumstances[1] have marginalized a
vast proportion of Nigerians and have increased the need for children to work
on the street for survival.

These difficult economic circumstances have also forced traders who previously traded exclusively in market shops and stalls to become street traders.
Previously established traders no longer can afford rents of market stalls.

---

[1]The Structural Adjustment Programme (SAP), which was evolved to develop a self-reliant
economy and assist the country in servicing its debt burden, has led to massive retrenchment,
forced retirement, and a high unemployment rate of adults.

There is consumer resistance to some consumer goods, which therefore have to be paraded to induce impulsive buying. Makeshift stalls near markets and residential accommodation have been eradicated. These circumstances have all combined to push traders and their children into the streets.

The findings of the two sets of studies indicate that the returns from children's street trading were attractive enough to encourage traders to sell on as many fronts as they had available children. Because women traders in Lagos reported that they may not realize as much as five naira per day in off-sale seasons, depending on the type of goods sold and stall location, the consistent finding that four fifths of child street traders in the three towns made more than five naira per day is significant.

The young subjects seemed to be aware of the importance of their economic activity for the welfare of their families and themselves. When the subjects were asked in a questionnaire to select one of six needs that they thought would suffer most if they stopped work, about half of the children in Kaduna and Calabar mentioned that their own food needs would suffer most. The second most mentioned need was school materials, which was indicated by 28% of children in the towns. Only 5% to 7% of the children thought no need would be adversely affected if they were to stop work.

The first four needs that were mentioned were those of children, followed by two adult needs—a clear indicator that children were working for their own survival. Other studies have shown that children in Nigeria are capable of distinguishing between their interests and predicaments and those of adults (Ministry of Social Development, Youth and Sports, 1984).

Apart from dire economic necessity, one of the rarely mentioned reasons for the greater involvement of children vis-à-vis adults in street trading in the present than in the past is associated with the fact that street-trading laws, which were not enforced in the past, are now being enforced. The enforcement of laws through frequent raids necessitates agile participants who can trade without being arrested. The physical agility and size of children protect them from being arrested as frequently as adults.

From the children's perspective, one of the incentives of street work is the private income, termed *gain*, that they derive from it. Child traders are never paid since they are perceived as contributing to their upkeep. The "gain" is the only monetary reward the children derive from their work. The private income represents the differential between the actual sale price of goods as stipulated by parents and the amount demanded by child vendors. About half the children in each of the three samples reported that they derived private income, which they spent on extra food and simple school materials, whereas approximately half denied that they generated private income. Whether children derived private income from trading depended on locality of trading, types of goods sold, work intensity, and work periods, among other things.

Because children from lower SES homes rarely obtained pocket money from their parents, those who street traded had more disposable income than those who did not. A few of the children who were interviewed in Lagos and observed in Ibadan were secretly involved in street work on their own initiative to generate pocket money.

INFORMAL EDUCATION AND STREET TRADING

Having provided examples of changes in the nature, scope, intensity, and physical and social environments of work, and having assessed the effects of some of these changes on the safety of working children, I proceed to examine adaptive and maladaptive functions of work from the perspective of children's adjustment to their social milieu and educational attainment.

The assessment of the amount and type of knowledge that children acquire during street work is as problematic as the evaluation of what children actually learn in schools. This is because children are simultaneously exposed to various aspects of living. Although some of their experiences can be articulated, some are latent and may not be accessible until much later. However, I attempted to assess learning benefits of children's work largely through participant observation and responses to interview items by children, mothers, teachers, and other experts.

One of the adaptive functions of street trading that was mentioned by women traders and teachers was that it provides children with a substantial knowledge of their socioeconomic milieu, such that they do not become emotionally distanced from it even when they achieved sustained schooling. What is a trader's socioeconomic milieu?

The informal sector, which is dominated by various categories of traders, is disadvantaged with respect to access to capital, regulation of market, scale of operation, too much ease of entry, volume of participation, and excessive competition (Fapohunda, 1985). The competition among informal sector workers is particularly intense among petty traders. They tend to cluster, sell similar goods, and therefore reduce the turnover and profit that could have accrued to them individually had they adopted a different strategy of trading. Petty traders have limited capital output and tend to depend on hard work and vertical and horizontal interpersonal relationships to survive.

Moreover, traders have to maintain cordial and affiliative relationships with their buyers to ensure steady sales. Unlike selling situations in the formal sector, in which sales persons adopt an impersonal and intimidating stance toward buyers, traders in the informal sector deliberately utilize interpersonal charm and conviviality to attract and even woo customers, in order to retain them.

The interpersonal norms and skills that are needed to function in the informal sector are intensified versions of some of those inculcated in extended families. However, the extended family exists in residual forms for a large number of urban dwellers. In some contexts, the customer relationship becomes the functional equivalent of extended family relationships, which have been eroded for certain groups of urban migrants.

Children's street trading constitutes one of the mechanisms for the socialization of adult traders. The competitive yet affiliative settings in which children work on the street tend to facilitate the acquisition of knowledge, attitudes, and skills necessary for the solution of problems associated with trading. Such skills include interpersonal ones, such as ability to (a) woo customers and sometimes induce impulsive buying in them, (b) distinguish bonafide customers from fraudulent ones, and (c) elbow other sellers away from the bargaining situation; as well as noninterpersonal ones, such as the ability to (a) gradually accumulate capital, (b) compute sales quickly and give correct change, and (c) account for sales without first recording them on paper. The concept of profit and probably the profit motive would be firmly entrenched in trading children, as found in a study of another group of African children (Jahoda, 1986).

In describing the skills that petty trading instills, I find some of Mills' (1951) categories of salesgirls appropriate, even though they were developed for a different social and sales context. Mills identified eight categories of salesgirls including the wolf, who pounces on potential customers; and the elbower, who is bent on monopolizing all the customers. Observers of the Nigerian scene readily recognize these two selling styles, among others, that children have acquired at tender ages.

The interpersonal skills that children learn during street trading deserve special discussion because of their complexity. On the one hand, street-trading children realize that their goal is to sell their wares quickly and profitably, ensuring that they make a private income for themselves. On the other hand, they seem to know that the goal of financial success should not be obtained at the expense of interpersonal relationships with their competitors, and hence they tend to minimize acrimony. In this respect, my findings are in agreement with a conceptual discussion of social intelligence among the Yoruba and other non-Western peoples (Mundy-Castle, 1974).

However, the social intelligence that the children manifest may be attributable to the fact that they work in groups and in competitive and harassed situations in which cooperation is necessary for survival. In passing, it should be observed that, even in the United States, harassed female vendors have been found to adopt some of the strategies used by these young subjects (Spalter-Roth, 1988). Because children sell in groups, which may be age and gender homogenous or heterogenous, harmony needs to be fostered so that members can provide mutual technical and social assistance, such as detecting forged currencies, protecting against criminal adults and youths, and alerting the group of the approach of law-enforcing officials.

One of the significant outcomes of group selling is that it affords opportunities for play, which is usually curtailed in the traditional and transitional homes from which young vendors originate. Overworked parents, especially mothers, attempt to get more work out of children by prohibiting play, which they perceive as a manifestation of indolence and hedonism that will be maladaptive in the future. Three types of play have been observed in working children: (a) nonabsorptive play, which is manifested in verbal interchanges such as repartee and mimicry; (b) competitive play, in which vendors attempt to out-walk, out-trot, or out-run one another purely for fun; and (c) full-blown play, which involves a temporary relinquishment of their trading roles and that could hardly occur in the subjects' home without reprimand and sometimes punishment.

In other words, the findings of the research agree with the previous assessments of adults who have traded in childhood and maintain that street trading provides its participants with a sense of freedom and independence that they would not have had otherwise. The effects of this latent function of street trading for different aspects of creativity have not been explored. The findings with respect to the subjects' self-reliance in difficult situations indicate that working children tended to be more self-reliant than their non-working counterparts.

The technical and social skills that children learn during trading constitutes part of their occupational preparation, despite their school attendance. This is so because of the unemployment of primary and secondary school graduates. The skills that children learn from street trading are not to be underrated in view of the following trends. First, in the immediate future, most unemployed female school graduates will earn their livelihood by assisting their mothers preparatory to their own later independent trading. The findings of the Lagos market-women study, which revealed that 57% of women traders had attended school and that 29% of these had secondary education, are indicative of the likelihood that an even higher proportion of younger primary and secondary educated females who have trading backgrounds may remain traders. Second, if the current trend in which professional women such as teachers, nurses, and clerks augment their incomes from formal employment by simultaneously carrying out petty to large-scale trading persists, only a few young subjects who can proceed to tertiary education will escape from trading at one time or another in the future.

MALADAPTIVE FUNCTION OF PRESENT TRADING
FOR SCHOOL ATTAINMENT

In some of the foregoing sections, it was reasoned that street trading constituted adaptation to poor socioeconomic circumstances, extremely competitive economic activity, and unemployment of primary and secondary school
leavers—graduates. But to what extent does street trading create obstacles
to adequate scholastic achievement, and hence impede further education and
social mobility of its participants? In other words, to what extent can working students in their student role effectively compete with their nonworking
counterparts given their physical exertion and preoccupation with work?

As admitted by working students, the work role tends to be associated
with irregularity of school attendance, lack of concentration in class due to
fatigue, and inability to carry out homework assignments in time to meet
deadlines. Moreover, working children, vis-à-vis their nonworking counterparts, tend to be disadvantaged by being unable to attend remedial lessons
that nearly all primary and secondary school students routinely attend for
reasons of prestige and the vested interests of teachers.

Comparison Between the Scholastic Attainment
of Working and Nonworking Children

In an attempt to assess the influence of work on the scholastic attainment
of working children, the two sets of surveys included nonworking children
who served as controls for their working counterparts. However, the two
sets of studies used different types of assessments and different types of control groups. In the Lagos study, academic attainment of the two samples was
assessed using guided teacher ratings of their continuous assessment and attainment in English, arithmetic, and general knowledge paper. The general
paper tests knowledge of history, geography, and social studies. Its approxi-
mate equivalent in the United States is civics. In the Kaduna–Calabar study,
educational assessment of working and nonworking children was based on
reading fluency in the English language and the mother tongue.

Findings of the Lagos Study

In the Lagos study, in which scholastic attainment was based on teachers'
assessments of the students attainment in English, arithmetic, and general
knowledge paper, the teachers were requested to categorize all the children
in their class into three groups: below average, average, and above average.
The assessments were based on the scores of the children in the continuous
assessments and examinations.

Table 10.1 presents a comparison of the scholastic attainment of working and nonworking children in three critical school subjects. The findings in the table indicate that the working students were rated consistently and significantly lower than their nonworking counterparts. The table shows that working children compared with nonworking children consistently had greater representation among those who were rated as manifesting below-average attainment in the three schools subjects. Correspondingly, nonworking children had significantly higher representation among those who were rated as manifesting average and above-average attainment.

Age and gender were significantly related to the attainment of working children. Age was significantly related to English ($p < .05$), arithmetic ($p < .001$), and general paper ($p < .001$). Gender was significantly related to English ($p < .001$), arithmetic ($p < .001$), and general paper ($p < .0001$). In the three subjects, younger children and boys out-achieved their counterparts, namely older children and girls, for reasons associated with greater physical and emotional involvement of girls and older children with work. The reported findings are consistent with those of an earlier study carried out in Ikorodu (Oloko, 1979).

Even though it is popularly believed that street trading facilitates greater arithmetical skills, a belief shared by a few of the subjects, my finding did not confirm that opinion. As a matter of fact, judging from the level of statistical significance obtained from the comparison of working and nonworking students in the three subjects, nonworking children out-performed their working counterparts most in arithmetic.

One explanation for the findings is that school tests have time limits. Working children may utilize informal procedures to solve arithmetical problems that may take longer than the conventional algorithms that their nonworking counterparts tend to use. The findings of a study carried out in another country showed that informal strategies of solving arithmetic problems take longer than conventional algorithms (Petitto & Ginsburg, 1982). Of course, in out-of-school contexts, especially in their own social milieu, working children may solve practical arithmetic problems more efficiently than their nonworking counterparts. This pattern agrees with the findings of Carraher, Carraher, and Schlieman (1985) and Saxe (1990) in Brazil, although those authors emphasized the positive aspects of child vendors' street math, rather than the negative aspects of their school math.

It is noteworthy that 28%, 21%, and 25% of working children were rated as manifesting above-average attainment in English, arithmetic, and general knowledge, respectively (Table 10.1). In view of the great odds against which these children study, this finding is impressive, especially if one considers the home lives of both working and nonworking children. Home life will be discussed later in this chapter. For now I focus attention on the educational attainment of working and nonworking children in Calabar and Kaduna.

TABLE 10.1
Representing the Scholastic Achievement Differences in Critical School Subjects Among Working and Nonworking Children in Lagos

Category	Achievement in English*				Achievement in Arithmetic**				Achievement in General Knowledge Paper***			
	Below Average	Average	Above Average	Total	Below Average	Average	Above Average	Total	Below Average	Average	Above Average	Total
Working	188 34%	206 38%	153 28%	547 100%	239 44%	186 35%	112 21%	537 100%	201 37%	208 28%	135 25%	544 100%
Nonworking	33 21%	68 44%	54 35%	155 100%	38 24%	74 48%	43 28%	155 100%	32 21%	73 47%	50 32%	155 100%

Note. *, $\chi^2 = 9.69$, $p = .0079$.
**, $\chi^2 = 20.05$, $p = .0000$.
***, $\chi^2 = 14.50$, $p = .0007$.

READING ABILITY IN ENGLISH AND MOTHER TONGUES: THE KADUNA–CALABAR STUDY

Because the Lagos study found that a significant proportion of working children manifested below-average performance in important school subjects, the Kaduna–Calabar study used a different criterion for assessing school achievement, reading ability in English and the mother tongues. Reading in the mother tongue is taught as a subject in schools in Kaduna and Calabar for at least 4 years of upper primary education, whereas English constitutes the teaching language. In the first two years of primary education, the mother tongue is used exclusively as a teaching language, whereas English is taught as a subject only.

It was felt that the ability to read, which had important implications for permanent literacy, would improve economic and social participation in a modernizing society, even if the subjects might not experience occupational mobility due to inability to excel in examinations and further their education.

The findings of the literacy test in English revealed that only one third of working children in the two towns were assessed as manifesting fluent reading ability. The reading ability of working children in both towns was compared with that of the control group. Although in Calabar there was practically no difference between working and nonworking children, in Kaduna nonworking children significantly out-performed their working counterparts. Although about two fifths of Kaduna working children were found to read fluently, about half of nonworking children were judged as fluent. These findings were consonant with several other findings of the study, in which Kaduna working children were relatively more disadvantaged vis-à-vis their nonworking counterparts than were Calabar working children. With respect to reading in the mother tongue, Kaduna nonworking children were evaluated as being more fluent than their working counterparts. However in Calabar, nonworking children performed more poorly than their working counterparts.

The Influence of Maternal Education

Maternal education was significantly correlated with reading ability in English in Calabar and Kaduna but was not significantly correlated with reading ability in the mother tongue in the two towns. The last finding was to be expected for two reasons. First, all children speak their mother tongue very well. The ability of their mothers to read in their mother tongue will not necessarily improve the reading ability of their children unless deliberate efforts are made by their mothers to expose their children to reading material in the local languages. Because reading materials are more abundant in English than in the mother tongue, mothers would be inclined to expose their children to reading materials in English if they attempted to accelerate their children's reading. Second, if children can speak their mother tongue well, attainment of reading skills will be relatively easier than in English, in which their verbal competence is doubtful.

Maternal literacy may be of no particular advantage because all children can speak their first languages well, and therefore can predict or guess sentence structures and meaning from earlier clues. Moreover, because local languages are written more phonetically than English, they facilitate the ability of children to read in their mother tongues.

I have touched on some aspects of the home lives of working children in the foregoing discussion in order to properly situate the educational disadvantages of working children vis-à-vis their nonworking counterparts. It is necessary to consider fuller descriptions of the home circumstances of the different groups of subjects, focusing particularly on maternal teaching styles. The interview schedule administered to young subjects in the Lagos and Kaduna–Calabar studies contained over 30 items that were designed to tap socioeconomic differences between and within the two groups of young subjects. Some representative responses to a few items are considered.

Although working and nonworking children resided in similar communities, working children tended to originate from poorer families than their nonworking counterparts. In the Lagos and Kaduna–Calabar studies, a greater proportion of nonworking subjects had mothers and fathers who had secondary and postsecondary education and who worked in the formal rather than the informal sector. Moreover, the families of nonworking children tended to have greater living spaces. Maternal education is a critical variable in this study because polygyny tends to place the control of the labor, education, and other activities of children in the hands of their mothers.

Although 15% and 48% of mothers of working children in Lagos and Calabar, respectively, were illiterates, only 5% and 23% of mothers of nonworking children, respectively, in the two towns were so identified. In the Lagos study, 21% of nonworking children had mothers who had postsecondary education, whereas only 7% of working children had such mothers (see Table 10.2). About 35% of mothers of nonworking children were shown as working in the formal sector. This proportion far exceeded that of mothers of nonworking children who had postsecondary education.

Only 9% of the mothers of working children were identified as working in the formal sector; this proportion is similar to that of mothers of working children who had postsecondary education. Recruitment into the formal labor force requires completion of at least secondary education, which many mothers of working children classified as having secondary education clearly did not have.

Having shown that working and nonworking children had different propor-

TABLE 10.2

Representing Some Parental Background Differences Among Working and Nonworking Children in Lagos

Category	No. of Rooms Rented in House*				Amount of Mother's Schooling**					Mother's Occupation***				Father's Occupation†		
	1	2	3 or more	Total	None	Primary	Secondary	Post-secondary	Total	Trading Groups		Formal	Total	Informal Sector	Formal Sector	Total
Working	170	248	206	624	63	150	179	31	423	506	27	52	585	214	362	576
	27%	40%	33%	100%	15%	36%	42%	7%	100%	86%	5%	9%	100%	37%	63%	100%
Nonworking	24	55	81	160	6	31	53	23	113	62	19	44	125	30	120	150
	15%	34%	51%	100%	5%	27%	47%	21%	100%	50%	15%	35%	100%	20%	80%	100%

Note. *, $\chi^2 = 19.56$, $p = .0001$.
    **, $\chi^2 = 23.52$, $p = .0000$.
    ***, $\chi^2 = 88.07$, $p = .0000$.
    †, $\chi^2 = 14.93$, $p = .0001$.

tions of mothers who were literate and illiterate, and having discussed the significance of maternal education for the reading ability of children, particularly in English, I now explore the mechanism by which maternal education or lack of it influences children's school enrollment and attainment. The findings of the two studies indicate that maternal literacy was associated with enrollment of children in school, whereas illiteracy tended to act as an obstacle to school enrollment. For example, in Kaduna, an educationally backward area, of the 102 children who admitted never attending school only 6 (6%) had mothers who were literate, whereas the remaining 96 (94%) had mothers who were illiterate. In contrast, only 66% of the children who had been to school had illiterate mothers.

The children who were not attending school gave reasons of finance, health, and parental reluctance. Of the 50 children who gave parental reluctance as a reason for not attending school, 44 were from Kaduna. Of these, 41 had illiterate parents, whereas only 3 had literate parents—a finding that underscores the role of parental literacy in school enrollment.

With respect to the educational attainment of children who had been enrolled in school, practical and attitudinal factors militate against working children who tend to have illiterate mothers or mothers who have not attained much schooling. The practical disadvantage that working children have is associated with the fact that their mothers, who are mostly traders, have a heavy economic work role. These women wake up early and work late to accomplish their routine tasks. Their children tend to maintain the same sleeping and waking habit as their parents. My findings indicate that working children and children whose mothers were illiterates reported earlier waking and later sleeping times than children of nonworking and literate parents. It is not surprising that the former tended to report more frequently than the latter that they experienced inadequate sleep and consequently slept during school lessons.

With respect to attitudes of literate and illiterate women to the schooling experiences of their children, it is difficult to generalize because of important mediating influences such as educational attainment of spouses, amount of exposure to urbanization, and extent of relative deprivation experienced vis-à-vis women who have gone to school. However, it may be valid to maintain that educated women, especially if they have the opportunity and means, tend to support the student role of their children more than their illiterate counterparts. This generalization is inferred from responses to several items in the Kaduna–Calabar study. Literacy status of mothers was significantly correlated in both Kaduna and Calabar with the (a) amount of education fathers had ($p < .001$), (b) period of day in which children traded ($p < .001$), (c) regulation of children's work ($p < .042$), and (d) type of punishment meted out when children sustained losses during trade ($p < .004$).

As expected, literate women were married to literate men—a situation that provided children with a double model and support for their student role. The children of literate women were significantly underrepresented among those who sold all day and at disadvantageous periods that exposed children to health and moral hazards. The children of literate mothers reported that their mothers merely reasoned with or scolded them when they sustained losses at work, whereas those who had illiterate mothers reported that they were physically beaten.

Previous studies of mother–child interactions have suggested pathways by which maternal education is associated with a developmental rather than a survivalist orientation (LeVine, 1987; Richman et al., 1988). Of the pathways suggested in the cited studies, the one that was confirmed by several of my findings was the tendency for schooling to be associated with social and psychological dispositions, which make educated women more developmentally oriented than their illiterate counterparts. To give an example, the responses to an item that requested Lagos women to opine whether the dignity of a child is the same as, more than or less than that of an adult indicated that literate women opined more frequently that a child's dignity is the same as that of an adult.

However, the age of mothers was more strongly correlated than maternal literacy with respect to opinion about child's dignity. Older women more than younger women perceived the dignity of a child as being the same or more than that of an adult. Similarly, when requested to indicate how often irresponsibility should be excused in children, literate and older mothers tended to be more permissive than illiterate and younger mothers. Literate mothers also tended to indicate that a child should hold onto his or her own opinion when right even if that opinion is contrary to those of his or her peers.

Possibly when these child-oriented responses are reinforced by direct parental encouragement, such as provision of remedial education and visits to schools, working children may be committed to their student role and tend to manifest adequate scholastic attainment. Maternal encouragement is facilitated by the better understanding of the student role on the part of literate women. Greater ability to understand and empathize with the student role facilitates goal setting with respect to years of schooling and quality of scholastic attainment. Of the Lagos market women who were interviewed, none desired that her children have less education than herself. For some of the illiterate mothers, even 2 years of schooling represented an acceptable advance over their own educational status.

Participant observation during the Lagos study revealed the ignorance of illiterate women about the student role when they, sometimes under work pressure, demanded that their children terminate "abstract" studies and attend to "sustenance" matters. Some of them also denigrated schooling and affirmed that common sense rather than "book knowledge" determines life success. Children of illiterate mothers who were found to be committed to their student role despite their work role sometimes faked school assignments in order to carry out spontaneous reviews of their schoolwork.

The illiteracy of some mothers of working children is only one of the factors that militate against them. The adoption of continuous assessment to replace the previous one-time assessment has tended to decrease the compensatory opportunities that working children need to manifest adequate scholastic attainment. As defined by the Federal Ministry of Education, Science and Technology (1985), continuous assessment is "a method of finding out what the pupil has gained from learning activities in terms of knowledge, thinking and reasoning, character development and industry" (p. 8). Experts' interpretations of continuous assessment is that it should systematically cover the whole spectrum of moral and academic components of school achievement, including values, attitudes, interests, and motivation. However, in reality, teachers tend to restrict assessment to academic achievement as assessed by tests. Because teachers refuse individual make-up tests for those who miss the class tests, children who cannot attend school regularly are consistently disadvantaged.

CONCLUSION

This chapter has discussed the adaptive and maladaptive functions of street trading, especially from the perspective of educational attainment. Even though changes have occurred in the nature, scope, and environment of work, the persistence of children's street trading into present time represents a continuity of past tradition. Structurally, those children who street trade, regardless of whether they attend school, may be regarded as manifesting a continuity, whereas those children who do not participate in street work, for whatever reasons, could be thought of as manifesting a kind of discontinuity.

However, from the perspective of the adaptive capacity of work for effective schooling and eventual adequate adaptation to a modernizing economic, social, and political environment, street work or its absence can be said to represent continuities for two groups of children—namely those from the lower classes who combine work with school and manage to excel in the latter, and middle-class children who refrain from trading in order to maximize the returns from their parents' investments in schooling. From this perspective, children who combine street work and schooling but manifest deficits in the latter, and those who do not attend school at all because of their involvement in trading, represent maladaptation to a modernizing economic, social, and political environment.

For the groups of children for whom street work represents continuities—namely those who participated in street work and schooling in the early phase of the introduction of schooling, those who combine street work and schooling in the present day and manifest excellence in the latter, and nonworking students—different mechanisms are responsible for their abilities to succeed. For children who participated in street work and schooling in the early phase of the introduction of formal schooling, the physically and socially safe environment of work and maternal encouragement facilitated academic attainment. Moreover, the school assessment method that predominated at that time (viz. the one-shot examination) provided children with opportunities to compensate for their periodic inability to attend schools punctually and regularly, thereby contributing to the scholastic success of working students in the past.

For present-day working students who excel in their academic pursuits, maternal literacy and encouragement, as well as the children's own determination to succeed, act as positive influences. The ability of literate mothers to provide meaningful models of educational attainment for their children, as well as specific acts of encouragement such as encouraging children to maintain adequate sleeping hours, provisions of remedial education, and visits to school, were found to offset some of the negative consequences of street work. Moreover, the opportunities that children have for play, and for manifesting self-reliance and resourcefulness on the street, tip the adult-oriented socialization in their families toward independence training, a prerequisite for school success.

For nonworking students, most of whose parents had adopted new achievement values through formal education, the mechanisms that promoted scholastic excellence, and hence intergenerational continuities, were (a) parental support and protection from street work, (b) parental literacy, and (c) specific acts of parental encouragement similar to those that were mentioned earlier for the first two categories of children.

For the two categories of children for whom street work represents discontinuities vis-à-vis modernization (viz. working students who manifest deficient achievement and street-trading children who either dropped out of school or never attended school), several mechanisms act as obstacles to their ability to adapt to a modernizing and education-conscious society. For failing or dropped-out working students, five negative trends were identified.

First, the trend whereby some children worked for distant relatives rather than parents has eroded the traditional mechanism that moderated and monitored street work. The absence of new regulatory strategies that could monitor children's street work has exposed children to exploitation in several ways.

Second, even among children who work for their parents, economic necessity has obliterated norms that traditionally undergirded children's street work to the extent that children presently work in hot and inclement weather.

Third, because of the unsafe physical and social environments of work, lack of parental surveillance of street work tends to encourage children to yield to distracting and sometimes deviant enticements in the work environment, such as truancy and membership in "street-corner societies."

Fourth, the high rate of unemployment of school leavers—graduates, combined with the illiteracy and semi-illiteracy status of mothers, yields negative maternal attitudes toward education. Illiterate mothers denigrate formal schooling, and thereby fail to provide adequate support for their children's student role. The tendency of young street vendors to enjoy street work because it satisfies their needs for private income, freedom, and play tends to reinforce parental attitudes toward schooling vis-à-vis work.

Fifth, the educational assessment method of continuous assessment, which was recently introduced, tends to militate against working students who cannot attend schools consistently, regularly, and punctually.

The most maladaptive aspect of street work occurred when it was found to prevent school enrollment and encourage dropping out of school. The immediate issue raised by lack of school enrollment and dropping out is the extent to which the earlier extensive discussion on some of the adaptive values of street work is definitive.

To what extent can informal education obtained on the streets compensate for lack of formal schooling? In the past, when the literacy rate was very low in society and particularly among traders, certain personality attributes could facilitate economic success, as occurred in the cases of well-known trading Amazons who were stark illiterates. However, in current times, when more than half of the sample of market women studied had received formal schooling, illiteracy undoubtedly would create obstacles to occupational success and mobility, as well as to personal development and meaningful political participation in an increasingly modern society.

This chapter also discussed the adaptive capacity for different groups of children of the value of familism or collectivism, which street trading fosters. It was maintained that early childhood working experience may constitute one of the important mechanisms by which the value of familism is maintained and the self-orientation that prolonged schooling inculcates is reduced.

Although adults who street traded in childhood were found to maintain active links with their extended family members and offered financial and educational assistance to their less privileged relatives, adults who had not worked in childhood manifested considerable self-orientation. The latter expended their financial and educational resources on members of their nuclear family and provided grudging assistance to deprived relatives only when they could not avoid such commitment.

In situations of rapid social change and unequal distribution of important resources, such as exists in Nigeria, the foregoing finding raises two issues. On the one hand, is self-orientation more adaptive than collectivistic orientation, which facilitates relatively wider distribution of scarce resources? On the other hand, lack of school success on the part of working children would eventually deny them needed resources with which to manifest reciprocity and redistribution, some key components of a collectivistic orientation.

ACKNOWLEDGMENTS

An earlier version of this chapter was prepared for the National Institute of Mental Health (USA) workshop on "Continuities and Discontinuities in the Cognitive Socialization of Minority Children," organized by P. M. Greenfield and R. R. Cocking, Washington, DC, June 1991. The research support of the Ford Foundation and UNICEF is acknowledged.

REFERENCES

Barry, H. III, Bacon, M. K., & Child, I. L. (1957). A cross-cultural survey of some sex differences in socialization. *Journal of Abnormal and Social Psychology, 55,* 327–332.

Barry, H. III, Child, I. L., & Bacon, M. K. (1959). Relation of child training to subsistence economy. *American Anthropologist, 61,* 51–63.

Carraher, T. H., Carraher, D. W., & Schliemann, A. (1985). Mathematics in the streets and in schools. *British Journal of Developmental Psychology, 3,* 21–29.

Coker, O. (1985, August). Street Trading Culture I. *Daily Times* (Lagos), p. 5.

Fapohunda, O. (1985). *The informal sector: An inquiry into urban poverty and employment.* Ibadan, Nigeria: Ibadan University Press.

Federal Ministry of Education, Science and Technology. (1985). *A handbook on continuous assessment.* Ibadan, Nigeria: Heinemann Educational Books.

Hill, P. (1969). Hidden trade in Hausaland. *Man, 4*(3), 392–409.

Inkeles, A., & Smith, D. H. (1974). *Becoming modern—Individual change in six developing countries.* Cambridge, MA: Harvard University Press.

Jahoda, G. (1986). A cross-cultural perspective on developmental psychology. *International Journal of Behavioral Development, 9*(4), 417–437.

LeVine, R. A. (1977). Child rearing as cultural adaptation. In P. H. Leiderman, S. R. Tulkin, & A. Rosenfeld (Eds.), *Culture and infancy: Variations in the human experience* (pp. 15–27). New York: Academic Press.

LeVine, R. A. (1987). Women's schooling, patterns of fertility and child survival. *Educational Researcher, 16*(9), 21–27.

McClelland, D. C. (1961). *The achieving society.* Princeton, NJ: Van Nostrand.

Mills, C. W. (1951). *The white collar.* New York: Oxford University Press.

Ministry of Social Development, Youth and Sports (1984). *The situation of children in Nigeria.* Enugu, Nigeria: Nkeora Associates.

Moore, E. W. (1965). *Industrialization and labour: Social aspects of economic development.* New York: Russell & Russell.

Mundy-Castle, A. C. (1968, December). . . . __ __ __ . . . . Paper presented at a workshop in social psychology organized by the Makerere Institute of Social Research and Syracuse University, New York.

Mundy-Castle, A. C. (1974). Social and technological intelligence in Western and non-Western cultures. *Universitas, 4,* 46–52.

Nadel, S. F. (1961). *Black Byzantium*. London: International African Institute.

Oloko, B. A. (1979). *Socio-cultural correlates of school achievement in Nigeria*. Unpublished doctoral dissertation, Harvard University, Department of Anthropology, Cambridge, MA.

Oloko, B. A. (1989). Children's work in urban Nigeria: A case study of young Lagos street traders. In W. E. Myers (Ed.), *Protecting working children* (pp. 11–23). New York: UNICEF.

Oloko, B. A. (1993). Children's street work in urban Nigeria as adaptation and maladaptation to changing socio-economic circumstances. *International Journal of Behavioral Development, 16*(3), 465–482.

Oloko, O. (1985, November). *Moral, scientific and technological values in modernisation*. Paper presented at the 14th international conference of the unity of the sciences [I.C.U.S.]. Houston, TX.

Parsons, T. (1951). *The social system*. New York: The Free Press of Glencoe.

Petitto, A. L., & Ginsburg, H. P. (1982). Mental arithmetic in Africa and America: Strategies, principles and explanations. *International Journal of Psychology, 17*, 81–102.

Pittin, R. (1976). *Social status and economic opportunity in Urban Hausa Society*. Paper presented at the Conference on Nigerian Women and Development in Relation to Changing Family Structure, Ibadan, Nigeria.

Pittin, R. (1979). *Marriage and alternative strategies: Career patterns of Hausa women in Katsina City*. Unpublished doctoral dissertation, University of London.

Richman, A. L., LeVine, R. A., New, R. S. Howrigan, G. A., Welles-Nystrom, B., & LeVine, S. E. (1988). Maternal behavior to infants in five cultures. In R. A. LeVine, P. M. Miller, & M. M. West (Eds.), *Parental behavior in diverse societies* (pp. 81–93). San Francisco: Jossey Bass.

Saxe, G. B. (1990). *Culture and cognitive development: Studies in mathematical understanding*. Hillsdale, NJ: Lawrence Erlbaum Associates.

Schildkrout, E. (1981). The employment of children in Kano. In G. Rodgers & G. Standing (Eds.), *Childwork, poverty and under-development* (pp. 81–106). Geneva: ILO Office.

Simmons, E. B. (1973). The economics of consumer-oriented processing technology in Northern Nigeria. *Samaru Agricultural Newsletter, 15*(2), 65–72.

Simmons, E. B. (1975). The small-scale rural food processing industry in Northern Nigeria. *Food Research Institute Studies, 14*(2), 147–161.

Spalter-Roth, R. M. (1988). The sexual political economy of street vending in Washington, DC. In G. Clark (Ed.), *Traders versus the state, anthropological approaches to unofficial economies* (pp. 165–187). Boulder, CO: Westview.

UNICEF (1989). *Children and women in Kaduna state, Nigeria: A situation analysis*. Lagos, Nigeria: UNICEF.

Whiting, B. B. (1963). *Six cultures: Studies of child rearing*. New York: Wiley.

Whiting, B. B., & Whiting, J. W. M. (1975). *Children of six cultures: A psycho-cultural analysis*. Cambridge, MA: Harvard University Press.

Yoloye, E. A. (1971). Socio-economic background and school population: A survey of the background of children in three types of schools in the Western State of Nigeria. *Teacher Education in New Countries, 12*, 5–18.

PART

III

ASIAN ROOTS

Mutual respect for learning, for knowledge, and for each other. United States, 1993.
Photograph by Lauren Greenfield

11

INDIVIDUALISM, COLLECTIVISM, AND CHILD DEVELOPMENT: A KOREAN PERSPECTIVE

Uichol Kim
Department of Psychology,
University of Hawaii

Soo-Hyang Choi
Korean Educational Development Institute

John Locke (1690) proposed that infants are born with a *tabula rasa* (a blank tablet) in which life experiences etch their messages. Similarly, William James (1890) suggested that an infant's initial experience is "one great blooming, buzzing confusion" (cited in Zimbardo, 1988, p. 66). These statements represent the empiricist's position, which assumes that infants are born into this world totally unprepared. They learn by experience how to translate a vast array of physical stimuli into psychological perception, cognition, and emotion.

Empirical studies of child development refute this traditional viewpoint. Researchers are discovering that infants are born with more than empty slates. They are born with a well-equipped capacity to selectively attend to salient cues, to organize information into a coherent whole, and to synthesize incoming information in a systematic manner (Masters, 1981). Infants learn that the world does not operate in a chaotic fashion, but in a systematic, coherent, and meaningful manner. Infants are "pre-wired" genetically to attend, perceive, and process a selected set of incoming information, and also to impose structure on it (Masters, 1981). They learn to develop and utilize internal schemas that provide coherence and meaning to a wide variety of sensations and experiences.

Cultures similarly provide collective strategies to organize, interpret, and represent their physical and social world (Berry, 1976). For example, infants have the capacity to learn any existing language. The cultural context in which they are raised shapes the acquisition of a particular language (Segall, Dasen,

Berry, & Poortinga, 1990). Cultural learning is passed on to subsequent generations. This process is known as cultural transmission (Boyd & Richardson,
1985). There are two types of cultural transmission: enculturation and socialization. Enculturation is learning without specific teaching. By an osmosis-
like process, children acquire values and norms of a particular culture (Segall
et al., 1990). Socialization refers to a deliberate attempt to shape, coax, and
mold children's behavior so that it is socially acceptable and desirable (Segall
et al., 1990). It is the explicit transmission of appropriate values, norms, and
skills.

Both enculturation and socialization take place in different contexts (e.g.,
in the family setting and in public institutions, such as the school or the workplace). Although the content of what is taught in each environment may vary,
there is usually a close correspondence between the goals of socialization
in the family and the goals of socialization in public institutions. The goal
is to create a common viewpoint and lifestyle. When children become adults,
these socialized aspects become perceived as being supremely "natural." As
Wirth (1946) observed, "the most important thing . . . that we can know about
a person is what he takes for granted, and the most elemental and important
facts about a society are those things that are seldom debated and generally
regarded as settled" (p. xxiv).

With social change and acculturation, a rift may appear between what is
taught in the family and what is emphasized in social institutions. Children
and adolescents often become victims of incompatible demands. As a reflection of this discrepancy, some children and adolescents may display symptoms
of maladjustment and delinquency (U. Kim, 1990b).

This chapter examines the relationship between child development and
the ecocultural context. The first part of this chapter examines effects of ecology and culture on child development. The second part of this chapter over-
views social and cultural change. The third part reviews the areas of
individualism and collectivism and how these two constructs relate to child
development. The fourth part of the chapter reviews the parent–child relationship in Korean culture. The fifth section provides a comparative analysis
of Korean culture and American culture (i.e., the United States). The final
section examines the effects of acculturation on parent–child relationships.
The first three parts of this chapter are a summary and elaboration of U. Kim's
(in press) analysis.

ECOLOGY AND CULTURAL ADAPTATION

Ecology is the natural environment that humans share with other living or-
ganisms. Ecology refers to the total pattern of relationships between life forms
and their environment. Climatic and natural conditions such as temperature,

humidity, water supply, soil conditions, and terrain affect the existence of various types of vegetation and life forms, including human beings (Segall et al., 1990). Early in human history, collective units such as families, clans, and tribes developed strategies to cope with, and adapt to, their ecology.

A crucial element of survival rested on the availability of food supply (Segall et al., 1990). Food supply was largely determined by ecological conditions. Various collective responses appeared in response to ecological pressures (i.e., subsistence economies). For people living in mountainous areas, jungles, or deserts, food supply was limited. When it was depleted, they had to move to another region in search of a new food source. Hunting and gathering tribes subsisted by moving with or toward the food supply.

Some of these migratory tribes found land where soil was rich, water was abundant, and terrain was flat. These favorable conditions were utilized to develop agriculture and animal husbandry. With increased agricultural efficiency, they could depend on the food produced from the land for subsistence. They no longer needed to migrate to a new food source. Enough food could be produced from the land to ensure a steady supply of food for themselves. The development of agriculture and animal husbandry reflects another form of collective human effort to adapt to and manage their environment.

Migratory tribes who lived in jungles, mountains, and deserts needed a specific set of skills to survive in their hostile environments. Barry, Child, and Bacon (1959) found that in migratory tribes socialization practices emphasized assertiveness, autonomy, achievement, and self-reliance. As a consequence, adults in the migratory communities tended to be individualistic, assertive, and venturesome. The authors viewed these characteristics as being adaptive and functional to their ecology. On the other hand, they found that in the agricultural communities socialization practices emphasized compliance, obedience, and responsibility. As a result, adults in the agricultural communities tended to be conscientious, compliant, and conservative. These characteristics were socialized into their children because they were qualities needed to survive in their respective ecologies.

Berry (1976) similarly found that the ecological context had profound effects on subsistence culture and individual functioning (i.e., cognitive style). Cognitive style refers to a consistent mode of functioning in which individuals organize, interpret, and interact with their perceptual world (Witkin & Berry, 1975). One dimension of cognitive style is field independence/dependence; considered a bipolar dimension. The field-independent cognitive style refers to an approach that is analytical and based on standards of judgment internal to the individual. The field-dependent cognitive style refers to an approach that is more global and based on an external frame of reference. Paralleling the cognitive domain, it has been found that field-independent individuals tend to be socially independent, autonomous, and distant, whereas field-dependent individuals tend to be socially dependent, which means being more sensitive to social cues and developing closer interpersonal ties (Berry, 1976). One might intuitively expect field dependence to characterize hunters and gatherers who are responsive to their ecological settings. However, the dimension is a psychological one, which means that hunters and gatherers use internal standards to make judgments about how they should respond to environmental demands. Berry found that for subsistence economies agricultural communities tend to be field dependent, whereas hunters and gatherers tend to be field independent. These results highlight a consistent pattern of relationships between ecology, culture, family, socialization, and individual functioning.

SOCIAL AND CULTURAL CHANGE

From about the 16th century, the ecological context began to be drastically altered in Western Europe. Human beings exerted greater control over their environment and significantly altered the ecological balance. Numerous factors contributed to this change: rise of international trade, formation of a merchant class, rise of city states, rapid developments in science and technology, greater agricultural efficiency, and increased industrialization. These changes resulted in a movement away from subsistence economies (largely determined by ecology) and toward market economies (created by human interventions).

More and more human intervention mediated the ecological influences. For example, people did not have to migrate to find new food sources or till their soil to have dinner on the table. They did not have to store their food for the coming winter. They did not have to sew to have shirts on their backs. They no longer needed the neighbors' help in putting up a barn. Instead, people worked for wages. Money they earned could be used to buy necessary goods and services, or it could be deposited in a bank for future use. Money acted as an intermediary commodity that created the efficient movement of resources.

These changes drastically altered cultures and lifestyles in Western Europe. With greater agricultural efficiency, many serfs and peasants were dislocated from their agricultural communities. They congregated in the newly formed cities to look for other forms of subsistence, generally being hired by industrial factories that paid wages for their labor. The new types of work demanded new sets of skills. People could no longer rely on the skills and knowledge that had been passed down from one generation to another. Workers produced specialized goods for distribution. The work involved acquiring new skills that resulted in a rapid increase in production and in efficient distribution.

Socialization in the industrial urban centers contrasted sharply with those of agricultural communities (Tonnies, 1887/1963). In traditional agricultural communities, trust, cooperation, and conservatism were important aspects of daily life. In these communities, *social intelligence* was highly valued (to use Mundy-Castle's, 1991, term). However, in the urban setting, *technological intelligence* began to play a prominent role. In subsistence economies, the goal of socialization was survival (Tapia-Uribe, LeVine, & LeVine, chapter 2, this volume). In the newly formed urban communities, socialization emphasized cognitive and linguistic skills that were necessary to compete in market economies.

Industrial urban settings were full of unrelated strangers. The relationship a person had with an employer was contractual, rather than based on any long-standing relationship of trust and obligation. Workers simply provided their services and they received a wage for their labor. This relationship was fueled by the law of supply and demand. When demand for labor was low and supply was high, workers were underpaid, underemployed, or unemployed. Many employers exploited their employees in search of a greater profit. In these settings, there was no one to protect the rights of these unrelated individuals.

Collective action began to appear to protest the working conditions and the working relationships. A new form of collective emerged in Europe defined by class (e.g., ruling class, merchant class, working class). Members of the working class began to organize and lobby their interests through demonstrations, confrontations, and revolutions. These collective actions resulted in the institutionalization of democratic changes that are part of modern Europe and North America.

This type of collective emerged with the separation from ascribed relationships such as family, community, and clans. It meant developing a new collective based on common interests, experiences, and goals. Cultures based on this type of re-alignment have been labeled as *individualistic*. Western European countries and the United States have been found to be highly individualistic (Hofstede, 1980). Cultures that maintain familial and communal relatedness have been labeled as *collectivistic*. Countries in East Asia have been found to be collectivistic (Hofstede, 1980).

INDIVIDUALISM AND COLLECTIVISM

In an international survey of 117,000 IBM employees in 50 different countries, Hofstede (1980) found four dimensions of cultural variations. One dimension was labeled as *individualism* and *collectivism*. Countries that were highest in *individualism* were the United States, followed by Australia, Great Britain, Canada, the Netherlands, and New Zealand. On the other end of the pole, countries low on the *individualism* scale (i.e., *collectivistic*) were Venezuela, Colombia, Pakistan, Peru, Taiwan, Thailand, Hong Kong, and Korea.

According to Hofstede (1980), *individualism* emphasizes the following:

1. "I" consciousness,
2. autonomy,
3. emotional independence,
4. individual initiative,
5. right to privacy,
6. pleasure seeking,
7. financial security,
8. need for specific friendship, and
9. universalism.

On the other hand, *collectivism* stresses the following:

1. "we" consciousness,
2. collective identity,
3. emotional dependence,
4. group solidarity,
5. sharing,
6. duties and obligations,
7. need for stable and predetermined friendship,
8. group decision, and
9. particularism.

Hofstede (1991) defined *individualism* and *collectivism* as follows:

> *Individualism pertains to societies in which the ties between individuals are loose: everyone is expected to look after himself or herself and his or her immediate family. Collectivism, as its opposite, pertains to societies in which people from birth onwards are integrated into strong, cohesive ingroups, which throughout people's lifetime continue to protect them in exchange for unquestioning loyalty.* (p. 51)

In a study of cross-cultural researchers, Hui and Triandis (1986) found similar results. Within an in-group, members of collectivistic cultures are more likely than individualistic cultures to: (a) emphasize the implications of their own behavior for others, (b) share resources, (c) emphasize harmony, (d) be controlled by shame, (e) share both good and bad outcomes, and (f) feel that they are a part of their in-group's life. On the other hand, people in individualistic cultures (a) share with their immediate nuclear family, (b) are less willing to subordinate their personal goals to those of a collective, (c) are willing to confront members of their in-groups, (d) feel personally responsible for their successes and failures, and (e) experience some degree of separation and distance from their in-groups.

This bipolar categorization has been further refined and elaborated. Both individualism and collectivism exist within each culture. U. Kim (1993) provided schematic representations of three types of individualism and three types of collectivism.

Individualism emphasizes distinct, autonomous, and independent individuals. The first type of individualism is depicted in Fig. 11.1a. It is labeled as an *aggregate mode*. In this model, the individual is the basic unit of analysis and other individuals serve as cues or stimuli for the focal person. Each individual is believed to be "an entity separate from every other and from the group" (Spence, 1985, p. 1288). This belief can "lead to a sense of self with a sharp boundary that stops at one's skin and clearly demarks self from non-self" (Spence, p. 1288). Sampson (1977) used the term *self-contained individualism*, which is defined as "the combination of firmly drawn self–other

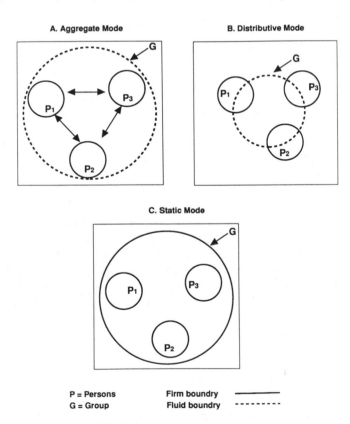

FIG. 11.1. Facets of individualism.

boundaries and an emphasis on personal control" (p. 16). It emphasizes the values of freedom, independence, self-determination, personal control, and uniqueness (Sampson, 1977). Both Spence and Sampson noted that this version of individualism is prevalent in the United States.

Empirical studies have supported the prevalence of the aggregate mode in the United States and Canada (Bellah, Madsen, Sullivan, Swindler, & Tipton, 1985; Chinese Cultural Connection, 1987; Hofstede, 1980). Bellah et al. (1985) found eight dominant themes in the content analyses of 200 interviews:

1. self-reliance, independence, and separation from family, religion, or community;
2. hedonism, utilitarianism, and an emphasis on exchanges and contracts;
3. competition, and being a distinguished person;
4. equity and fairness;
5. trust in others;
6. emphasis on competence;
7. equality and rejection of arbitrary authority; and
8. self as the only source of reality (cited in Triandis, Leung, Villareal, & Clack, 1985).

In the United States, individuals are strongly encouraged to separate from their ascribed relationships such as family, relatives, community, and religion (Bellah et al., 1985; Hsu, 1971; Maday & Szalay, 1976) and encouraged to form achieved relationships based on common interests and goals. Maturity in the United States is defined by a movement away from ascribed relationships to an aggregate mode.

The aggregate mode emphasizes principles (such as equality) and rules (such as equity) for governing individuals. Because members are independent and unrelated individuals, theoretically no one individual enjoys special privileges. Decisions are made equally based on majority approval. Resources are shared equitably based on merit and performance. Individuals are "democratically" elected to represent the group, arbitrate grievances, oversee the fair distribution of resources, and implement policy and programs on behalf of the group. The core values and functions are deeply embedded and are abstracted from reality. Individuals who share these implicit values, goals, and aspirations define the boundary of a group. The core values are rarely discussed because they are usually accepted and never questioned. They are accepted as being "natural" and "universal" because they are not linked to a particular person or context.

When a group is explicitly defined, it constitutes a *distributive mode*, to paraphrase Harré's (1984) term (see Fig. 11.1b, Diagram B). It can be described as a group that "arises by each member having some similar attributes to every other" (Harré, 1984, p. 930). The boundary is defined by commonality and fluidity. Voluntary organizations, interest groups, and recreational clubs are examples of this type of collective. Because the form and degree of participation is voluntary, permanent loyalty is not demanded from each member. The collective persists if it satisfies the needs and interests of its members. It dissolves when it fails to do so.

Another form of a distributive mode is defined by a contract. For example, a contract defines a relationship between professionals (who provide services) and clients (who pay a fee for the services). Doctors, lawyers, accountants, teachers, counselors, and professors provide specialized services to anyone in need of those services. Similarly, labor and management represent collective entities in which the relationship is defined by a contract. In this type of a collective, an individual or a group (as in the case of the union) is seen as a basic unit that is capable of interacting with, and benefiting from, the group.

Figure 11.1, Diagram C, depicts the third version of individualism: the static mode. In the United States, the government exists to protect freedom and uphold justice for all self-contained individuals. Because individuals are unrelated to one another, they may not always act in a responsible, moral, sane, and altruistic manner. In fact, they may exploit or commit crimes against one another and against society. Laws and regulations are established to protect the rights of all citizens and the viability of public institutions. No one person can step beyond the boundaries of the static mode. If they do so, these individuals are identified, punished, and often incarcerated. The legal system, correctional system, military, and the internal revenue service are examples of the static mode. Everyone in a culture is bound by these laws, and theoretically no one enjoys special privileges.

Figure 11.2 provides a schematic representation of the three types of collectivism. In these diagrams, collectivities are presented as a unit—an entity. A collective unit is considered more than a mere sum of individuals. An undifferentiated mode is depicted in Fig. 11.2a. The current research on collectivism is representative of this perspective (e.g., Hofstede, 1980; Hui & Triandis, 1986; Triandis, 1988; Triandis et al., 1985). Triandis (1988) described collectivism as putting greater emphasis on:

1. the needs and goals of the in-group rather than on the individual,
2. social norms and duties rather than on individual pleasures,
3. beliefs and values that are shared by the in-group members rather than those that distinguish individual members, and
4. readiness to cooperate with the in-group members rather than competing with them.

The undifferentiated mode emphasizes a firm and distinct collective unit and relatively loosely defined individuals.

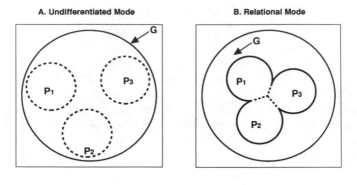

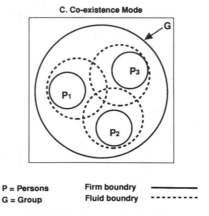

FIG. 11.2.   Facets of collectivism.

Kashima (1990) articulated the need to distinguish two types of collectivism: substantive and relational. The substantive model focuses on the characteristics of a collective unit (i.e., the undifferentiated mode). The relational model emphasizes the internal characteristics of a collective (i.e., the relational mode). Figure 11.2, Diagram B, depicts the relational mode, which focuses on the relatedness of individual members. The relational orientation has been discussed by numerous researchers (Azuma, 1986; Doi, 1981, 1985; Ho, 1982; Kagitcibasi, 1987). The relational orientation focuses on constructs of *amae* ("interdependence"; Doi, 1981), empathy, and naturalism (Lebra, chapter 12, this volume). It is elaborated in the next section.

In India, a different form of group is found. Sinha and Tripathi (in press) provided the co-existence mode where diverse elements, including contradictory elements, co-exist within a culture and within a person (see Fig. 11.2, Diagram C). He noted that collectivist values such as family loyalty and interdependence co-exist along side of individualistic values such as self-cultivation and personal endeavor. Co-existence does not imply dissonance in the Indian culture. It appears in all facets of Indian culture: in childrearing practices, in interpersonal relationships, in intergroup relations, and in public institutions. The co-existence mode was empirically verified in series of studies in India (Mishra, in press; Sinha, in press; Sinha & Verma, 1987).

Doi (1985) noted that in the Japanese culture there are two sides to virtually all social phenomena. He used the distinction between *omote* ("face") and *ura* ("mind, heart, and soul"), *soto* ("outside") and *uchi* ("inside") (Azuma, chapter 13, this volume), and *tatemae* ("principles, rules, and conventions") and *honne* ("true intentions, or the inner self"). Within the psychological space, these contrasting elements co-exist as two contiguous principles (Doi, 1985). Lebra (chapter 12) describes such differentiations as "social zoning."

At the cultural level, *tatemae* represents the official ideology and *honne* reflects the indigenous perspective, often hidden to outside observers (Azuma, 1986). *Tatemae* is reflected in the official ideology of Confucianism, which emphasizes patriarchical lineage (see Ho, chapter 14, this volume). The father–son relationship is considered to be the most important dyad (Azuma, 1986; Hsu, 1971), and it serves as a prototype for other formal relationships (e.g., master–servant, teacher–student, husband–wife, elder–younger, superordinate–subordinate). These relationships required benevolence, authority, responsibility, and wisdom from superordinates and loyalty, obedience, and dedication from subordinates. Roles and obligations are socially prescribed and each individual is expected to fulfill them. Hsu suggested that in China and Japan the father–son relationship occupies a dominant position and the mother–son dyad occupies a subdominant position. However, Azuma suggested that this view represents *tatemae* and not *honne*.

Although the father is the symbolic head of the family, in reality he is in the periphery (Befu, 1986). The husband becomes dependent on his wife and is considered "more burdensome and harder to control than other children" (Azuma, 1986, p. 8). Azuma noted that "according to *tatemae*, the father is the head of the household, but according to *honne*, he is psychologically dependent" (p. 8). Within a family, the most important relationship is the mother–child *amae* relationship. Outside of home (*soto*), women occupy subjugated positions with very few individual rights and little power. Inside one's home (*uchi*), women, as mothers, hold stable and powerful positions. Azuma noted that: "in many families the position of the father is peripheral. The formal head of the family, he is accorded respect. However, this respect is symbolic; in reality he does not exert much control" (p. 8).

SOCIALIZATION AND KOREAN CULTURE

Traditional Korean cosmology emphasized a triarchic balance among nature, spirits, and humans. With the adoption of Confucianism, the emphasis on human relationships became dominant (Han, 1974). Within the Confucian philosophy, human relationships occupy the central place (Chung, 1970). D. S. Lee (1980) noted that Korean culture can be viewed as a "relationship culture." The fundamental principle for governing relationships among individuals, family, society, world, and beyond is best articulated in the writing of Confucius, entitled "Righteousness in the Heart." He stated:

> *If there be righteousness in the heart,*
> *   there will be beauty in character,*
> *If there be beauty in character,*
> *   there will be harmony in the home.*
> *If there be harmony in the home,*
> *   there will be order in the nation.*
> *If there be order in the nation,*
> *   there will be peace in the world.*
>   (From the "Great Learning," adapted from J. Legge's translation, 1960, pp. 358–359)

Confucius did not consider individuals as independent entities. They are linked to others in a web of interrelatedness. Family is considered as the prototype for all relationships (King & Bond, 1985; S. W. Lee, 1990). S. W. Lee noted that "according to Confucianism, social relations are nothing more than an expansion of this family relationship" (p. 2). Confucianism viewed father–son relationship, based on hierarchy central to all relationships. This represents the official ideology (i.e., *tatemae*), but the father is only a symbolic head. It is the mother who cultivates the relational mode (i.e., *honne*) who is the central person in a child's life.

The relational mode is the most important and prototypical unit of analysis in Korean culture. It emphasizes a sense of relatedness. It is depicted by a porous boundary between persons that allows thoughts, ideas, and emotions to flow freely without any impediments (see Fig. 11.2b, Diagram B). It emphasizes oneness and bonding of persons. Its qualities have been discussed through the concepts of *amae* (Doi, 1981) and *omoiyari* ("empathy"; Lebra, chapter 12, this volume) in Japanese culture. It is highlighted by the following analysis of four key concepts in Korean culture: *t'aekyo, maternal dew, uri,* and *chong.*

T'aekyo: A Traditional Form of Prenatal Care

According to Yu (1984), there were two important concepts emphasizing a mother's relatedness to her child: *t'aekyo* (the traditional form of prenatal care) and maternal dew (an indigenous concept of a mother's intrinsic love for her child). *T'aekyo* contained explicit guidelines outlining dos and do nots for pregnant women.[1] These prescriptions were based on the belief that a mother's experience during her pregnancy would directly affect the baby inside her womb and leave long-lasting imprints on the child.

In the book entitled *T'aekyo Sin Ki*, it was stated that "In life, one's temper is innate, but personality is learned. Thus, it is the parents' responsibility to culture the child's personality in a correct manner. . . . In teaching a child, the first ten months in the mother's womb are more important than the ten years later in school" (Yu, 1984, p. 35).

These prescriptive guidelines help prevent infantile death in traditional Korean society. These recommended prohibitive behaviors, such as resenting, swearing, or getting angry, are found to have positive benefits, such as reducing stressful effects on the body system of expectant mothers and the fetus (T. C. Kim, 1972). Beyond the medical benefits, the psychological intent of *t'aekyo* is to cultivate a keen sense of relatedness with the unborn child.

T'aekyo articulates in great detail the need to adopt the perspective of the child inside the womb. The mother must become a part of the unborn child if she is to successfully adhere to the prescriptive guidelines. For instance, when a mother eats something, she must presume that it is the unborn child who is consuming the food.[2] When a mother makes a move, it must be imagined that the child in her womb is the agent of the movement.[3] Unless a mother psychologically synchronizes herself with the unborn child, she cannot possibly hope to observe all the rules stipulated by *t'aekyo*. Within *t'aekyo*, a mother believes that every aspect of her experience during her pregnancy affects the unborn child. A mother ensures that she experiences pleasant events and sees things that are precious, noble, and beautiful (such

---

[1]Prohibited behaviors included: harming other people, harboring an intention to kill living things, cheating, envying, stealing, resenting, swearing, getting angry, gesturing (with fingers) when speaking, showing gums (when speaking or laughing), teasing, reprimanding (the subjects), reprimanding animals, slandering, whispering, spreading rumor (or stories), being talkative, peeping through a hole, squinting, pouting, scoffing, kicking, or pointing.

[2]Prohibited foods are: fruits in crooked shapes or rotten, fresh vegetables (for fear of parasites), cold dishes, food with a bad smell, unripened produce, produce out of season, meat, crayfish, horse meat, fish with no scales (might lead to miscarriage), garlic (might digest umbilical cord), buckwheat noodle (might cut umbilical cord), peach, dog meat (might make the baby dumb), lamb liver (might invite mishaps), chicken meat or eggs eaten with glutinous rice (might give parasites to the baby), duck meat, sparrow meat, crab, ginger, food served at funeral or ancestral worship, liquor, burnt food, incompletely cooked rice, chicken feet, and eyes of animal or fish.

[3]Prohibited behaviors are: sharing a bed with one's husband, dressing too warmly, eating too much, sleeping too much, sitting on a cold or dirty seat, smelling bad odors, climbing high places, going out at night or when it rains or snows, going to mountains, going near a well, entering an old shrine, passing by dangerous places, lifting heavy things, pushing anything too hard, receiving acupuncture indiscreetly, rearing silkworms, pricking fingers with a needle, cutting living things, sitting crookedly, taking things from a high place, picking up things from the ground when standing, looking back over one's shoulders, washing hair in the last month, running in haste, lying on one's stomach, leaving the door open, and many others.

as white jade or a peacock). She avoids coming in contact with hideous, un-
pleasant, and ominous creatures and objects.

The rigors of *t'aekyo* lead a mother to become keenly aware of the unique
psychological and biological bonds she has with her unborn child. A mother
observing *t'aekyo* is constantly reminded of her role as surrogate *umwelt* for
her child. As the unborn child grows in her womb, so does the relational
bond between her and the child. By the time the baby is actually in her arms,
she has already developed a potent sense of relatedness to her child.

Maternal Dews: The Psychological Nutrient

According to A. C. Yu (1981, 1984, 1985), mothers in traditional Korean society had a belief that children need more than just their milk: They also need
symbolic "dews" coming down from a mother. The exact nature of the maternal dews is not clear. It is interpreted as a symbolic representation of the
intrinsic bond between mothers and children. From a psychological viewpoint, the concept of maternal dews reflects a mother's unfaltering belief in
the unseen but powerful bond between a mother and her child.

A child's psychological and physical well-being are considered the prime
responsibility of the mother. She needs to remain close to the child and in-
dulge the child with this essential psychological nutrient—the maternal dews.
In traditional society, if a child had to sleep in a separate room away from
the mother, the mother would leave the door open to clear a "passage" that
would allow her dews to travel to her child. When adopting a child, people
calculated the physical distance between the residence of the biological
mother and the adopting family. A preference was given to a child whose
biological mother lived in close proximity (i.e., within the reach of the maternal dews).

Maternal dews are perceived to have special healing powers. When an
infant came down with jaundice, a mother used to wash the infant with water
with which she washed herself. A mother's spittle was the first aid to a child's
cut or scrape wound. A mother's hair was often used to remove a child's warts.
When a baby developed a rash, a mother's skirt became a huge "bandage"
for the child. People believed that when the child was asleep in the skirt,
the rash would disappear.

The Present Situation

Although social change has significantly altered the social ecology of Korea,
the core concepts sustaining the Korean family system have not changed significantly in recent years (J. S. Choi, 1987). External features such as status
distinction, hierarchical relationship, filial piety, maternal and paternal

sacrifice, and devotion are still the major tenets of the Korean family system. The internal features such as emotional and relational intimacy between parents and children still remain strong. They are considered binding forces in a family. The traditional and the modern mother–child relationship share two common features: leniency and devotion. A number of studies have reported that Korean mothers are very lenient and indulgent toward their children (J. E. Kim, 1981; Lee & Lee, 1987; S. K. Yu, 1985).

Indulgence

The weaning program often does not come up until the age of 3 or 4 (Lee & Lee, 1987). Children are not forced to eat by themselves until the age of 3. Even at this age, if children do not show any intention to do so they are not pressured. Lee and Lee found that a majority of mothers wait until a child spontaneously comes to acquire that skill.

Bedtime is another area wherein Korean mothers appear to be highly flexible. Regardless of their educational backgrounds, Korean mothers do not specify exact sleeping hours (Lee & Lee, 1987). A similar observation is made in regards to toilet training. When and how to introduce this basic task is of little importance to Korean mothers. It is when a mother perceives a child's need, through nonverbal channels such as facial expressions or body movement, that she takes the child to the toilet. These practices closely parallel the belief of naturalism in Japan (Lebra, chapter 12, this volume).

J. E. Kim (1981) similarly found that Korean mothers are not discipline oriented. They are often inconsistent in their socialization methods: Sometimes they appear to be authoritarian, and other times they appear to be democratic. A behavior often prohibited at one point is unchecked at another point. Situational whims, rather than any particular principle of the mothers, have been described as the norm (J. E. Kim, 1981).

There are several possible explanations for this observed inconsistency. A lack of a particular socialization orientation of the mothers could be the cause. Second, it is possible that mothers possess a specific socialization orientation but they are not able to practice it. The most likely possibility is that mothers are psychologically enmeshed with their children. They do not see their children as objects of discipline; they have a clear empathic understanding of them. Ho (1986) offered a similar interpretation in Chinese socialization:

> The reason for leniency toward the younger child is that he or she is considered to be not yet capable of "understanding things," and therefore should not be held responsible for his or her wrongdoings. . . . It is thought that training cannot be expected to accomplish much for infants or young children; they are viewed as passive dependent creatures who are to be cared for, and whose needs are to be met with little delay or interference. (p. 4)

The other side of this lenient socialization process is the role of the mothers as major caregivers because their young children are viewed incapable of taking care of themselves. A Korean mother's significant maternal role, however, does not necessarily imply greater maternal sensitivity to the needs of an individual child.

Devotion

In an ethnographic study done by S. H. Choi (1990), an interesting cross-cultural difference between Korean mothers and Canadian mothers was found in their maternal attitudes. Whereas Korean mothers place a greater weight on their role as caregivers, Canadian mothers assign equal emphasis on their role as caregivers and on their own personal development. Korean mothers feel little or no conflict in sacrificing their careers to devote themselves to their children. In contrast, Canadian mothers indicate their dual perception (as autonomous individuals and as caring mothers). Although they recognize their devotion as mothers, they feel personal career development to be equally important. Although they are very much satisfied with their role as mothers, they have regrets about the curtailment of their career development. They hope to resume their personal development once their children are self-reliant.

Similar conflicts arise for Korean women (Lee & Kim, 1979). However, Korean mothers view unselfish devotion as a critical feature of their personhood and motherhood (J. E. Kim, 1981). For many Korean women, their motherhood is their single most important role. A Korean mother's personhood is not deserted but fused with that of her children. It is not a case of self-denial but of self-transformation. Becoming one with their children, Korean mothers are not self-interested persons pursuing their own independent goals. They become closely and intrinsically attached to their children.

In the relational context, Korean mothers see their children as extensions of themselves. Children's accomplishments become their own. Children vicariously fulfill their unaccomplished dreams and goals. For Korean mothers, attaining this vicarious gratification is one of the most important aspects of motherhood. It is the most valued meaning that Korean mothers have in raising their children (Gallup, 1985). Similarly, when a child misbehaves or fails, a mother is often held responsible for the outcome (S. H. Choi, 1990).

The relational orientation of Korean mothers is best evidenced by their persistent and enduring support for their children throughout their lives. In a cross-national comparison with the United States, England, Germany, France, and Japan, Korean parents are second only to Japanese parents in the amount they contribute financially to their children's college education (Gallup, 1983). In terms of eagerness or willingness to pay for their children's college education, Korean parents exceed all the other nations. Korean parents are also at the top in their willingness to pay off their children's debts and in paying for their children's wedding expenses (Gallup, 1983).

Support and caring are not unilateral processes. As children mature, they need to reciprocate the unconditional support provided for them. Table 11.1 lists the obligations that children must fulfill to their parents.

TABLE 11.1
Duties of Children Toward Their Parents

Duties	Examples
1. Obeying: Children must respect their parents' opinions and authority. This respect must be expressed through their daily behavior.	Example 1: Children must consult with their parents and seek agreement or permission from them in making decisions. If parents do not approve the decisions, children must stop insisting on their own ideas (*Kuk-mong-yo-keul*). Example 2: When called, children must immediately answer. If their mouths are full, they must empty their mouths first and then answer (*Myong-Shin-Bo-Kam*).
2. Attending: Children must take care of their parents' every need.	Example 1: When parents are ill, attending to their illnesses must be given priority by children (*Kuk-mong-yo-keul*). Example 2: Children must take care of their parents' bedding before and after their sleep (*Yi-Ki*). Example 3: Parents must be kept warm in winter and cool in summer, and laid down at night (for sleep) and greeted with "good morning" at dawn (*So-hak*). Example 4: Children must constantly check if their parents are in need of anything (*So-hak*).
3. Supporting: Related to the attending category, teaching emphasizes more materialistic comforts for parents.	Example 1: Children must make sure that parents are comfortably housed, fed, and dressed (*Dong-Mon-Seun-Sup*).
4. Comforting: Whereas Categories 2 and 3 are concerned with physical comfort, Category 4 focuses more on creating psychological ease and entertainment, by not worrying them.	Example 1: Children must let their parents know their coming in, going out, and whereabouts (*Myong-shim-bo-kam*). Example 2: Children must be careful not to expose themselves to danger (*Yi-ki*).
5. Honoring: Even after their parents pass away, children are encouraged to honor their parents' achievements, fulfill their intentions, complete their undertakings, and sustain their social networks.	Example 1: Children must restrain themselves from dietary and sexual pleasure for 3 years after their parents' death (*So-hak*). Example 2: In extreme cases, even the concubine of a father must be taken good care of by the children after their father's death (*So-hak*).

Communication Patterns

The indulgence orientation of Korean mothers provides a pattern of communication with their children that is different from that of Canadian mothers
(S. H. Choi, 1985, 1990). In Korea, a mother speaks *for* the child, on behalf
of the child, rather than *to* the child. S. H. Choi (1990) has found that Korean
mothers' questions do not usually seek information from children, but they
prompt the children to confirm what they have already presented to them.
All the children have to do is to express whether they agree with their
mothers' perceptions. From the children's perspective, the world is put forward to them by their mothers. Children are not encouraged to assert their
own ideas. Even if children's ideas are creatively presented, they are often
not appreciated.

S. H. Choi (1990) found that, compared with Canadian mothers, Korean
mothers produce utterances that are not thematically related to the children's
earlier utterances. In terms of communicative responsiveness, Korean mothers
fall behind Canadian mothers. Korean mothers show greater initiative and
spontaneous patterns of interaction, which are often not necessarily coordinated with the children's prior attempts.

Korean mothers do not dissociate themselves from their children's reality. Children are not perceived as separate beings to deal with, to discipline,
or to converse with rationally. The leniency of Korean mothers reflects the
strong sense of relatedness to them. Being related, mothers are very much
aware of their children's reality. Because of this peculiar psychosocial topog-
raphy, Korean mothers cannot help thinking, behaving, or feeling from their
children's perspective.

Father–Child Relationship

Devotion is an important element in both the mother–child and father–child
relationships. In a mother–child relationship, it is complemented with indulgence. A mother shows her devotion to her child through indulgence (i.e.,
it flows downward, from a mother to a child). In a father–child relationship,
devotion is complemented with strictness. Children display their devotion
to their fathers through obedience, respect, and compliance (i.e., it flows upward, from a child to a father). Thus, the roles that fathers and mothers play
are both different and complementary. The contrast is best summarized in
a popular Korean phrase, *om bu ja mo* (translated literally it means "strict
father, benevolent mother"; Rohner & Pettengill, 1985).

Although a father's role is only symbolic in a family, he represents a
link between the family and the outer world. Through the father, children
are linked across time (i.e., through his lineage) and across space (i.e., through

his position in a community). It is his responsibility to maintain, propagate, and elevate the position of the family. When making a decision, he must simultaneously consider implications of such a decision on a particular individual (e.g., a child), on the family, on the lineage, and on the community. Thus, wisdom and foresight are seen as essential ingredients of his decision-making process. Children are considered not capable of understanding such a complex process, and thus they are required to obey, respect, and abide by their fathers' decision. From children's perspective, it often means sacrificing personal interests for the benefit of the family. The difference between the role of a father and a mother is further described by Lebra's (chapter 12, this volume) articulation of *boundary socialization* in Japan.

INDIVIDUALISM AND COLLECTIVISM:
A COMPARISON BETWEEN KOREA
AND THE UNITED STATES

Maday and Szalay (1976) empirically verified the importance of family relations in Korean culture and the self in the United States. They conducted an empirical study to examine the psychological connotations of "me" with a sample of Korean and American respondents. The results support the claim that Koreans emphasize the relational mode and that Americans stress the aggregate mode. The four most important categories for Korean responses to "me" in descending order are:

1. family, love;
2. ideals, happiness, freedom;
3. hope, ambition, success; and
4. money, materials, and goods (Maday & Szalay, 1976).

The four most frequent themes for U.S. respondents in descending order are:

1. I, person, individual
2. other people;
3. tired, lonely, physical appearance; and
4. good, friendly, sociable (Maday & Szalay, 1976).

Maday and Szalay noted that the American conception of "me" focuses on the individuated self. Americans are detached from their family members and are surrounded by strangers. There is an emphasis on negative emotions such as "tired" and "lonely," rather than on the positive emotions found in the Korean sample such as "happiness, hope, and ambition." They commented that Koreans and Americans relate to a different set of significant others. For Koreans, the family occupies the central place. Individual members are contributors to a family's happiness and material success. On the other hand, Americans need to prove their worth to strangers. Thus, appearance, friendliness, and sociable behavior are emphasized.

Two Korean concepts of relatedness, *uri* ("we") and *chong* ("affection"), were investigated by Choi, Kim, and Choi (1993). *Uri* in Korean denotes an inclusive group: we or us. It is a word used to denote a group of people (such as "our family"), an entity (such as "our nation"), and even possessions (such as "our house"). It is most often used to denote a group of people.

Open-ended questions were given to a sample of Koreans in Korea and Euro-Canadian students. They were asked to write down psychological connotations of "we" in Canada and *uri* in Korea. In the Korean sample, the word *uri* elicited three major themes: positive affect (especially *chong*), oneness or wholeness, and the priority of the group over the individual. For the Korean sample, the group took precedence over the individual members. The affective bond, *chong*, was the key that united members of a group into a coherent whole. The Korean responses indicated that the dominant form of the primary group in Korea is the relational mode followed by the undifferentiated mode.

The Canadian responses indicated that the majority of the respondents view a group as an aggregate mode, a form of individualism diagrammed in Fig. 11.1. A group is typically viewed as an aggregate of plural individuals around the focal person "I." The distributive model also emerged as another common theme of "we." Respondents emphasized the cognitive awareness of similarity shared by the members of the group. A group is often united by common interests or hobbies.

Chong is the affective bond that unites and integrates in-group members together in Korean culture. *Chong* is not directly acquired. Through an osmosis-like process, it circulates among the members to bind them together. For this reason, the relational mode emphasizes a porous boundary between members of a group. The porous boundary allows *chong* to flow naturally without any impediments.

The results of an open-ended questionnaire indicated that *chong* arises from a closely knit family and friends who spend a long time together (S. C. Choi et al., 1993). Characteristics that are associated with *chong* are: unconditionality, sacrifice, empathy, care, sincerity, and shared experience. *Chong* does not develop in a contractual, commercial, and rational relationship. Someone without *chong* is described as being conditional, uncaring, selfish, cool, hypocritical, apathetic, rational, and logical. He or she is also an individual who is self-reliant, independent, and autonomous.

The Korean mother–child relationship is the epitome of *chong*. *Mo chong* is translated as a mother's (*mo*) love or affection (*chong*) for her children. It is associated with maternal wholeheartedness and broadmindedness. It is more than a mother's deep love and generosity. It goes beyond rationality. For instance, when a child's faults and flaws are found, a mother tries to accept, embrace, forbear, or even overlook them. In a rational mode, a mother tries to teach her children to learn from their mistakes and to prevent the same behavior from being repeated in the future. She critically appraises situations with the children and explains the proper behavior. The rational approach can be considered more constructive and desirable in some ways. However, it does not represent a relationship based on *chong*. In such a relationship, a mother tries to understand from the child's perspective and empathically relate her disappointments. The emotional arousal can be a powerful force that shapes a child's behavior. Similar observations are made in the Japanese mother–child relationship (Doi, 1981; Lebra, chapter 12, this volume).

Rohner and Pettengill (1985) found similar contrasts when they compared parent–child relationships in the United States and in Korea. In the United States, strict parental control (along the dimension of strictness–permissiveness) is perceived by adolescents as a manifestation of parental hostility, aggression, distrust, and overall rejection. This view is consistent with the fact that American parents, by and large, encourage independence and self-reliance. Rohner and Pettengill noted that for the American sample "parental strictness infringes upon the youths' sense of their right to be autonomous and self-directing" (p. 527). Parental strictness is exerted when adolescents behave in an inappropriate or disruptive manner. In the United States, parental strictness is antithetical to a warm and harmonious parent–child relationship.

In Korea, however, the results were reversed. Korean adolescents view parental strictness as an indication of parental warmth and low neglect. This result is consistent with the fact that in a relational mode parental involvement is an essential ingredient. Parental involvement is necessary to ensure the success of children. Parental strictness is not viewed as control but as an essential component necessary for academic, economic, and social success.

ACCULTURATION

Acculturation is defined as culture change that results from continuous first-hand contact between two distinct cultural groups (Redfield, Linton, & Herskovits, 1936). It is differentiated from social change, which is more gradual, diffuse, and mediated. For Koreans living in Korea, exposure to Western influences are mediated by their own cultural filters and frame of reference.

For Korean immigrants moving to North America,[4] this frame of reference is shifted to the host society. The host society (i.e., Canada or the United States) defines the context of acculturation by setting up limitations, boundaries, goals, and the endpoint of acculturation. It provides a norm of what is accepted, tolerated, and encouraged. Members of the acculturating groups can adjust, adapt, reject, or change the given context (U. Kim, 1990a).

During the process of acculturation, individuals may experience five types of changes: physical, biological, cultural, social, and psychological (Berry, Kim, Minde, & Mok, 1987). First, physical changes may occur, such as a new place to live, new housing, and new climate. Second, biological changes may occur, such as new nutrition, new disease, and interracial marriages. Third, cultural changes may occur, with the original political, economic, religious, social, institutional and linguistic systems becoming replaced. Fourth, a new set of social relationships may be formed based on a reclassification of in-group and out-group (e.g., based on race or ethnicity). Finally, psychological changes may occur, including shifts in attitude, values, behaviors, and lifestyles. The type and degree of changes that individuals experience depend largely on the characteristics of the two cultures in contact.

Koreans are relatively recent immigrants to North America. A vast majority of Korean immigrants (over 90%) came after the Immigration Reform Act of 1965 (Arnold, Minocha, & Fawcett, 1987; U. Kim, 1984). Korean immigrants tend to be young and well educated, with professional-managerial backgrounds prior to emigration, and they are often accompanied by young children or have children in their host country (Barringer & Cho, 1989; Hurh & Kim, 1984; U. Kim, 1984, 1988).

In an acculturation study of Korean immigrants to Canada, U. Kim (1988) examined five major areas of adaptational difficulties corresponding to the five types of changes that they may experience. They reported having greatest difficulties adapting to cultural differences (i.e., communication problems, self-centeredness of people, emphasis on materialism, and lack of knowledge of Canadian society) and overcoming institutional barriers (lack of social foundation, finding an appropriate occupation, and lack of recognition in Canada for Korean job experience and education). The second set of problems dealt with a lack of social support (e.g., not having someone to confide in and not having close friends). The third set of problems focused on psychological feelings of loneliness, nostalgia, and powerlessness. Adapting to physical changes (e.g., differences in weather) and biological changes (e.g., differences in food) were not considered to be problematic.

There is a common strand underlying these adaptational difficulties of Korean immigrants: the transition from the relational mode to the aggregate

---

[4]*Koreans* refers to these people emigrating from South Korea. *North America* is used to denote Canada and the United States.

mode. As discussed earlier, children raised in North America are socialized in the aggregate mode model. In Korea, however, the relational mode is instilled at an early age. As mature adults emigrating to North America, Koreans report having difficulties shifting their frame of reference from the relational mode to the aggregate mode (U. Kim, 1988). This dilemma is best depicted in parent–child relationships.

For Korean immigrants living in North America, one of the most significant challenges is the maintenance of a harmonious parent–child relationship. This challenge stems from three critical factors: cultural differences between Korea and the United States and Canada (as described earlier), a differential rate of assimilation for parents and children, and change in occupational status. As described earlier, when Koreans emigrate to North America, they report having significant difficulties adapting to cultural and social changes. Children who are born in North America or who came at an early age (i.e., before the age of 10) adapt more easily and quickly than their parents (U. Kim, 1984). In a study conducted by U. Kim, adults who came to Canada after the age of 20 reported significant difficulties learning English and participating in Canadian society. Participating in Korean organizations and maintaining Korean language were not considered to be problems for them. On the other hand, Korean children and adolescents became fluent in English within several years and were able to participate actively in Canadian society. However, they reported difficulties in maintaining Korean language fluency. As a result, children and adolescents are influenced by two cultures: Korean culture in the home environment propagated by their parents, and Canadian culture outside of their home environment.

Korean-Canadian and Korean-American children and adolescents adopt individualistic values relatively quickly. They accept a view of the parent–child relationship that is consistent with Canadian and American culture, which encourages independence, autonomy, and self-reliance. On the other hand, their parents maintain a traditional collectivistic orientation that emphasizes a strong sense of relatedness, devotion, and interdependence. This difference becomes the basis of parent–child conflicts (Pettengill & Rohner, 1985).

The second major change is a shift in occupational status. Although many Korean immigrants come to North America with college degrees and professional backgrounds, these qualifications are often not recognized. Moreover, poor proficiency in English limits their ability to land attractive jobs (U. Kim, 1988). Due to these structural and linguistic barriers, many Korean immigrants turn to labor-intensive small businesses for livelihood, such as grocery stores, dry cleaners, fast-food restaurants, and garment manufacturing (Bonacich, 1973; U. Kim, 1988). According to the 1980 U.S. Census, Korean immigrant males report more than three times the national average in self-employment (24% vs. 7%, respectively; Shin & Han, 1990).

These small businesses require members of a family, especially wives, to become full-time participants in the business. Prior to immigration, most Korean wives stayed home with their children. After immigration, for the first time in their lives they spend a large portion of their time outside of their homes working in the family businesses. As a consequence, they have difficulties providing unconditional support for their children and maintaining the relational mode.

Pettengill and Rohner (1985) further explored the nature of the parent–child relationship with a sample of Korean-American respondents. They found that, like other Americans and unlike Koreans, Korean-American adolescents perceive parental strictness as a sign of hostility, aggression, distrust, and overall rejection. In addition, parental strictness was correlated with conflicts they experienced with their parents.

U. Kim (1992) conducted a series of studies to further explore the parent–child relationship with Korean, Korean-Canadian, and Korean-American samples. Two samples were collected from Korea: Grade 9 students from a working-class community ($n = 259$) and Grade 12 students from a middle-class community ($n = 269$). In Toronto, Canada, a sample was obtained from various Korean community churches ($n = 86$). In Hawaii, a sample was obtained from a Korean language school ($n = 31$).

In all samples, the Parental Acceptance-Rejection Questionnaire (measuring the dimensions of parental warmth, hostility, neglect, and rejection) and the Parental Control Questionnaire (measuring parental strictness; Rohner, 1984) were administered. In addition, Korean Values Survey (an adapted version of the Chinese Value Survey; Chinese Cultural Connection, 1987) was administered to the two Korean samples and the Korean-Canadian sample. In the Hawaii sample, the 25-item Conflict Questionnaire (an adapted version of Pettengill & Rohner's, 1985, scale) was also administered. The Conflict Questionnaire assessed the degree to which Korean-American adolescents experienced conflicts with their parents in their personal, social, and cultural lives. In addition, a 13-item Knowledge Questionnaire (from U. Kim, 1988) was administered. It assessed perceived parental knowledge of various aspects of the United States, such as history, geography, politics, business, and finance.

Across four samples, sample means did not differ on dimensions of parental control, rejection, neglect, and hostility. The two acculturating samples (Korean Canadians and Korean Americans) scored slightly higher on the perceived parental warmth dimensions than their Korean counterparts. The overall correlational results replicated Rohner and Pettengill's (1985) and Pettengill and Rohner's (1985) pattern of results. In the two Korean samples, parental control was correlated with high parental warmth and low neglect, and slightly with parental hostility and rejection (see Fig. 11.3. Only statistically significant results are depicted in the figure. None of the correlations was significant for fathers in the Korean-American sample). The reverse pattern was observed for the two acculturating samples. For the Korean-Canadian and

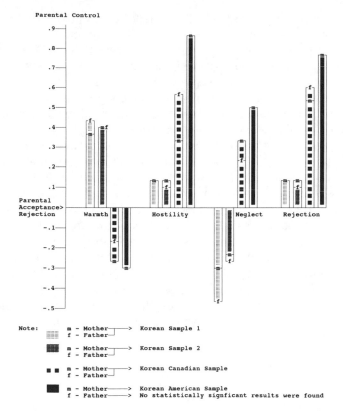

FIG. 11.3. Correlations between parental acceptance–rejection and parental control.

Korean-American samples, parental strictness was correlated with low warmth and high hostility, neglect, and rejection. Because of altered family conditions (less involvement of the mother) and altered societal contexts (the individualistic value of independence), parental control, a positive feature of the parent–child relationship in Korea, turned into a negative for the adolescent children of Korean immigrants to the United States and Canada. In this way, an individualistic societal context can rob a collectivistic childrearing practice of its psychological adaptiveness.

Results from the Korean Values Questionnaire provide support that Korean cultural values are mediating factors that affect perceived parent–child relationships. The three subscales (Internal Striving, Interpersonal Harmony, Social Order) correlated with high parental warmth and with low hostility, neglect, and rejection for both the Korean samples and the Korean-Canadian sample. Those adolescents, both Koreans and Korean Canadians, who identified with Korean values viewed their parents as more accepting, and less hostile, neglecting, and rejecting.

In the Korean-American sample, those adolescents who reported experiencing greater conflicts (as measured by Conflict Questionnaire) with their mothers perceived them to be more hostile, neglecting, and rejecting. Second, those adolescents who perceived their parents to be less knowledgeable about the United States also perceived them to be more hostile, neglecting, and rejecting. Third, those adolescents who identified themselves as Americans (rather than Korean Americans or Koreans) perceived their fathers as being more hostile, neglecting, and rejecting.

The overall pattern of results reveals the tension between Korean parents and adolescents living in North America. First, although parental control was perceived as parental acceptance in the Korean samples, it was perceived as parental rejection in the two acculturating samples. Second, perceived parental control was correlated positively to conflicts that adolescents experience with their parents in the Korean-American sample. Third, those parents who were believed to know less about the United States were perceived as more rejecting. Fourth, assimilated Korean Americans perceived their fathers as more rejecting. This pattern of results suggests that the acculturation process challenges cultural values at their core: how one thinks about self and relates to others. Acculturation disrupts the relational orientation of Koreans, which could lead to familial, social, and cultural disintegration (U. Kim, 1988).

CONCLUSION AND IMPLICATIONS

The goal of this volume is to examine the cognitive socialization of children living in culturally continuous versus culturally discontinuous environments. This chapter provides a descriptive overview of Korean culture and American culture, and documents the differences between the two cultures. Although Koreans living in Korea are confronted with Western influences, Korean institutions and society provide a reference frame and allow for a mediated response to these external influences. However, Korean immigrants emigrating to North America must confront these contrasting value systems with very little institutional or societal support. They experience incompatibilities between the two contrasting cultures, and struggle to adapt in their new environment.

A possible solution for Korean immigrants is to give up their heritage culture in favor of the host culture (i.e., assimilation). This implies a separation from, and abandonment of, their culture, community, and family. The emotional and psychological costs of such a decision could be enormous. Another option is to cling to their heritage culture and remain loyal to their families (i.e., separation). This mode of acculturation cannot be viewed as a successful adaptation because it is correlated with low life satisfaction and high mental health problems (Berry & Kim, 1988; Berry et al., 1987; U. Kim, 1988, 1990a).

The third option is to synthesize, integrate, or adopt both cultures (i.e., integration). Integration refers to a bicultural mode of acculturation in which individuals maintain their heritage culture while participating actively in the larger society. Integration is an additive mode of acculturation, whereas assimilation and separation are subtractive modes. The goal of integration is to acquire, synthesize, or integrate new cultural elements so that individuals can function effectively in both cultures. In a multicultural context, it encourages individuals to function effectively in many different environments. The additive model allows a relatively smooth transition from a monocultural context to a bicultural context, and even to a multicultural one. It allows the propagation of a continuous sense of personhood, family integrity, and cultural identity. It is the option that Korean immigrants and various ethnic groups prefer (Berry, Kim, Power, Young, & Bujaki, 1989; U. Kim, 1988, 1990a). It is correlated with high life satisfaction and low mental health problems in Canada (Berry, Kim, & Boski, 1987; U. Kim, 1984, 1988) and the United States (Delgado-Gaitan, chapter 3, this volume; Joe, chapter 5, this volume; Suina & Smolkin, chapter 6, this volume; Wong-Rieger & Quintana, 1987).

Compatibility of values is an important factor in child development. U. Kim (1990b) reviewed three empirical studies that revealed that if the goal of socialization in the family is compatible with the goal of socialization in the school setting, then children experience little or no conflict and benefit maximally from their educational experiences. When the goal is not compatible, children do not fully benefit from their educational experiences and they also may display problem behaviors. The Kamehameha Early Education Program created a school environment for Native Hawaiians that was compatible with their family environment (Tharp, chapter 4, this volume; Tharp & Gallimore, 1988). When this was accomplished, the Native Hawaiians, who were the lowest achieving minority group in the United States, soon reached the national average. Similarly, Kagitcibasi, Sunar, and Bekman (1989) created community-based learning centers to educate mothers of young children. They developed a program that is compatible with the Turkish culture. When they worked with mothers to create a more compatible home environment for learning, significant improvements were seen in the academic achievement of the children. Stevenson et al. (1986) showed that the phenomenal success in educational attainment of Japanese students, especially in mathematics, is attributable to the socialization practices of mothers, which are compatible with practices supported by the Japanese schools. Finally, Misumi (1985) attributed the economic success of Japan to the development of small-group processes that are compatible with the relational orientation. These studies emphasized the importance of cultural compatibility and of the continuity of socialization values in different contexts (i.e., family, community, and society).

In an acculturation context, compatibility and continuity are often disrupted. They are not likely to exist in countries that emphasize subtractive acculturation (i.e., countries that pursue a policy of assimilation, segregation, or ethnocide; see Kim & Berry, 1986, for a review). Compatability and continuity are theoretically possible in a country that pursues a policy of multiculturalism (such as Canada; see Berry, 1991, for a review). At the individual and community level, this policy allows individuals to maintain their heritage culture and ethnic loyalty. One aspect of this policy encourages diversity at individual and community levels. The other aspect encourages unity and cooperation at the national level. At the national level, the diversity of individuals and ethnic groups is not seen as a problem but an asset. Multiculturalism (at the national level) and integration (at the individual level) promote and propagate compatibility and continuity for all members of a society. They are associated with healthy human development in the psychological, social, economical, and political spheres (U. Kim, 1988; Murphy, 1975; Ward & Hewstone, 1985; Wong-Rieger & Quintana, 1987).

ACKNOWLEDGMENTS

The author gratefully acknowledges the financial support provided by the Department of Psychology, College of Social Sciences, and the Center for Korean Studies, University of Hawaii.

REFERENCES

Arnold, F., Minocha, U., & Fawcett, J. T. (1987). The changing face of Asian immigration to the United States. In J. W. Fawcett & B. V. Carino (Eds.), *Pacific bridges: The new immigration from Asia and the Pacific Islands* (pp. 105–152). Staten Island, NY: Center for Immigration Studies.

Azuma, H. (1986). Why study child development in Japan? In H. Stevenson, H. Azuma, & K. Hakuta (Eds.), *Child development and education in Japan* (pp. 3–12). New York: W. H. Freeman.

Barringer, H. R., & Cho, S. N. (1989). *Koreans in the United States: A fact book*. Honolulu: University of Hawaii Press.

Barry, H. III, Child, I. L., & Bacon, M. K. (1959). Relations of child training to subsistence economy. *American Anthropologist, 61*, 51–63.

Befu, H. (1986). The social and cultural background of child development in Japan and the United States. In H. Stevenson, H. Azuma, & K. Hakuta (Eds.), *Child development and education in Japan* (pp. 13–27). New York: W. H. Freeman.

Bellah, R. N., Madsen, R., Sullivan, W. M., Swindler, A., & Tipton, S. M. (1985). *Habits of the heart: Individualism and commitment in American life*. Berkeley, CA: University of California Press.

Berry, J. W. (1976). *Human ecology and cognitive style: Comparative studies in cultural and psychological adaptation.* New York: Wiley.

Berry, J. W. (1991). Understanding and managing multiculturalism: Some possible implications of research in Canada. *Psychology and Developing Studies, 3,* 17–49.

Berry, J. W., & Kim, U. (1988). Acculturation and mental health: A review. In P. Dasen, J. W. Berry, & N. Satorius (Eds.), *Cross-cultural psychology and health: Towards application* (pp. 207–238). Newbury Park, CA: Sage.

Berry, J. W., Kim, U., & Boski, P. (1987). Psychological acculturation of immigrants. In Y. Y. Kim & W. B. Gudykunst (Eds.), *Cross-cultural adaptation: Current approaches* (pp. 62–89). Newbury Park, CA: Sage.

Berry, J. W., Kim, U., Minde, T., & Mok, D. (1987). Acculturative stress in Canada. *International Migration Review, Special Issue on Migration and Health, 21,* 491–511.

Berry, J. W., Kim, U., Power, S., Young, M., & Bujaki, M. (1989). Acculturation attitudes in plural societies. *Applied Psychology: An International Review, 38,* 185–206.

Bonacich, E. (1973). A theory of middlemen minorities. *Sociological Review, 38,* 583–594.

Boyd, R., & Richardson, P. J. (1985). *Culture and the evolutionary process.* Chicago: University of Chicago Press.

Chinese Cultural Connection. (1987). Chinese values and the search for a culture free dimension of culture. *Journal of Cross-Cultural Psychology, 18,* 143–164.

Choi, J. S. (1987). *The study of Korean family system* (in Korean). Seoul: Il-Ji-Sa.

Choi, S. C., Kim, U., & Choi, S. H. (1993). Korean culture and collective representation. In U. Kim & J. W. Berry (Eds.), *Indigenous psychologies: Experience and research in cultural context* (pp. 193–210). Newbury Park, CA: Sage.

Choi, S. H. (1985). *Social class differences in Korean mothers' speech.* Unpublished masters' thesis, University of Alberta, Edmonton, Canada.

Choi, S. H. (1990). *Communicative socialization processes: Korea and Canada.* Unpublished doctoral dissertation, University of Alberta, Edmonton, Canada.

Chung, Y. H. (1970). Comparative research on theories of emotion: With main emphasis on social emotion. *The Korean Journal of Psychology, 1,* 77–90.

Doi, T. (1981). *The anatomy of dependence.* Tokyo: Kodansha International.

Doi, T. (1985). *The anatomy of self: The individual versus society.* Tokyo: Kodansha International.

Gallup. (1983). *The Koreans' family life and children's education* (in Korean). Seoul: Korea Survey (Gallup) Polls.

Gallup. (1985). *The Korean children and mothers* (in Korean). Seoul: Korea Survey (Gallup) Polls.

Han, W. K. (1974). *The history of Korea.* Honolulu: The University of Hawaii Press.

Harré, R. (1984). Some reflection on the concept of "social representation." *Social Research, 51,* 927–938.

Ho, D. Y. F. (1982). Asian concepts in behavioral science. *Psychologia, 25,* 228–235.

Ho, D. Y. F. (1986). Chinese patterns of socialization: A critical review. In M. H. Bond (Ed.), *The psychology of the Chinese people* (pp. 1–37). Oxford: Oxford University Press.

Hofstede, G. (1980). *Culture's consequences: International differences in work-related values.* Beverly Hills, CA: Sage.

Hofstede, G. (1991). *Organizations and cultures: Software of the mind.* New York: McGraw-Hill.

Hsu, F. S. L. (1971). Psychosocial homeostatsis and jen: Conceptual tools for advancing psychological anthropology. *American Anthropologist, 73,* 23–44.

Hui, C. H., & Triandis, H. C. (1986). Individualism-collectivism: A study of cross-cultural researchers. *Journal of Cross-Cultural Psychology, 17,* 225–248.

Hurh, W. M., & Kim, H. C. (1984). Adhesive sociocultural adaptation of Korean immigrants in the U.S.: An alternative strategy of minority adaptation. *International Migration Review, Special Issue on Migration and Health, 18,* 188–217.

Kagitçibasi, Ç. (1987). Individual and group loyalties: Are they compatible? In Ç. Kagitçibasi (Ed.), *Growth and progress in cross-cultural psychology* (pp. 94–103). Lisse: Swets & Zeitlinger.

Kagitçibasi, Ç., Sunar, D., & Bekman, S. (1989). *Preschool education project*. Ottawa: IDRC, Government of Canada.

Kashima, Y. (1990). *Substantive and relational model of individualism and collectivism*. Paper presented at the First International Conference on Individualism and Collectivism, Seoul, Korea.

Kim, J. E. (1981). *The psychology of Korean families* (in Korean). Seoul: Chang-Ji-Sa.

Kim, T. C. (1972). *The reality of mother–child's health* (in Korean). Seoul: Korean Family Planning Institute.

Kim, U. (1984). *Psychological acculturation of Korean immigrants in Toronto: A study of modes of acculturation, identity, language, and acculturative stress*. Unpublished master's thesis, Queen's University, Kingston, Ontario, Canada.

Kim, U. (1988). *Acculturation of Korean immigrants to Canada: Psychological, demographic and behavioural profiles of emigrating Koreans, non-emigrating Koreans, and Korean-Canadians*. Unpublished doctoral dissertation, Queen's University, Kingston, Ontario, Canada.

Kim, U. (1990a). Acculturation of Korean immigrants: What are the hidden costs? In H. C. Kim & E. H. Lee (Eds.), *Koreans in America: Dreams and realities* (pp. 193–216). Seoul: Institute of Korean Studies.

Kim, U. (1990b). A desirable and just society for youth: Historical and cross-cultural perspectives. In Korean Institute for Youth and Children (Ed.), *Proceedings of the First International Conference on Youth and Culture: Reconstructing society with youth as major participants* (pp. 165–225). Seoul: Korean Institute for Youth and Children.

Kim, U. (1992). *The parent–child relationship: The core of Korean collectivism*. Unpublished manuscript, University of Hawaii, Department of Psychology, Honolulu.

Kim, U. (in press). Individualism and collectivism: Conceptual clarification and elaboration. In U. Kim, H. C. Triandis, C. Kagitcibasi, S. C. Choi, & G. Yoon (Eds.), *Individualism and collectivism: Theory, method and applications*. Newbury Park, CA: Sage.

Kim, U., & Berry, J. W. (1986). Predictor of acculturative stress: Korean immigrants in Toronto, Canada. In L. Ekstrand (Ed.), *Ethnic minorities and immigrants in a cross-cultural perspective* (pp. 159–170). Lisse: Swets & Zeitlinger.

King, A. Y. C., & Bond, M. H. (1985). The Confucian paradigm of man: A sociological view. In W. T. Tseng & D. Wu (Eds.), *Chinese culture and mental health* (pp. 29–46). New York: Academic Press.

Lee, D. S. (1980). Traditional norms in family and problems of modern family (in Korean). In D. S. Lee (Ed.), *Traditional values and establishment of new values*. Seoul: Institute of Korean Studies.

Lee, E. H., & Lee, K. W. (1987). *The Korean mothers' socialization process for children* (in Korean). Seoul: Ehwa Women's University.

Lee, S. J., & Kim, J. O. (1979). The value of children: Korea (in Korean). *ED, 186*, 324.

Lee, S. W. (1990, July). *Koreans' social relationship and Cheong space*. Paper presented at the 1st International Conference on Individualism and Collectivism: Psychocultural Perspectives from East and West, Seoul, Korea.

Legge, J. (1960). *The Chinese classics, Vol. 1: Confucian analects, the great learning, the doctrine of the mean*. Hong Kong: Hong Kong University.

Locke, J. (1975). *An essay concerning human understanding*. Oxford: P. H. Nidditch.

Maday, B. C., & Szalay, L. B. (1976). Psychological correlates of family socialization in the United States and Korea. In T. Williams (Ed.), *Psychological anthropology* (pp.). Hague: Mouton.

Masters, J. C. (1981). Developmental psychology. *Annual Review of Psychology, 32*, 117–151.

Mishra, R. C. (in press). Individualistic-collectivistic orientations across generations. In U. Kim, H. C. Triandis, C. Kagitcibasi, S. C. Choi, & G. Yoon (Eds.), *Individualism and collectivism: Theory, method and applications*. Newbury Park, CA: Sage.

Misumi, J. (1985). *The behavioral science of leadership*. Ann Arbor, MI: University of Michigan Press.

Mundy-Castle, A. C. (1991, June/July). Discussion paper presented at conference, "Continuities and Discontinuities in the Cognitive Socialization of Minority Children," Washington, DC.

Murphy, H. B. M. (1975). Low rate of mental hospitalization shown by immigrants to Canada. In C. Zwingmann & G. Pfister-Ammendes (Eds.), *Uprooting and after*. New York: Springer-Verlag.

Pettengill, S. M., & Rohner, R. P. (1985). Korean-American adolescents' perceptions of parental control, parental acceptance–rejection and parent–adolescent conflict. In I. R. Lagunes & Y. H. Poortinga (Eds.), *From different perspective: Studies of behavior across cultures* (pp. 241–249). Lisse: Swets & Zeitlinger.

Redfield, R., Linton, R., & Herskovits, M. J. (1936). Memorandum on the study of acculturation. *American Anthropologist, 38,* 149–152.

Rohner, R. P. (1984). *Handbook for the study of parental acceptance and rejection*. Storrs, CT: University of Connecticut Press.

Rohner, R. P., & Pettengill, S. M. (1985). Perceived parental acceptance–rejection and parental control among Korean adolescents [Special issue]. *Child Development, 56,* 524–528.

Sampson, E. E. (1977). Psychology and the American ideal. *Journal of Personality and Social Psychology, 35,* 767–782.

Segall, M. H., Dasen, P. R., Berry, J. W., & Poortinga, Y. H. (1990). *Human behavior in global perspective: An introduction to cross-cultural psychology*. New York: Pergamon.

Shin, E. H., & Han, S. K. (1990). Korean immigrant small businesses in Chicago: An analysis of the resource mobilization process. *Amerasia Journal, 16,* 39–60.

Sinha, D., & Tripathi, R. (in press). Individualism in a collectivist culture: A case of co-existence of opposites. In U. Kim, H. C. Triandis, C. Kagitcibasi, S. C. Choi, & G. Yoon (Eds.), *Individualism and collectivism: Theory, method and applications*. Newbury Park, CA: Sage.

Sinha, J. B. P., & Verma, J. (1987). Structure of collectivism. In C. Kagitcibasi (Ed.), *Growth and progress in cross-cultural psychology* (pp. 123–129). Lisse: Swets & Zeitlinger.

Spence, J. (1985). Achievement American style: The rewards and costs of individualism. *American Psychologist, 40,* 1285–1295.

Stevenson, H., Lee, S. Y., Stigler, J., Kitamura, S., Kimura, S., & Kato, T. (1986). Achievements in mathematics. In H. Stevenson, H. Azuma, & K. Hakuta (Eds.), *Child development and education in Japan* (pp. 3–11). New York: W. H. Freeman.

Tharp, R. G., & Gallimore, R. (1988). *Rousing mind to life: Teaching, learning and schooling in social context*. Cambridge: Cambridge University Press.

Tonnies, F. (1963). *Community and society*. New York: Harper & Row. (Original work published 1887)

Triandis, H. C. (1988). Collectivism vs. individualism: A reconceptualization of a basic concept in cross-cultural social psychology. In C. Bagley & G. K. Verma (Eds.), *Personality, cognition and values: Cross-cultural perspectives of childhood and adolescence* (pp.). London: Macmillan.

Triandis, H. C., Leung, K., Villareal, M. J., & Clack, F. L. (1985). Allocentric versus idiocentric tendencies: Convergent and discriminant validation. *Journal of Research in Personality, 19,* 395–415.

Ward, C., & Hewstone, M. (1985). Ethnicity, language and intergroup relations in Malaysia and Singapore: A social psychological analysis. *Journal of Multilingual and Multicultural Matters, 6,* 271–296.

Wirth, L. (1946). Preface. In K. Manheim (Ed.), *Ideology and utopia: An introduction to sociology of knowledge*. New York: Harcourt, Brace.

Witkin, H. A., Berry, J. W. (1975). Psychological differentiation in cross-cultural perspective. *Journal of Cross-Cultural Psychology, 6,* 64–87.

Wong-Rieger, D., & Quintana, D. (1987). Comparative acculturation of Southeast Asian and Hispanic immigrants and sojourners. *Journal of Cross-Cultural Psychology, 18,* 345–362.

Yu, A. C. (1981). *The traditional children's play in Korea* (in Korean). Seoul: Jung-Min-Sa.

Yu, A. C. (1984). *The child rearing practices in the traditional Korean society* (in Korean). Seoul: Jung-Min-Sa.

Yu, A. C. (1985). *The traditional psychotherapies for children in Korea* (in Korean). Seoul: Jl-Ji-Sa.

Yu, S. K. (1985). *A study of the childhood socialization process in Korea* (in Korean). Seoul: The Korean Academy of Science.

Zimbardo, P. G. (1988). *Psychology and life* (12th ed.). Glenview, IL: Scott, Foresman.

12

MOTHER AND CHILD IN JAPANESE SOCIALIZATION: A JAPAN–U.S. COMPARISON

Takie Sugiyama Lebra
University of Hawaii

Child development goes hand in hand with the child's communicative interaction with adult members of society who have internalized some notions of cultural manuals on childrearing and act them out intentionally or unintentionally. Inevitably, then, child growth amounts to or interlocks with socialization and enculturation in a particular society.

What complicates socialization is the possibly universal and inevitable fact that it involves both continuity and discontinuity between the child being socialized and the socializing adult agent, or between generations. The child must bond and attach to his or her parental figure but also has to learn self–other distinction and separation. Put another way, encouragement of interdependence goes hand in hand with autonomy, and indulgence with discipline. I assume, however, that there is cultural variation in the mode of managing this double process of socialization. I further argue that such variation has a good deal to do with whether the overall cultural value highlights continuity or discontinuity.

In this chapter, I first delineate Japanese strategies in implementing double socialization in early childhood. Then, at the risk of overgeneralizing, I characterize the mother–child dyad as a cultural trope for other relationships. Finally, I offer another comparable model for North Americans in contradistinction to the common claim that the mother–child dyad is a universal model. Central to this comparison is the differential emphasis on continuity and discontinuity with the parental generation.

THREE STRATEGIES OF SOCIALIZATION

The primacy of the mother–child dyad is manifested in the following characteristics of Japanese socialization. First, the child is conceived and treated as naturally or bodily tied to the mother in association with the natural process of reproduction and birth, granted that *nature* and *body* are culturally defined. This **naturalism** underlies the significance of body contact between mother and child as a communication channel.

In the well-known study by Caudill and Weinstein (1986) on 3- to 4-month-old infants and maternal caregivers in Japan and the United States, it was found that Japanese mothers hold their babies or otherwise have bodily contact with them more frequently than do American mothers, and that the latter chat with their infants more often. Caudill and Weinstein observed that this difference in style of maternal care shows up in the different way that infants behave: American babies tend to be more vocal and "happily" so, whereas Japanese babies, who are more "lulled," soothed, and quieted down, sound unhappy when they make vocalizations. This particular difference in the modality of sound production was more or less underscored by Bornstein, Azuma, Tamis-LeMonda, and Ogino (1990) as "distress versus nondistress" vocalization.

For the Japanese dyad, it appears as if the intensity of body communication does away with the cultural or linguistic means of communication (viz. talking), whereas the reverse holds for the American dyad. To borrow further from the same study, the Japanese mother turns out to be "passively present" in the infant's room, without necessarily doing caregiving activities even while the infant is asleep. The American mother, if present, engages in caregiving activities and leaves the baby sleeping alone. For her, infant care is an in-and-out matter, her separate identity alternating with her maternal identity. I detect a naturalistic symbiosis in the Japanese pair, and a purposeful interaction in the American pair.

The Japanese sense of bodily connection between mother and child seems to relate to their attitudes toward abortion and mother–child "double suicide." Paradoxical as it may sound, I think the mother–child inseparability, in which the child is looked upon as part of the mother's body, accounts for Japanese' greater acceptance, compared with Americans, of abortion and killing the child in joint death. Conversely, I consider the American right-to-life advocacy a gross manifestation of separation, distance, or even alienation between mother and child. It is quite alien to Japanese to think of the existence of a fetus independent of the uterine body, so independent as to claim its right, even at the risk of its nurturer's life.

The Japanese lifestyle, which is partly changing, has allowed such bodily intimacy. Sleeping arrangements in particular attracted attention from American researchers, who discovered, among other things, that co-sleeping takes place between child and parents (mother, particularly), sometimes even if this necessitates separate sleeping for the couple (Caudill & Plath, 1986). In my research, middle-aged and older women disclosed in interviews that they had slept with their children, in some cases, beyond the infancy stage. According to a grandmother, in her days "no children slept alone" (Lebra, 1984, p. 176). Co-sleeping was facilitated by the quilt beddings spread in a mat-floored common room, which have been largely replaced by Western-style beds or bunks for children placed in their own hard-floored rooms. Less changed is co-bathing as another opportunity for body contact between child and caregiver. The Japanese deep bathtub (furo) necessitates that the caregiver hold her child tight to herself to enjoy co-soaking.[1]

Naturalism runs through the image of idealized childhood as unhampered by artificial restrictions of the adult world. If asked about their childrearing strategies, Japanese mothers emphasize letting their children grow up *shizen ni, nobi nobi to* (naturally and freely). The child should be childlike (*kodomo-rashii*), which can mean natural and spontaneous, and the mother is expected to feel naturally like accepting its childish behavior. Thus, naturalism merges with indulgence, which is framed in Japanese vernacular as *amae* relationship. *Amae* refers to one's inclination to depend on or accept another's nurturant indulgence, including one's dependency wish, typically applied to the mother–child relationship. *Amayakasu*, referring to the mother's indulgent behavior toward the child's *amae*, verges on spoiling the child.

Indeed, the Japanese mother is contrasted to the American mother in not exercising her parental authority (Conroy, Hess, Azuma, & Kashiwagi, 1980; Hess et al., 1986), as if she would rather let the child's nature take its course than impose unnatural means of curbing it. The result is that many young kids behave so wildly and obstreperously in supermarkets, trains, or other public places, as to annoy foreigners. At home, some of my sample mothers[2] found that their children, to their regret, turned into insatiable tyrants due to their earlier indulgence, leaving the mothers at a loss (Lebra 1984). A mother's refusal to resort to her authority in disciplining her child seems to be reproduced by preschool teachers. Peak (1989) stressed a radical shift from the family to preschool life for the children, a shift that replaces the intrafamilial *amae* indulgence by group discipline. Yet, I see preschool teachers, as described by Peak, as more continuous with mothers in letting a few unruly boys have their own way rather than chastising them (also see Tobin, Wu, & Davidson, 1989). The lenient, nonauthoritarian reactions of mothers and

---

[1]Such parent–child body contact, especially in co-sleeping, raises the eyebrow of a few Westerners because of a total misunderstanding. An American psychoanalyst, excited when he read the passages on co-sleeping in my book (Lebra, 1984), wrote me, to my astonishment, commending my candidness in revealing the widespread incestuous practice in Japan!

[2]This information is based on interviews conducted as part of fieldwork in a provincial city in 1976–1977.

nursery school teachers seem to derive from the common belief that ob-
streperous conduct is age specific and will soon disappear as a matter of the
natural life course. Implicit herein is the functional optimism that nature is
self-regulative in the long run.

Thus, naturalism stresses continuity in body between child and mother,
but at the same time recognizes a certain autonomy of the child as an age-
bound organism that cannot be entirely controlled by his or her caregiver
in conformity to a cultural norm. Looked at more positively, the child is believed to have a natural capacity for growing up apart from the caregiver's
nurturance.

Yet, the lack of discipline is only one side of Japanese childhood. In fact,
most children exhibit contradictory patterns of behavior: spoiled and yet disciplined, spontaneous but programmed, unruly but reserved, free but con-
forming. Is discipline a product of socialization outside the home, involving
the child's emotional severance from its mother, as argued by Peak (1989)?
My contention is that it is part of maternal socialization. To understand this,
one must move from naturalism to a second dimension of mother–child socialization (i.e., appeal for empathy). *Omoiyari*, a rough equivalent of empathy, "refers to the ability and willingness to feel what others are feeling, to
vicariously experience the pleasure or pain that they are undergoing, and
to help them satisfy their wishes" (Lebra, 1976, p. 38). It is at the opposite
pole from egocentricity. I place *omoiyari* on top of the moral-value hierarchy in Japanese culture, judging from the frequency of its appearance in people's self-reflective talks, media, and various campaign slogans (including traffic
safety campaigns). Parents, including my sample women, want their children
to develop the *omoiyari* feeling in depth.

Who could be a better embodiment of empathy than the mother? The
mother cannot afford to be egocentric but must always be concerned with
her child. My sample women (Lebra, 1984) stressed how they had been entirely occupied by their children from their infancy up through their marriage to the extent that they neglected their husbands. Hence, the child
became the mother's life (*ikigai*), or the mother "became" the child in the
extreme state of empathy.

The mother's personal experience and the child's perception of it actually
vary from case to case, and yet these are both affected by the culturally shared
image of motherhood, which is loaded with the virtues of empathy, selflessness, and sacrificial hardship. Motherhood is played up and dramatized in
the Japanese media, and I would say there is at least one drama series going
on at any time depicting a mother as the protagonist. To be sure, not all depic-
tions are favorable and not all mothers are motherlike: Some chase after their
boyfriends in total neglect of their children, and some are more egocentric
than child centered. Nevertheless, the producer's message is loud and clear

about what the "true" mother is like, and it is reinforced by the portrayal of an opposite type of mother.

The mother, assimilating the culturally idealized motherhood, stands as the finest exemplar of empathy, sending quiet messages for her child to imitate her and reciprocate her in empathy. Verbally, too, she cultivates empathy in her child, asking him or her to feel the way she does. Once she succeeds in sensitizing her child to her feeling, pain, and wishes she can then discipline him or her in the direction of her choice. Thus, the child's egocentric, free, and natural behavior, although tolerated and indulged as an age-specific propensity, can come under control through exchange of empathy with his or her mother. Indeed, when compared with American mothers, Japanese mothers were found to appeal more to "feelings" in disciplining their children (Hess et al., 1986). The child may learn to refrain from disruptive behavior that "hurts" his or her mother's feeling, to obey his father because that is what his or her mother wants, and to be well mannered toward house visitors because she would be "ashamed" otherwise. From this stage on, the child learns to empathize with people other than the mother.

Empathy involves the child's feelings as well as the mother's feelings (*kokoro, kimochi*), which are stimulated in two directions: outward and inward. Outwardly, the child is supposed to develop social sensitivity to his or her mother's feelings and, through her, to other people's feelings. This is reflected in the fact that many Japanese, young and old, men and women, find it mandatory to avoid causing worry (*shinpai*) or trouble (*meiwaku*) for others, and not to reveal their natural inclinations under the self-imposed social restraint (*enryo*). Thus, empathy goes a long way to control the child's social behavior and to counter naturalistic spontaneity. On the other hand, empathy training takes an inward direction. Central here is the child's interior in contrast to the socially sensitized exterior, subjectivity in contrast to outer self-presentation, and volition in contrast to social constraint. It is implied that social rules cannot be enforced unless the child is subjectively ready to understand and accept them or to comply with them voluntarily. Thus, empathy socialization results in fostering self-reflectiveness, inner motivations, strength, perseverance, and determination to overcome externally encountered adversities.

Empathy is a psychological mainstay that reinforces and generalizes continuity between the child on the one hand and the mother and others through her on the other hand. It is also evident from this discussion that, through empathy training, the child learns the separate identities of mother and self— the identities that are to be reciprocally acknowledged.

This leads to a third dimension, what I call *boundary socialization*. I consider the zoning of social or personal space into interior and exterior, inside and outside (*uchi* and *soto*), feeling and conduct, or private and public. This dimension becomes more important as the child grows older, beyond the infancy stage, even though it begins earlier.

Cultural messages regarding the two zones are somewhat ambivalent. On the one hand, they are considered to merge into one. Given the likelihood of discrepancy between role and personhood, obligation and volition, and external constraint and inner feelings, it behooves the socializing agent to voluntarize the child's conformity. A Japanese saying facilitates this task by pointing up the interreflexivity or interpenetration of interiority and exteriority, spirit and form, and *kokoro* and *katachi*. A person's inner state of mind is bound to surface, Japanese would say, in his or her appearance, and the latter therefore serves as a true reflection of the former. Hence, an untidy, sloppy style of dressing is taken as a sign of laxity of the mind (*Fukuso no midare wa kokoro no midare*).

Reflexivity is a two-way street. If the mind is manifested in the appearance through "surfacing," the appearance shapes up the mind through inward "penetration." Thus, so-called "spiritual" education, given at various stages of life, typically and paradoxically begins with an imposition of minute rules of external manners and conduct. Child training in etiquette such as greetings begins early at home and is intensified through preschool and grade school. The training process is not just to teach socially addressed skills but as an effective method to straighten out the child's inner character. Many schools today control their students through minutiae of rules such as the length of hair and skirt, width of pants, minimum physical distance between boy and girl in conversation, prohibition of cosmetics and perms, regulation of what personal possessions should or should not be brought to school, and so forth.[3] These rules are ridiculous to the general public even in Japan, and yet most parents support such discipline largely because of the described concept of surfacing/penetration reflexivity.

National obsession with academic achievement, which is measured and validated by the prominence of the school one is admitted to (not just at university level but at each entry level from kindergarten on) is deplored by many Japanese because it neglects or victimizes a child's personhood. Critics see a wide discrepancy between inner motivations and obligatory study, and condemn the whole educational system as demoralizing and stifling. Critics and *kyoiku-mama* (education mothers) alike concur that a child's inner volition is essential to the fruitfulness of study. On the other hand, there are many mothers in my study who, although they do not voice their opinion in public, claim that studying hard to face examination hurdles strengthens the character of their children (Lebra, 1984). According to these mothers, the

---

[3]Control over possessions can be so stringent that, according to a mother, a pupil (and his or her mother, too) is punished for bringing four or two pencils, instead of three—the number specified by his or her teacher.

"examination hell," far from damaging a child's personhood, contributes to the buildup of his/her strength. Furthermore, many mothers succeed in voluntarizing their children to persevere in meeting the role requirement of academic endeavor.

The unity of the two zones is an ideal. However, in practice there tends to be a discrepancy in the sense that the boundary between inner and outer zones is not entirely permeable. In fact, the two zones are looked on as dichotomous and oppositional, and as such are to be kept apart. Thus, children are gradually taught to hide their inner feelings if they are not socially acceptable, to smile when they really feel unhappy, and to be more circumspect in their conduct once they step outside the house.

This socialization strategy directly counters naturalism discussed previously. It is here that the intimate microcosm of the mother–child dyad serves as the primary point of departure forming the inner, natural, private sanctuary for the child, from which the outer, rulebound, public realm is removed. The latter realm is impressed on the child as in opposition to the former. A sense of discontinuity is instilled between the family on the one hand, and neighbors, friends, school, strangers, and so on on the other, so that the child builds up a package of double or multiple identities.

Peak's (1989) observation on radical discontinuity between home and preschool, family and peers, *amae* and *enryo*, self-centeredness and discipline held perfectly valid in this respect. I want to note again that it is the mother who prepares and encourages the child to reorient his or her habit by 180 degrees now that he or she is going to belong to the outer world as well. It is the mother who is the first to foster in the child a new, anticipatory identity as a pupil and member of a class and school. Instead of opposing her authority to that of the teachers, family integrity to the child's peer-group solidarity, the Japanese mother presents herself as a compliant agent of the school, as expected by the school, renouncing her right to be an independent home educator.[4]

It is through exposure to the zone external to the intimate mother–child dyad and yet under the mother's strong instigation that the child undergoes *positional*, rather than *personal*, socialization, to borrow Douglas' (1970) typological terms. Positional socialization inculcates the rules of conduct vested in the position or role that the child is expected to hold in relation to others at present or in the future. The male child is trained to act or present himself in a proper way as a boy, as an elder brother, as a son and heir of a doctor,

---

[4]This is one of the points that surprise and irritate U.S. mothers married to Japanese men who send their children to Japanese preschools or regular schools. Imamura (1989) quoted one such mother: "They (school) really expect a lot and there's so much competition among the women to produce. I was really surprised. The first six months of his [my son's] kindergarten this year I was really surprised at the way the women have dedicated themselves body and soul to the kindergarten" (p. 21).

as a school child, as a first grader, as a pupil, as a neighbor, as a train passenger, and so forth. Others around the male child play various positional roles relative to his: complementary (e.g., the roles of parent, teacher), opposite (girl, adult), peer, model, or rival (fellow first grader), and/or audience (neighbor, classmate). It is largely in the context of positional training that the Japanese refer to *rashii* or *rashiku*, meaning "like." The male child is told to appear or conduct himself "like a boy," "like a nursery school pupil," and so forth. The like behavior stands for a role-specific behavior bounded from the rest of the child's total existence, distinct from his nature.

Positional socialization is universal inasmuch as society cannot exist unless a sufficient number of members perform their respective roles properly in sufficient frequency. It may be said that Japan goes beyond the United States in the degree to which role propriety or role obligation, together with positional hierarchy, is stressed, articulated, and elaborated in child socialization. Positional socialization begins with learning a particular role (e.g., being a nursery school boy), and extends to a cluster of roles to be assumed at once. The ultimate purpose of positional socialization lies in inculcating the significance of role fitness as part of the individual's self-identity and inducing the generalized readiness to assume whatever role one is assigned, regardless of one's personal preference. When driven to an excessive degree, it may end up producing a role robot.

I have covered a wide range of socialization strategies under three dimensions that are attributed to the mother–child dyad: naturalism, empathy, and boundary. I noted that in each dimension both continuity and discontinuity between self and other are in operation. Yet, there is increasing emphasis on discontinuity as socialization shifts from naturalism to empathy to boundary making. It is in the boundary socialization that the most strict discipline is imposed to counteract the earlier naturalism, and even to suppress the personal feeling that is so crucial in empathy training. In natural and empathic socialization, mother and child are more continuous physically or psychologically, with no boundary separating them. Painful separation comes with the boundary training that is supposed to enable the child to live in two zones, inner and outer, and to cross the zonal boundary whenever needed.

Despite this drastic change, the primary tie of mother and child is not dissolved but preserved in the tiny, inner, private sanctuary. This is, to be sure, because of the overwhelming impact of naturalistic and empathic socialization. But it is also because of the *boundary training* that discourages one zone from annihilating or transcending another. Underlying this zonal pluralism is the preserved image of natural motherhood. In short, naturalistic continuity between mother and child does not come to an end with training in zonal discontinuity but remains more or less intact in its own zone.

THE MOTHER–CHILD DYAD AS A CULTURAL TROPE

In this section, I try to underscore the idea that the mother–child dyad I have described is a cultural construct more than a natural product. I show how this dyad is extended, generalized, or appropriated as a trope to various kinds of social relationship in the adult world, which in turn provides a model for child socialization. Let me illustrate with examples. In marriage, as far as domestic life is concerned, the Japanese husband expects his wife to be an overall caregiver for him, including body care, as if he saw a mother substitute in his wife. The wife is amused to call her husband her "oldest child" who demands the greatest attention and nurturance. A woman said in an interview, "Every morning, I put out one thing after another, saying, 'Here are your socks, here's your shirt, here's your handkerchief and so forth.'" The wife may help her husband dress and undress. She does not go as far as to bathe him (but I know a few women who wash their husbands' bodies) but may prepare everything necessary so that all he has to do is take a dip. Another woman told me that her husband, a medical doctor, refused to do anything by himself: If he did not find a G-string right there after bathing he would walk out of the bathroom totally nude. If shoes were not placed in front of him when about to go out, he would stand there waiting for his wife to rush over (Lebra, 1984). No wonder the husband, when he is at home, is likened to a huge pile of junk (*sodaigomi*): useless but unremovable. Nowadays, Japanese husbands joke about becoming such junk or are seriously resocializing themselves not to end up *sodaigomi*.

This kind of childlike dependency does not hurt the husband's macho image but, quite to the contrary, does enhance his male status. The idealized mother–child image, when applied to the marital relationship, is thus converted into an extreme gender hierarchy of male master and female servant. (As a matter of fact, however adored she is, the mother also serves her child like a maid. Thus, the "education mother" becomes an "education maid," monitoring the child's health and study and delivering food and snacks to him or her, devoted to her child master around the clock particularly during the examination season.)

Does the same model hold for extramarital relationships? In a small bar (the type that exists in abundance particularly in the vicinity of train stations to catch commuting workers), a middle-aged bar hostess, standing behind the bar, not only serves drinks but prepares food in front of the drinking men. "Mamasan," well named, appears more like a nurturant mother who is looked up to by her male customers waiting to be fed as if they were reliving their childhood. At the same time, this mother behind the bar pays lip service to gender hierarchy by addressing her customers by their titles such as "*sensei*" and "president."

One might think that romantic affairs involving a married man and a mistress would not fit the described picture. They probably do not fit during the initial phase of excitement but indications are that even such relationships tend to settle down to that of caregiver and care receiver. Televised "home-drama" series depict mistresses, if they are to be viewed favorably by the audience, as attractive housewives of sorts who take good care of their quasi-husbands. The husband may rationalize this relationship by saying, "When I am with her, I feel at full rest (*kokoro ga yasumaru*)," implying that his wife is incapable of providing such a relaxing home environment. The audience may condone the affair under this circumstance because the Japanese male worker is stereotyped as overworked and in need of nothing but rest and relief from work stress.

Interestingly, romance in this context has less to do with libidinal impulse and a display of virility than with a mental and physical vacation. In my view, *rest*, *relief*, and *relaxation* all refer to a childlike, free, natural state of body and mind, where the man feels free to lie around like a log or a "pile of junk" without worrying about his family's disapproval. The wife may complain about her husband being useless and constantly demanding her attention, and may prefer his absence; as a proverbial saying goes, "The best husband is in good health and in absence." But the "true" mother, who may be represented by a mistress, would embrace a childlike man and care for him as he is or as he returns to nature.

Housewifely domesticity, with maternal dedication and care, was a main theme that I found in an autobiography of a *geisha* turned concubine (Ando, 1927). As a concubine of Taro Katsura, who was prime minister three times between 1901 and 1913, Ando was most concerned about Katsura's stressful political life and heavy responsibility as the top leader of the nation; she took it as her duty to help him rest during his occasional visit. The reader is not given a clue about how Katsura felt about this concubinal arrangement, but one is told by the author that he was introduced to her by a group of his colleagues and friends who were worried about his health and stress as an overworked prime minister; she was expected to provide diversion and relaxation for him.

There are many other relationships featuring the mother–child dyad as a model. In a company organized by modern bureaucracy, one finds a chief (of a section, department, or division, or entire company) responsible for "raising" his or her subordinates into promising company workers or future leaders. In this case, it is the superior who takes a maternal role, and a successful boss displays such nurturance. If the boss happens to be a woman, the mothering role may be played up all the more.

In 1985, I interviewed 12 businesswomen in Tokyo who head companies as presidents to listen to their retrospective narratives on their business careers. Among them was a woman in her 70s who leads an internationally based company that employs 100 workers, predominantly male. She regards her company as a family and her employees as her children, likens the company's rapid expansion to the children's growth, and sees the labor union's threat of strike as symptomatic of the rebellious stage of childhood. Her maternal love has succeeded, she says with confidence, in bringing the union to self-dissolution (see Lebra, 1992, for details).

Another example comes from the same study. Service industries in Japan offer a great variety of "package" deals that allow customers to relax throughout the cycle of given services. Thus, the mother–child model is reproduced by the motherlike vendor and childlike customer, and is exemplified by the travel industry. One of my interviewees, a female president of a travel agency, tries to overcome the seemingly inevitable evanescence of the traveler–agency relationship by intensifying the pretour through posttour interaction and succeeds in securing regular customers. She plans each and every trip so meticulously and in such detail that no traveler has to make a single choice of his or her own throughout. An hourly calendar is printed with instructions and information on each site, and the staff is available 24 hours a day. Thus, the agency, with such perfect programming, provides much more than any mother can in terms of caregiving. It is well said that "customers are gods," as children are.[5] What is remarkable is that Japanese customers are willing to pay the price of autonomy and options to buy the privilege of being so totally programmed, dependent, and cared for.

Care for the elderly also tends to imitate the mother–child model (e.g., the elderly being looked after like children). In an institutional home for the elderly in Japan, Bethel (1992) observed how a family was forged out of strangers, and how young caregivers on staff were expected to be like mothers for the elderly in residence, who in turn assumed the role of a childlike care receiver. Campbell (1984) also saw the staff members in Japanese nursing homes treat their charges like "cute" children.

I could go on to cite many more examples but enough has been said about the mother–child dyad as a cultural trope. That Japanese carry the mother–child dyad over into many sectors of adult life suggests that they do not hold much ambivalence, if any, regarding motherhood or what mother represents—the kind of ambivalence found in other cultures. This unambivalent acceptance of motherhood may have to do with the fact that the dyad does not represent a hierarchical supersubordination in a simple, unilateral fashion. The maternal figure represents power in one sense but is like a servant in another—vis-à-vis the child figure. While a superior in a bureaucracy

---

[5]There are childlike gods and motherlike gods. If Shinto gods are to be opposed to Buddhist gods in disregard of the historical fusion of the two, I speculate that the former are more childlike and to be protected by human intervention, whereas the latter are more motherlike, compassionate, and forgiving toward humans.

may act like a caring parent, his or her subordinate may reciprocate by being a servile caregiver for him or her. For that matter, the mother herself embodies a whole spectrum from power to vulnerability, from sanctity to servitude. Thus, motherhood is multivocal, and I claim that multivocality is inherent in anything culturally salient. I have argued for the cultural saliency of motherhood or the mother–child dyad in Japan. Next, I contextualize this claim in a comparative perspective by a brief discussion of the American counterpart of socialization and its function as a basic model or cultural trope.

A COMPARISON OF JAPAN AND THE UNITED STATES IN SOCIALIZATION MODELS

I think the key model for the U.S. lifestyle, socialization, selfhood, and human relations is adolescence, male adolescence in particular. There are enormous cultural pressures on a child to reach the adolescent stage. Hence, a child in the United States looks much more mature than a Japanese child, of the same age, who is expected to be childlike as a matter of nature. Conversely, adults in the United States seem compelled to retain or return to the youthful stage of life, which accounts for many more over-aged adolescents observable in the United States than in Japan.

What does adolescence stand for? It is a prelude to adulthood—a stage of rebirth for a child to shed dependence and to start his or her own life. This is in opposition to the mother–child model, in that adolescence symbolizes a final and irreversible cut off of the umbilical cord. It is a stage of second birth, which presupposes self-severance from one's past, one's first birth, and one's parents. Independence from the parental generation and from maternal nurturance becomes a maxim that touches everyone's heart. From then on, every person is supposed to be self-made. Such rebirth highlights U.S. high school life most dramatically. As Rohlen (1983) described, the U.S. high school, unlike its Japanese counterpart, is a stage for self-creation, self-exploration, and self-experimentation. Sex, drugs, and delinquency are part of such explosive freedom. However, the culture of rebirth and independence seems to pervade everywhere in the United States—through life stages before and after high school as well.

For highly individuated Americans, there is something anomalous about the relation between parents and children because the biologically normal dependence of children on adults is perceived as morally abnormal:

> [C]hildren must leave home, find their own way religiously and ideologically, support themselves, and find their own peer group. This process leads to considerable amnesia about what one owes to one's parents. The tendency to for-

get what we have received from our parents seems, moreover, to generalize to a forgetting of what we have received from the past altogether. (Bellah, Madsen, Sullivan, Swidler, & Tipton, 1985, p. 82)

Children's forgetfulness and denial of dependence on their parents are complemented by their parents' ambivalence toward their children. Bellah et al. (1985) continued, "Conversely, many Americans are uneasy about taking responsibility for children" (p. 82). In my observation, U.S. parents encourage their children to stand on their own two feet. For that purpose they encourage children to have work experience while being students, "loan" instead of giving money to them (a shock to Japanese students), and worry if their children stay around them too long. Socialization in separation and independence begins earlier in the U.S. child's life; signs already appear in the infant care practices described earlier. The American mother lets her child become aware of a separate existence from her: The child's self-expression and even mother–child hugging are felt necessary because of this separation.

I assume that the culture of rebirth ties in with the immigrant culture of the United States; this culture keeps alive the utopian folklore of a second birth, leaving the native, parental culture behind. Adolescent rebirth is a sort of temporal replay of spatial immigration, in which one's ascribed origin is muted or rejected. In contrast, the trope of mother–child bonding calls attention to one's origin, roots, and ancestry. It is no coincidence that Japanese religious life centers around the ancestor cult and memorial rites.

Rebirth in adolescence goes not only with the independence and separation of the reborn, but with a buildup of sexual identity and formation of sexual partnership. Thus, the American version of independence and individualism is accompanied by involvement with the sexual dyad as a cultural model that is incompatible with the mother–child dyad. Above all, independence is a sexual independence from kinship dependence. Intergenerational discontinuity is inherent in the primacy of the sexual alignment of every generation.[6]

Is the Japanese child, bonded with his or her mother, stagnant? Does he or she not go through rebirth at all? Yes, he or she also undergoes a series of life transitions. The difference lies in the goal. For the Japanese, life transitions, or resocializations, are not for the individual's independence or separation from his or her parents. Rather, a transition is often prepared and helped by the mother herself, as stated earlier regarding the shift from home to

---

[6]This point may be significant for gender issues. I am inclined to generalize that for Americans gender is primarily a sexual issue, including homosexuality, whereas for Japanese, it is entrenched in motherhood. Both sexuality and motherhood are regarded either as detrimental to the feminist cause or as what is to be integrated to strengthen it. Women's rights, if phrased as mothers' rights, would meet much less resistance among conservative men and women in Japan.

preschool. In fact, the goal of each transition is even to reconfirm the primary ties, either literally or metaphorically.

Indeed, the mother–child bond is strategically recharged in various programs for resocialization, rebirth, or therapy. In Naikan therapy, which is regarded as truly Japanese, the client is supposed to self-reflect on what someone did to benefit him or her and how the client—the beneficiary—has been ungrateful and has even hurt his or her benefactor. The mother is considered the best benefactor to be recalled; her culturally loaded image as a paragon of love, selflessness, empathy, and sacrifice is appropriated to arouse a resonant empathy and heart-felt repentance in the client. Recollections typically go back to the client's childhood (Lebra, 1976; Murase, 1986; Reynolds, 1983). Psychoanalytically oriented Western therapy also draws on the client's childhood recollection, but the mother is often recalled as a major source of the child's suffering—opposite to the desired outcome of Naikan therapy.

Another example was given by Kondo (1990). As part of her anthropological field work in Japan, Kondo participated in a program called "Ethics Retreat" with her company "co-workers." Trainees were subjected to a variety of sessions involving semi-religious discipline, military-style regimentation, strenuous work and exercise, meditation, and physical pain. One of the instructional themes on which the trainees were induced to reflect was filial piety to be recaptured. For example, they were told, "Recall the faces of your mother and father when they saw you off, recall their faces when they took care of you when you were sick" (Kondo, 1990, p. 93). The excruciating knee pain, caused by sitting Japanese style on the hard floor, was said to be "only one-thousandth of the pain your mother felt in bearing you." After an even more tortuous exercise of walking barefoot on a path covered with rocks and gravel, the trainees were again admonished to think about the mother's childbearing pain. In other words, the trainees were reminded of their natural tie of reproduction and birth with their mothers. Rebirth here amounts to an imaginary reenactment of the first, natural birth. Both Naikan and Ethics Retreat seem to find it necessary to restore the mother–child continuity to the clients' contemporary world of separation in order to achieve a new level of revitalized selfhood.

CONCLUDING REMARKS

This comparison between Japan and the United States in socialization models and tropes suggests gender-associated attributes as identified by many Western scholars including Chodorow (1974) and Gilligan (1982). The mother–child dyad, which I condensed as a cultural trope for Japanese human relations and socialization, involves what emerges as the feminine character, orientation, and identity focused on relationality, interdependency, connectedness, empathy, and caring. Conversely, the youth or sexual dyad, which I delineated as an American trope, represents the masculine character with emphasis on separation, independence, individuation, and self-creation. One sides with continuity, whereas the other sides with discontinuity. This gender dichotomy cuts across cultural boundaries, reminding one of the universal aspect of double socialization for continuity and discontinuity, which brings me back to the beginning of this chapter.

Both Japanese and U.S. cultures must handle the problem of the continuity–discontinuity opposition. This chapter has attempted to delineate cultural differences in relating one to the other. Briefly stated, Japanese culture, with its overall emphasis on continuity, as best embodied by the mother–child dyad, tends to frame discontinuity within continuity so that one does not have to squash or repress the other. Even when the discontinuity phase comes to center stage, as in boundary training, the continuous identity is retained and recharged. The notion of boundary makes continuity and discontinuity compatible by creating multiple selves. American culture, which focuses on adolescence and sexual identity, is more committed to discontinuity, independence, and separation, with a greater emphasis on second birth than first birth and cultural rebirth more than natural birth. As a result, discontinuity and continuity tend to be mutually exclusive (i.e., one must repress the other). For people in the United States, continuity is associated with immaturity something to be overcome.

If the contrast I have drawn between Japan and the United States is valid, one can imagine what kind of cultural dilemma Japanese Americans may have to go through. It is likely that while carrying on some aspects of "a culture of continuity," as well as racial heritage from their ethnic ancestors, they are under double pressure to separate from their Japanese parents or ancestry symbolically or psychologically, not only as an inevitable process of maturation but because they have to establish themselves in "a culture of discontinuity." It is also possible that, in the course of ambicultural conflict and struggle, they can reach a new plane of bicultural flexibility and transcultural understanding. Many of my Japanese-American friends and colleagues are successfully doing exactly that.

ACKNOWLEDGMENTS

While preparing this manuscript, I was assisted by a University of Hawaii Japan Studies Endowment Faculty Research Award.

REFERENCES

Ando, T. (1927). *Okoi monogatari* [Okoi's tale]. Tokyo: Fukunaga Shoten.

Bellah, R. N., Madsen, R., Sullivan, W. M., Swidler, A., & Tipton, S. A. (1985). *Habits of the heart: Individualism and commitment in American life.* New York: Harper & Row.

Bethel, D. L. (1992). Life on *Obasuteyama*: A Japanese institution for the elderly. In T. S. Lebra (Ed.), *Japanese social organization* (pp. 109–134). Honolulu: University of Hawaii Press.

Bornstein, M. H., Azuma, H., Tamis-LeMonda, C., & Ogino, M. (1990). Mother and infant activity and interaction in Japan and in the United States: A comparative macroanalysis of naturalistic exchanges. *International Journal of Behavioral Development, 13,* 267–287.

Campbell, R. (1984). Nursing homes and long-term care in Japan. *Pacific Affairs, 57,* 78–89.

Caudill, W., & Plath, D. W. (1986). Who sleeps by whom? Parent–child involvement in urban Japanese families. In T. S. Lebra & W. P. Lebra (Eds.), *Japanese culture and behavior: Selected readings* (rev. ed., pp. 247–279). Honolulu: University of Hawaii Press.

Caudill, W., & Weinstein, H. (1986). Maternal care and infant behavior in Japan and America. In T. S. Lebra & W. P. Lebra (Eds.), *Japanese culture and behavior: Selected readings* (rev. ed., pp. 201–246). Honolulu: University of Hawaii Press.

Chodorow, N. (1974). Family structure and feminine personality. In M. Z. Rosaldo & L. Lamphere (Eds.), *Woman, culture, and society* (pp. 43–66). Stanford, CA: Stanford University Press.

Conroy, M., Hess, R. D., Azuma, H., & Kashiwagi, K. (1980). Maternal strategies for regulating children's behavior: Japanese and American families. *Journal of Cross-Cultural Psychology, 11,* 153–172.

Douglas, M. (1970). *Natural symbols: Explorations in cosmology.* New York: Vantage Books.

Gilligan, C. (1982). *In a different voice: Psychological theory and women's development.* Cambridge, MA: Harvard University Press.

Hess, R., Holloway, S., McDevitt, T., Azuma, H., Kashiwagi, K., Nagano, S., Miyake, K., Dickson, W. P., Price, G., & Hatano, G. (1986). Family influences on school readiness and achievement in Japan and the United States: An overview of a longitudinal study. In H. Stevenson, H. Azuma, & K. Hakuta (Eds.), *Child development and education in Japan* (pp. 147–166). New York: W. H. Freeman.

Imamura, A. E. (1989). Interdependence of family and education: Reactions of foreign wives of Japanese to the school system. In J. J. Shields, Jr. (Ed.), *Japanese schooling: Patterns of socialization, equality, and political control* (pp. 16–27). University Park, PA: The Pennsylvania State University Press.

Kondo, D. K. (1990). *Crafting selves: Power, gender, and discourses of identity in a Japanese workplace.* Chicago: University of Chicago Press.

Lebra, T. S. (1976). *Japanese patterns of behavior.* Honolulu: University of Hawaii Press.

Lebra, T. S. (1984). *Japanese women: Constraint and fulfillment.* Honolulu: University of Hawaii Press.

Lebra, T. S. (1992). Gender and culture in the Japanese political economy: Self-portrayals of prominent businesswomen. In K. Shumpei & H. Rosovsky (Eds.), *The political economy of Japan: Vol. 3. Cultural and social dynamics* (pp. 364–419). Stanford, CA: Stanford University Press.

Murase, T. (1986). Naikan therapy. In T. S. Lebra & W. P. Lebra (Eds.), *Japanese culture and behavior: Selected readings* (rev. ed., pp. 388–397). Honolulu: University of Hawaii Press.

Peak, L. (1989). Learning to become part of the group: The Japanese child's transition to preschool life. *Journal of Japanese Studies, 15,* 93–123.

Reynolds, D. K. (1983). *Naikan psychotherapy: Meditation for self-development.* Chicago: University of Chicago Press.

Rohlen, T. (1983). *Japan's high schools.* Berkeley: University of California Press.

Tobin, J. J., Wu, D. Y. H., & Davidson, D. H. (1989). *Preschool in three cultures: Japan, China, and the United States.* New Haven, CT: Yale University Press.

13

TWO MODES OF COGNITIVE SOCIALIZATION IN JAPAN AND THE UNITED STATES

Hiroshi Azuma

Shirayuri College, Tokyo

In Lebra's (chapter 12, this volume) conceptualization, Japanese socialization practices are a synthesis of empathic and positional socialization. Each mode sends a different message, and the dialectics that synthesize them are important in understanding Japanese childrearing practices. Basic to the two modes of socialization is the *uchi–soto* dichotomy, as Lebra points out. *Uchi*, or inside, is the sphere of private and intimate interpersonal relationships. *Soto*, or outside, is a sphere of public and formal relationships. Positional socialization is for *soto*, and empathetic socialization is for *uchi*. This distinction is not unique to Japan. In any culture, children are to some extent socialized into distinguishing between *uchi* and *soto*. In Japan, however, the ecological validity of this distinction is strikingly high.

Soto is governed by the principle of patriarchal hierarchy, which is perhaps rooted in the Confucian ethics (cf. Ho, chapter 14, this volume), long the officially backed code of conduct. There, a person is defined by his or her social role, and the distal mode of interpersonal communication prevails. On the other hand, *uchi* is governed by the maternal principle of nurturant egalitarianism, which derives perhaps from pre-Confucian native culture (Doi, 1971; Kawai, 1971).

In Korea, for example, Confucianism is a principle regulating much of intrafamilial relationships, as well as the relationships in the external society (cf. Kim & Choi, chapter 11, this volume). Inside Japanese families, this is not the case. The reverence for elders and the worship of ancestors is much less stressed compared with traditional China. For this reason, I have some reservation about Ho's labeling of Japan as a Confucian country (Ho, chapter 14, this volume).

An illustration of the extent of the effect of this differential socialization can be seen in one of the results of a cross-national survey conducted by Japan's government some years ago (Sorifu,[1] 1981). Among other items, they administered a test patterned after the Rosenzweig Picture Frustration Test. Children of different countries were shown two cartoon pictures, both depicting a child being reprimanded by an adult. In one of the pictures the adult is the teacher, and in another the adult is the mother. Children were to provide verbal responses for the child in the picture, projecting their own feelings. The percentages of obedient/receptive responses are shown in Fig. 13.1.

In every country, the percentage of obedient responses to the reprimanding mother is somewhat less than that to the reprimanding teacher, showing that a certain degree of *uchi–soto* differentiation is universal. Indeed, despite the influence of Confucianism in Korean families, empathy socialization, characteristic of the *uchi* zone, is emphasized in Kim and Choi's account of the Korean mother–child relationship (chapter 11, this volume).

But according to this survey, only in Japan is this discrepancy between obedience to the mother and teacher strikingly large. The majority of Japanese responses to the reprimanding mother are disobedient, whereas the majority of the responses to the teacher are obedient. The rate of obedience to the teacher is higher in Japan than in most of the countries surveyed, except Korea. From this we see that the socialization of *uchi–soto* differentiation is carried much further in Japan than in other countries. Children are expected to be obedient and respectful in the *soto* sphere but may behave differently in *uchi*. What characterizes the interpersonal relationships in *uchi* is close and empathetic interdependence, the *amae-amayakashi*, as White and Levine (1986) called it. *Soto* is governed to some extent by authoritative hierarchy reminiscent of Confucian patriarchism, whereas *uchi* is governed by maternal egalitarianism.

Although the core of the *uchi* is the family, the boundary between *uchi* and *soto* is neither physical nor institutional. As the child grows, there develops a gradation of *uchi*-ness. Close peers become a part of *uchi*. Schools try, not quite successfully, to make *soto*-mode and *uchi*-mode behavior styles co-exist. Children are more manageable in *soto* mode, but more alive and imaginative in *uchi* mode. Formal institutions like industries and companies may occasionally take on *uchi*-ness on occasions planned to make intimacy override formality.

The strain of adjustment to the unempathic demands of *soto* may be

---

[1]*Sorifu* is a government department of general affairs that, among other things, has conducted a number of survey works. *Sorifu* has recently changed its name to *Somucho*.

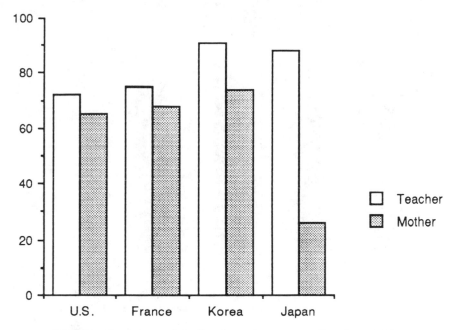

FIG. 13.1. Percentages of obedient/receptive responses (based on statistics from Sorifu, 1981).

reduced by finding a niche there where the *uchi*-mode behavior is acceptable. The ability to perceive the extent to which the *uchi* behavior pattern is appropriate in a given situation becomes an important social skill.

In any culture, toddlers and very young children are protected inside the interdependence or *uchi*-ness of the family. In the West, however, they are expected to outgrow it as soon as possible and become independent. In Japan, *uchi* persists and co-exists with *soto*. The attainment of independence is less an immediate developmental goal for young children in Japan than in the West. Rather, in Japan the early development of behavior traits that facilitate familial harmony is hoped for strongly. Figure 13.2 compares Japanese and American mothers of 4-year-old children concerning how early they expect different developmental goals to be attained (based on results reported in Azuma, Kashiwagi, & Hess, 1981). As expected, emotional maturity and compliance, two traits that contribute to familial harmony, are expected earlier in Japan, whereas social initiative and verbal assertiveness, two traits that contribute to independence, are expected earlier in the United States.

A second example comes from one of our studies in which we asked both U.S. and Japanese mothers what they would say if their child were to refuse to eat the vegetables they had prepared for dinner (Azuma, Kashiwagi, & Hess, 1981). Mothers in both countries say they would first give some kind of reason why the child should eat the vegetable. If that move is unsuccessful,

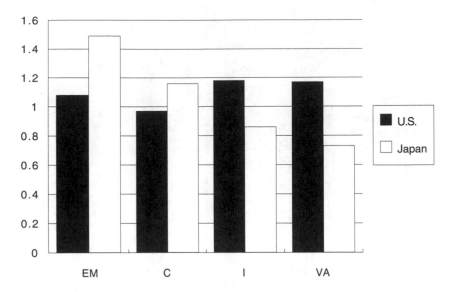

FIG. 13.2. Maternal expectations for early mastery (average age level). EM
= emotional maturity; C = compliance; I = social initiative; VA = verbal assertiveness.

U.S. mothers get stronger and stronger: "Eat it, please," "You must eat it,"
and then the child eats. In contrast, Japanese mothers become weaker and
weaker: "All right, just try a little bit," and "Okay, then tomorrow you will
eat vegetables." I asked one mother if the child would eat vegetables the
next day. "No, never," she said. "He is like my husband; he will never change."
The mother looked very happy. This is not because she thinks discipline is
unimportant but because she thinks it is more important to sustain the feeling of oneness necessary for socialization by empathy, which she is practicing.

The second synthesis of *uchi* and *soto* in Japanese childrearing is seen in
educational methods. Elsewhere, I distinguished two models of teaching and
socialization: verbal teaching and osmosis (Hess & Azuma, 1991). Verbal teaching is what one sees in ordinary classrooms. There is a teacher and at least
one learner. The differentiation of the two roles is clear and distinct. The
teacher has the knowledge or skill that the learner wants to acquire. One
is benefactor and the other is beneficiary. Hence comes the authority of the
teacher. The acknowledgment of this authority, or expert–novice, relationship by both parties is essential. The teacher intentionally imparts his or her
knowledge through verbal media, and the learner receives the message with
the intention to learn. Because the two parties are different and distinct, the
distance between the two has to be bridged by a distal communication medium, typically verbal language.

Osmosis, on the other hand, is a less intentional influence of the social environment, the effect of which is based primarily on modeling on the side of the teacher and incidental learning on the side of the learner. Acquisition of accents, mannerisms, eating habits, and so on are examples of osmosis. The value orientations of parents are often transmitted to the child without intentional teaching. Knowledge and skills are also imparted from the parents to the child even when the parents do not have the slightest intention to teach, as when the mother simply, and even reluctantly, responds to the inquisitive child. When the learner is in close and empathic interdependence with the socializing agent or teacher, more frequent occurrence of modeling and incidental learning is to be expected. By just staying close with secure attachment, children learn a great deal from parents and parent substitutes.

The motivation to imitate a model is reduced if the learner perceives a large distance between the model and him or herself. The affectionate identification of the learner with the model or the teacher is the condition for effective osmosis. Authority relationships beyond a certain minimum block osmosis and are therefore avoided in osmosis-oriented educational environments. The teacher takes the role of a nurturant collaborator in learning, rather than that of an authoritative source of knowledge.

In any culture, socialization and education follow both models. However, the prevailing model of teaching depends on the stress given to independence or interdependence by the general culture. Within a culture that stresses the independence and individuality of a person, a learner is likely to be expected to be independent from the teacher as an individual. There, effective education requires an authoritative relationship from teacher to learner in order to create the one-way flow of information and verbal exchange that bridges the separation between two independent parties. In the collectivistic culture of Japan, a greater stress on interdependence allows the interpersonal closeness required for the osmosis model to prevail.

A comparative study of Japanese and U.S. mothers' reported strategies for teaching their 4-year-olds to read reveals differential use of the two models in the two cultures, as expected. Although the majority of U.S. mothers described more than two teaching methods (e.g., spelling with alphabet blocks, reading to the child), Japanese mothers made fewer attempts and many answered that they did not teach. They would say that children started to read without teaching, using the phrase *shizen ni*, or by nature.

But of course people do not learn to read by nature. What must have taken place was a series of unintentional teaching episodes. For example, the child might come to the mother when he or she is reading, look at the page, point to a character, and ask how it is pronounced. The mother would give him or her the pronunciation simply to get rid of the interference without intending to teach. The child might pick up another character, and then another, until the mother got irritated and told the child to leave her alone. The mother's knowledge of and attitude to reading would, in this way, get transmitted to the child without intentional teaching because mother and child are close, because the child feels that it can interfere with the ongoing engagement of the mother, and because the two are in empathic interdependence that characterize *uchi*-mode interrelations.

Inside *uchi*, personal boundaries in the Lewinian model become thin and permeable, thus allowing an effective osmosis. Verbal messages are less important than they are in *soto*-mode verbal teaching. In our cross-national study mentioned earlier (Azuma et al., 1981), we also compared the verbal messages used by mothers in teaching children how to sort a bunch of wooden blocks of different shapes. Contrary to our expectation, the average number of message units did not significantly differ between Japan and the United States. The difference was in the content of those messages. The American mothers would typically teach step by step, verbalizing how to do it and asking for verbal responses. Japanese mothers would show in a wholistic fashion how to sort blocks, and use verbal messages to engage children to look carefully, to think better, and to do it right. The Japanese mothers do not teach verbally, but use verbalization to get the child involved, capitalizing on empathic identification.

This osmosis model also prevailed in the training of traditional arts and crafts in Japan. The master would not teach. Instead, the live-in disciples, called *uchideshis*, would "steal" the art, together with the professional living style and work ethic, while helping the master with his work and doing household chores. The *uchideshi* system was also common until the Meiji Reform of the late 19th century, even in academic schooling.

Modern schooling in Japan started after the Meiji Reform, which took place some 120 years ago. The method of teaching at that time was closely patterned after Euro-American schools. But in the course of more than a century, there was a substantial amount of assimilation to Japanese culture. One notable shift from the original model is the permeation of *uchi*-mode egalitarianism into the method of elementary education.

For example, the present course of study prepared by the Japanese Ministry of Education requires that science classes should make pupils explore, observe, experiment, and think. What should be explored, observed, experimented with, and thought through is specified for each grade level and for each season of the year. An obvious approach would be to tell the pupils to observe, experiment, and so forth. Textbooks published by private publishers based on this course of study, however, do not use this imperative style.

Out of about 2,500 sentences that appear in Grades 4–6 textbooks published by Dainippon-Tosho absolutely none uses the imperative form. Instead of saying "do this" or "do that," the expressions such as "let's do this," "what will happen if we do that?" "let's find out why it is shaped like that," and so forth are used. As one of the editorial members of this textbook, I at one time proposed reducing the use of this hypocritical egalitarian expression in favor of more imperative forms. This proposal was turned down by the strong opposition of the classroom teachers who were members of the same editorial board. Their point was that the directive style would destroy the nice, creative atmosphere of good science classes. Having seen classes in the United States where clear, snappy directions from the teacher led to exciting discoveries, I do not believe that what our teachers said represents the universal truth. It nevertheless reflects the belief prevailing in Japanese school practices.

Thus, even school education patterned after the Western model reflects the traditional osmosis orientation typical of *uchi* culture. One consequence of this is the lowering of the boundary separating family from school.

In the United States, the mother plays the role of teacher at home when the child is young, and then hands the role over to the teacher as the child starts school. The mother removes herself from instruction, and the school is somewhat insulated from family influence. In Japan, family culture penetrates into the school life of the child by way of common *uchi*-ness. The family's influence on school learning continues to be stronger in Japan than it is in the United States.

Figures 13.3a and 13.3b show the correlations of mothers' interaction styles observed when children were under age 5 with the academic skills and achievements 6–7 years later. Solid arrows show significant correlations, and dotted arrows show significant partial correlations after partialing out school readiness at ages 5–6. Values of partial correlations are shown in Table 13.1 (see p. 283).

Although most maternal variables are correlated with school readiness at ages 5 and 6 in both countries, the patterns of partial correlation are radically different. In the United States, maternal variables influence readiness and relate to later achievement by way of differences in readiness. In Japan, maternal variables affect progress even after children have started school. Particularly, the variable called mother's expectation, which primarily represented the level of education that the mother expected the child to attain, was found to exert a strong influence on the child's progress in school. Assessment of this expectation was made when the child was 3 years old but it would not be unreasonable to assume that many mothers kept the same expectation until their children were older. Although this variable was obviously confounded with social class, most of this social class effect had been partialed out as a component of school readiness skills at age 6. I infer that a mother's expectation permeated the child through years of close empathic identification, shaping his or her aspirations and in turn affecting the child's school achievement. The corresponding partial correlation in the United States was insignificant (Table 13.1).

Is this model compatible with the notorious phenomenon of "education

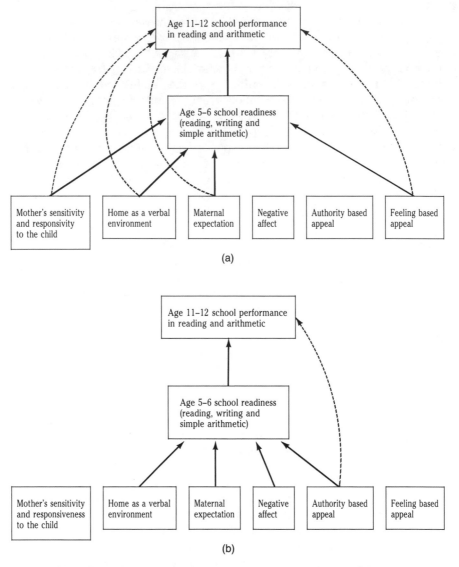

FIG. 13.3.   (a) Correlation of preschool mother variables with ages 5–6 school readiness and their correlation with ages 11–12 performance after partialing out the school readiness (Japan). (b) Correlation of preschool mother variables with ages 5–6 school readiness and their correlation with ages 11–12 performance after partialing out the school readiness (United States).

TABLE 13.1

Partial Correlation of Preschool Maternal Variables with Ages 11–12 School Achievement,
Ages 5–6 Cognitive Achievements Being Partialed Out

Country	Mother's Sensitivity	Home as a Verbal Environment	Maternal Expectation	Negative Effect	Authority-Based Appeal	Feeling-Based Appeal
Japan	0.32	0.34	0.42	n.s.	n.s.	−0.32
United States	n.s.	n.s.	n.s.	n.s.	−0.29	n.s.

Note. n.s. = not significant.

mothers" in Japan? The education mother is a mother deeply preoccupied by the education of her child, especially his or her performance on entrance exams. About 60% to 70% of Japanese mothers fall in this category. But when one looks closely, one sees that Japanese mothers prepare good learning environments for their children. They rarely teach directly. The ethnographic observation of a Japanese-American mother helping her child to write a poem by Schneider, Hieshima, Lee, and Plank (chapter 16, this volume) is very relevant to this point. The mother does not teach him or her how to write. Instead, she prepares an environment where the child can write a good poem. In general, the Japanese mother maintains the position of a quiet cheerleader, not a coach. The child's empathy for the quiet but eagerly cheering mother turns into what Schneider et al. view as intrinsic motivation in Japanese-American children. In Japan, I found that pleasing mother was one of the top three reasons for doing well on tests for the great majority of fifth graders in my sample.

To conclude, the Japanese cultural tradition of education and socialization, which places more weight on osmosis than is the case in the United States, has influenced not only mother–child relationships but also teacher–pupil relationships, school–family relationships, and even the schools' teaching methods. Schneider et al. (chapter 16, this volume) strongly suggest that this tradition survives even in the families of third-generation Japanese immigrants to the United States. Family involvement in education and schooling, which is part of this tradition, would have contributed to the academic success of Japanese-American children, as Schneider et al. point out. On the other hand, it is not impossible that this tradition, because it is different from prevailing culture in the United States, has caused adjustment difficulties for a certain portion of immigrant Japanese children. Further studies of Japanese Americans will contribute much to clarifying issues of continuity and discontinuity with Japanese culture and current societal context.

REFERENCES

Azuma, H., Kashiwagi, K., & Hess, R. D. (1981). *The influence of attitude and behavior upon the child's intellectual development*. Tokyo: University of Tokyo Press.

Doi, T. (1971). *The anatomy of dependence*. New York: Kodansha International.

Hess, R. D., & Azuma, H. (1991). Cultural support for schooling: Contrasts between Japan and the United States. *Educational Researcher, 20*, 2–8.

Kawai, H. (1971). *Boshi-shakai Nippon no Byori* [The pathology of Japan as a maternalistic society]. Tokyo: Chuko-Sosho.

Sorifu. (1981). Children and mothers of Japan. Tokyo: Bureau of Printing of the Ministry of Finance.

White, M. J., & LeVine, R. (1986). What is an Iiko (good child)? In H. Stevenson, H. Azuma, & K. Hakuta (Eds.), *Child development and education in Japan* (pp. 55–62). New York: W. H. Freeman.

14

COGNITIVE SOCIALIZATION IN CONFUCIAN HERITAGE CULTURES

David Y. F. Ho
University of Hong Kong

Investigators of cognitive socialization in Confucian heritage cultures are confronted with a paradox. On the one hand, it is commonly believed that in these cultures a high value is placed on educational achievement, and that children are highly motivated to succeed in school. Given that a culture tends to excel in what it values, it is hardly surprising that tangible dividends in terms of actual achievement have been obtained. Superior levels of achievement in mathematics and/or science by Chinese and Japanese children have been consistently reported in cross-national studies (Comber & Keeves, 1973; Garden, 1987; Husen, 1967; Rodd, 1959; Stevenson et al., 1990; Stevenson, Lee, & Stigler, 1986).

In North America, the superior educational and occupational achievements of Asians are well documented (Vernon, 1982). Asian Americans have higher levels of educational achievement than the national average, as indicated by percentages of high school and college graduates, grades, and finalists and winners in prestigious competitions (Sue & Okazaki, 1990). The image of Asian "whiz kids" has captured the attention of educators and has even entered the public consciousness.

On the other hand, critics of Confucian educational systems point to their many ills: (a) the authoritarian atmosphere in the classroom in general and of the teacher–student relationship in particular; (b) outmoded instructional methods; (c) overemphasis on examinations; (d) lack of cultivation of creativity and independent, critical thinking; and (e) excessive pressure to succeed, often at the expense of the students' mental health. Thus, the question must be raised: What are the costs to psychological development of the lopsided emphasis on academic achievement? Further, do the cultural values leading to the ills of the educational systems also have adverse implications for cognitive socialization in general?

Confronting the paradox provides a convenient framework for the organization of the present chapter. I first identify the core Confucian values underlying socialization. Then I present evidence pertaining to the psychological consequences of these values for cognitive socialization. Next, I make explicit expectations pertaining to cognitive socialization in several important areas of research and examine the extent to which they are supported by evidence. The learning environment in school and at home is then described. A discussion of three themes follows: (a) continuities and discontinuities with cultural heritage, (b) socialization for social and technical intelligence (Mundy-Castle, 1974), and (c) socialization for survival and educational development (LeVine, 1987).

A comparison of the cognitive socialization patterns between Asian and Asian-American children throws light on continuities with and departures from tradition. How social and technological intelligence relates to collectivism and individualism is explored. LeVine's (1977) argument about the different goals of socialization was grounded in a general thesis: Consciously or unconsciously, adults try to inculcate in children, through childrearing practices, cognitive, linguistic, motivational, and social competencies that are adaptive in their particular cultural milieu. I give illustrations of how this thesis applies in Confucian heritage cultures. Finally, I deal with the paradox through a discussion of psychological and educational issues.

Given its great ethnic, linguistic, and cultural diversity, it would be pretentious and impossible to speak of Asia as a whole. I chose to confine myself to the Far East because societies in the Far East, specifically Chinese, Japanese, and Korean, share a common cultural heritage—the oldest with an unbroken Confucian heritage—that has been extensively studied by scholars.

Although an extensive behavioral science literature on socialization in Confucian societies is available, it is rather uneven and has serious lacunae of knowledge. Asian-American studies tend to ignore the literature on Asian studies, especially when it is from non-English language sources—as if Asian Americans can be understood without a fuller understanding of Asia and Asians. For instance, a perusal of the 1990 *Child Development* special issue on minority children reveals that the Asian literature was rarely consulted. Therefore, an integration of knowledge is needed. I rely on studies of Chinese children primarily and Japanese children secondarily, and draw on studies of Chinese-American and Japanese-American children where appropriate. In this respect, my chapter complements that of Kim and Choi (chapter 11, this volume), who discuss Korean, Korean-American, and Korean-Canadian child development in relation to the Confucian tradition (albeit with somewhat different emphasis).

CONFUCIANISM, CHILD TRAINING, AND COGNITIVE SOCIALIZATION

In a seminal article, Greenwald (1980) argued for a conception of the totalitarian ego as an organization of knowledge, characterized by three cognitive biases: (a) egocentricity (self as the focus of knowledge), (b) beneffectance (perception of responsibility for desired, but not undesired, outcomes), and (c) cognitive conservatism (resistance to cognitive change). His psychological portrait of what he called the totalitarian ego bears a striking correspondence to the portrayal of totalitarian political systems by political scientists. In this chapter, I investigate the nature of cognitive biases, particularly cognitive conservatism, in the context of Confucian heritage cultures.

The influence of Confucianism on cognitive socialization may be conceived in two ways. The first concerns the usual interest in the child's learning experiences; the second concerns the representation of reality transmitted to, and subsequently experienced and internalized by, the child.

Concerning the second, Confucian thinking on morality and, by extension, knowledge in general assumes that there is a fundamental distinction between right and wrong—one that cannot be disputed because it is an extension of the cosmic principle into the realm of knowledge. The human mind is capable of discerning this distinction, and the function of education is to enforce making it. Therefore, children must be taught the correct knowledge, not to question it. This knowledge is contained in the teachings of sages in the classics. The written word is sacred and comes to be identified with truth. Thus, Confucianism sets the stage for cognitive socialization through inculcating into the child's mind its representation of reality. The learning experiences that follow are in conformity with this representation.

In Confucian societies, the guiding principle governing socialization is embodied in the ethic of filial piety. This principle organizes and stamps the child's learning experiences. Among the filial precepts are: obeying and honoring one's parents, providing for the material and mental well-being of one's aged parents, performing the ceremonial duties of ancestral worship, taking care to avoid harm to one's body, ensuring the continuity of the family line, and in general conducting oneself so as to bring honor and not disgrace to the family name. Traditional parental attitudes and child training, rooted in filial piety, exert a pervasive influence on cognitive socialization in the (a) definition of the teacher–student relationship, (b) attitudes toward learning, and the (c) cognitive aspects of personality functioning.

The evidence from psychological studies strongly suggests that the influence of filial piety is predominantly and consistently negative from a contemporary perspective on human development. Thus, fathers' and mothers' subscription to the precepts of filial piety tends to result in high rigidity and low cognitive complexity in their children (Boey, 1976). Individuals holding traditional attitudes toward filial piety and/or child training tend to be poorer in verbal fluency; to adopt a passive, uncritical, and uncreative orientation toward learning; to hold fatalistic, superstitious, and stereotypic beliefs; and to be authoritarian, dogmatic, and conformist (Ho, 1990). This constellation of attributes points toward cognitive conservatism—a disposition to preserve existing knowledge structures described by Greenwald (1980).

The significance of the evidence described is that it establishes a linkage between external cultural knowledge and internal individual cognition: Cognitive conservatism operating within the individual mirrors the Confucian conservatism governing human relationships, as well as educational and sociopolitical institutions. On the basis of this evidence, it is possible to make explicit a number of expectations about cognitive socialization and functioning in Confucian heritage cultures. In the following, I state these expectations and examine the extent to which they are empirically confirmed in each of five important research areas: maternal and infant behavior, relative differences in cognitive abilities, achievement motivation, beliefs and attributions of academic success or failure, and learning styles and strategies.

Maternal and Infant Behavior

Expectation 1. Given the emphasis on social control in the Confucian tradition Chinese and Japanese children are socialized to achieve an early mastery of impulse control, which is a precondition for academic success later. In Confucian heritage cultures, impulse control and academic achievement may be identified as two of the most important goals of socialization. The former is more fundamental than the latter: Impulse control is an imperative requirement for meeting the demands of social control regardless of one's level of academic achievement. The more stringent the social control, the greater is the pressure to exercise impulse control.

In particular, given the highly disciplined nature of formal schooling, beginning from the lower grades and even kindergarten, an early mastery of impulse control is essential for school readiness. In other words, the distant goal of academic success is predicated on the immediate goal of impulse control—no less than on the development of cognitive skills. The literature has recognized the roles of the father and the teacher as disciplinarians. I believe that no less attention should be paid to the mother as the chief agent of impulse control in the earliest period of the child's life. This is the topic of the next section.

Complementarity Between Maternal and Infant Behavior.   There is evidence to suggest that the emphasis on impulse control is reflected very early in the infant's behavior. Cross-cultural studies have found that Chinese (Freedman, 1974; Freedman & Freedman, 1969; Kagan, Kearsley, & Zelazo, 1978) and Japanese babies (Bornstein, Azuma, Tamis-LeMonda, & Ogino, 1990; Caudill & Weinstein, 1969; Otaki, Durrett, Richards, Nyquist, & Pennebaker, 1986) differ from Euro-American babies on the dimensions of excitability and temperament. For example, Chinese and Japanese tend to be less happily vocal, less active, and less exploratory—a cluster of qualities indicative of a disposition toward quiet calmness. However, this cannot be considered an established finding, in view of the conflicting results on infant activity reported in Japanese-American studies (see review by Bornstein, 1989).

In each culture, infant behavior appears to show a high degree of complementarity with maternal behavior. Thus, Caudill and Weinstein (1969) found that Japanese mothers were in greater bodily contact with their infants and soothed them toward physical quiescence and passivity with regard to their environment. By contrast, mothers in the United States were in greater vocal interaction with their infants and stimulated them to greater physical activity and exploration. A follow-up study (Caudill & Schooler, 1973) found that consistent cross-cultural differences in the behavior of children and their caregivers persisted into early childhood. Bornstein, Miyaki, and Tamis-LeMonda (1985–1986) found that mothers on the island of Hokkaido in the far north of Japan stimulated their infants to the environment less than mothers in New York City. However, the study by Bornstein et al. (1990) found no significant group differences in maternal activities between Tokyo and New York City, suggesting that urbanized Japanese mothers are becoming more like their Western counterparts. Still, the data point to mutual attunement (synchronization of activities) in mother–infant dyads in both groups.

A genetic interpretation of ethnic differences in infant excitability and temperament was favored by Freedman and Freedman (1969) based on their studies of newborns. The evidence also supports a cultural role. The complementarity between maternal and infant behaviors has already been mentioned. Unlike Japanese infants, third-generation Japanese-American infants are like Euro-American infants: They both respond to greater stimulation from their mothers with high levels of happy vocalization and physical activity (Caudill & Frost, 1973).

In the study by Kagan et al. (1978), with the exception of heart-rate change, significant differences between Chinese- and Euro-American infants were not found until 6–12 months, and they were more pronounced among infants from the working class than the middle class. Thus, there is good reason to believe that familial experiences contribute to these differences.

Of course, both genetic and cultural factors may be operative. The reader is referred to Bornstein (1989) for a more detailed discussion of the genetic-versus-culture issue.

To conclude, early Chinese and Japanese socialization patterns are in line with the demands of Confucian heritage cultures in which overriding importance is attached to impulse control. I interpret the disposition toward inhibition, if indeed manifest as early as the newborn period, as a precursor of the same disposition to be found in adulthood. This disposition is adaptive in the Confucian cultural context, characterized by its great demands of social control, intolerance of deviancy, and pressure toward conformity.

Early Socialization for Educational Development. Early socialization patterns appear closely related to parental conceptions of the young child's capacity for learning and expectations of the mastery of developmental skills. Traditionally, Chinese parents do not regard young children as capable of "understanding things," and therefore do not hold them responsible for their wrongdoings or failures to meet expectations (Ho, 1986, 1989a). Young children are viewed as passive, dependent creatures who are to be cared for and whose needs are to be met with little delay or interference; training cannot be expected to accomplish much for them. Although little or no systematic attempt is made to develop the child's cognitive skills, overriding importance is attached to the mastery of impulse control. Although passive oral needs are typically met without hesitation, active or exploratory demands tend to be thwarted even during infancy and early childhood. Research is needed on the effects of such parenting on cognitive development, creativity in particular.

There are indications that parental conceptions of childhood are changing. For instance, an intergenerational study (Ho & Kang, 1984, Study 2) showed that, in comparison with grandfathers, fathers in Hong Kong were less traditional in their attitudes toward child training and seemed to be more aware of the young child's capacity for learning. A cross-cultural study of mother–infant teaching interactions (Steward & Steward, 1973) found that Chinese-American mothers were very specific in their instructions and provided a high proportion of enthusiastic, positive feedback to their 3-year-old sons.

A cross-cultural study (Hess, Kashiwagi, Azuma, Price, & Dickson, 1980) found that the overall levels of maternal expectations of developmental tasks in Japan and the United States were virtually identical. However, Japanese mothers expected early mastery on skills indicating emotional maturity, self-control, and social courtesy. By contrast, mothers in the United States expected mastery at an early age on items indicating verbal assertiveness and social skills with peers. Maternal expectations were found to correlate with children's performance on tests of school aptitude when they reached 6 years of age. A follow-up study (Hess, Azuma, Kashiwagi, Holloway, & Wenegrat, 1987) showed that maternal behavior was significantly related to readiness at both 5 years and achievement test scores at 11 or 12 years of age. The association of maternal behavior with children's school-related performance increased between preschool and follow-up periods in Japan, but declined in the United States. Thus, it appears that early maternal expectations and behavior are strategically adaptive to educational development in each culture; the mastery of skills indicative of impulse control is, in actuality, more relevant to academic performance than has been previously recognized. (Note that a contrasting interpretation of this study is provided by Azuma, chapter 13, this volume.)

Relative Differences in Cognitive Abilities

Expectation 2. Chinese and Japanese people should show a relative weakness in verbal compared with nonverbal abilities. This expectation assumes that cognitive conservatism is more closely related to verbal than nonverbal functions. Vernon (1982) observed that "there is the curious but unanimous finding that Orientals of all ages in any cultural setting score higher relative to Euro-Americans on spatial, numerical, or nonverbal intelligence tests, and less well on verbal abilities and achievements" (p. 271). This "unanimous finding" remains controversial, however. It is possible that the relative differences in cognitive abilities across ethnic groups also have their origin in infancy, although admittedly the supporting evidence is weak. Here, I limit myself to a discussion of verbal abilities. (It is too involved to get into the possibility that the superior spatial abilities have to do with the Chinese ideographic system of writing and its implications for brain functions.)

Kagan et al. (1978) found that Chinese infants at 7 months of age and older generally vocalized and smiled less than Euro-American infants in response to laboratory events. They were also poorer in concept formation at 29 months and in language development at 20 months. The authors suggested that these observations may be explained by a complementary relation between two mechanisms: less parental reinforcement for affective display and language development, and a temperamental disposition for a lower threshold for uncertainty toward discrepant experience among the Chinese infants.

Caudill and Weinstein (1969) and Caudill (1972) found that Japanese mothers have less vocal interaction with their infants than American mothers; they do not seem to encourage vocal responsiveness but act in ways that they believe will soothe and quiet their babies. Again, the lack of reinforcement for early language development by both Chinese and Japanese mothers should be interpreted in the context of cultural expectations for adult behavior: Like physical aggressiveness, verbal assertiveness has to be restrained.

Expectation 3. Because of cognitive conservatism, the cultivation of creativity is neglected. Accordingly, Chinese people are relatively weak in divergent thinking abilities.

In contrast to the attention devoted to intelligence and academic achievement, there is a dearth of research on creativity. Ho, Spinks, and Yeung (1989) made a quantitative analysis of 361 educational psychological studies pertaining to Chinese people, most of which were published in The People's Republic of China, Taiwan, and Hong Kong. Each study was indexed using subject terms selected from the *Thesaurus of Psychological Index Terms* (American Psychological Association, 1985). The results indicate that the subject term *achievement* ranked first in frequency (108) and *academic achievement* ranked third (62)—again, a reflection of that with which the researchers have been preoccupied. Significantly, *creativity* registered less than 10.

What little available evidence there is conforms in general to the expectation that Chinese people do not fare well in comparison with people from the United States on tests of creativity or divergent thinking, especially originality. Subjects from Grade 2 to second-year university were tested with a Chinese version of the verbal Torrance Tests of Creative Thinking (Liu & Hsu, 1974). On all three measures (i.e., fluency, originality, and flexibility), the Taiwan norms were below the U.S. norms. Paschal, Kuo, and Schurr (1980–1981) administered a figural (nonverbal) version of the Torrance tests to 120 randomly selected U.S. and Chinese college students. It was found that the Chinese students scored significantly lower on originality but higher on fluency than the U.S. students.

Ripple (1983) tested Hong Kong-Chinese subjects aged 9–60 on three divergent thinking abilities: fluency, flexibility, and originality. The measures were derived from free, written responses to groups of acoustic stimuli recorded on a cassette tape, conceptually similar to the Sounds and Images test (Cunnington & Torrance, 1965). It was found that all age groups scored lower than their U.S. counterparts on all three measures, particularly on originality. They also scored lower than South-African subjects on fluency and flexibility but not on originality. These results are difficult to interpret on account of methodological difficulties. First, the subjects compared were not matched on relevant variables except age. Second, they were required to respond in writing to the acoustic stimuli but the difference in the speed of writing Chinese versus English was not taken into account. The factor of speed may be important because it takes about three times as long to write a Chinese page as its English equivalent (Taylor, 1981).

Adding to the interpretive difficulty in Ripple's (1983) study is the result that comparable scores were obtained between secondary school students from an expatriate school responding in English (Group 1) and those from an Anglo-Chinese school responding in the language of their choice (Chinese or English; Group 2) or a Chinese school responding in Chinese (Group 3).

Group 2 scored higher than Group 3 on flexibility and originality but not on fluency—a result that seems to negate the factor of speed. Students from an Anglo-Chinese school who were forced to respond in English (Group 4) were dramatically inferior to the other three groups on all three measures, indicating that the production of divergent thoughts was severely inhibited when students were required to respond in a non-native language. The devastating effect of language shift was found even for university students, who would be expected to have a good command of English. The same group responding in English performed poorer by far on all three measures than when they were responding in Chinese. It appears that responding in English has an inhibitory effect that is too potent to be compensated for by the speed factor. However, to obtain unambiguous results, the factors of speed as well as the subjects' bilingual proficiency have to be adequately controlled.

Achievement Motivation

Expectation 4. Because of the Confucian emphasis on education, Chinese children are socialized to achieve academically. Accordingly, academic achievement motivation should be exceedingly strong.

It is beyond dispute that great importance is attached to academic achievement in Confucian societies. For instance, Simmons and Wade (1988) reported that Japanese 14-year-olds attached supreme importance to studying, passing examinations, and entering high school, whereas English 15-year-olds were more concerned with getting a job. Biggs (1990) found that in Hong Kong, Chinese and other Asian students were significantly more achievement oriented than European students. Mitchell (1972) reported that, among Form 5 (Grade 11) students, 34% indicated that they "would like to attend" and 26% indicated that they would "very much like to attend" a university; 58% stated that their parents wanted them to do so; and "doing well in school" was the most frequently mentioned quality or behavior most likely to be approved by their father and mother. A more recent survey ("Youth in Hong Kong," 1988, table 3.7.3) showed that 52% of respondents aged 10–25 preferred to attain a postsecondary level of education. Educational and occupational aspirations appeared closely related: 24% of the respondents preferred to be professionals (e.g., scientists, doctors, and teachers) in the future.

I now examine the motivational context within which such stress is placed on academic achievement. Earlier reports suggested that achievement motivation was lower in Chinese than in U.S. society, as revealed in a content analysis of children's readers (McClelland, 1963) and Thematic Apperception Test (TAT) stories collected from college students (Hsu, 1963). However, the reverse was found when self-report inventories were used as measuring instruments (see the review by Yang, 1986). This inconsistency may be attributed, at least in part, to problems of measurement, bearing in mind that zero or very low correlations between projective and self-report measures have been reported in the literature on achievement motivation.

Still, diachronic data obtained with similar measurement techniques point to an increase in achievement motivation: Content analysis of children's reading materials collected at different time periods reveal an increase in the salience of achievement-related activities in the People's Republic of China (see review by Ho, 1986).

Among both fathers and grandfathers in Hong Kong, the most frequently mentioned personal characteristics expected of their children when they grew up were those concerned with, in a descending order, (a) competence and achievement, (b) moral character, (c) sociability, and (d) controlled temperament (Ho & Kang, 1984, Study 2). As to cross-cultural comparisons, Lin and Fu (1990) reported that Chinese parents in Taiwan and immigrant Chinese parents tended to rate higher than Euro-American parents on (a) parental control, (b) emphasis on achievement and, contrary to what has been commonly believed, (c) encouragement of independence. Expression of affection showed no significant differences between groups. Taken together, the evidence suggests that achievement motivation has been gaining strength in Chinese societies, even surpassing the United States.

Expectation 5.   Chinese achievement motivation is rooted more firmly in the collectivistic than in the individualistic orientation. As a derivative of filial piety, collectivism links individual achievement to family-oriented achievement.

In comparing Chinese and U.S. achievement motivation, Wilson and Pusey (1982) pointed out that independence training was not the decisive factor for Chinese—in contradiction to McClelland's (1963) theory of achievement motivation. Furthermore, Chinese achievement motivation was positively associated with face consciousness and group orientation. Salili (1987) explored the meaning of achievement among groups of male and female British and Chinese secondary school students and Chinese adults in Hong Kong. For the Chinese groups, positive correlations, mostly moderate in magnitude, were obtained between importance ratings of success in academic, career, and financial situations and those in personal-social life and in family relationships. In contrast, negligible or negative correlations were obtained for the British students.

These results invite one to question the universality of McClelland's theory, one rooted in the ideology of individualism, which DeVos (1973) did in his studies of achievement motivation in Japan. The results also point to a high degree of commonality between Chinese and Japanese achievement motivation.

Studies linking achievement motivation directly to filial piety are rare. Ho (1990) reported that filial piety was correlated with both individual achievement and family-oriented achievement. The difference between these two correlations was not significant at the .05 level. Individual achievement and family-oriented achievement were correlated. Yu (1974) found that filial piety was correlated with verbal statements on achievement but uncorrelated with achievement motivation as measured by TAT stimuli. Verbal statements on achievement correlated more highly with extended familism than with nuclear familism, supporting the contention that Chinese achievement motivation is rooted more firmly in the collectivistic than in the individualistic orientation. Further support to this contention may be found in studies summarized by Ho (1986), Yang (1986), and Yue and Yang (1987).

More recently, Ho and Chiu (in press) cautioned against the indiscriminate characterization of Chinese culture as exemplary of collectivism or as antithetical to individualism. They reported that, among Hong Kong university students, attitudes toward self-reliance and cooperation (i.e., toward ideas of both individualism and collectivism) are positively correlated. Also, a content analysis of 9,995 Chinese popular sayings reveals the importance of recognizing the multidimensional nature of the individualism–collectivism construct.

According to the analysis, the number of sayings that affirm, advocate, or endorse ideas of collectivistic achievement (e.g., cooperation and relying on group efforts) is greater than those that negate, disavow, or oppose those ideas. Regarding individualistic achievement (e.g., competition and relying on individual efforts), the reverse is found: Ideas of relying on individual efforts (e.g., doing things by oneself) to achieve goals are especially negated.

However, on another dimension both interdependence (a component idea of collectivism emphasizing reciprocity in self–other relationships) and self-reliance (a component idea of individualism emphasizing individual responsibility, needs, interests, security, etc.) are clearly affirmed. Thus, the content analysis identifies individualistic achievement and self-reliance as two distinct component ideas of individualism; the negation of the former does not entail the negation of the latter. It also shows that ideas of both individualism and collectivism may be affirmed (or negated) within Chinese culture.

From both a methodological and a conceptual point of view, it is important to develop different measures for collectivistic and individualistic achievement motivation. Yue and Yang (1987) provided strong evidence to support their contention that what they termed *social-oriented* and *individual-oriented* achievement motivation are two distinct psychological constructs. For instance, a near-zero correlation was obtained between highly reliable measures of these two types of achievement motivation. After reviewing the evidence, Yang (1986) concluded that social-oriented achievement motivation is declining in Chinese society in the process of modernization, whereas individual-oriented achievement motivation is gaining ascendancy.

Beliefs and Attributions

Expectation 6. Confucian educators believe that diligence is key to successful academic performance. Therefore, effort is regarded as the main determinant of success or failure.

The traditional Chinese belief in learning through hard work is embodied in the popular saying: "The sea of learning knows no bounds; only through diligence may its shore be reached." It is also consistently reflected in studies conducted in Hong Kong. For example, Hau and Salili (1991) found that secondary students rated effort as the most important determinant of academic performance. Among university students in Taiwan, Yang (1982) reported that effort was approximately equal to ability in attributions of academic success. However, lack of effort was stronger than lack of ability in attributions of failure. In a cross-cultural study of family beliefs about children's performance in mathematics, Hess, Chang, and McDevitt (1987) found that mothers in mainland China attributed their children's failures predominantly to lack of effort, whereas Chinese-American mothers viewed effort as important but also considered other factors. In contrast, Euro-Americans attributed failure least to effort.

A psychological corollary of the belief in effort places the emphasis on internal rather than external attributions. As Chan-Ho (1990) reported, Hong Kong students attribute both success and failure more to internal than to external causes. The implication is that one would expect them to be highly achievement oriented, in accordance with Weiner's attribution theory of achievement-related behavior (Weiner, Heckhausen, Meyer, & Cook, 1972). Research conducted in Taiwan (see review by Bond & Hwang, 1986) has shown that achievement motivation is positively related with internal attributions to effort and ability, and negatively related with external attributions to luck and task difficulty. However, academic achievement is not related to causal attribution.

However, the emphasis on effort over ability may have some unfortunate consequences. Parents, teachers, and students tend not to give ability due consideration in cases of academic failure; often the goals of educational attainment are unrealistically high. This heightens the pressure placed on and felt by students who fail. Many repeat the same grade or take the same university entrance examination, often more than once, only to have their sense of frustration intensified. Mitchell (1972) reported that, among Form 5 students in Hong Kong, 38% have repeated a grade one or more times. Indeed, "Failure is the mother of success" is a belief strongly held by Chinese people. Hence, the prescriptive principle for action is: "If you don't succeed, try again."

Learning Styles and Strategies

Expectation 7. Because of the sacred quality of the written word in Confucianism, learning styles emphasize memorization and repeated practice, at the expense of understanding and discovery. In accord with the Confucian emphasis on mastering a body of correct knowledge, students are preoccupied with examinations and are syllabus-bound in their approach to study.

A survey (Liu, 1984) found that most teachers in public schools in Taiwan still require pupils to memorize every lesson in the Chinese language textbooks. The stress on repeated practice is reflected in the fact that Chinese schoolchildren spend an inordinate amount of time on homework (see the following section). Not surprisingly, there is evidence that such traditional learning styles are not conducive to the development of critical intellectual faculties advantageous for learning at higher levels of education. For instance, compulsive study orientation (stressing belief in (a) what the book says, (b) the hardship of learning, and (c) the need for memorization, compulsion, and punishment in the learning process) was positively correlated with measures of belief stereotypy, authoritarianism, conformity, dogmatism, and traditionalism (Ho, 1987). However, it was negatively correlated with measures of academic performance by university students in Hong Kong (Ho & Spinks, 1985).

The results of another study (Gow et al., 1989) are typical: Hong Kong tertiary students (a) are preoccupied with examinations; (b) strategically concentrate their efforts on materials covered by the syllabus; and (c) typically rely on handouts or notes taken in lectures, and use texts and/or recommended readings only as supplements. In view of these results, it is difficult to imagine why they would need to spend, according to a survey (Asian Commercial Research, 1990), an average of 20 hours and 47 minutes at home per week doing their studies (in addition to 33 hours and 36 minutes spent at school).

LEARNING ENVIRONMENTS IN SCHOOL AND AT HOME: THE INFLUENCE OF CONFUCIANISM

The School Environment

As stated in *The Three-Character Classic*, a chief primer for beginners produced in the 13th century and memorized by countless Chinese children until recent times: "Rearing without education is the fault of the father; teaching without strictness is the negligence of the teacher." It appears that the injunction on strictness has persisted to the present day. The Chinese school environment is orderly and authoritarian; strict discipline is emphasized. In line with the Confucian ideal of filial piety, teachers are authority figures who are not to be questioned or challenged. Their role is to impart knowledge—to instruct, not to stimulate, students. The typical teaching methods are formal, expository, and teacher initiated.

Students are treated as passive recipients, not active seekers, of knowledge. Students soon learn an implicit behavioral rule in the classroom: Avoid making mistakes and thereby being ridiculed. Therefore, the safest strategy is to keep silent.

A study by Stevenson et al. (1986) reported that Chinese and Japanese children are led by the teacher for higher percentages of the time than U.S. children (about 90%, 70%, and 50%, respectively). Correspondingly, Chinese and Japanese teachers spend proportionally more time imparting information than U.S. teachers (58%, 33%, and 21%, respectively). Concerning the People's Republic of China, Hawkins (1983) stated:

> Chinese teachers have utilized an approach over the past 30 years that remains surprisingly traditional—the teacher-centered classroom. Despite revolutionary rhetoric, massive social-change efforts, and period of political disruption, Chinese students have been cast as passive recipients of whatever form of instruction has prevailed at the time. (p. 168)

How do students react to their authoritarian school environment? Available evidence suggests that in the future tension may be increasingly felt. Wu and Chen (1978) reported that junior secondary school students in Taiwan generally expected their teachers to provide democratic leadership; the greatest "expectation distance" was found for authoritarian teachers. The greater the expectation distance, the poorer was the students' academic achievement, belief in internal control, achievement motivation, and personal and social adjustment. On the other hand, teachers' democratic leadership correlated positively with these variables.

Socioeconomic Status, Family Structure, and Family Environment

At the outset, it is useful to distinguish three classes of variables: socioeconomic status (SES), family structure (e.g., number of children, ordinal position, and gender of siblings), and familial environment (e.g., press for achievement, intellectual stimulation, parental attitudes, and parental involvement). Of these three, only familial-environment variables are psychological in nature and translate directly into differences in the child's enculturation experience; the other two have indirect effects mediated by their influence on various aspects of the child's environment.

Yang (1985) reviewed relevant studies done in Taiwan and concluded that low SES has adverse consequences for children's self-concept, social adjustment (as indicated by behavioral disturbance and delinquency), attitudes toward learning, intelligence, and academic achievement.

However, there is some evidence to suggest that the effects of parental education per se are negligible or very small. In the study by Yue and Yang (1987), correlations of fathers' and mothers' education with either individual-oriented or social-oriented achievement motivation were very low (less than .15). Ho (1979) reported that mostly near-zero correlations were obtained between fathers' and mothers' levels of education and measures of verbal intelligence and academic performance among Hong Kong schoolchildren.

The pressure on students to study hard and to do well in examinations, which is notorious in Hong Kong, may be present regardless of parental education. Among Form 5 students whose fathers and mothers attained only the primary level of education or lower, 50% stated that their parents wanted them to attend a university (Mitchell, 1972, table 7.1).

Asian-American children show a similar pattern. The report by Coleman et al. (1966) showed that, at Grade 6, correlations between nonverbal ability and familial-environment variables (reading materials and consumer items in the home) or family structure (number of siblings) were higher than they were for the Euro-American children, but this was reversed for parental education. Among these predictors, environmental variables had the highest and parental education had the lowest predictive power for the Asian-American children. In the United States, as in Asia, this finding is consonant with a uniformly high value placed on education, in accord with the Confucian tradition.

Results obtained by Jensen (unpublished data, cited in Vernon, 1982) showed nonsignificant or very low correlations between parental SES and child intelligence or achievement. Yee and LaForce (1974) also found that social class, as measured by residence and fathers' occupation, was not correlated with Wechsler Intelligence Scale for Children (WISC) scores for American-born Chinese fourth graders. In sum, familial-environment variables appear to be more potent predictors than family-structure or SES variables—in line with the conclusion that Marjoribanks (1972) reached for Western children.

Homework and Parental Involvement

Given the emphasis on effort in the Confucian tradition, it is hardly surprising that Chinese children are expected to and do spend a great deal of time on homework. Given the Confucian emphasis on the role of the family in children's education, parental involvement in children's homework would also be expected.

In a cross-cultural examination of homework, Chen and Stevenson (1989) reported that Chinese children (both mainland and Taiwan) were assigned more homework and spent more time on homework than Japanese children, who in turn were assigned more and spent more time on homework than did U.S. children. Chinese children also received more help from family members with their homework than did U.S. and Japanese children, and had more positive attitudes about homework than did U.S. children. There was no consistent linear or curvilinear relation between the amount of time spent on homework and achievement in reading and mathematics within cultural groups. Moreover, the amount of time mothers spent helping their children with their homework was mostly correlated negatively with achievement.

Similarly, surveys conducted in Hong Kong indicate that students spend an enormous amount of time on homework, leaving precious little time for outside reading, leisure, or other activities. Secondary and tertiary students spend an average of 36 hours and 9 minutes and 33 hours and 36 minutes, respectively, at school; and 17 hours and 1 minute and 20 hours and 47 minutes, respectively, at home per week on academic work (Asian Commercial Research, 1990). Among Form 5 students, 24% spend 3–4 hours, and 29% spend 4 or more hours each day "doing homework *outside* of school" (Mitchell, 1972, pp. 308–309).

Primary and junior secondary schoolchildren (Grades 4–9) spend an average of 13 hours and 33.6 minutes on homework (exclusive of other activities), but only 1 hour and 12 minutes on outside reading per week ("Research Report," 1979; calculated from tables 2.2 and 2.9). For Primary 5 schoolchildren, the average time spent on homework per week is 15 hours and 10.2 minutes. This is far longer than those for fifth graders elsewhere reported by Chen and Stevenson (1989)—equivalent to, for instance, 2.1 times (estimated by mothers) and 3.6 times (estimated by teachers) the amount spent by children in the United States.

The findings add credence to the view, long held by educators and parents alike, that children's schoolwork is a major parental preoccupation fraught with contradictions and difficulties in Hong Kong and Taiwan. For example, by far more parents (63%) in Hong Kong found children's schoolwork to be "difficult to handle" than in the case of other problems (Against Child Abuse, 1986).

A study conducted by Griffin and Mok (1990) used the Hong Kong dataset from the International Educational Achievement mathematics study. Parental pressure was measured by students' perceptions of the importance their parents attach to mathematics, the encouragement given to them, and how much their parents wanted them to do well in class. Parental involvement was measured by the students' perceptions of how much their parents liked mathematics and their parents' ability to help them with mathematics homework. The results indicate that parental pressure and parental involvement represent two different aspects of home influence: Parents who want their children to do well may not have the ability to help them. More importantly, parental pressure has a negative effect, greater for males than for females, on the students' achievement.

Lin (1988) investigated three classes of predictors of academic performance, as measured by two sets of examination results, by elementary school students in Taiwan. The results show that personal factors alone (gender, time spent on outside reading, and time spent on homework) accounted for only about 1% of performance variances; family background alone (parental education, occupation, attitudes toward education, and expectations of the child's educational attainment) accounted for about 10%; and parental involvement (time spent on helping the child in schoolwork, level of participation in decision making, communication with the school, homework, outside reading, and extracurricular activities), by itself accounted for about 5% and 6%. Together, the three classes of predictors accounted for about 12% and 14% of performance variances. Also, parental involvement was found to be positively associated with family background.

Apparently parents spend a large amount of time, ranging from less than one-half hour to more than 3 hours per day, helping their children in schoolwork. However, this variable tends to be negatively associated with academic performance, which I interpret as reflecting poorer students' need to demand more time from their parents, who are prepared to go to extreme lengths to help them. Moreover, that time spent on homework by the child has a negligible effect on academic performance should raise questions about the learning strategies adopted. That outside reading has a similar negligible effect should raise questions about the relevance and meaningfulness of examinations in particular, as well as about the goals of education in general.

In conclusion, it is prudent to ask if overstressing the amount of homework to be done represents a misguided belief that quantity automatically translates into quality. Are the children, especially in Hong Kong, being deprived of the time for play, outside reading, and other activities essential for balanced psychological development? Will something of lasting value be gained from all that hard work? I know of no evidence to suggest that there is any. However, there is evidence that points to mental health costs incurred on account of the pressure to succeed in school, such as: (a) high levels of anxiety, (b) depression, (c) school phobia, and (d) psychosomatic and neurotic disorders (see Cheung, 1986, for a summary). Disturbed parent–child relations, which as a clinical psychologist I have had plenty of opportunities to witness, add to the high costs.

A DISCUSSION OF THREE THEMES

Continuities and Discontinuities

The theme of continuities and discontinuities applies to two separate, but related, domains. One concerns continuities with and departures from the Confucian tradition. The other concerns the degree of compatibility or incompatibility of the Confucian tradition with mainstream formal schooling in the United States.

The Confucian Tradition. In reviewing the literature on Chinese patterns of socialization in diverse geopolitical communities, Ho (1989a, 1989b) concluded that discontinuities appear less salient when gauged against continuities with the traditional pattern. Ho (1989b) argued that:

> Authoritarian moralism (vs. democratic-psychological orientation) and collectivism (vs. individualism) capture succinctly the distinctive character of Chinese socialization patterns. The former entails impulse control (vs. expression); the latter entails interdependence (vs. autonomy) and conformism (vs. unique individuation). Authoritarian moralism and collectivism underlie both the traditional and the contemporary ideologies governing socialization, and thus preserve its continuity. (p. 144)

The evidence supports the contention that the roots of authoritarian moralism and collectivism may be traced to the Confucian ethic of filial piety.

A powerful impetus toward discontinuity stems from lowered rates of birth and infant mortality in recent decades, leading to an alteration of priorities. The population policy of having one child per married couple in the People's Republic of China, in particular, is bound to have unprecedented psychosocial consequences. If the policy is successfully implemented, future generations will find having cousins, uncles, or aunts an unusual experience. It is mind-boggling to contemplate the consequences of such a radical transformation of the kinship structure.

Ho (1989b) observed that children are now valued, especially within the family, more so than ever before. Children seem to enjoy priority in the allocation of limited material resources. Chinese society has shown unmistakable signs of becoming less age centered and more child centered. Often the child is the center of attention, whose needs and interests are to be met above all else. What may be called a precious-child syndrome may be readily observed.

Ho (1989b) predicted that this child centeredness will lead to an ascendancy of individualism, placing a greater value on individuality, self-reliance, and fulfillment of self-interests and aspirations. I also predict that socialization for maximizing educational development will strengthen as the low birthrate continues; and that changes in formal schooling, more in keeping with the ascendancy of individualism, will accelerate.

Among Asian-Pacific Americans, both continuities and discontinuities with their traditional parenting style may be discerned. Asian-American students tend to come from families high on authoritarianism and permissiveness and low on authoritative characteristics—the opposite of Euro-American students; their parents had the lowest level of involvement among the ethnic groups studied (see Dornbusch, Prescott, & Ritter, 1987; Dornbusch, Ritter, Leiderman, Roberts, & Fraleigh, 1987; Ritter & Dornbusch, 1989), in contrast to the high level of parental involvement found for Chinese-American and Japanese-American students.

The evidence suggests that academic performance declines with increased acculturation, presumably in association with a decline of the Asian values of hard work, discipline, and respect for education. Dornbusch et al. (1987) and Ritter and Dornbusch (1989) reported that Asian-American academic performance tends to be inversely related to the number of generations in the United States. In the study by Stevenson et al. (1990), although Asian-American children received higher scores in mathematics than other ethnic groups of American children, their scores were significantly lower than those of children in Beijing. Evidently, the superiority of Asian students carries over—but only to a degree—to Asian-American students.

Compatibility and Incompatibility.   Advocates of culturally compatible education (e.g., Tharp, 1989; Delgado-Gaitan, chapter 3, this volume; Suina, chapter 6, this volume) argue that it would result in improved educational outcomes for ethnic minority children. Accordingly, instead of demanding these children to conform to mainstream requirements, the schools should become more congenial and adaptive to the children's cultural backgrounds. When it comes to Asian-American children (particularly Chinese and Japanese), however, the cultural compatibility hypothesis runs into apparent paradoxes. Confucian heritage cultures can hardly be viewed as "compatible" with mainstream U.S. culture; yet, children from these cultures excel academically. One has seen that, as these children acculturate and hence become more compatible with the school environment, their academic performance may drop. Would this not argue against cultural compatibility? On the other hand, if the school environment were to become more compatible with their cultural backgrounds, would the children perform even better?

Incompatibilities between Confucian heritage and U.S. cultures in education are to be expected, and observing them is a good lesson in cross-cultural encounters. Predictably, immigrant parents from Hong Kong and Taiwan often complain that not enough homework is assigned to their children. Teachers in the United States, in turn, complain that the newly arrived students typically do not participate actively in class, show little interest in extracurricular activities, and are too preoccupied with examinations. Yet, one must not assume that all students from Confucian heritage cultures find the U.S. school environment incompatible. Stifled or rejected by the authoritarian educational system in these cultures, many obtain a new lease on their academic career and flourish in the openness of education in the United States.

Clearly no one would argue that the school environment should become more authoritarian, or that the students should be regarded as passive recipients of knowledge, as a rigid interpretation of cultural compatibility would recommend. I argue that cultural incompatibility is not necessarily a bad thing. Rather, incompatibility presents a challenge to the student, and thus an opportunity to grow. *Bienculturation* and *multienculturation* (two newly coined terms) offer an attractive alternative to cultural compatibility. They promise to produce bicultural and multicultural individuals. No longer viewed as marginal, these individuals may even serve as models of enculturation for the creation of world citizens in the not-too-distant future.

Social and Technological Intelligence

Mundy-Castle (1974) made a distinction between social and technological intelligence. The distinction was made on the basis of the relative importance a culture attaches to social skills in relation to people versus technology in relation to things. Cross-cultural observations led him to argue that in African cultures the primary goal of socialization is to develop social intelligence. In Western cultures, the primary goal is to develop technological intelligence.

It is tempting to associate collectivistic orientation with social intelligence and individualistic orientation with technological intelligence. Thus, Chinese cognitive socialization, being rooted more firmly in collectivistic than in individualistic achievement motivation, would be conducive to the development of social intelligence. There are reasons for casting doubt on the fruitfulness of this line of reasoning.

To begin with, as Ho and Chiu (1990) argued, explanations of cross-cultural differences based on a dichotomous conception of individualism and collectivism may be faulted on conceptual, methodological, and empirical grounds. Conceptually, it does no justice to the complexity of the two concepts, individualism and collectivism, each of which is composed of a number of interrelated component ideas. The two concepts are distinct: One is not reducible to be simply the antithesis of the other. The complexity and heterogeneity of each concept is captured in the scheme presented by Kim and Choi (chapter 11, this volume).

Methodologically, therefore, individualism and collectivism should not be construed as opposite ends of a continuum or continua. There is no necessary contradiction for a person to hold individualistic and collectivistic views at the same time. Empirically, it has been found that component ideas of both individualism and collectivism are affirmed or negated in Chinese culture (see the previous section on Achievement Motivation). What comes closer to the truth is that both collectivistic and individualistic tendencies of varying strengths co-exist, as they do in other cultures.

An alternative framework and methodology rests on what Ho (1993) called relational orientation. It gives full recognition to the central importance of relational contexts of achievement, regardless of cultural variation. Therefore, the unit of analysis is not the individual but individual-in-relations. Relational orientation confronts the bias toward methodological individualism in contemporary social psychology. It makes a demand on the theorist to consider how social relationships are defined before attempting to interpret the behavior of individuals. Therefore, an adequate explanation entails making explicit the normative expectations and behavioral rules governing role relationships.

From this perspective, collectivism in Chinese culture is viewed as specific to role relationships. That is, the collectivistic orientation of individuals depends on the normative expectations and behavioral rules associated with the role relationship involved. As has been seen, role relationships within the family are particularly important in Chinese and Japanese achievement motivation.

A dichotomous conception of social versus technological intelligence also poses difficulties. Mundy-Castle (1974) explicitly eschewed such a conception. He stated: "[Social and technological intelligence] constitute different strategies of adaptation involving distinctive patterns of culturally determined skills. . . . A truly adaptive strategy would incorporate both" (p. 48). Likewise, Dasen (1984) avoided making a dichotomy. He considered whether technological intelligence is conceived of as a means to serve social ends (as in African cultures) or as an end in itself (as in Western cultures). Still, regardless of cultural context, social intelligence (e.g., cooperation) is relevant and would apply to the solution of technological problems (e.g., building a hut or an aircraft carrier). Likewise, it is hard to conceptualize technological intelligence as purely an end in itself, devoid of any social context.

Given the difficulties posed in both dichotomous conceptions, attempting to relate individualism–collectivism to social–technological intelligence is surely ridden with intellectual traps. For instance, consider the literacy tradition of Confucian heritage cultures. According to Mundy-Castle (1974), literacy is the key to the development of technological intelligence. At the same time, however, these cultures are generally viewed as collectivistic; moral socialization reigns supreme, implying that the development of social intelligence has priority over that of technological intelligence. Thus, the implications of the social–technological intelligence formulation are far from clear. An examination of the contemporary formal schooling for Chinese and Japanese children reveals that there is nothing incompatible in the development of social and technological intelligence.

Survival and Educational Development

The notion of socialization for survival and for educational development is due to LeVine (1987). In subsistence societies, maternal behavior is strategically aimed to meet the immediate needs that ensure infants' survival, not to educate them. In industrialized societies, where survival is usually not in question, maternal behavior is strategically aimed to achieve the long-term goal of developing cognitive skills. A revision of this notion (LeVine, Miller, & West, 1988) argues that childrearing strategies are complex patterns for investing time, energy, and attention. Optimal strategies then depend on cultural context and on what is needed to ensure survival, and strategies become maladaptive when cultural change takes place too rapidly.

Again, a dichotomous formulation of survival versus educational development should be avoided. It would not apply in Confucian heritage cultures without posing difficulties. First, according to LeVine (1987), in societies where survival is a major concern, maternal behavior is characterized by close physical contact with the infant. But this characteristic is also observed among present-day Chinese-American (Kagan et al., 1978) and Japanese mothers (Caudill & Weinstein, 1969), for whom survival is no longer a major concern.

Second, in traditional Chinese society, given its high birthrates and high infant mortality, ensuring infant survival was indeed a major concern. Yet, it was not an exclusive concern. Aspirations of social ascendancy through educational achievement, despite very limited opportunities, were a potent motive. Thus, socialization for survival did not preclude socialization for educational development. Rather, the early concern with survival was to ensure that the hope for later educational achievement by the child could remain alive.

THE GOALS OF EDUCATION

I now return to the paradox stated at the beginning of the chapter. To do so, let me first examine the evidence on the alleged academic success in Confucian societies. At what psychological costs is the academic success achieved? How meaningful is it? Most important, what is education for?

The most extensive research involving Asian children in cross-national comparisons of cognitive abilities and academic achievement was conducted by Stevenson and his colleagues. The main findings may be summarized as follows.

1. The cognitive abilities of Chinese (Taiwan), Japanese, and U.S. children are similar. Stevenson et al. (1985) concluded: "By the time they are enrolled in the fifth grade of elementary school, the most remarkable feature of their performance is the similarity in level, variability, and structure of their scores on the cognitive tasks" (p. 734).

2. Chinese (both mainland and Taiwan) and Japanese children consistently surpass U.S. children in mathematics achievement. As reported in an earlier study (Stevenson, Lee, & Stigler, 1986), by Grade 5 both Chinese (Taiwan) and Japanese children surpassed U.S. children. A later study (Stevenson et al., 1990) involved computations and word problems as well as the application of knowledge about mathematics. Again, the performance of Chinese (mainland China) first and fifth graders was consistently superior to their U.S. counterparts. Differences among the Chinese (mainland and Taiwan) and Japanese children were not consistently significant.

3. The reading achievements of the three countries compared are, in descending order: China (Taiwan), United States, and Japan. The rank order is consistent from kindergarten through Grade 5. However, the differences are less extreme than those in mathematics (Stevenson, Lee, & Stigler, 1986).

4. Large differences exist in the children's life in school, the attitudes and beliefs of their mothers, and the involvement of both parents and children in schoolwork (Chen & Stevenson, 1989; Stevenson, Lee, & Stigler, 1986).

Because of its methodological rigor and richness of data obtained, the research by Stevenson and his colleagues may serve as a focal reference for discussion. In particular, the finding concerning mathematics achievement is consistent with those from an earlier cross-national study (Rodd, 1959), the first International Educational Achievement (IEA) studies of achievement in mathematics (Husen, 1967) and science (Comber & Keeves, 1973), and the second IEA mathematics study (Garden, 1987). The remarkable consistency of all these findings has seldom been matched in educational research. It has established the superior achievement in mathematics by Chinese and Japanese children on a firm empirical ground.

As a phenomenon, the cross-national differences in mathematics achievement call for an explanation. Cognitive abilities are ruled out as an explanatory factor because of their similarity across the three national groups. They also provide strong evidence against claims made by various authors (e.g., Lynn, 1977; Vernon, 1982) that some Asian groups may be superior to Euro-Americans in intelligence. The level of achievement in elementary school mathematics does not appear to be closely related to the content of the curriculum (Stigler, Lee, Lucker, & Stevenson, 1982). Thus, Stevenson and his colleagues were led to look for an explanation in the children's experiences in school and at home.

Upon reflection, the superior achievement of Chinese and Japanese children in mathematics is hardly surprising at all, given that people usually do better on tasks to which they attach importance and on which they spend a great deal of time. Indeed, one would be hard put to give an explanation if they did not achieve higher levels than children in the United States. It is more meaningful to ask: Will the achievement in elementary school carry over to the university and beyond, and translate into an advancement of knowledge in science and mathematics? Mathematics is only one subject, important to be sure, that has to be learned in school. Performance in this subject is only one indicator of current academic achievement, which does not predetermine future academic achievement. More fundamentally, academic achievement, too often narrowly conceived of and measured by the mere acquisition of knowledge, is not an ultimate goal of cognitive socialization, much less of education. I submit that the development of critical thinking (cf. Delgado-Gaitan, chapter 3, this volume), creativity, and an intrinsic motivation for learning have a prior claim in the scale of educational values.

With regard to Asian-American achievements, Sue and Okazaki (1990) proposed the notion of relative functionalism, according to which Asian Americans are highly influenced by the opportunities for upward mobility in educational *and* noneducational areas (e.g., career opportunities). Sue and Okazaki contrasted relative functionalism with an explanatory perspective based on a consideration of Asian cultural values.

However, relative functionalism has its roots in Confucian societies, from where it is exported to the United States. Traditionally, Chinese people do not regard low socioeconomic status as an insurmountable barrier to educational achievement. On the contrary, scholastic success is a passport to high status. This tradition is rooted in the availability of an imperial ladder of social ascendancy in traditional China: achieving upward mobility through education—more precisely, success in imperial examinations. Thus, regarding education as a means to an end has long been identified as one of the ills of Chinese education. I term this orientation *utilitarian pragmatism*. Unfortunately, it has persisted to the present day.

In Hong Kong, utilitarian pragmatism reaches new heights and takes on a new twist. In a study of tertiary students, Gow et al. (1989) stated: "The students' motives for higher education were to get good jobs. They wanted to do well and were therefore strategic in their studies. They were examination-oriented and studied only the materials on which they would be examined" (p. 57).

In each culture, formal education reflects a philosophy underlying cognitive socialization. The findings of Stevenson and his colleagues may be rightfully viewed as an indictment of American elementary education in mathematics and science. I hope that these findings are not construed as a vindication of the education that children receive in Confucian heritage cultures. In conclusion, the present chapter has revealed extremes in the educational systems across the Pacific: Excesses in one mirror deficiencies in the other, and vice versa. An appreciation of these contrasts is an educational experience for educators. Each system has something from which the other urgently needs to learn.

ACKNOWLEDGMENT

I gratefully acknowledge the financial support to the present research from the University of Hong Kong.

REFERENCES

Against Child Abuse. (1986). *Survey report on child rearing in Tuen Mun*. Hong Kong: Author.

American Psychological Association. (1985). *Thesaurus of psychological index terms* (4th ed.). Washington, DC: Author.

Asian Commercial Research. (1990). *Daily life in Hong Kong*. Hong Kong: Author.

Biggs, J. B. (1990). Effects of language medium of instruction on approaches to learning. *Educational Research Journal, 5*, 18–28.

Boey, K. W. (1976). *Rigidity and cognitive complexity: An empirical investigation in the interpersonal, physical, and numeric domains under task-oriented and ego-oriented conditions*. Unpublished doctoral dissertation, University of Hong Kong.

Bond, M. H., & Hwang, K. K. (1986). The social psychology of Chinese people. In M. H. Bond (Ed.), *The psychology of the Chinese people* (pp. 213–266). Hong Kong: Oxford University Press.

Bornstein, M. H. (1989). Cross-cultural developmental comparisons: The case of Japanese-American infant and mother activities and interactions. What we know, what we need to know, and why we need to know. *Developmental Review, 9*, 171–204.

Bornstein, M. H., Azuma, H., Tamis-LeMonda, C., & Ogino, M. (1990). Mother and infant activity and interaction in Japan and the United States: I. A comparative macroanalysis of naturalistic exchanges. *International Journal of Behavioural Development, 13*, 267–287.

Bornstein, M. H., Miyaki, K., & Tamis-LeMonda, C. S. (1985–1986). A cross-national study of mother and infant activities and interactions: Some preliminary comparisons between Japan and the United States. *Annual Report of the Research and Clinical Center for Child Development* (pp. 1–12). Sapporo, Japan: University of Hokkaido Press.

Caudill, W. A. (1972). Tiny dramas: Vocal communication between mother and infant in Japanese and American families. In W. P. Lebra (Ed.), *Mental health research in Asia and the Pacific: Vol. 2. Transcultural research in mental health*. Honolulu: The University Press of Hawaii.

Caudill, W. A., & Frost, L. (1973). A comparison of maternal care and infant behavior in Japanese-American, American, and Japanese families. In W. P. Lebra (Ed.), *Mental health research in Asia and the Pacific: Vol. 3. Youth, socialization, and mental health*. Honolulu: The University Press of Hawaii.

Caudill, W. A., & Schooler, C. (1973). Child behavior and child rearing in Japan and the United States: An interim report. *Journal of Nervous and Mental Disease, 157*, 323–338.

Caudill, W., & Weinstein, H. (1969). Maternal care and infant behavior in Japan and America. *Psychiatry, 32*, 12–43.

Chan-Ho, T. F. I. (1990). *The relationship between motives, learning strategies, attributions for success and failure and level of achievement among secondary school students in Hong Kong.* Unpublished master's thesis, University of Hong Kong, Hong Kong.

Chen, C., & Stevenson, H. W. (1989). Homework: A cross-cultural examination. *Child Development, 60,* 551–561.

Cheung, F. M. C. (1986). Psychopathology among Chinese people. In M. H. Bond (Ed.), *The psychology of the Chinese people* (pp. 171–212). Hong Kong: Oxford University Press.

Coleman, J. S., Campbell, E., Hobson, C., McPartland, J., Mood, A., Weinfield, F., & York, R. (1966). *Equality of educational opportunity.* Washington, DC: U.S. Government Printing Office.

Comber, L. C., & Keeves, J. P. (1973). *Science education in nineteen countries.* Stockholm: Almquist & Wiksell.

Cunnington, B. F., & Torrance, E. P. (1965). *Sounds and images.* Lexington, MA: Ginn.

Dasen, P. R. (1984). The cross-cultural study of intelligence: Piaget and the Baoule. In P. S. Fry (Ed.), *Changing conceptions of intelligence and intellectual functioning: Current theory and research* (pp. 107–134). New York: North-Holland.

DeVos, G. A. (1973). *Socialization for achievement: Essays on the cultural psychology of the Japanese.* Berkeley, CA: University of California Press.

Dornbusch, S. M., Prescott, B. L., & Ritter, P. L. (1987, April). *The relation of high school academic performance and student effort to language use and recency of migration among Asian- and Pacific-Americans.* Paper presented at the meeting of the American Educational Research Association, Washington, DC.

Dornbusch, S. M., Ritter, P. L., Leiderman, P. H., Roberts, D. F., & Fraleigh, M. J. (1987). The relation of parenting style to adolescent school performance. *Child Development, 55,* 1244–1257.

Freedman, D. G. (1974). *Human infancy: An evolutionary perspective.* Hillsdale, NJ: Lawrence Erlbaum Associates.

Freedman, D. G., & Freedman, N. C. (1969). Behavioural differences between Chinese-American and European-American newborns. *Nature, 224,* 1227.

Garden, R. A. (1987). The second IEA mathematics study. *Comparative Education Review, 31,* 47–68.

Gow, L., Bella, J., Kember, D., Stokes, M., Stafford, K., Chow, R., & Hu, S. (1989). Approaches to study of tertiary students in Hong Kong. *Bulletin of the Hong Kong Psychological Society* (Nos. 22/23, pp. 57–77).

Greenwald, A. G. (1980). The totalitarian ego: Fabrication and revision of personal history. *American Psychologist, 35,* 603–618.

Griffin, P. E., & Mok, M. C. (1990). Student gender, home support, and achievement in mathematics among Hong Kong secondary students. *Educational Research Journal, 5,* 43–50.

Hau, K. T., & Salili, F. (1991). Structure and semantic differential placement of specific causes: Academic causal attributions by Chinese students in Hong Kong. *International Journal of Psychology, 26,* 175–193.

Hawkins, J. N. (1983). The People's Republic of China (mainland China). In R. M. Thomas & T. N. Postlethwaite (Eds.), *Schooling in East Asia.* Oxford: Pergamon.

Hess, R. D., Azuma, H., Kashiwagi, K., Holloway, S. D., & Wenegrat, A. (1987). Cultural variations in socialization for school achievement: Contrasts between Japan and the United States. *Journal of Applied Developmental Psychology, 8,* 421–440.

Hess, R. D., Chang, C. M., & McDevitt, T. M. (1987). Cultural variations in family beliefs about children's performance in mathematics: Comparisons among People's Republic of China, Chinese-American, and Caucasian-American families. *Journal of Educational Psychology, 79,* 179–188.

Hess, R. D., Kashiwagi, K., Azuma, H., Price, G. G., & Dickson, W. P. (1980). Maternal expectations for mastery of developmental tasks in Japan and the United States. *International Journal of Psychology, 15,* 259–271.

Ho, D. Y. F. (1979). Parental education is not correlated with verbal intelligence or academic performance in Hong Kong pupils. *Genetic Psychology Monographs, 100,* 3–19.

Ho, D. Y. F. (1986). Chinese patterns of socialization: A critical review. In M. H. Bond (Ed.), *The psychology of the Chinese people* (pp. 1–37). Hong Kong: Oxford University Press.

Ho, D. Y. F. (1987). Prediction of foreign language skills: A canonical and part canonical correlation study. *Contemporary Educational Psychology, 12,* 119–130.

Ho, D. Y. F. (1989a). Continuity and variation in Chinese patterns of socialization. *Journal of Marriage and the Family, 51,* 149–163.

Ho, D. Y. F. (1989b). Socialization in contemporary mainland China. *Asian Thought and Society, 14,* 136–149.

Ho, D. Y. F. (1990). *Filial piety, child training, and cognitive socialization: An integration of available evidence.* Manuscript submitted for publication.

Ho, D. Y. F. (1993). Toward an Asian social psychology: Relational orientation. In U. Kim & J. Berry (Eds.), *Indigenous psychologies: Research and experience in cultural context* (pp. 240–259). Newbury Park, CA: Sage.

Ho, D. Y. F., & Chiu, C. Y. (in press). Component ideas of individualism, collectivism, and social organization: An application in the study of Chinese culture. In U. Kim, H. C. Triandis, & G. Yoon (Eds.), *Individualism and collectivism: Theoretical and methodological issues.* Newbury Park, CA: Sage.

Ho, D. Y. F., & Kang, T. K. (1984). Intergenerational comparisons of child-rearing attitudes and practices in Hong Kong. *Developmental Psychology, 20,* 1004–1016.

Ho, D. Y. F., & Spinks, J. A. (1985). Multivariate prediction of academic performance by Hong Kong university students. *Contemporary Educational Psychology, 10,* 249–259.

Ho, D. Y. F., Spinks, J. A., & Yeung, C. S. H. (Eds.). (1989). *Chinese patterns of behavior: A sourcebook of psychological and psychiatric studies.* New York: Praeger.

Hsu, F. L. K. (1963). *Clan, caste, and club.* New York: Van Nostrand.

Husen, T. (Ed.). (1967). *International study of achievement in mathematics: A comparison of twelve countries.* New York: Wiley.

Kagan, J., Kearsley, R. B., & Zelazo, P. R. (1978). *Infancy: Its place in human development.* Cambridge, MA: Harvard University Press.

LeVine, R. A. (1977). Child rearing as cultural adaptation. In P. H. Leiderman, S. R. Tulkin, & A. Rosenfeld (Eds.), *Culture and infancy* (pp. 15–27). New York: Academic Press.

LeVine, R. A. (1987). Women's schooling, patterns of fertility, and child survival. *Educational Researcher,* 21–27.

LeVine, R. A., Miller, P. M., & West, M. M. (Eds.). (1988). *Parental behavior in diverse societies: Vol. 40. New directions for child development.* San Francisco: Jossey-Bass.

Lin, C. Y. C., & Fu, V. R. (1990). A comparison of child-rearing practices among Chinese, immigrant Chinese, and Caucasian-American parents. *Child Development, 61,* 429–433.

Lin, Y. N. (1988). Family socioeconomic background, parental involvement, and students academic performance by elementary schoolchildren. *Journal of Counseling* (National Taiwan Institute of Education), *11,* 95–141. (In Chinese, with an English abstract)

Liu, I. M. (1984). *A survey of memorization requirement in Taipei primary and secondary schools.* Unpublished manuscript, National Taiwan University, Taipei.

Liu, I. M., & Hsu, M. (1974). Measuring creative thinking in Taiwan by the Torrance test. *Testing and Guidance, 2,* 108–109.

Lynn, R. (1977). The intelligence of the Japanese. *Bulletin of the British Psychological Society, 30,* 69–72.

Marjoribanks, K. (1972). Environment, social class, and mental abilities. *Journal of Educational Psychology, 63,* 103–109.

McClelland, D. C. (1963). Motivational patterns in Southeast Asia with special reference to the Chinese case. *Journal of Social Issues, 19,* 6–19.

Mitchell, R. E. (1972). *Pupil, parent, and school: A Hong Kong study.* Taipei: Oriental Cultural Service.

Mundy-Castle, A. C. (1974). Social and technological intelligence in Western and non-Western cultures. *Universitas, 4,* 46–52.

Otaki, M., Durrett, M. E., Richards, P., Nyquist, L., & Pennebaker, J. W. (1986). Maternal and infant behavior in Japan and America: A partial replication. *Journal of Cross-Cultural Psychology, 17,* 251–268.

Paschal, B. J., Kuo, Y. Y., & Schurr, K. T. (1980–1981). *Creative thinking in Indiana and Taiwan college students.* Paper presented at the Fifth International Conference of the International Association for Cross-Cultural Psychology, Bhubaneshwar, India.

Research report on current leisure activities among Hong Kong schoolchildren. (1979). Hong Kong: The Boys' and Girls' Clubs Association. (In Chinese)

Ripple, R. E. (1983). Reflections on doing psychological research in Hong Kong. *Hong Kong Psychological Society Bulletin, 10,* 7–23.

Ritter, P. L., & Dornbusch, S. M. (1989, March). *Ethnic variation in family influence on academic achievement.* Paper presented at the meeting of the American Educational Research Association, San Francisco, CA.

Rodd, W. G. (1959). A cross-cultural study of Taiwan's schools. *Journal of Social Psychology, 50,* 3–36.

Salili, F. (1987). *Age, sex, and cultural differences in the meaning of achievement.* Paper presented at the Annual Convention of the American Psychological Association, New York.

Simmons, C., & Wade, W. (1988). Contrasting attitudes to education in England and Japan. *Educational Research, 30,* 146–152.

Stevenson, H. W., Lee, S. Y., Chen, C., Lummis, M., Stigler, J., Fan, L., & Ge, F. (1990). Mathematics achievement of children in China and the United States. *Child Development, 61,* 1053–1066.

Stevenson, H. W., Lee, S. Y., & Stigler, J. W. (1986). Mathematics achievement of Chinese, Japanese, and American children. *Science, 231,* 693–699.

Stevenson, H. W., Stigler, J. W., Lee, S., Lucker, G. W., Kitamura, S., & Hsu, C. (1985). Cognitive performance and academic achievement of Japanese, Chinese, and American children. *Child Development, 56,* 718–734.

Steward, M. S., & Steward, D. S. (1973). The observation of Anglo-Mexican and Chinese-American mothers teaching their young sons. *Child Development, 44,* 329–337.

Stigler, J. W., Lee, S., Lucker, G. W., & Stevenson, H. W. (1982). Curriculum and achievement in mathematics: A study of elementary school children in Japan, Taiwan, and the United States. *Journal of Educational Psychology, 74,* 315–322.

Sue, S., & Okazaki, S. (1990). Asian-American educational achievements: A phenomenon in search of an explanation. *American Psychologist, 45,* 913–920.

Taylor, I. (1981). Writing system and reading. In G. E. MacKinnon & T. G. Waller (Eds.), *Reading research: Advances in theory and practice* (Vol. 2, pp. 1–51). New York: Academic Press.

Tharp, R. G. (1989). Psychocultural variables and constants: Effects of teaching and learning in schools. *American Psychologist, 44,* 349–359.

Vernon, P. E. (1982). *The abilities and achievements of Orientals in North America.* New York: Academic Press.

Weiner, B., Heckhausen, H., Meyer, W., & Cook, R. E. (1972). Causal ascriptions and achievement behavior: The conceptual analysis of effort. *Journal of Personality and Social Psychology, 21,* 239–248.

Wilson, R. W., & Pusey, A. W. (1982). Achievement motivation and small business relationship in Chinese society. In S. L. Greenblatt, R. W. Wilson, & A. A. Wilson (Eds.), *Social interaction in Chinese society.* New York: Praeger.

Wu, W. T., & Chen, H. J. (1978). Teacher leadership behavior as related to students' expectation, achievement and adjustment. *Bulletin of Educational Psychology, 11,* 87–104. (In Chinese)

Yang, K. S. (1982). Causal attribution of academic success and failure and their affective consequences. *Acta Psychologica Taiwanica, 24*, 65–83. (In Chinese)

Yang, K. S. (1985, November). *Family factors and children's behavior: A critical analysis of research in Taiwan*. Paper presented at the Second International Conference on Modernization and Chinese culture, Chinese University of Hong Kong. (In Chinese)

Yang, K. S. (1986). Chinese personality and its change. In M. H. Bond (Ed.), *The psychology of the Chinese people* (pp. 106–170). Hong Kong: Oxford University Press.

Yee, L. Y., & LaForce, R. (1974). Relationship between mental abilities, social class, and exposure to English in Chinese fourth graders. *Journal of Educational Psychology, 66*, 826–834.

Youth in Hong Kong: A Statistical profile (1988). Hong Kong: Central Committee on Youth, The Information and Research Committee.

Yu, E. S. H. (1974). Achievement motive, familism, and hsiao: A replication of McClelland-Winterbottom studies. *Dissertation Abstracts International, 35*, 593A. (University Microfilms No. 74-14, 942)

Yue, A. B., & Yang, K. S. (1987). Social-oriented and individual-oriented achievement motivation: A conceptual and empirical analysis. *Bulletin of the Institute of Ethnology* (Academia Sinica), *64*, 51–98. (In Chinese, with an English abstract)

15

MOVING AWAY FROM STEREOTYPES AND PRECONCEPTIONS: STUDENTS AND THEIR EDUCATION IN EAST ASIA AND THE UNITED STATES

Harold Stevenson
University of Michigan

I am increasingly skeptical about many of the conceptions held in the West, and actually about some of the conceptions that are held in the East about what happens in the East. One hears about child development in East Asia, but I often wonder about the reliability of some of the information. Let me give some examples.

I recently had a conversation with a group of principals and head teachers in Beijing's elementary schools. They were telling me about their teaching schedules: The typical elementary school teacher teaches 2 or 3 hours a day, with the exception of some homeroom teachers who spend up to 4 hours with their classes. The rest of the time is available to teachers for preparing lessons, discussing their work with other teachers, grading their students' papers, working with students individually, and so on.

I described my meeting to a well-known Chinese child psychologist. I mentioned the remarkable difference between the schedules of Chinese and American teachers. "Oh, no," was the reply, "that is not possible. Chinese teachers teach many more hours a day than the number you are quoting."

Because of the authoritative tone of this reaction, I worried that I had misunderstood the teachers or had remembered the data incorrectly. Members of our research group had interviewed 120 elementary school teachers in Beijing the previous year, and in the interview we had included questions about their teaching loads. When I returned to the United States, I reviewed the results of the interviews. What the Chinese expert had said was incorrect. The expert obviously had not been in elementary schools recently or frequently enough to find out what was happening in the schools of the city. The comments of the principals and teachers were in line with the data.

One needs reliable data, not hearsay. Popular articles offer many descriptions of what occurs in the schools and homes of East Asia. Unfortunately, these are often reports of conversations or informal observations, with no objective data to support or confirm what is being reported.

Here is another example. One reads a great deal about the competitiveness of entering prestigious schools in Japan. Even Japanese preschools are reported to subject 3-year-olds to mental testing before considering them for admission. In her book about Japanese preschools Peak (1991) investigated this matter. When she looked at the data, she found that only 1% of the preschools in Japan have such examinations—hardly what we have been led to think.

PSYCHOLOGICAL ADJUSTMENT

Here is yet another example. Many discussions of the need to raise standards in U.S. schools eventually lead to a discussion of the influence on mental health of studying too hard. Might not this result in problems for American students similar to those found among students in East Asia (cf. Ho, chapter 14, this volume)? After all, the questioner usually suggests, should not we be concerned about the high suicide rate of students in East Asia and about the severe stress and accompanying psychological problems that occur as a consequence of having to study so hard and of being pushed so relentlessly by their parents and teachers?

We checked current statistics about the suicide rate of students in Japan. The incidence of suicide among Japanese teenagers differs from that in the United States by approximately 0.7 per 100,000 persons, with the slightly higher rate of suicides occurring in the United States. Statistics that have been quoted in the American press are apparently from the 1950s, when, following the defeat of Japan in World War II, youths despaired about the bleak future that seemed to face their country. The teenage suicide rate in Japan during that period was nearly four times that found in the United States.

Also relevant are the comparative data we have collected about the psychological adjustment of high school students in East Asia and in the United States. We are just completing a study involving more than 1,000 American, 1,400 Chinese, and 1,200 Japanese 11th graders selected to constitute a representative sample of students in large metropolitan areas (Minneapolis, Sendai in Japan, and Taipei in Taiwan). Our collaborators include native speakers of Chinese and Japanese, and all English-speaking colleagues know either Chinese or Japanese. Therefore, we were able to construct questionnaires and interviews simultaneously in the three languages. Items were always written so that the nuances of meaning were similar in each language. If we could not find satisfactory words in all three languages, we did not include questions about that topic. This approach is quite different from that found when questions are first written in English and then translated into the other languages. We asked about such factors as stress, depression, anxiety, aggression, and psychosomatic symptoms.

There were small differences in these indices between East-Asian and American youth. In rating the frequency with which they felt stress, it was actually students in the United States, not East Asia, who indicated more frequent feelings of stress (see Fig. 15.1). Such data do not support what many Westerners accept as a fact: That Asian students suffer much greater stress than students in the United States. What was the major source of stress for U.S. students? School.

Here is another example of the 11th graders' responses. Figure 15.2 presents the average frequency of occurrence of psychosomatic symptoms checked by students out of a list of eight, including such things as being tired; overeating; loss of appetite; and having headaches, stomachaches, or trouble sleeping. There were no strong trends for Chinese and Japanese adolescents to show a greater incidence of psychosomatic symptoms than American adolescents. In fact, Japanese students reported the lowest frequency of complaints about somatic ailments.

We asked the students about their feelings of depression. Students in Taiwan indicated somewhat more frequent depression than American and Japanese students but there was no strong indication of widespread depres-

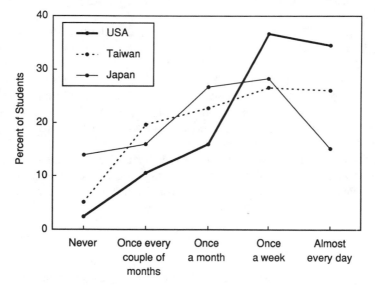

FIG. 15.1. Frequency distribution of feelings of stress by American, Chinese, and Japanese high school students.

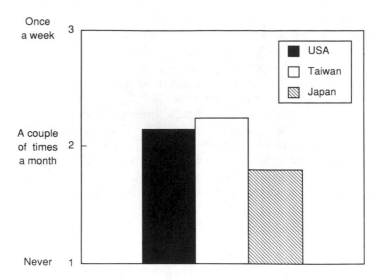

FIG. 15.2. Mean number of somatic complaints made by American, Chinese, and Japanese high school students.

sion among the students from any of the cultures. Cross-cultural differences were also small for feelings of anxiety and aggression.

So when one asks large, representative samples of Chinese and Japanese students to respond to questions about common indications of stress, their answers are not in line with the stereotypes of tense, unhappy, overburdened adolescents.

It is not only Chinese and Japanese high school students who report low frequencies of stress. We also gathered data from teachers of first graders in Beijing and Chicago. As part of a study of children's adaptation to school, we asked first-grade teachers about the children's first few weeks at school. The teachers reported that children in China, in comparison with children in the United States, less frequently did not want to go to school, were disorganized or nervous, wanted their parents to stay with them, or had difficulty following directions (see Fig. 15.3).

According to their teachers, it was the U.S. children, not the Chinese children, who displayed a higher frequency of fidgeting; inattentiveness; and seeking physical contact; and who complained of being tired, not wanting to go to school, and having stomachaches and headaches.

TEACHING STYLE

Similarly erroneous impressions of the teaching styles found in Chinese and Japanese classrooms are also common. Our observations do not agree with these descriptions. Systematic observations yield images very different from

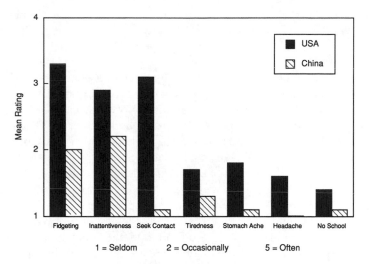

FIG. 15.3. Teachers' reports of the percentage of first-grade students who displayed various types of behavior during their first weeks at school.

those of teachers spending their time lecturing to passive, robotlike students who respond in mechanical unison and acquire large amounts of unintegrated information in a rote fashion. This type of negative image is presented by Ho (chapter 14, this volume).

East-Asian and U.S. classrooms have seldom been compared in formal observational studies employing standard observational schemes. My colleagues and I have done two large observational studies, one of which has been published so far (Stevenson et al., 1987). In a second, more recent study, we visited 40 first-grade classrooms and 40 fifth-grade classrooms in Chicago; 20 first-grade and 20 fifth-grade classrooms in Taipei; and the same numbers in Sendai and Beijing. These classrooms constituted a representative sample of the classrooms in each city.

We observed in each classroom during mathematics lessons on four different, randomly chosen days. Two native speakers trained as observers were present. One followed a time-sampling procedure in which checks were made if predefined categories of behavior occurred during each brief observational interval. The other observer compiled a narrative record of everything that happened during the class period. Details were filled in by reference to audio recordings. We then broke these observations down into units defined by changes in classroom activities and entered coded summaries of each unit into the computer. This made it possible to quantify the narrative observations.

Based on these data and my personal observations, I believe that some of the most remarkable teaching in the world goes on in Chinese and Japanese elementary school classrooms. The teaching is done with skill, energy, and finesse. We described this in a book, *The Learning Gap* (Stevenson & Stigler, 1992), and have made a half-hour video program, *The Polished Stones* (Stevenson & Lee, 1989), that presents examples of daily life in East-Asian classrooms.

What are the most simple structural features of a good lesson? It begins with an introduction of what will be discussed, continues with an elaboration of the content, and ends with a summary of what has been presented. For example, when we compared first-grade and fifth-grade classrooms in Chicago and Beijing, we found that Beijing teachers followed this format more frequently than the Chicago teachers. In following this format, they also avoided vague, unrelated discussions to a greater degree than the Chicago teachers. (I should add that the schools we observed were in metropolitan Chicago, which included North Shore communities and western suburbs.)

Most people would also agree that good teaching occurs when: (a) there is frequent interaction between students and the teacher, (b) material is presented in a meaningful context, (c) there are not long uninterrupted periods of seatwork, (d) there is frequent feedback, (e) students are called on to explain their answers, (f) young children have experience with concrete objects before being presented with abstract operations, and so forth.

One would get little disagreement from laymen, teachers, or educational theorists that these statements describe good teaching. Yet when we compared classrooms in Taipei, Sendai, and Beijing with those in Chicago, we found that the practices were followed less frequently in Chicago than in the East-Asian cities. Here are some examples: Among the fifth-grade class periods in Sendai, less than 10% spent time on non-math topics and/or had interruptions to the class. This occurred in over 40% of the class periods in Chicago. Teachers elaborated on children's answers to clarify or emphasize their main points in nearly 50% of the class periods in Sendai but in less than 30% of the periods in Chicago. Japanese first-grade teachers provided experience with concrete, manipulable objects in more than 40% of the class periods; Chicago teachers did this in less than 15% of the periods.

ROLE OF TEACHERS

The East-Asian teacher acts as a knowledgeable guide. Indeed, the two characters in the Japanese term for teacher (*sensei*) mean "living or being before"— one who has had the experience and now can guide others through it. The teacher is not a lecturer but nevertheless knows what should be learned and the types of techniques that will lead children to learn. The teacher does not act as an authoritarian dispenser of knowledge and judge of what is correct but leads children to construct knowledge and evaluate the reliability of their own and others' solutions.

In American classrooms, students were often not responding at all. Chicago children were left to work alone at their seats on seatwork nearly 40% of the time. Not only was a great deal of time spent on seatwork but the time was not used well. In East Asia, the typical pattern was for the teacher to teach for a while, then give the children seatwork or boardwork so they could practice what they had just learned. During the seatwork time, the teacher monitored the class to see that the children were proceeding properly. After this brief interval of seatwork was completed, some form of feedback was given by the teacher or was elicited from the students. This cycle was repeated frequently during each lesson.

Seatwork was the last thing happening during the Chicago mathematics classes. The teacher was through teaching. The students did their seatwork and class ended. Nearly half of the time the children received no feedback.

Why do American teachers use seatwork in this manner? American teachers are in front of classrooms nearly every hour all day long. Teachers must have time to rest and prepare for the next class. Seatwork time is the only time during which they are free to do this. I was recently talking to a teacher in one of the large American school systems in which we have been working. The half hour teachers had for preparation has been eliminated in a new effort to economize.

In short, contrary to popular stereotypes, East-Asian teaching is dynamic and interactive. The teacher is an authority but this authority is used to stimulate learning with understanding, not to discipline or coerce rote memorization. Ho (chapter 14, this volume) takes a highly critical perspective on education in cultures with a Confucian heritage. Some of the differences may lie in a difference in educational levels. Ho concentrated on students in the upper grades and in the university, whereas I focused my attention on elementary schools. Another part of the difference may lie in the discipline. My recent observations have been in mathematics classes. Mathematics is a highly structured discipline that may lend itself to a type of teaching different from that found for other subjects.

As Lebra (chapter 12, this volume) pointed out, Ho and I are each insiders and possibly more critical of our own culture than of the other cultures we have observed. Undoubtedly, each system has its strengths and weaknesses. From my perspective, the greatest strength of East-Asian education lies in its elementary schools, whereas in the United States it lies in its universities.

REFERENCES

Peak, L. (1991). *Learning to go to school in Japan.* Berkeley: University of California Press.
Stevenson, H. W., & Lee, S. Y. (1989). *The polished stones* (videotape). Ann Arbor, MI: Center for Human Growth and Development, University of Michigan.

Stevenson, H. W., & Stigler, J. W. (1992). *The learning gap: Why our schools are failing and what we can learn from Japanese and Chinese education.* New York: Summit Books.

Stevenson, H. W., Stigler, J. W., Lucker, G. W., Lee, S. Y., Hsu, C. C., & Kitamura, S. (1987). Classroom behavior and achievement of Japanese, Chinese, and American children. In R. Glaser (Ed.), *Advances in instructional psychology* (pp. 153–204). Hillsdale, NJ: Lawrence Erlbaum Associates.

16

EAST-ASIAN ACADEMIC SUCCESS IN THE UNITED STATES: FAMILY, SCHOOL, AND COMMUNITY EXPLANATIONS

Barbara Schneider
National Opinion Research Center and
The University of Chicago

Joyce A. Hieshima
Northeastern Illinois University

Sehahn Lee
The University of Chicago

Stephen Plank
The University of Chicago

The academic success of Chinese-, Korean-, and Japanese-American students has been well established in large-scale quantitative studies such as High School and Beyond, and in smaller, more qualitative field-based investigations (Coleman, Hoffer, & Kilgore, 1982; Matute-Bianchi, 1986; Peng, Owings, & Fetters, 1984; Schneider & Lee, 1990; Tsang, 1988; Wong, 1980). Consistently, East Asian-American students outperform their Euro-American counterparts on standard achievement tests. Similar results are found when comparing the academic performance of U.S. students with their peers in other East-Asian countries (Garden, 1987; Husen, 1967; Stevenson et al., 1990; Stevenson, Lee, & Stigler, 1986). Although these differences in academic performance among different groups are documented, few investigators have attempted to explore what accounts for the success of particular minority groups. (A notable exception is Stevenson, Lee, Chen, Stigler et al. 1990.)

Concerned with providing new understandings for why a disproportionate number of East Asian-American students experience school success, a field-based study was initiated at Northwestern University (Evanston, IL) to compare East-Asian with Euro-American sixth- and seventh-grade students with respect to (a) family background characteristics; (b) family and student educational attitudes and aspirations; (c) time spent in and out of school; (d) academic performance; (e) classroom behaviors; and (f) relationships with parents, teachers, and peers.[1] Using ethnographic techniques, 73 students, 62 of their parents, and 16 teachers and administrators were interviewed; 90 days of in-school observations were conducted, school records were reviewed, and student essays were collected in two Chicago area public elementary schools. Results strongly link the academic success of East-Asian students to (a) the values and aspirations they share with their parents, (b) the home learning activities in which they participate with their families, and (c) the expectations they share and the interactions they have with their teachers and classmates (Schneider & Lee, 1990).

This Chicago field-based study explored a new conceptual model of academic achievement that incorporated both cultural macrolevel explanations (Gibson, 1988; Ogbu, 1983, 1987; Ogbu & Matute-Bianchi, 1986) and microlevel interactions and instructional activities (Erickson, 1987; Moll & Diaz, 1987; Trueba, 1986, 1988) for interpreting variations in academic performance and educational attainment among dominant and minority groups. Moving away from explanations that focus on traditional family background measures or cultural values that are compatible and consistent with U.S. public schools, we sought to link both macro- and microlevel approaches for explaining differences in academic performance among East-Asian and Euro-American students. We developed our model on theories that emphasize (a) the home environment (Hess & Holloway, 1984), (b) the communication style between teacher and learner (Erickson, 1987; Heath, 1983), and (c) the socializing influences of society (Ogbu, 1987; Gibson, 1988).[2]

Results from the Chicago field-based study spurred an interest to learn more about the educational orientation of East Asian-American families. In this preliminary work, differences were found between East Asians and Euro-Americans with respect to the educational and occupational expectations that parents had for their children, the type of home learning activities the families engaged in, and the extent of monitoring and control of student time outside of school. Differences in behavior among these groups were traced to strong East-Asian cultural values that emphasize the importance of educa-

---

[1]In the Chicago field-based study, East-Asian Americans referred to first-, second-, and third-generation Chinese, Japanese, and Korean families. The term *first generation*, as used in this chapter and by Japanese Americans themselves, is equivalent to the term *immigrant generation*, as used by Delgado-Gaitan (chapter 3, this volume) for Mexican Americans. Delgado-Gaitan's first-generation families would be considered second generation in the terminology of the present chapter.

[2]For an extensive review of family influences on achievement, including (a) effects of verbal interaction, (b) affective relationship between parent and child, (c) discipline and control strategies, and (d) parental beliefs and attributions, see Hess and Holloway (1984).

tion for self-improvement, a respect for authority, and a sense of duty and honor to the family. East-Asian American families stressed to their children that their actions in school reflected on their family and their family's country of origin. Duty and sense of responsibility to one's country of origin help to reinforce a collective value orientation. Such a collective orientation has roots in U.S. society but it has been counteracted by a tension between collectivism and competitive individualism (Bellah, Madsen, Sullivan, Swidler, & Tipton, 1985).

In the Chicago study, the number of third- and fourth-generation East-Asian American families was limited. Therefore, it is difficult to discern if the strong traditional values and activities of "immigrant groups" has broken down as each successive generation has become more susceptible to U.S. values, and has perhaps encountered a lesser incidence of discrimination in the larger societal systems such as the workplace, educational institutions, and housing market.

We were especially interested in Japanese Americans because they represented a unique group among the East Asians. Many Japanese families living in the United States today, unlike Chinese and Koreans, are likely to have emigrated to the United States before World War II. During the 1950s and for part of the 1960s, emigration of Japanese families to the United States was nearly nonexistent. From 1965 to 1984, approximately 3% of Asian immigrants to the United States were Japanese, and in the latter part of the 1980s Japanese immigrants to the United States dropped to 1.7% of the total immigration population from Asia (Takaki, 1989). Japanese families that have come to the United States since the late 1970s for the most part are Japanese nationals who plan on returning to Japan. Many of these Japanese nationals tend to send their children to Japanese private schools in the United States.

Due to this trend of reduced immigration from Japan, Japanese Americans have become primarily an American-born ethnic group: In 1980, 72% were citizens by birth and predominately English speaking. A large number of these third- (*Sansei*) and fourth-generation (*Yonsei*) Japanese Americans represent a somewhat culturally detached immigrant group. During World War II, the ties many first-, second-, and third-generation Japanese Americans had with their country of origin were severed. At this time, familial relationships with relatives in Japan were oftentimes disrupted and emotionally strained. Even years after World War II, relatives in Japan are often regarded by many Japanese Americans as distant. Forced into internment camps and then into resettlements, these Japanese are very unlike Chinese and Korean immigrants, who have never suffered such massive displacement and destruction of their communities in the United States.

As a result of the strained familial ties and the lack of a strong social community network, opportunities for many third- and fourth-generation Japanese Americans to become proficient with the Japanese language have been limited. In fact, they are virtually monolingual in English. Very few *Sansei* and *Yonsei* are able to speak Japanese at all (Takaki, 1989). Given the historical experiences of Japanese Americans in the United States, we questioned whether third- and fourth-generation Japanese Americans would continue to maintain the values and activities often associated with more recent East-Asian immigrant groups and with others who have lived in the United States for several generations.

To answer this question, we conducted 10 supplementary interviews with Japanese-American families and 11 child interviews using the same protocol as in the Chicago field-based study (see, e.g., Lee, 1987). In addition to these new interviews, we also undertook an analysis of a new study, the National Education Longitudinal Study of 1988 (NELS:88), initiated by the National Center for Education Statistics. This large-scale random sample of 26,000 eighth-grade students and their parents, teachers, and administrators includes an oversample of East-Asian students representing both recent immigrants and those who have been in the United States for several generations.

Findings of this study reveal that East-Asian students (not controlling for length of time in the United States) outperform their Euro-American counterparts on academic achievement tests and grades (Hafner, Ingels, Schneider, & Stevenson, 1990). However, recent additional analyses of NELS:88 indicate that, among the East-Asian American groups sampled (i.e., Chinese, Japanese, and Koreans), there are differences in various student outcome measures. These group differences can be linked to variations in social resources that families allocate to certain educational activities, such as parental involvement in school activities, volunteering in school, and discussing school matters at home.

This chapter integrates results from the new Japanese-American interviews, the Chicago field study, and recent analyses of NELS:88 to further explore differences and similarities in values held by and activities undertaken by Chinese, Korean, and Japanese American families to ensure their children positive educational futures. The general approach of our work is based on the model of academic achievement used in the Chicago field study. This model is especially useful for our work because it links specific family behaviors to larger social systems.

MODEL OF ACADEMIC ACHIEVEMENT

To explain differences in academic performance among East-Asian American groups, the model we developed combines macro- and microlevel approaches. At the macrolevel, the focus is on the economic and cultural history of the family's country of origin, as well as that of the country to which they have immigrated. At the microlevel, the focus is on the interactive process among children, their parents, their teachers, and their peers (see Schneider & Lee, 1990, for a detailed description of the model.)

The rationale for integrating a macro- and microlevel analysis is based on work by Spindler and Spindler (1987a, 1987b), in which they argued that culture operates at both collective macrosocial and micropsychological levels. From our perspective, a microlevel analysis provides an opportunity to systematically observe how individuals translate their experiences, thoughts, and feelings into behaviors. Yet, if only a microlevel analysis is employed, one can obfuscate how interactions are linked to family values and attitudes, as well as to larger social structural systems. As Ogbu (1987) contended, microlevel ethnographies that neglect to examine the wider societal systems cannot demonstrate how educational performance is linked with the nation's economy, political system, local community social structure, and belief systems of minority groups served by the schools.

Our model views East-Asian academic success and high educational aspirations as the results of a multilevel process of interactions among parents, children, teachers, and peer groups. Consequently, the model is both dynamic and interactive. Family and school interactions are examined in light of socioeconomic and cultural factors. For example, how families structure and monitor the learning activities of their children at home are dependent on family members' expectations. These expectations are formed in turn through family members' cultural and economic experiences, the expectations of the school and community, and family resources, such as the amount of time parents can devote to an activity. The relationship between macrosociocultural factors and microinterpersonal interactions is diagrammed in Fig. 16.1.

We assume that the value a minority group places on education is historically determined and interfaces with the group's socioeconomic position in the host society. Historically, education in East-Asian societies was limited to the privileged classes. However, as the societies became more industrial-

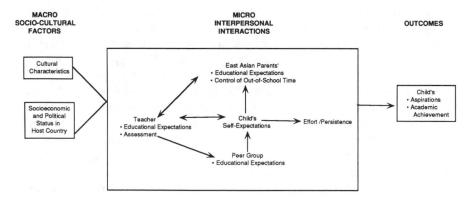

FIG. 16.1. A model to explain East-Asian academic success.

ized, education became a means to achieve upward mobility, social respect, and self-improvement (Lee, 1987). The availability of education within East-Asian countries helped to foster an even stronger commitment to learning among all the social classes. Thus, when East-Asians came to the United States, they already had been socialized in their countries of origin to believe that additional education leads to economic and social rewards. Nevertheless, the economic rewards for investing in education for East Asians in the United States have been lower than they have been for Euro-Americans (Barringer, Takeuchi, & Xenos, 1990; Gibson, 1988; Lee, 1987). This lower reward indicates the operation of political forces affecting relative power or status.

East Asians may be willing to accept these lower economic rewards because they expect that future benefits may be accrued either in the United States or when returning to their country of origin. Thus, East Asians encourage their children to acquire more education beyond high school, despite the relatively lower economic rewards they receive from additional schooling as a means to enhance their lives in the future. Further, noneconomic cultural values such as self-improvement and upholding the family honor may mediate the actual economic benefits of education.

We expect that sociocultural factors will be transmitted by, and thus visible in, microlevel relationships that East-Asian American children have with their parents, teachers, and peer groups. We assume that children develop academic self-expectations based on their own past experiences, as well as the educational expectations that their parents, teachers, and peer groups hold for them. Aware of others' expectations, it appears that children set certain self-expectations, or standards, for their own achievement, and then translate these standards into performance through persistence in coping with particular learning situations or tasks.

In addition to cultural and socioeconomic factors, the academic expectations parents have for their children are likely to be influenced by their children's self-evaluation and by teacher assignments (Wong, 1980). Teacher expectations, which we perceive to be formed in part by societal views of East-Asian success, are affected by interactions with East-Asian students and their parents. We suspect that teachers' attitudes toward East-Asian students are expressed openly in the classroom. Such teacher perceptions frequently communicated to East-Asian American children at school, coupled with high parental expectations at home, most likely have a strong positive effect on children's expectations for their own academic achievement.

Influenced by their teachers' and parents' attitudes toward other children, as well as by their own observations, children formulate educational expectations for their peers. Students are accustomed to having their academic performance judged by their teachers. If teachers consistently give high grades to and make positive comments about the performance of certain groups of children, such teacher behaviors are likely to positively affect the opinions that students have toward their classmates. Expressed positive teacher opinions of East Asians can also arouse envy of and eventual discrimination against these students by their Euro-American peers. Thus, Euro-American students could expect East Asian Americans to do well in school, and at the same time resent the likelihood of their future academic success. We assume that the behavior of East-Asian American students in school is influenced by the expectations of their peers, which in turn is consonant with the views held by their teachers.

We also hypothesize that East-Asian parents are more likely to stress certain norms such as industriousness, diligence, and respect, which reinforce behaviors highly valued by teachers in the United States, who are usually Euro-American. The closeness of East-Asian families and the clearly delineated lines of parental authority within them enhance the parents' ability to control their children's behavior regarding activities such as the use of time. Such control would be exercised by closely monitoring their children's division of time between academic and social pursuits. The children would be unlikely to resist such control and to conscientiously fulfill parental expectations because of certain cultural values and norms that relate academic achievement to family honor.

In the Chicago field-based study, we explored each of the components of this model through interviews and observations in two public schools. We were limited in our school selections because few schools had 20 or more Chinese, Japanese, and Korean American students in Grades 6 and 7. The recent release of NELS:88 allowed us to look at our model using a national random sample of students throughout the United States. Because of the NELS:88 design, we used data sources (parents, teachers, and peer group), values, and behaviors similar to those in the Chicago study, with the additional benefit of a nationally random representative database.

The National Longitudinal Study of 1988 Design and Sample

Conducted by the National Center for Education Statistics (NCES), NELS:88 is the third in a series of national longitudinal studies of American student cohorts that began in 1972. NELS:88 differs from other longitudinal studies in that the first data collection phase occurred when the students were in eighth grade. The two previous NCES studies began when the students were in 10th and 12th grade in high school and followed them through postsecondary school into adulthood. A substantial subsample of the NELS:88 students were resurveyed in 1990 as sophomores, and will be surveyed again next year when they are high school seniors.

Substantively, NELS:88 was designed to examine student achievement over time, as well as to focus on family, community, school, and classroom factors that may promote or inhibit educational success. Other issues addressed by NELS:88 that were consistent with our interests include: (a) what role the family plays in shaping educational attitudes and behavior; (b) how teacher judgments of student motivation, performance, and potential influence student achievement; and (c) how students are assigned to particular programs and how these program assignments affect academic performance and future career choices.

The NELS:88 base-year study collected data from students, parents, teachers, and school administrators. Self-administered questionnaires and tests represented the principal modes of data collection. The student questionnaire solicited information on basic demographic variables and a range of other topics including schoolwork, aspirations, and social relationships. Students also completed a series of curriculum-based cognitive tests. One parent of each student was asked to respond to a parent survey that gauged (a) parent aspirations for their children, (b) family willingness to commit resources to their children's education, (c) home educational supports, and (d) other family characteristics related to achievement. Two teachers of each sampled student also completed a teacher questionnaire designed to collect data about (a) teacher evaluations of selected students, (b) course content and classroom teaching practices, and (c) school and teacher characteristics. A school administrator questionnaire completed by the school principal requested information about the school's (a) teaching staff, (b) climate, (c) student body characteristics, and (d) policies and offerings.

Sample

The base-year survey employed a two-stage, stratified sample design, with schools being the first stage and students within the selected schools being the second stage. To ensure a balanced sample, schools were first stratified by region, urbanicity, and percentage minority prior to sampling. The school sample was restricted to "regular" public and private schools (including independent, Catholic, and their types of religious schools) with eighth graders. From a national frame encompassing 39,000 schools with eighth grades, a total of 1,057 schools participated in the study.

Within each school, approximately 26 students were randomly selected. In sampled schools with fewer than 24 eighth graders, all eligible students were selected. In schools where 26 students were surveyed, 24 regularly sampled students (which included standard racial and ethnic groups; i.e., African Americans, Native Americans, Asian/Pacific Islanders, Hispanics, and Euro-Americans) and 2 supplementary Hispanic and Asian/Pacific-Islander students were included. This oversample of Asian Americans makes the NELS:88 study particularly valuable for examining issues related to East-Asian American academic success. The final sample of 24,599 students included 1,527 Asian/Pacific Islanders, 3,009 African Americans, 3,171 Hispanics, 299 Native Americans, and 16,317 Euro-Americans (in 276 cases, race and ethnic identity information was missing). The Asian/Pacific-Islander category includes a wide range of groups: Chinese, Filipino, Japanese, Southeast Asians (Vietnamese, Laotian, Cambodian/Kampuchean, Thai), Pacific Islanders (Samoan, Guamanian), and others. (For a complete description of the base-year sample design, see Spencer, Frankel, Ingels, Rasinski, & Tourangeau, 1990.) For purposes of our work we have subsampled Chinese (N = 313), Japanese (N = 95), Koreans (N = 191), and Euro-Americans (N = 15,692) from this group.

RESULTS FROM THE NELS:88 STUDY

The NELS:88 data illustrate that East Asians continue to outperform Euro-American students on tests scores with some exceptions (see Table 16.1). As shown in Table 16.1, Chinese- and Korean-American students are overrepresented in the upper percentile range. Japanese-American students also appear to be overrepresented in the upper percentile range but the difference is not significant, possibly due to sample size. (Other results show a similar pattern: Results for Japanese- and Korean-American students are often skewed in the hypothesized direction but they are not statistically significant. We strongly suspect that this is an artifact of the data.) However, results for grades seem to indicate a somewhat different trend. Chinese- and Korean-American student grades differ significantly from those of Japanese-American and Euro-American students, whereas Japanese-American and Euro-American student grades are not significantly different from one another. Chinese- and Korean-American students clearly are overrepresented in the upper percentile range for grades. In contrast, Japanese-American and Euro-American students are nearly evenly distributed among the three categories. Finally, in examining postsecondary plans, we find that Chinese-, Japanese-, and Korean-American students are overrepresented in the highest category (i.e., East-Asian Americans are more likely than Euro-Americans to indicate that they plan to attend graduate school).

The family background characteristics of the East-Asian American families, when compared with those of Euro-Americans, support some conventional notions but not others (see Table 16.2). Looking at parent education, we find that Chinese Americans, Japanese Americans, and Korean Americans are overrepresented among the highest education levels. However, at the highest education level only Chinese parents are significantly different from Euro-Americans. (Parent education is calculated by the highest degree held by either parent.) With respect to income, the results show that Japanese-American families far surpass all other groups in total family income, followed

TABLE 16.1
Differences in Grades, Test Scores, and Postsecondary Plans
Among Racial and Ethnic Groups

	Racial and Ethnic Groups			
Outcome Measures	Chinese American	Japanese American	Korean American	Euro- American
Grades[a]				
Lowest 25th percentile	17.8*	36.2	9.9*†	33.7
25th to 75th percentile	21.3*	33.3	28.0	34.0
Upper percentile	60.9*†	30.5	62.0*†	32.3
Test Scores				
Lowest 25th percentile	11.0	8.9	6.5*	18.2
25th to 75th percentile	39.8	41.6	31.9*	50.3
Upper percentile	49.1*	49.5	61.5*	31.5
Postsecondary Plans				
Won't finish high school	1.2	.0*	.0*	1.3
Will graduate from high school	1.7*	3.6	1.8*	10.3
Vocational or trade school	2.6*	3.7	.8*	9.2
Will attend college	7.9	13.5	3.6*	11.9
Will graduate from college	39.2	35.2	32.3	45.4
Will attend graduate school	47.5*	44.1*	61.4*	22.0

[a]k is the number of relevant simultaneous comparisons being made in each row, following from the questions addressed in the text. For grades and test scores, $k = 5$; for postsecondary plans, $k = 3$.[3]

*Chinese, Korean, or Japanese American significantly different from Euro-American (one-tailed, $p < .05/k$).

†Chinese or Korean American significantly different from Japanese American (one-tailed, $p < .05/k$).

---

[3]To compare Chinese, Korean, Japanese, and Euro-American responses on various items, t statistics were computed using the following formula:

$$t = (P1 - P2) / SQRT(SE1*SE1 + SE2*SE2)$$

where $P1$ and $P2$ are the estimates to be compared and $SE1$ and $SE2$ are estimates of their corresponding design-corrected standard errors. Estimates for the standard errors were carried out as described in the *NELS:88 Base Year Data File User's Manual* (Ingels, Abraham, Karr, Spencer, & Frankel, 1990). Design-corrected standard errors for a proportion of the sampled population can be estimated by using the following formula:

$$SE = DEFT * SQRT(p (1-p)/n)$$

where *DEFT* is the mean root design effect, p is the weighted proportion of respondents giving a particular response, n is the size of the subsample (e.g., number of Chinese responding to the question about post-high school plans).

For Chinese, Korean, and Japanese subgroups, we used the mean *DEFT* for the entire Asian/Pacific-Islander population based on parent questionnaire data. We used the *DEFT* from the parent questionnaire because the data for the analyses undertaken in this chapter were taken exclusively from the parent questionnaire. The use of the Asian/*PI DEFT* tends to be an overestimate

TABLE 16.2
Differences in Family Background Characteristics
Among Racial and Ethnic Groups

Family Background Factors	Racial and Ethnic Groups			
	Chinese American	Japanese American	Korean American	Euro- American
Parent Education[a]				
Didn't finish high school	11.0	3.0	8.1	5.9
High school graduate	13.1	2.3*	17.1	20.7
Post high school	30.4*	31.8	13.6*	43.4
College graduate	16.9	40.6*	31.4	16.1
Masters	15.1	10.9	14.7	9.4
Ph.D, M.D.	13.6*	11.3	15.1	4.5
Income				
Lowest 25th percentile	31.7†	6.4*	24.3	23.8
25th to 75th percentile	22.8	18.5	23.4	29.1
Upper percentile	45.4†	75.1*	52.3	47.1
Family Composition				
Mother and father	84.2*	83.7	79.0	68.1
Parent and stepparent	4.0*	5.7*	6.0*	14.4
Mother only	8.2	7.6	12.4	12.7
Father only	1.3	0.0*	.5	2.6
Other	2.3	2.9	2.1	2.1

[a]k is the number of relevant simultaneous comparisons being made in each row, following from the questions addressed in the text. For all rows in this table, $k = 3$.[3]

*Chinese, Korean, or Japanese American significantly different from Euro-American (one-tailed, $p < .05/k$).

†Chinese or Korean American significantly different from Japanese American (one-tailed, $p < .05/k$).

Source: U.S. Department of Education, National Center for Education Statistics, "National Education Longitudinal Study of 1988: Base Year Survey."

---

of the *DEFT*s for the subgroups, meaning that our findings are likely to be more conservative than if we had separate *DEFT*s for each subgroup. For the Euro-Americans we used the *DEFT* for "White" based on the parent questionnaire data.

To make multiple simultaneous comparisons, we followed the Bonferroni procedure. Here we have six potential comparisons for each questionnaire response. But in some cases it was apparent that a significant contrast would not be found, and thus the corresponding claims were not made in the text. Specifically, significant differences between Chinese and Korean subgroups were consistently absent. Thus, contrasts between these subgroups were not discussed in the text and this was not counted as one of the simultaneous comparisons being made. Similarly, in some other cases, other potential contrasts were not discussed in the text, thus reducing the number of simultaneous comparisons being made.

As a result, our number of simultaneous comparisons was either three, four, or five for each questionnaire response. We divided the alpha level by either three, four, or five, accordingly. That is, for a set of five claims to hold simultaneously at alpha level .05, the critical value for each comparison would be the t associated with alpha = .01 ($t = 2.326$).

by Korean-Americans, Euro-Americans, and Chinese Americans. The sharpest (and statistically significant) contrast is between Japanese Americans at the high end and Chinese Americans at the low end. Regarding family composition, we find that East Asians are overrepresented in traditional homes where both the mother and father are present. Relative to Euro-Americans, East Asians are less likely to be in melded families.

In summary, the findings for family background factors seem to mirror the original field work in Chicago. East-Asian American parents tend to have higher than average educational levels but this does not always translate into higher incomes, particularly for the Chinese. As a group, East Asian Americans seem less likely than Euro-Americans to experience some of the major shifts in the structure of the American family. East Asian-American students are more likely than Euro-American students to live in traditional two-parent homes.

One of the prevailing assumptions about East-Asian Americans is that they are less likely to contact the school regarding student educational matters. Japanese-American parents seem to dispel this assumption because they contact the school with the same frequency as Euro-Americans. Table 16.3 shows that Chinese Americans and Korean Americans are less likely to contact the school regarding academic matters than are Japanese-American and Euro-American families. Similar results can be found for contacting the school for behavioral reasons but they are not so robust as those for contacting the school for academic reasons. As for contacting the school for volunteer work, such as lunchroom duty, Great Books leader, and so on, Euro-Americans have the highest rates, followed by Japanese Americans.

One possible explanation for these results may be related to English proficiency. Using the NELS:88 data, Muller (1991) found that English proficiency is significantly related to the frequency of parental contacts with the school regarding student academic and behavioral concerns and parent volunteer work. Relatively high family income and English language dominance make Japanese Americans, particularly those who are third and fourth generation, very unlike more recent East-Asian immigrants.

We suspected that such family characteristics as high income and English language dominance would enhance the likelihood that Japanese Americans would live in communities where they had established solid social networks and frequently communicated about their children's schools with neighbors. This assumption is fairly reasonable because, when looking at the number of parents who know their children's friends' parents, the Japanese responses more closely resemble those of Euro-American families than Chinese-American and Korean-American ones.

When examining what happens to the children at school, we find that East Asian-American children are much more likely than Euro-Americans to be enrolled in algebra classes (see Table 16.4). Here is where Japanese-American

TABLE 16.3
Parental Relations with the School Among Racial and Ethnic Groups

	Racial and Ethnic Groups			
Parental Relations with the School	Chinese American	Japanese American	Korean American	Euro-American
Contact with the School About Academic Performance[a]				
Never	70.9*†	45.3	65.2	46.3
Once or twice	25.5	49.0	21.9	36.8
More than three times	3.5*	5.7	6.9	16.9
Contact the School About Student Behavior				
Never	91.1*	78.4	87.5	72.5
Once or twice	6.9*	20.0	11.6	20.2
More than three times	1.9*	1.6	.9	7.3
Contact the School About Doing Volunteer Work				
Never	88.7*	82.1	92.4*	79.1
Once or twice	9.3	14.3	5.4*	15.2
More than three times	1.9	3.6	2.2	5.7
Parent Relations with Community				
Know the Parents of Child's Friends				
No friends	39.3*†	15.4	26.9*	9.2
One to three	51.5	53.6	59.9	50.7
Over four	9.2*†	30.9	13.2*	40.1

[a]k is the number of relevant simultaneous comparisons being made in each row, following from the questions addressed in the text. For the first six rows of this table, $k = 4$; for the last six rows, $k = 5$. (See footnote 3, pp. 332–333.)

*Chinese, Korean, or Japanese American significantly different from Euro-American (one-tailed, $p < .05/k$).

†Chinese or Korean American significantly different from Japanese American (one-tailed, $p < .05/k$).

Source: U.S. Department of Education, National Center for Education Statistics, "National Education Longitudinal Study of 1988: Base Year Survey."

and Euro-American students differ: Japanese-American students are as likely as other East-Asian Americans to be enrolled in algebra classes. It may be that placement in algebra is more a function of test scores than grades, which would be consistent with the fact that Japanese Americans and Euro-Americans are ranked very similarly with respect to grades but less similarly with respect to test scores. Grades, which are typically negotiated and often the result of social interactions between students and teachers, do not seem to have the same sorting implications of test scores. Enrollment of eighth-grade students in algebra classes is noteworthy because taking algebra in eighth grade typically leads to a college preparatory track in high school (Hallinan, 1991; Oakes, 1985). Thus, despite their grades (Table 16.1),

TABLE 16.4
Difference in Student Activities at School Among Racial and Ethnic Groups

	Racial and Ethnic Groups			
Parental Attitudes Toward:	Chinese American	Japanese American	Korean American	Euro- American
Academic Activities/Enrolled in Algebra[a]				
Yes	59.7*	61.9*	62.2*	36.1
No	33.2*	35.4*	32.3*	60.7
Don't Know	7.2	2.7	5.5	3.2
Extra Curricular Activities/Participate on a Sports Team				
Yes	26.0*†	51.7	38.7*	68.1
No	74.0*†	48.3	61.3*	31.9

[a]k is the number of relevant simultaneous comparisons being made in each row, following from the questions addressed in the text. For all the rows in this table, $k = 5$. (See footnote 3, pp. 332–333.)

*Chinese, Korean, or Japanese American significantly different from Euro-American (one-tailed, $p < .05/k$).

†Chinese or Korean American significantly different from Japanese American (one-tailed, $p < .05/k$).

Source: U.S. Department of Education, National Center for Education Statistics, "National Education Longitudinal Study of 1988: Base Year Survey."

Japanese-American students are likely to be tracked into college-preparatory programs.

Chinese/Americans and Korean Americans are underrepresented in their participation in school sports. Chinese Americans are the least likely to participate in sports, followed by Korean Americans and Japanese Americans. Euro-Americans are the most likely to participate in sports. The dominance of East-Asian Americans in academic pursuits and the lack of participation in sports seems to suggest that in-school "education-related" activities are more highly valued than athletic ones.

East Asian-American parental attitudes toward school are generally more positive than those of Euro-Americans. As indicated in Table 16.5, Chinese Americans, Japanese Americans, and Korean Americans are more likely than Euro-Americans to report that parents have an adequate say in school policies. With respect to perspectives of "academic press" at their child's school, Chinese Americans and Korean Americans are more likely than Euro-Americans to say that their child is working hard at school. Here again we see Japanese Americans responding more similarly to Euro-Americans than to Chinese Americans or Korean Americans. Nearly identical patterns are also found for the item that asks parents whether the school is preparing their child for high school. Chinese-American and Korean-American parents (although responses are not significantly different in any group, differences are in the hypothesized direction) are more likely to report that the school

TABLE 16.5
Parental Attitudes Toward Education Among Racial and Ethnic Groups

	Racial and Ethnic Groups			
Parental Attitudes Toward:	Chinese American	Japanese American	Korean American	Euro- American
Having an Adequate Say in School Policy[a]				
Agree	75.3*	80.4*	77.7*	60.5
Disagree	24.6*	19.5*	22.3*	39.5
Child Working Hard at School				
Agree	90.2*	79.9	86.9*	73.1
Disagree	9.8*	20.2	13.1*	26.9
School Preparing Students Well for High School				
Agree	94.6*	79.5	91.4	83.5
Disagree	5.4*	20.5	8.6	16.5

[a]k is the number of relevant simultaneous comparisons being made in each row, following from the questions addressed in the text. For the first two rows of this table, $k = 3$; for the last four rows, $k = 4$. (See footnote 3, pp. 332–333.)

*Chinese, Korean, or Japanese American significantly different from Euro-American (one-tailed, $p < .05/k$).

Source: U.S. Department of Education, National Center for Education Statistics, "National Education Longitudinal Study of 1988: Base Year Survey."

is adequately preparing their child for high school than Euro-American and Japanese-American parents. Japanese-American parents have the lowest level of agreement with this statement.

The similarity of responses between Japanese-American and Euro-American families could be interpreted as another indication of acculturation by the Japanese into American societal values because they may be more willing to express dissatisfaction with the school. However, the level of dissatisfaction is hardly overwhelming because it hovers around one fifth of the population (see Table 16.5).

The type of activities that East-Asian Americans are likely to spend time on outside of school are education related. East-Asian Americans are more likely than Euro-Americans to report that they have a computer in the home (see Table 16.6). Not only are East-Asian Americans more likely to have education materials in the home but they are more likely to engage in activities outside the home that are arguably directly related to school learning. For example, Table 16.6 indicates that Japanese-, Korean-, and Chinese-American parents are more likely than Euro-American parents to have their child attend a language school outside of regular school. Even more remarkable are the rates for having a child study music outside of school. A little over half of the Japanese- and Korean-American families report that their eighth graders

TABLE 16.6
Family Activities at Home Among Racial and Ethnic Groups

| | Racial and Ethnic Groups | | | |
| | Chinese | Japanese | Korean | Euro- |
Activities at Home	American	American	American	American
Child Attends Language School Outside of Regular School[a]				
Yes	20.3*	32.5*	29.7*	2.9
No	79.7*	67.5*	70.3*	97.1
Child Studies Music Outside of Study				
Yes	31.3	51.6*	52.5*	27.5
No	68.7	48.4*	47.5*	72.5
Family Has Rules About Household Chores				
Yes	72.4*	73.4	66.4*	89.4
No	27.6*	26.6	33.6*	10.6
Family Has Rules for Television Programs Students May Watch				
Yes	50.9*	48.0*	49.0*	69.8
No	49.1*	52.0*	51.0*	30.2
Family Has a Computer in Home				
Yes	44.6*	40.9	52.8*	27.8
No	55.4*	59.1	47.2*	72.2

[a]k is the number of relevant simultaneous comparisons being made in each row, following from the questions addressed in the text. For all rows in this table, $k = 3$. (See footnote 3, pp. 332–333.)

*Chinese, Korean, or Japanese American significantly different from Euro-American (one-tailed, $p < .05/k$).

Source: U.S. Department of Education, National Center for Education Statistics, "National Education Longitudinal Study of 1988: Base Year Survey."

study music outside of school. In both situations, families have to expend additional resources to enroll the student in classes, arrange for transportation, monitor assignments, and, in the case of music lessons, supervise practice.

Although East-Asian Americans are more likely to participate in educational activities outside the home that encourage student self-discipline, they are less likely than Euro-Americans to require their children to do family chores (see Table 16.6). Furthermore, East-Asian Americans are less likely to have rules concerning what television shows can be watched. What these results seem to suggest is that the authoritative, disciplinary structure being enacted in East-Asian homes may be decidedly different from the socialization process traditionally associated with American families. This is further corroborated by findings related to communication (see Table 16.7).

Table 16.7 provides a summary of measures of factors associated with communicating about school at home. Looking at the table, we see that Euro-American and Japanese-American parents are much more likely than Chinese-

TABLE 16.7
Communications About School at Home Among Racial and Ethnic Groups

	Racial and Ethnic Groups			
Communication Activities	Chinese American	Japanese American	Korean American	Euro-American
Talk About School Experiences[a]				
Not at all	4.7	.6	3.2	.3
Occasionally	46.6*	29.5	51.4*	17.4
Regularly	48.7*	69.9	45.4*	82.3
Talk About High School Plans				
Not at all	5.2	.7	4.7	1.6
Occasionally	62.8	59.1	71.1*	53.4
Regularly	32.0*	40.1	24.2*	44.9

[a]k is the number of relevant simultaneous comparisons being made in each row, following from the questions addressed in the text. For all rows in this table, $k = 4$.

*Chinese, Korean, or Japanese American significantly different from Euro-American (one-tailed, $p < .05/k$).

Source: U.S. Department of Education, National Center for Education Statistics, "National Education Longitudinal Study of 1988: Base Year Survey."

and Korean-American parents to talk generally with their children about school experiences. Euro-Americans are also more likely to talk about high school plans. Japanese-American families appear to engage in similar patterns of communication with their children. Results for communication seem to point to a different form of communication in Chinese- and Korean-American families. We suspected that differences in communication patterns among the groups may be culturally derived, in contrast to more conventional interpretations that stress lack of familiarity with the American educational system.

The Japanese Americans represent an extremely interesting group because their responses on many of the NELS:88 questions are more similar to the Euro-Americans than are the Chinese Americans and Korean Americans, especially for certain items that measure parent involvement in the schools and patterns of communication. Yet on other factors, such as parental educational expectations, the Japanese-American responses more closely resemble those of the Chinese Americans and Korean Americans. The differences in responses for the Japanese Americans, in comparison to the other East Asian-American families, appear to illustrate the results of an immigrant group in the process of assimilation. Their activities seem to represent an accommodation between East-Asian values and those of "mainstream" American society. We suspect that more intensive in-depth interviews with Japanese-American families would help us gain new insights into how Japanese values and traditions become incorporated in the assimilation process.

Specifically, we were interested in learning more about the influences of culture and family in the formation of the student's academic self-expectations and performance. We were interested in learning if third- and fourth-generation Japanese Americans (*Sansei* and *Yonsei*) emphasized some of the same traditional cultural values as the Chinese Americans and Korean Americans. In the Chicago field study, the number of Japanese Americans interviewed was considerably smaller than the number of Chinese- and Korean-American families. Therefore, we decided to expand the sample by interviewing additional Japanese-American families.

To replicate as closely as possible the same design as the Chicago field study, we contacted Japanese-American families with children in elementary school who live in neighborhoods similar to those of the original sample. The interview protocols were identical to the Chicago study instruments, and the same procedures were employed. Eleven Japanese-American students and one parent of each student were interviewed. The number of parent interviews totaled 10 because two children were interviewed in one family. The interviews were free flowing and as informal as possible. All of the interviews were recorded and transcribed. In addition to the interviews, the students were also asked to complete three essays, one on each of three subjects: "my home," "my school," and "my future."

RESULTS OF THE JAPANESE-AMERICAN INTERVIEWS

Unlike the Chinese- and Korean-American families in the Chicago study, but similar to the NELS:88 sample of Japanese Americans, the Japanese-American families had high income and occupational levels. With the exception of family composition, the demographic profiles of the Japanese-American families more closely resembled the Euro-American families in the Chicago study than the East Asian-American ones. Yet the Japanese Americans demonstrated higher educational expectations and standards for their children than did the Euro-Americans.

In the Chicago study, we found that the differences in educational expectations between East-Asian Americans and Euro-Americans could be traced to the East-Asian cultural tradition, which places a high value on education for self-improvement, self-esteem, and family honor, and the determination of some East Asian-American families to overcome occupational discrimination by investing in education (cf. Sue & Okazaki, 1990). Although clearly "making it" in American society monetarily, overall the Japanese-American families we interviewed retained the same values found among the Chinese- and Korean-American families in the Chicago study.

Unequivocally, the value of education was evident across all of the Japanese-American families, as demonstrated in the following quotations from several parents:

> I think the emphasis in most Asian-American families is on education and it comes from the parents and the culture. Asian parents, from what I can see, will find any opportunity to improve the education of their children. They're willing to put time and energy into it.

> I expect him to go to college because I want him to have the most options for later life. Hopefully, he will have the qualifications to do whatever he wants and then he can pick and choose. I want him to be prepared and have as many opportunities as possible and not be forced into a position because he is unprepared or unqualified.

> Education is important from an altruistic point of view. Education widens your perspective; it makes your life a lot richer. I think education is very, very, important, so that you can become more global. Not only in terms of what you know but how you think and how flexible you can become. From a pragmatic point of view, education is very important because it is the ticket to a better job, and especially for a nonmainstream person you are stalemated without it.

As implied in the last quote, Japanese Americans recognize that there is still a great deal of racial discrimination, and that access to certain occupations and advancement within particular fields is still limited for Japanese Americans. This is particularly disconcerting because all of the parents interviewed for this study were born and raised in the United States and all of the children are *Yonsei* or 4th-generation Japanese Americans. All but two of the parents interviewed reported experiencing racial discrimination both personally and professionally.

The parent interviews clearly support Ogbu's (1983, 1987) position that such experiences can be used as a strong incentive to invest in education as a mechanism to overcome prejudice and discrimination. Education is seen as the strategy to thwart the vestiges of racial discrimination:

> Due to social status and discrimination, you need "education," otherwise you haven't got a chance, and it's very sad. Today college is a given. It's an automatic part of how life is.

> Without an education you have real difficulty. Although even with an education there are problems. There is definitely a ceiling in terms of a corporation. Take for instance the company I work at now. You could probably count the number of Asian Americans and certainly Japanese Americans. You probably would count 20 Asian Americans in a work force of 13,000, and there are potentially 4 Japanese Americans at the top and none of them are higher than middle management. And from my experiences with the company I knew that Asians were feared, because they are seen as overly competent and therefore setting a new pace. Yes, there definitely is a ceiling effect, especially in the administrative power positions.

Racial and ethnic discrimination is not limited to the labor force. The overwhelming majority of Japanese-American families and their children report incidents of racial discrimination at school. The continued harassment of Japanese Americans, who are perceived by their peers and teachers to excel at school (Schneider & Lee, 1990), demonstrates a negative tension between those who are perceived as immigrants and mainstream Americans, despite the ethnic or racial group's accomplishments. Thus, even in educational situations where Japanese Americans are succeeding they continue to experience discrimination.

The underlying racial tensions experienced by Japanese-American students are vividly articulated by parents and students in 19 of the 21 interviews. A sample of the parent stories include the following:

> During the Gulf War, I guess a couple of boys in her class made a comment about how Japan didn't send an army. The boys asked my daughter why Japan didn't send an army. She replied, "I don't know, I'm not Japanese, I'm American." I was glad she said that. The way I took it is the boys see her as non-Caucasian, so although she does everything just like them, her skin color is not the same. They probably feel that way because of their parents. As much as we Japanese Americans say we don't see racial discrimination, it's always here, and we feel it.

> When my daughter switched from private preschool and into public schools, then she didn't want to walk by herself to school. It turned out that there was a boy who would call her something on the playground. He was saying, "Hey Chinese girl, stop, or I'll kick you." She would say, "Well, I'm not Chinese, I'm Japanese." When I went to the school I was really angry. I didn't really realize how upset I was. That was the first time in my child's life that she had been called something other than her name.

From the *Yonsei* children, a similar story of discrimination:

> I usually get made fun of because I'm Japanese or Oriental.

> Yes, I've been called names in school and after a while I got really sick of it. I told the teacher, but she didn't do much. They got detention and stuff, and then they still did it. They were making fun of me because I'm Japanese and picking on me and making fun of me. My mother said, "Oh, well, give them one more chance." My dad said, "Sock him in the mouth!" So, I took my dad's advice and they didn't bother me anymore.

> There's like this taboo that Japanese kids are smarter and are taking over. It's not really true. The smartest kid in the grade is Greek. It's funny though. People joke about that Orientals are taking over, but it's not true.

The continued discrimination experienced by these Japanese-American families in the labor force and their children at school could potentially undermine the Japanese commitment to education. Repeated incidents of discrimination over successive generations could eventually become an ingrained part of their culture and result in an eroding confidence in the instrumental value of education. One likely reason why Japanese Americans may remain steadfast in their position on education is the continued strength of Japanese cultural values, which hold education to be fundamental to personal fulfillment. It is important to emphasize this cultural aspect because it constrains the argument that Asians invest in education primarily for economic and self-advancement desires (Ogbu, 1983; Sue & Okazaki, 1990).

By stressing the intrinsic value of education, the benefits of education are self-perpetuating rather than dependent on external rewards such as job advancement. Going to college becomes a given not only because it is a ticket to opportunity but also because it enhances the personal development of the individual.

> Ideally, the primary goal of education is to help children discover their unique talents, to be excited about learning and discovery and that it is lifelong, and to acquire tools for that discovery. It gives them the tools to think and to evaluate. Education allows them to look around on their own and make sense of what's around them. That gives them the tools to explore, gain understanding, and knowledge.

> Education is very important. It is something that you need, and if you have it, no one can take it away from you. You can build on it. I think it is critical to life.

> Going to college is just assumed. If you have a college education, it may not actually be necessary for what you want to do, but it's not a handicap either. If you want to do other things, you have an education as a base.

Getting good grades, like attending college, is an unquestioned expectation. A tacit understanding exists between the parents and the child about the value of education, putting forth one's greatest effort, and bringing the family honor through successful academic performance. Parental expectations for getting good grades are not typically communicated verbally, nor are they exclusively treated as "goods," as in many Euro-American families, which if acquired result in a tangible reward such as money or special privileges. As one parent comments, "In our family, grades are not held out with condition, if you do this, then you get this." The benefits of getting good grades are mutually understood to be intrinsic and not subject to a negotiated exchange between the student and the parents or the school.

> I don't have to say anything about bad grades. My kids have high expectations of their own. If they don't do well, they're mad at themselves.

> With my son, I don't have to comment about his report card. His grades are excellent. On his last report card, he got one grade that was one step down

from excellent. He was very disappointed about that. So I try to focus on the positive side of things, because he drives himself so hard. He doesn't need me to make negative comments. So it is for me just basking in the glow with him.

My daughter is an A student and pretty much self-motivated. I just want her to learn how to think. I would like her to develop more critical thinking. I don't want to impose myself on her because some day I'm not going to be around.

The child interviews are consistent with the comments of the parents: The expectation for achieving good grades is assumed and controlled by (a) self-motivation, (b) sense of efficacy, and (c) commitment to family. Failure to achieve scholastically is personally humiliating to the individual as well as his or her family. Relying on internalized norms of performance rather than external rewards appears to be the primary incentive for achieving academic success.

I really feel good when I get a good report card [for this child all As is a good report card]. I feel I can tell everyone about my report card without feeling embarrassed or anything like that.

I would literally die if I got a D.

Interviewer: Do you get rewards for your grades?
Child: No.
Interviewer: What do your parents do if they are not pleased with your grades?
Child: I don't know. I guess they would just talk to me. I guess I would feel bad enough, that they wouldn't do anything.

The tacit understandings that operate for getting good grades also pertain to homework. As with getting good grades, the families articulate a belief that the motivation for completing one's homework is self-initiated. In contrast to the Chicago study, we did not find that Japanese-American families establish a specific time for study or carefully monitor their children's use of time. Rather, parents rely on their children's understanding of self-discipline to meet expectations.

I can't complain about studying. The minute she gets home she gets right to her homework. I don't know where that comes from. I never had to say, "Get started."

I just leave it to her that she knows when she has something to do and I expect her to get it done. I assume she knows that she should only watch a certain amount of T.V. and her taste in the programs she watches is pretty innocuous.

I don't put a lot of restrictions on them for doing homework because I feel they need to develop that for themselves. I pretty much let them be responsible.

Although parents do not report carefully monitoring the students' time at home, all of the parents indicate that their children engage in some type of education-related activities outside of school. All of the parents indicate using the public libraries on a regular basis (usually weekly). Seven out of the 11 students take either piano, clarinet, flute, or *taiko* (Japanese drums). Two of the children attend a Japanese language school. One student reported attending a special private school after public school that uses *Kumon*, a Japanese method for teaching mathematics (see Finn, 1989). However, we also found that seven of the students engaged in other activities (e.g., gymnastics, soccer, swimming, tennis, and scouts), which we did not find among the Chinese Americans and Korean Americans in the Chicago study.

Although the children are engaged in many different activities, the families report spending a lot of time together. Children and parents feel that they spend 95%–99% of their time outside of work and school together. Among all of the Japanese-American families, there seems to be a strong emphasis on just being together, whether reading, watching television, or completing household chores. It is important to underscore that the nature of this time is very child centered. That is, the families organize their time around activities that are perceived to be enriching for the development of their children.

On weekdays, it's work, school. In my free time, getting organized, getting the boys organized, sitting and talking to them, and reading with them, and taking them to their activities, having their friends over, or taking them to friends' homes. Sometimes we go on an after school excursion to the library or to a museum. It's pretty much centered around the home and spending time together. On weekends we get a little more loose. We don't have immediate deadlines; it's more laid back. The boys build forts and bike and help me in the garden. Friends come over or we go on a day trip.

The close relations between the family members help to reinforce cultural traditions and values as one parent explains:

For me it just seems like the Asian-American students do better than other students. You see it in the paper about the sciences and math. In the competitions, there's always one or two Asians. I just can't help but think it's a lot of heritage and background and the emphasis on family, education, and discipline. It's not to say that other ethnic groups do not put education any higher, it's just that . . . I think a lot of it is just family structure and the discipline.

We suspect that it is not just these values that motivate the behavior but also the mechanisms by which these beliefs are transmitted. One parent's story illustrates how values and understandings are communicated and reinforced. In this instance, in which the mother uses symbolism and relies on conceptual understandings to motivate her child to write a poem, it is important to note that there is no material reward. Rather, the reward is a feeling of self-accomplishment.

My son had to write a poem about his people, and wasn't sure how to start. He was really having trouble with it. I asked him to explain to me what a poem was. Then I asked him to simply think of words and I would write them down. I would ask him about these things when he was with his grandmother or in a Japanese restaurant. Then I put him in his room at his desk. Nothing happened for awhile. Then I brought in some Japanese dolls that represented a family, a Japanese art book, and a Japanese scroll. After some more time he came out with a very nice poem. He was very happy. We gave him much reinforcement. I think these types of experiences are self-motivating.

In this example, the mother helps the child establish his identity with the Japanese people conceptually through symbols. The poem in many ways reflects this conceptual and symbolic orientation.

My People

People dressed in beautiful robes
Dark hair, respectful, bowing
  are my people.
Quiet, peaceful, loving,
  simple, strong, and wise.
Warriors of a different kind
  are my people.

Overall, we find that these Japanese-American parents stress particular values at home that forge a tripartite relationship between cultural continuity, family obligation, and academic performance. This relationship is strengthened by specific educational activities undertaken at home that are directly connected to academic performance and high educational aspirations.

Although we find evidence of strong identification with the Japanese culture, we also detect some tension as these families try to accommodate to both American and Japanese cultures. At one level these families are very "Americanized": They are involved at school and in their communities, their children play sports, and as a family they participate in a wide variety of recreational activities. On the other hand, they also maintain some of the strong East-Asian traditions, such as high educational expectations, reliance on tacit understandings to monitor and motivate performance, and respect for authority. Thus, it could be said that they behave like Americans socially and think like Japanese. This emerging identity represents somewhat of a hybrid of American and Japanese values.

My mother speaks pretty much only Japanese. I have learned a broken Japanese. As an adult, I have returned to it more, mostly to understand my mother better. And in a way, in studying the language [she has been studying Japanese at a local university], I've come to understand myself a lot more and how the

Japanese language develops and molds the character of the people. And it's been interesting, I have found out the ways that I am Japanese and the ways I am American. Having traveled to Japan in 1970 while my father was still alive, it was a way to find out that I really am American. Most of my values mark me as an American, although I think that the way we raise our children is a combination of both. I think my values are both Christian and my values are old world, too. We believe very strongly in the role of parents, and we're strict parents. We have a great deal of emphasis on the kids studying with a focus toward excellence. Maybe a little more lenient and understanding than our parents. . . I would like my children to retain a sense of heritage, but I would like them to have a sense that we're all human beings, we're all in this together, that would be fine with me.

SUMMARY

Findings of NELS:88 and the in-depth interviews provide some new insights into the behaviors and changing norms of Japanese-American families. Third- and fourth-generation Japanese Americans represent in some ways the most "Americanized" of the East Asian-American groups, primarily because of their historical experiences in American society over the last 50 years. As with all ethnic and racial groups that have emigrated to America, we expect that they would retain some of the cultural traditions and customs from their country of origin. What is of interest here is the accommodation process in which some Japanese characteristics remain as fundamental to the family, whereas other features of family life become "Americanized."

Results suggest that the strongest continuity between Japanese Americans and other East-Asian Americans is the focus on values. This is perhaps most pronounced in the area of education. Like other East Asians, Japanese Americans value education for self-improvement, self-esteem, and as a means for social mobility. It is important to underscore that Japanese Americans, like other East-Asian groups, place a high intrinsic value on education, which some may argue is not representative of mainstream American values, which tend to stress education primarily for occupational mobility.

Not only do the Japanese Americans share the same educational values as other East-Asian Americans but they also transmit these values using the same "tacit" mechanisms as other Asian groups. This is perhaps most obvious in the transcripts describing homework and grades. Japanese-American parents do not explicitly require, monitor, or supervise homework assignments. Similarly, they do not directly place demands on their children to get good grades. Rather, these expectations and values are transmitted indirectly and symbolically.

It appears from the comments of families and their children that homework and good grades are not negotiated. That is, the Japanese-American children do not respond that if they do their homework they receive tangible rewards such as extra time to watch television or talk on the phone. Instead, the children treat homework as an activity that has intrinsic value to them personally. Failure to complete it reflects not only their lack of effort but also their parents' inability to instill appropriate values. In essence, the "responsibility for completing homework" has high internal worth to the student, and the value and responsibility associated with it is stressed by the family.

The transmittal of values appears to occur "tacitly" through concepts and symbols. This is perhaps best exemplified by the story of the mother who explains how she helped her child write a poem. The mother does not sit down with the child and help him think of rhymes or words, but instead tries to stimulate his imagination through cultural symbols that tie the child to his historical roots. These symbols become personified in the child's poem, which offers further evidence of how concepts are used metaphorically: "warriors of a different kind are my people."

We suspect that this reliance on conceptual symbols as a mechanism for communication is particularly efficacious for school achievement. The high level of achievement of Japanese Americans on standardized tests in mathematics and science has been well documented. One conventional explanation for this result has been that Asians lacking language proficiency in English focus their energies on subjects that are not language based. The language explanation seems less salient for Japanese Americans, who, with the exception of a small number of first-generation Japanese, are proficient in English. It may be that Japanese-American educational success in mathematics and science, which require abstract cognitive skills, could be the result of the symbolic value socialization process stressed in the families.

REFERENCES

Barringer, H., Takeuchi, D., & Xenos, P. (1990). Educational prestige and income of Asian Americans. *Sociology of Education, 63*(1), 27–43.

Bellah, R., Madsen, R., Sullivan, W., Swidler, A., & Tipton, S. (1985). *Habits of the heart: Individualism and commitment in American life.* New York: Harper & Row.

Coleman, J., Hoffer, T., & Kilgore, S. (1982). *High school achievement: Public, Catholic, and private schools compared.* New York: Basic Books.

Erickson, F. (1987). Transformation and school success: The politics and culture of educational achievement. *Anthropology and Education Quarterly, 18*(4), 335–356.

Finn, C. (1989, July 12). Made in Japan: Low-tech method for math success. *The Wall Street Journal,* p. 16.

Garden, R. (1987). The second IEA mathematics study. *Comparative Education review, 31,* 47–68.

Gibson, M. (1988). *Accommodation without assimilation: Sikh immigrants in an American high school.* Ithaca, NY: Cornell University Press.

Hafner, A., Ingels, S., Schneider, B., & Stevenson, D. (1990). *National education longitudinal study of 1988, A profile of the American eighth grader: Student descriptive summary.* Washington, DC: U.S. Department of Education.

Hallinan (1991, October). *Middle school teaching.* Invited presentation, Ogburn-Stouffer Center, University of Chicago.

Heath, S. (1983). *Ways with words: Language, life and work in communities and classrooms.* Cambridge, England: Cambridge University Press.

Hess, R., & Holloway, S. (1984). Family and school as educational institutions. In R. Parke (Ed.), *Review of child development research* (pp. 179–222). Chicago: University of Chicago Press.

Husen, T. (Ed.). (1967). *International study of achievement in mathematics: A comparison of twelve countries* (Vols. 1–2). New York: Wiley.

Ingels, S., Abraham, S., Karr, R., Spencer, B., & Frankel, M. (1990). *National education longitudinal study of 1988, Base year: Student component data file user's manual.* Washington, DC: U.S. Department of Education.

Lee, Y. (1987). *Academic success of East Asian Americans.* Seoul, Korea: Seoul National University, American Studies Institute.

Matute-Bianchi, M. E. (1986). Ethnic identities and patterns of school success and failure among Mexican-descent and Japanese American students in a California high school: An ethnographic analysis. *American Journal of Education, 95*(1), 233–255.

Moll, D., & Diaz, S. (1987). Change as the goal of educational research. *Anthropology and Education Quarterly, 18*(4), 300–311.

Muller, C. (1991). Unpublished tabulations, University of Chicago.

Oakes, J. (1985). *Keeping track: How schools structure inequality.* New Haven, CT: Yale University Press.

Ogbu, J. (1983). Minority status and schooling in plural societies. *Comparative Education Review, 27*(2), 168–190.

Ogbu, J. (1987). Variability in minority school performance: A problem in search of an explanation. *Anthropology and Education Quarterly, 18*(4), 312–334.

Ogbu, J., & Matute-Bianchi, M. (1986). Understanding sociocultural factors: Knowledge, identity, and school adjustment. In *Beyond language: Social and cultural factors in schooling language minority students* (pp. 73–142). Los Angeles: Evaluation, Dissemination and Assessment Center, California State University.

Peng, S., Owings, J., & Fetters, W. (1984, April). *School experience and performance of Asian American high school students.* Paper presented at the annual meeting of American Educational Research Association, New Orleans.

Schneider, B., & Lee, Y. (1990). A model for academic success: The school and home environment of East Asian students. *Anthropology and Education Quarterly, 21*(4), 358–377.

Spencer, B., Frankel, M., Ingels, S., Rasinski, K., & Tourangeau, R. (1990). *National education longitudinal study of 1988. Base year sample design report.* Washington, DC: U.S. Department of Education.

Spindler, G., & Spindler, L. (1987a). *The interpretive ethnography of education: At home and abroad.* Hillsdale, NJ: Lawrence Erlbaum Associates.

Spindler, G., & Spindler, L. (1987b). Cultural dialogue and schooling in Schoenhausen and Roseville: A comparative analysis. *Anthropology and Education Quarterly, 17*(4), 255–259.

Stevenson, H., Lee, S., Chen, C., Lummis, M., Stigler, J., Fan, L., & Ge, F. (1990). Mathematics achievement of children in China and the United States. *Child Development, 61*(4), 1053–1066.

Stevenson, H., Lee, S., Chen, C., Stigler, J., Hsu, C., & Kitamura, S. (1990). Contexts for achievement: A study of American, Chinese and Japanese children. *Monographs of the Society for Research in Child Development, 55*(1–2).

Stevenson, H., Lee, S., & Stigler, J. (1986). Mathematics achievement of Chinese, Japanese, and American children. *Science, 231*, 693–699.

Sue, S., & Okazaki, S. (1990). Asian-American educational achievements: A phenomenon in search of an explanation. *American Psychologist, 45*(8), 913–920.

Takaki, R. (1989). *Strangers from a different shore.* New York: Penguin.

Trueba, H. (1986). [Review of *Beyond language: Social and cultural factors in schooling language minority students.*] *Anthropology and Education Quarterly, 19*(3), 270–287.

Trueba, H. (1988). Culturally based explanations of minority students' academic achievement. *Anthropology and Education Quarterly, 17*(4), 255–259.

Tsang, S. (1988). The mathematics achievement characteristics of Asian American students. In R. R. Cocking & J. P. Mestre (Eds.), *Linguistic and cultural influences on learning mathematics* (pp. 123–136). Hillsdale, NJ: Lawrence Erlbaum Associates.

Wong, M. (1980). Model students? Teachers' perceptions and expectations of their Asian and white students. *Sociology of Education, 54*(4), 236–246.

17

CONTINUITIES AND DISCONTINUITIES IN THE COGNITIVE SOCIALIZATION OF ASIAN-ORIGINATED CHILDREN: THE CASE OF JAPANESE AMERICANS

Ruby Takanishi

Carnegie Council on Adolescent Development,
Carnegie Corporation of New York

Research on Asian-American children is comparatively rare. Thus, it is a challenge, especially from an empirical base, to contrast continuities and discontinuities in the cognitive socialization of Asian and Asian-American children. A literature search of diverse databases spanning the psychological, sociological, educational, and anthropological disciplines indicates that there is little research on the cognitive socialization (or socialization generally) of children in America whose parents or ancestors originated in Asia (Southwest Educational Development Laboratory, 1983; Tsang, 1988). Since 1970, about 25 published studies have addressed the cognitive socialization of Asian-American children (Slaughter-Defoe, Nakagawa, Takanishi, & Johnson, 1990).

To provide a context for discussion, three points are important in thinking about the cognitive socialization of children of Asian origins in the United States.

1. *The Asian-American population is diverse, in terms of countries of origin; generational status in the United States or recency of immigration; sociohistorical circumstances of immigration; English language facility; and educational and social class status before entering the United States* (General Accounting Office, 1990; Hing, 1993). All of these sources of potential variation may affect cognitive socialization and educational achievement in the United States. The nature of this diversity has been well documented (Fuchs, 1990; General Accounting Office, 1990; Takaki, 1990). But the linkage of this diversity in

Asian-American groups to the cognitive socialization of their children in the United States is only beginning, as the chapters in this volume illustrate.

The Census Bureau definition of *Asian Americans* currently includes 28 Asian countries of origin or ethnic groups. Based on the 1980 Census, Chinese, Pilipino, Japanese, Indian, Korean, and Vietnamese groups constituted about 89% of the Asian-American population (General Accounting Office, 1990). If one disaggregates East Asian-American students (i.e., Chinese, Japanese, and Korean Americans), there are differences in their educational achievement (Schneider, Hieshima, Lee, & Plank, chapter 16, this volume). At the very least, an empirical justification for aggregating Asian Americans into one group (e.g., Southeast Asian) needs to be demonstrated. As a concrete example, it is not unusual to see samples in journals identified as "Asian American" without specific reference to national or ethnic origins or generational status. In some studies, it may be that the category of Asian Americans includes a number of different Asian groups from East and Southeast Asia and of mixed generational status.

2. *The extent to which bicultural or two-cultural socialization takes place, drawing on values from the countries of origin and from the United States, is largely unknown and likely to vary by specific Asian groups and within those groups.* Increasing assimilation with each succeeding generation should not be automatically assumed (Delgado-Gaitan, chapter 3, this volume). Thus, it is not a simple matter of continuities or discontinuities but a more complex, bidirectional dynamic. The concept of a "moving target" merits serious consideration. Depending on social, economic, and historical circumstances surrounding the immigration of the specific group, varying degrees of continuities and discontinuities are likely to co-exist even in a specific ethnic group residing in the same geographical location, as described by Delgado-Gaitan (Matute-Bianchi, 1986). For Pilipinos, foreign-born have more education than American-born, due to the 1965 immigration laws favoring professionals.

U.S. Immigration policies (Hing, 1993) and social and cultural changes occurring in the country of origin attest to the fact that attending to the dynamics and content of these changes and their implications for socialization practices when the group migrates to the United States are very crucial (Hsia, 1988; Tapia Uribe, LeVine, & LeVine, chapter 2, this volume; Hing, 1993; Portes & Zhou, in press). Once the family is in the United States, children, through their exposure to schools and other influences, are likely to influence parents' behavior. Developmental change should also be included but is neglected because the luxury of longitudinal research is even more evident when children and youth of color are involved.

3. *The assumptions and potential biases of studying cognitive socialization among Asian Americans should be fully examined.* Obviously, one wants

to understand the processes and outcomes of cognitive socialization to increase one's knowledge about the universality and diversity of human development and experience. But in the case of several Asian groups, there is another agenda. Several chapters in this volume (Ho, chapter 14; Kim & Choi, chapter 11; Schneider, Hieshima, Lee, & Plank, chapter 16; Stevenson, chapter 15) point to cross-national comparisons of educational achievement between U.S. and Asian students (typically Japanese and Chinese in the People's Republic of China and Taiwan), and to comparisons within the United States in the educational performance of children of Asian origins (Schneider, Hieshima, Lee, & Plank, chapter 16, this volume). There is a fascination with high educational performance and what can be learned from it.

Unlike the study of African-American children and youth, which has been criticized as focusing on deficits and problems (McLoyd, 1990; Slaughter-Defoe et al., 1990), research on children and adolescents of Asian origins seems to assume that all members of the group are healthy and academic superstars. They are held up as a "model minority" (Kitano & Daniels, 1988). There is little attention to (a) the downsides, particularly mental health ones (pressures to succeed or the ramifications of average or low academic performance and its consequences; but cf. Ho, chapter 14, this volume); (b) disadvantaged or poorly achieving Asian Americans; or (c) the sources of variation within and between groups. The 1980 Census indicates wide variations among different Asian-American groups in income, educational levels, employment, and participation in welfare programs (General Accounting Office, 1990). In mathematics achievement, Tsang (1988) documented a larger spread in the distribution of scores for Asian Americans than for other ethnolinguistic groups. Chapter 16 by Schneider, Hieshima, Lee, and Plank addresses the issue of between-group variation in Asian-American socialization and development.

There must be a more balanced orientation to studying the socialization of children of Asian origins. This principle should apply to the study of all children, with a view to understanding both universals and sources of diversity. Theoretically and practically, there may be other interesting areas for comparative research with Asian-American samples, one candidate being socialization for social roles based on gender, age, parental roles, worker roles, and citizen roles. Another area for research would be the influence of the family and the school in constraining career opportunities for Asian-American students, particularly toward science, mathematics, and engineering (Tsang, 1988), to the neglect of a fuller range of occupational possibilities.

For the purposes of the present discussion, I limit my remarks to a brief, comparative, sociohistorical overview of Japanese Americans; and identification of issues of continuity and discontinuity in Japanese Americans based on the chapters in this volume.

BRIEF HISTORICAL OVERVIEW

Japanese Americans began to immigrate to the United States in the late 19th century (Kitano & Daniels, 1988; Takaki, 1990). For the most part, this immigration was chosen to pursue economic and educational opportunities that were limited by their circumstances in Japan. These immigrants were likely to be relatively literate, given the strong emphasis the Meiji and succeeding governments placed on broadly educating the population for competing in a world from which Japan had isolated itself. Immigrants to America were mainly from rural and agricultural areas. Unlike current Korean and Pilipino immigrants, they were not members of urban, professional, or upper income classes in their countries.

Many Japanese Americans (*Issei*) saw immigration as temporary, and initially planned to return to Japan once they were economically able to do so. For most, this did not occur, and their children (*Nisei*) saw themselves as Americans foremost and had little interest in returning to their mother country.

Like many other ethnic groups, Japanese Americans experienced severe discrimination. They also underwent physical and mental hardships involved in mass internment during World War II (Loo, 1990). The small sample of Japanese Americans in Chicago today (Schneider, Hieshima, Lee, & Plank, chapter 16, this volume) report that racism and discrimination remain salient in their daily lives.

Japanese Americans are four to five generations removed from their original immigration. Immigration for permanent residence is now virtually nonexistent. Half of Japanese Americans marry outside their ethnic group. They are widely dispersed in housing even in the regions of greatest concentration of Asian Americans (e.g., Los Angeles).

CONTRASTING CONTEMPORARY JAPANESE AND JAPANESE-AMERICAN SOCIALIZATION

Comparing the socialization of Japanese and Japanese-American children is fraught with minefields. The research from any discipline is presently sparse. Bits and pieces exist. What is available comes from different historical periods. A theoretical structure that links different levels of analyses is lacking.

Research on Japanese Americans from 1970 to 1988 has stressed the cultural compatibility theory of Caudill and DeVos (1973). Educational achievement is attributed to the idea that traditional Japanese values are consistent or compatible with American values, thus making achievement more likely. These studies have shed little light on actual processes of socialization in the family and the roles of other agents such as schools and peers.

At this time, it is probably accurate to say that the case of socialization in Japanese society (as described by Caudill for mother–infant interactions) and Japanese-American society (no comparable mother–infant data exist) represents a strong integration of both socialization for survival (i.e., survival for intense group life) and socialization for technological and educational development, which is driven by the values and attitudes shared between society and parents (Ho, chapter 14, this volume; Lebra, chapter 12, this volume). The Japanese mother, as described by Caudill and DeVos (1973), tends to have very close physical relationships with her children, to the extent that she sleeps with the very young ones and is almost totally devoted to the needs and educational success of the older children (White, 1987). The presence of nonmaternal caregivers is virtually nonexistent. Birthrates are correspondingly low as is infant mortality; maternal education is relatively high. The mother–child relationship, as described by Lebra, is the foundation for socialization for educational achievement and for group life in contemporary Japanese society.

The intense social-emotional nature of the mother–child relationship (i.e., the development of finely tuned social intelligence) becomes the foundation by which the Japanese child shapes him or herself to parental expectations, congruent with technological and skill requirements of the larger society. This suggests that in a particular culture or set of circumstances, highly developed social intelligence is not necessarily exclusive of developing technological intelligence, and that the former may be essentially interlinked with the latter (Ho, chapter 14, this volume).

In contrast, today Japanese-American mothers and their mothers (*Nisei* [second-generation children of *Issei* immigrants] and some *Sansei* [third-generation children of *Nisei*]) tend to work outside the home in large numbers. This is in marked contrast to the almost exclusive maternal role of their counterparts in Japan, although this is changing. This probably weakens physical and verbal contact and affects the intensity of the parent–child relationship. Thus, in studies (Schneider, Hieshima, Lee, & Plank, chapter 16, this volume) of middle-income Japanese-American families in Chicago, compensatory mechanisms appear to exist so that these families probably spend more time together, particularly in activities that promote the broad development of their children, than do non-Japanese families of similar economic status. (This may be partially due to the social dispersion of Japanese-American families in housing patterns, combined with barriers to socializing with families of other racial and ethnic backgrounds.)

In contemporary Japanese society, socialization clearly is oriented toward respect for hierarchical authority relations. Although there seem to be some cracks in these relationships and some sanctioned zones of temporary violation, overall Japanese children are socialized early on for these relations, which are characteristic of relations in the workplace and the family (White, 1987).

In contemporary Japanese-American families, the research evidence is limited. However, an adaptation may have occurred wherein Japanese-American children are socialized for such hierarchical authority relations within the family, including the extended family, while they are also socialized, according to Schneider's work (Schneider, Hieshima, Lee, & Plank, chapter 16, this volume), to be individualistic outside the family, thus adapting to school and workplace requirements in the host society. This is what Lebra (chapter 12, this volume) calls "situational code switch" and "positional socialization." These socialization practices need to be tested further but seem a reasonable avenue to explore.

One hypothesis is that Japanese-American children are explicitly and implicitly socialized to recognize the contextual press of situations and to adapt their behavior accordingly. This presents an opportunity to look at the idea that continuity between the teaching practices of the home and school is necessary for children to learn optimally (Suina & Smolkin, chapter 6, this volume; Tharp, chapter 4, this volume). It may be true for some ethnic groups but not necessarily for others.

The role of families, especially the mother, in intensive investment and socialization of their children seems to occur both in Japanese and U.S. society. Although Japanese-American mothers are likely to work outside the home (Hsia, 1988), children still report that their families monitor their activities closely (Schneider, Hieshima, Lee, & Plank, chapter 16, this volume), and for longer periods of time through adolescence. Although the nature of family relations is not as intensive as in Japan, the Japanese-American child is likely to experience more parental and family time overall than his or her counterparts. For example, the use of babysitters and other nonmaternal caregivers is likely to be less. The time that parents spend without children is also likely to be less than other groups. The overall monitoring of child behavior and activities is also likely to be more.

Overall, the interviews of Schneider, Hieshima, Lee, and Plank (chapter 16, this volume) indicate that Japanese-American parents spend a great deal of time with their children; they invest in educational activities and interact directly with their children. In a series of comparative interviews, Schneider and Lee (1990), found that East-Asian parents (i.e., Korean American, Chinese American, and Japanese American in descending order of frequency in the sample) put more time and investment into educational activities than did Euro-American parents.

When all the descriptive data on Japanese and Japanese-American families (and the lack thereof) are taken together, Coleman's (1988) idea of social capital provides a powerful heuristic framework to organize future research. Social capital refers to the nature and intensity of relations between parents and children, specifically the time, attention, and effort spent by parents in stimulating the cognitive development of their children. Social capital is not necessarily related to the human capital of parents that is measured by their educational attainment. Interestingly, Coleman cited the Japanese (*kyoiku*, education) mother (White, 1987) as one example of social capital.

Coleman (1988) argued that when parents are centrally involved with their children (i.e., are "there" for them physically and intellectually), social capital leads to the formation of individuals with highly developed human capital (i.e., skills and capabilities that enable children to learn new ways). In Japanese-American groups and other Asian-originated groups, social capital may decline in succeeding generations in the United States, and this may lead to a decline in educational achievement at the group or individual level.

What seems to be lacking in existing studies, but may prove to be important, is families' perceptions of job and economic opportunities and their expectations for their children regarding the linkage of education and opportunity, creating a climate supportive of learning. According to Coleman (1988) these expectations also constitute components of social capital. Schneider, Hieshima, Lee, and Plank (chapter 16, this volume) find that the Japanese-American families in their sample look to education to prepare a child for multiple opportunities, and yet education is not directly seen as linked to financial status. Whether this would hold for other groups, including other Asian-American ones, is not yet known.

Given the long hours that some immigrants spend working outside the home (e.g., Chinese-American women and men in New York City's Chinatown, Pilipino-American women caring for children as housekeepers and nannies, Korean-American families involved in small enterprises such as restaurants and stores), much of the microdynamics of family, primarily mother–child interactions, do not take place or take place with less frequency. Once in the United States, communication of parental expectations of children and their behavior, rather than maternal–child interactions, may be more powerful shapers of their children's outcomes (Hansell & Mechanic, 1990).

SOME POTENTIAL AVENUES FOR RESEARCH

One cross-cutting theme of the chapters in this volume is the paucity of theoretical or conceptual frameworks within which to organize existing research findings. (To a considerable extent, existing findings can also lead to formulations of such frameworks.) Two approaches seem especially promising in future research on cross-national comparisons of Asian children and youth. The first approach, based on the social capital concept (Coleman, 1988) discussed previously, seems especially relevant to the cognitive socialization of Japanese and Japanese-American children and should be seriously considered in the design of future studies.

The second approach is represented in the research of Feldman and associates (Feldman, Rosenthal, Mont-Reynaud, Leung, & Lau, 1991; Rosenthal & Feldman, 1991) involving cross-national comparisons of Chinese (Australia, Hong Kong, and United States) and European-origin (United States and Australia) adolescents in school performance and misbehavior. These studies illustrate that although there are differences in measures of school effort, grades, and factors hypothesized to lead to educational outcomes, the patterns of relationships between family, personal factors, and self-reported educational performance are similar across European and Chinese cultures. These findings suggest that processes that lead to good educational performance may be shared across cultures. The work of Feldman and associates implies the need to peel the layers within the broad rubric of culture to take account of both processes and patterns of relationships among variables in understanding cultural variation. Rosenthal and Feldman (1991) noted that factors that differentiate cultural groups did not account for individual differences within a cultural group. Factors related to individual differences in educational outcomes were not always those that resulted in cultural differences.

Because the research base is limited, there are many potential avenues for research. I suggest but a few.

Because different Asian groups are dispersed throughout the world, it would be useful to look at how each group adapts to different countries and the cultural frames of reference prevalent there, taking into account potential selection factors involved in immigrating to specific countries (e.g., Japanese in Hawaii, mainland United States, Peru, and Brazil; Chinese in Canada, Australia, Hawaii, United States, Taiwan, Hong Kong, and countries in Southeast Asia; Koreans in mainland United States, Hawaii, and Canada; Kim & Choi, chapter 11, this volume). These investigations provide an opportunity to examine the potential influences of sociocultural contexts and processes on cognitive socialization. The Asian diaspora provides a rich laboratory for exploring continuities and discontinuities in child socialization.

It may also be productive to look at the generational status of different Asian-American groups, the circumstances under which they immigrated, and their economic and occupational status prior to immigration. Schneider, Hieshima, Lee, and Plank (chapter 16, this volume) make an important start in this direction. Studies tend to overlook generational status, which provides a clue to continuities and discontinuities in socialization. At one end, there are the immigrations of the Japanese, Chinese, and Pilipinos in the late 19th century. Japanese immigration has virtually ended (except for temporary Japanese nationals); Chinese and Pilipino immigration continues at currently high levels (with different historical and educational backgrounds of these immigrants from those at the turn of the century). There are changes over time in the economic and educational backgrounds of Vietnamese and

Southeast-Asian immigrants (Caplan, Whitmore, & Choy, 1991; General Accounting Office, 1990; Myers & Milne, 1988; Tsang, 1988).

One hypothesis related to generational status is that educational achievement declines in succeeding generations due to assimilation. The differences that Schneider, Hieshima, Lee, and Plank (chapter 16, this volume) find between 4th- and 5th-generation Japanese-American students and immigrant and first-generation Korean- and Chinese-American students is suggestive in this regard. Two recent studies (Dornbusch, Prescott, & Ritter, 1987; Rosenthal & Feldman, 1991) indicated no differences between first- and second-generation Chinese Americans. However, Dornbusch, et al. reported a change in the third generation for Chinese students.

The values, attitudes, educational attainment, and economic status of Asian immigrants prior to immigration may make for a critical difference in the socialization patterns for their children in the United States, especially in terms of their educational performance. When Asian immigrants, like the Hmong, are from rural areas without a tradition of formal education and written literacy, they are likely to experience similar problems as those immigrants from other areas of the world who come to these shores with similar backgrounds. In contrast, the children of parents who were middle-class professionals in Korea (now running small convenience stores) are likely to have the values and attitudes, and experience family socialization practices, that place great emphasis and pressure on educational performance and economic success.

If one were to control for length of time in the United States and circumstances of entry into the United States (voluntary immigrants or refugees), what differences among the Asian-American groups might result? As one high-visibility example, the so-called "Asian" winners of the Westinghouse Talent Search are not Japanese Americans. Instead, they are, for the most part, children of Korean physicians and scientists (including notably two parents in the sciences) and are first-generation children of these highly educated immigrants.

Much research has focused on family socialization. Less research has focused on how the educational systems encountered by these children and families reinforce, modify, and counter the socialization processes and outcomes in families (Myers & Milne, 1988; Southwest Educational Development Laboratory, 1983; Tsang, 1988). Direct observations of and data collection from Asian-American children within schools are seriously lacking. Schneider and Lee (1990) and Schneider, Hieshima, Lee, and Plank (chapter 16, this volume) provide important exceptions. The fascination with achievement differentials between children in the United States and Asia is likely to fuel continuing studies of how these students fare in schools.

CONCLUSION: DÉJÀ VU AND HOPE

Many of my remarks have been somewhat speculative because the empirical research sources in Asia and in the United States are still sparse in relation to the questions raised in the chapters. There is much that can be done to understand both shared processes and those that are distinctive to different Asian groups, as well as similarities and differences with groups outside Asia (Feldman et al., 1991; Rosenthal & Feldman, 1991).

The chapters in this volume address continuities and discontinuities in socialization practices when a cultural group moves from its traditional national setting to another. The research reviewed indicates that the issue is not simply what remains constant and what changes. Except for rare instances, when immigration occurs in isolation from the receiving country (e.g., the case of unmarried men in New York City's Chinatown), even those aspects of socialization that remain constant are embedded in a different sociocultural context.

What is defined as *change* or *discontinuity* may be the result of specific adaptations to maintain core socialization practices and values. One potential example is the change in the amount of time Japanese-American mothers spend in contact with their children. Although there is a discontinuity from practices in the home country, the Japanese-American mother, when not at work, may spend comparatively more time in direct contact with her children than non-Japanese mothers. When this social capital is coupled with parental beliefs about effort and expectations for high performance that are continuous with the home country, the conditions for good educational performance are maximized. A core value is manifest in a different way under different societal conditions.

The expectations of the host country and schools that Japanese Americans are a group that performs well are not to be minimized. In cases where peers from the same group are available, a reinforcing influence exists along with families and schools. Thus, the available research points to complexity and the interaction of several institutions; it challenges simple cultural explanations.

In closing, I raise a question: Why is the research on Asian Americans so sparse (see also Hsia, 1988)? About 8 years ago, the Committee on Child Development Research and Social Policy of the National Academy of Sciences investigated the possibility of focusing on the socialization of minority children, but nothing materialized. In 1986, the National Institute of Child Health and Human Development held a one-time competition for research proposals. No clear commitment to research on ethnic minority populations has emerged from the public or the private sectors (Slaughter-Defoe et al., 1990). But there are hopeful signs, fueled by the changing demography of the nation's children and youth and the need to better understand our country's diverse populations, that funding patterns may change.

Analogous to the controversy about women and their underrepresentation in health research, a similar movement may develop for the inclusion of racial and ethnic minorities in health, behavioral, and social science research. Our science and understanding of cultural universals and diversity will undoubtedly be enhanced.

ACKNOWLEDGMENTS

I very much appreciate the research assistance and administrative support of Linda L. Schoff and Annette Dyer in the preparation of this chapter. Rodney Cocking provided many insights that led to the revision of the original draft.

REFERENCES

Caplan, N., Whitmore, J. K., & Choy, M. H. (1991). *Children of the boat people: A study of educational success*. Ann Arbor, MI: University of Michigan Press.

Caudill, W., & DeVos, G. (1973). Achievement, culture, and personality: The case of the Japanese Americans. In G. DeVos (Ed.), *Socialization for achievement: Essays on the cultural psychology of the Japanese* (pp. 220–247). Berkeley: University of California Press.

Coleman, J. S. (1988). Social capital in the creation of human capital. *The American Journal of Sociology, 94*, S95–S120.

Dornbusch, S. M., Prescott, B. L., & Ritter, P. L. (1987, April). *The relation of high school academic performance and student effort to language use and recency of migration among Asian- and Pacific-Americans*. Paper presented at the Annual Meeting of the American Educational Research Association, Washington, DC.

Feldman, S. S., Rosenthal, D. A., Mont-Reynaud, R., Leung, K., & Lau, S. (1991). Ain't misbehavin': Adolescent values and family environments as correlates of misconduct in Australia, Hong Kong, and the United States. *Journal of Research on Adolescence, 1*(2), 109–134.

Fuchs, L. H. (1990). *The American kaleidoscope: Race, ethnicity, and the civic culture*. Hanover, MA: University Press of New England.

General Accounting Office. (1990). *Asian Americans: A status report* (GAO Report No. HRD-90-36FS). Washington, DC: Author.

Hansell, S., & Mechanic, D. (1990). Parent and peer effects on adolescent health behavior. In K. Hurrelmann & F. Losel (Eds.), *Health hazards in adolescence* (pp. 43–65). New York: Aldine De Gruyter.

Hing, B. O. (1993). *Making and remaking Asian America through immigration policy*. Stanford, CA: Stanford University Press.

Hsia, J. (1988). *Asian Americans in higher education and at work*. Hillsdale, NJ: Lawrence Erlbaum Associates.

Kitano, H. H. L., & Daniels, R. (1988). *Asian Americans: Emerging minorities*. Englewood Cliffs, NJ: Prentice-Hall.

Loo, C. M. (1990). *An integrative-sequential treatment model for post-traumatic stress disorder: A case study of the Japanese American internment and redress.* Unpublished manuscript, University of Hawaii at Manoa, Department of Psychology.

Matute-Bianchi, M. E. (1986, November). Ethnic identities and patterns of school success and failure among Mexican-descent and Japanese-American students in a California high school. *American Journal of Education, 95,* 233–255.

McLoyd, V. (1990). Minority children: Introduction to the special issue. *Child Development, 61*(2), 263–266.

Myers, D. E., & Milne, A. M. (1988). Effects of home language and primary language on mathematics achievement: A model and results for secondary analysis. In R. R. Cocking & J. P. Mestre (Eds.), *Linguistic and cultural influences on learning mathematics* (pp. 259–293). Hillsdale, NJ: Lawrence Erlbaum Associates.

Portes, A. & Zhou, M. (in press). The new second generation: Segmented assimilation and its variants among post-1965 immigrant youth. *The Annals of the American Academy of Political and Social Sciences.*

Rosenthal, D. A., & Feldman, S. S. (1991). The influence of perceived family and personal factors on self-reported school performance of Chinese and Western high school students. *Journal of Research on Adolescence, 1*(2), 135–154.

Schneider, B., & Lee, S. (1990). A model for academic success: The school and home environment of East Asian students. *Anthropology and Education Quarterly, 21*(4), 358–377.

Slaughter-Defoe, D. T., Nakagawa, K., Takanishi, R., & Johnson, D. J. (1990). Toward cultural/ecological perspectives on schooling and achievement in African- and Asian-American children. *Child Development, 61*(2), 363–383.

Southwest Educational Development Laboratory. (1983). *Limited English proficiency project* (Research Rep., The Cantonese study). Los Alamitos, CA: Southwest Educational Development Laboratory.

Takaki, R. (1990). *Strangers from a different shore.* New York: Penguin.

Tsang, S. L. (1988). The mathematics achievement characteristics of Asian-American students. In R. R. Cocking & J. P. Mestre (Eds.), *Linguistic and cultural influences on learning mathematics* (pp. 123–136). Hillsdale, NJ: Lawrence Erlbaum Associates.

White, M. (1987). *The Japanese educational challenge.* New York: The Free Press.

CONCLUDING PERSPECTIVES

Exploration of cross-cultural roots is a frequent theme at the Bellagio Road Newcomers School. Los Angeles, California, USA, 1993.
Photograph by Lauren Greenfield

18

FROM CULTURAL DIFFERENCES TO DIFFERENCES IN CULTURAL FRAME OF REFERENCE

John U. Ogbu
University of California

For more than 20 years, I have studied minority education from a comparative or cross-cultural perspective. My research focuses on issues of school or academic achievement, as well as social and economic adaptations of minorities. The study of academic achievement inevitably involves cognitive socialization and cognitive behavior or "intelligence." This research covers minorities in the United States and in other urban industrial societies, including England, Israel, Japan, and New Zealand. I compare minority groups within the same countries, such as African Americans and Chinese Americans in the United States, and the same minority group in different countries, such as West Indians in Britain, Canada, and the United States; the Burakumin in Japan and the United States. Finally, my study includes examination of the school experience of non-Western peoples attending Western-type schools, such as Africans attending schools established by the French, British, or Americans.

Findings from these studies lead one to conclude that there are differences in social and cultural adaptations that have implications for the intelligence characteristic of different populations. Different modes of sociocultural adaptation seem to require different "intelligences" or repertoires of cognitive skills. These are functional cognitive skills that members of the population transmit to their children through various techniques of socialization (Ogbu, 1981). People do not possess a repertoire of cognitive skills or a particular type of intelligence (e.g., technological intelligence, social intelligence) merely because they have been socialized to do so. Rather, children are socialized to acquire the cognitive skills or pattern of intelligence that exist already in their culture because their culture requires it; it is functional in the culture. Socialization is an intermediate variable, a means or formula through which people transmit that which already exists in the culture.

A society that is technologically advanced will possess a repertoire of cognitive skills appropriate for advanced technological culture. That is, members of a technologically advanced culture are going to possess technological intelligence because it is the appropriate intelligence and a prerequisite for functioning competently in that culture. In contrast, members of a nontechnologically advanced culture are not going to possess technological intelligence because it is not the intelligence appropriate for the culture, nor is it required for competence in the culture. Whether such people will possess social intelligence or another kind of intelligence is a matter of empirical study. I suspect that it is not a matter of either technological intelligence or social intelligence. In a modern industrial society like the United States, I further suspect that both technological intelligence and social intelligence co-exist.

My position is that differences in intelligence among populations with different sociocultural adaptations within their distinct political boundaries are primarily due to cultural differences. For example, the French with their advanced technological culture have technological intelligence appropriate for their technological culture. On the other hand, the Baoulé of Ivory Coast have a different type of intelligence appropriate for their nontechnological culture (Posner, 1982). The French socialize their children to acquire technological intelligence, and the Baoulé of Ivory Coast socialize their own children to acquire nontechnological intelligence.

But when one turns to minorities in modern industrial societies like the United States, differences in intelligence become more than a matter of differences in culture and socialization. That is, in my view, Euro-Americans and African Americans do not differ in intelligence simply because Euro-Americans have a technological culture and African Americans do not. Nor are the two populations different in intelligence only because African Americans practice to some degree the cognitive socialization that can be traced to African origins. Rather, the differences between some minorities such as African Americans and Euro-Americans arise in important part from the status of the minorities *qua* minorities (i.e., from their minority status and all that it implies). Furthermore, there are different types of minority status, and each type seems to have different implications for intellectual and academic behaviors of the group members. My argument is that for minorities in urban industrial societies, it is not merely cultural differences and differences in cognitive socialization that distinguish the groups in measured intelligence; their measured intelligence and academic performance are also influenced by other factors generated by their minority status, such as their cultural frame of reference (i.e., how they perceive and interpret the cultural differences between them and the dominant group).

INTELLIGENCE AND CULTURE

According to ability theory, intelligence is like a genealogical tree, with the generalized intelligence (the g factor) at the base; above it are specialized types of abilities (such as verbal, numerical, spatial-perceptual, memorizing, reasoning, and mechanical intelligence; Cole, Gay, Glick, & Sharp, 1971; Jensen, 1969; Vernon, 1969). IQ tests are developed to tap these processes, which are believed to be universal.

The ability theory of intelligence makes no allowance for the fact that subjects from different cultures may perceive the test items and situation differently and may approach the test with different strategies from those intended by the testers (Cole et al., 1971; DeVos & Hippler, 1969; LeVine, 1970; Segall, Herskovits, & Campbell, 1966).

Contrary to ability theory, IQ does not equal intelligence, and IQ tests measure only a set of cognitive skills functional in Western middle-class culture. The cognitive problems posed by the technoeconomic environment of Western middle-class culture require and promote a distinct set of cognitive skills and strategies involving grasping relations and symbolic thinking. According to Vernon (1969), to some extent these have come to permeate all learning activities at school, at work, and in daily life. But they are not universally valued, nor equally functional; other cultures require and stimulate the development and use of other cognitive skills for coping with their environments. In other words, members of other cultures possess different intelligences.

In contrast to the ability theory, I present an alternative view of intelligence based on cross-cultural and historical studies. I adopt Vernon's (1969) distinction among Intelligences A, B, and C. This distinction also allows one to see how the intelligence or IQ of Western middle-class people is related to the cognitive demands of their cultural tasks and historical experience.

According to Vernon, intelligences A and B correspond to the geneticist's distinction between the genotype and the phenotype. Intelligence A, the genotype, is the innate capacity that children inherit from their ancestors through the genes, which determines the limits of their mental or cognitive growth. Similarly, for members of a culture, Intelligence A represents their genetic potential for acquiring cognitive skills. But there is no way a psychologist can directly observe or measure Intelligence A (Vernon, 1969).

Intelligence B, the phenotype, is a product of both nature (genetic equipment) and nurture (environmental pressures and forces). It refers to the everyday observed behavior of individuals and the behavior that is considered intelligent or nonintelligent by members of a given culture. Because Intelligence B is culturally defined, it differs from culture to culture in its attributes, even though the underlying processes may be the same. For example, the kinds of behavior and cognitive and perceptual skills that are included by middle-class Americans in their definition of *intelligence* differ in some respects from those included by the Ibos of Nigeria or the Eskimos of Alaska in their own definitions of *intelligence*.

But presumably all groups, although differing in their definitions, draw from the same pool of behavior and cognitive and perceptual skills available to the human species. In this connection, Scribner and Cole (1973) noted that capacities for categorizing, remembering, generalizing, forming concepts, abstracting, and logical reasoning appear to be universal, although the ways these things are done vary cross culturally. That is, members of every known population or culture can categorize, remember, generalize, form concepts, operate with abstraction, and reason logically; but they may categorize differently, remember differently, and differ in their logical reasoning. Thus, Intelligence B is not simply a matter of cultural definition but also denotes the cognitive skills and strategies selected from a common species' pool by a given cultural group for adaptation to its specific environment (Ogbu, 1978).

Intelligence B is not fixed; a person's cognitive capacity may change as a result of some significant changes in his or her environment (e.g., a move from a rural to an urban residence, or participation in an advanced technology or economy), education, or personality. These changes make the person appear more intelligent or less intelligent relative to his or her contemporaries. Similarly, the Intelligence B of a given cultural group may change after significant changes in the group's environment or activities. A good example is the change that occurred in the cognitive skills of the Western middle class as a result of the emergence of bureaucratic urban industrial economy and formal education.

Today, the United States and other urban, industrial societies are undergoing further changes in middle-class cognitive skills because of emerging computer technology and "high-tech" jobs with their emphasis on "cognitivism." The Committee of Correspondence on the future of Public Education (1984) has suggested that cognitive skills required by the new computer technology includes precise definitions, linear thinking, precise rules and algorithms for thinking and acting. In the United States, people are acquiring the new cognitive skills or intelligence by "learning computer" at home, at school, and in the workplace (e.g., Greenfield, 1984); they are also modifying their children's upbringing and education to enable the latter to acquire the new cognitive skills. Schools in the United States are rewriting their curricula and modifying their instructional techniques under public pressures to emphasize cognitive skills compatible with computer thinking and emerging cultural tasks relying on computer and "high-tech" know-how (Ogbu,

1987). However, the new cognitive development is not limited to the middle class because nonmiddle-class Americans participate in computer media applications, such as video games (Greenfield, 1984).

Under the impact of Western education, technology, and urbanization, many cultural groups in the Third-World nations of Africa and Asia are probably experiencing changes in their Intelligence B. Indeed, empirical evidence is both growing and convincing that when non-Western people participate in Western-type schooling, their cognitive skills are significantly affected and their cognitive transformations arise because schooling requires and promotes ways of thinking that are distinct from those required and promoted by indigenous cultural activities (Greenfield, 1966; Scribner & Cole, 1973).

What about Intelligence C, the measured intelligence or IQ? This refers to those cognitive skills usually sampled by IQ tests. The tested skills are, of course, a part of the cognitive skills that make up Intelligence B. But Intelligence C differs from Intelligence B in that the skills sampled by IQ tests are selected to serve a particular function (i.e., to predict scholastic performance or ability to perform other specific tasks). Thus, IQ or Intelligence C may not correspond to what members of a society consider intelligent or unintelligent behavior or thinking.

Generally, in contemporary Western cultures, IQ tests are constructed to measure specific aspects of Intelligence B vital for solving specific problems associated with industrialization, bureaucracy, urbanism, and the like. One should bear in mind that the cognitive skills tapped by these tests are those that Western cultures emphasize in their formal schooling. Historical evidence indicates that the transmission of such cognitive skills was first institutionalized in formal education and later formed the basis on which IQ tests were constructed to predict school performance (Alland, 1973; Brookover & Erickson, 1965; Gartner & Riessman, 1973). Hence, the primary purpose of IQ tests is to predict how well children in Western cultures learn the cognitive skills taught in Western schools, families, and other settings, cognitive skills that are required for successful participation as adults in the occupational environment of Western industrial societies.

If people living in the Arctic or a tropical forest, who had made a different sociocultural and economic adaptations, were to construct intelligence tests, they would probably include other psychological tasks that measure those cognitive skills and strategies required for effective adaptation to their environment, rather than the tasks that tap the cognitive skills emphasized in contemporary Western tests of intelligence or IQ. In cross-cultural studies, contemporary Western IQ tests tend to measure mainly those cognitive skills of individuals and groups that enable them to participate effectively in Western schools and in an industrial economy, not the skills and strategies they have developed to adapt effectively to their own largely traditional environment (LeVine, 1970).

The argument that the Intelligence C (IQ) measured by intelligence tests is derived from Intelligence B, which is culture bound, is supported by the history of intelligence testing. The cultural context of IQ is well illustrated by the changes that have accompanied the adaptation of the Binet Intelligence Test in various industrialized societies. This test was first developed in France, where it measured relatively well the Intelligence C of the French people. When the test was brought to the United States it proved inadequate for testing or measuring the Intelligence C of American people. Therefore, the French test was modified by removal of certain standardized tasks "unsuitable" for American children and the substitution of "more appropriate" tasks based on American experience. This revision resulted in the American Stanford-Binet Scale. Similar revisions took place in Britain and Japan.

Thus, the French Binet Scale, the British Binet Scale, the American Stanford-Binet Scale, and the Japanese Tanaka-Binet Scale are not exactly interchangeable because the Intelligence C measured in each country is also influenced by the Intelligence B of its people. Intelligence C, IQ, is not an index of Intelligence A, the genotype, but an index of Intelligence B, the phenotype, which is cultural behavior.

INTELLIGENCE AND CULTURAL DIFFERENCES

One has learned from cross-cultural studies that the cognitive skills of members of a given culture usually reflect their prior cultural experience. That is, the kinds of activities that the members of the given culture are engaged in tend to stimulate the development and expression of those cognitive and perceptual skills necessary for competence in their culturally valued activities. For example, in a study in Mexico, Price-Williams, Gordon, and Ramirez (1969) showed that experience with pottery making (and therefore manipulation of clay materials) resulted in the development of conservation skills, especially conservation of a continuous solid substance.

Dennis' (1970) cross-cultural study of the Goodenough Draw-A-Man test showed that there is a strong relationship between an involvement of a given group with representational art and the test scores of its children. For example, among the Japanese villagers where women rather than men were highly involved with artwork, girls scored higher than boys. In contrast, in the Native-American groups where men rather than women were involved with artwork, boys scored higher than girls.

Another example comes from Dasen's (1974) study of cognitive development among Australian aborigines and Euro-Australian children. He found that Euro-Australian children (like their European and Euro-American peers) develop logico-mathematical concepts before they develop their spatial concepts; among the aborigines, the order of development was reversed. Dasen's interpretation was that the aborigines develop spatial concepts earlier than logico-mathematical concepts because the former are more important for their nomadic hunting and gathering economy or adaptation.

My final example concerns the influence of cultural activities on mathematical skills. Posner (1982) and Saxe and Posner (1983) reported this phenomenon for two West-African cultures whose economic activities differ with regard to their use of numerical skills. In one group, the Dioula, the people are merchants whose principal economic activities require extensive use of numerals; their culture not only values mathematical skills but also provides children with many opportunities to practice and develop these skills. In the second group, the Baoulé, the people are subsistence farmers whose major economic activities do not depend on numerical skills, therefore they do not value these skills strongly enough to stress them for their children to the same degree as the Dioula. Children from the two groups who had not been to Western-type schools performed differently when tested for mathematical skills. Dioula children, the merchant group, were superior.

CULTURAL BIAS IN IQ TESTING

Because of differences in the cultural value of different cognitive skills and behaviors, a test of cognitive behavior (e.g., IQ test) designed to suit members of one population or group will almost inevitably discriminate against members of other populations or cultures. Consequently, IQ tests that adequately measure Western middle-class intelligence—an intelligence "especially well adapted for scientific analysis, for control and exploitation of the physical world, for large-scale and long-term planning and carrying out of materialistic objectives" (Vernon, 1969, pp. 89–90)—will discriminate against people of other cultures who have developed other Intelligence Bs better suited for other kinds of cultural tasks. This is particularly true in the measurement of IQ of tribal and peasant peoples in the Third World.

For example, it has been found that among some people Western mathematical concepts may not have equivalents in the indigenous mathematical systems or that their application is different (Closs, 1986; Cole et al., 1971; Gay & Cole, 1967; Lancy, 1983). Nevertheless, as a result of Western influence, such people eventually overcome the initial difference, undergo a kind of cognitive acculturation, and learn more or less successfully in Western-type schools.

In the United States (Jensen, 1969; Mayeseke, Tetsuo, Beaton, Cohen, & Wisler, 1973; Slade, 1982; Wigdor & Garner, 1982), Britain (Parliamentary Select Committee on Immigration and Race Relations, 1972–1973), Japan (De-Vos, 1973), and New Zealand (Harker, 1977), some minorities do not do well on IQ tests. Their low performance has usually been attributed to cultural bias in the tests, which is inevitable. On the other hand, there are other minorities in the same countries who do quite well in the same IQ tests (Taylor & Hegarty, 1985; Vernon, 1982). Curiously enough, the failure of the first group of minorities and the success of the second group are both attributed to culture. In one case, minority cultures work against their performance, whereas in the second group minority cultures enhance their performance.

MINORITY STATUS, CULTURAL DIFFERENCES

Compatibility between the ancestral values of minority groups and the dominant value orientations of the societies in which they reside cannot explain the differential academic performance of various minorities. One major problem with cultural compatibility as an explanation is that the minorities who are doing relatively well are, in fact, those closest to their ancestral cultural practice in socialization and social orientation, not those closest to the Western model. For example, immigrant Blacks from Africa and the Caribbean are more likely to be doing better than African Americans in the United States, and Mexican immigrants are more likely to be doing better than Mexican Americans or Chicanos (see Gibson, 1976, 1991; Matute-Bianchi, 1986, 1991). Asians who are doing well in the United States include pariah groups (e.g., Japanese Buraku) who do not perform well in Asia (DeVos, 1973; Ogbu, 1978; Shimahara, 1991).

How, then, does one explain the differential performance of the minorities? There are at least two prerequisites for understanding the performance of minorities in contemporary urban industrial societies. The first is to distinguish among different types of minority status that have different implications for cognitive and academic behaviors. The second is to distinguish different types of cultural difference.

TYPES OF MINORITY STATUS

In our comparative work, we have learned that the academic problems of minority children are due to complex factors in schools, classrooms, homes, and individuals, as well as in broader historical, economic, and sociocultural domains. But one finding is that persistent and disproportionate problems of school adjustment and academic performance are associated with some minorities but not with others. This finding has led me to classify minorities into the two types described next.

Voluntary or immigrant minorities are people (and their descendants) who have moved more or less voluntarily to the United States or to any other society because they believe that this will lead to more economic well-being, better overall opportunities, and greater political freedom. These expectations continue to influence the way the immigrants perceive and respond to obstacles that confront them in their host society, including discrimination in education. What makes immigrants voluntary minorities is twofold: (a) they chose to come to the United States instead of going to Japan or Britain; and (b) they were not forced by Euro-Americans against their will to come to the United States, either through conquest, slavery, or colonization. That people are "forced" to flee their country by war, famine, political upheaval, and so forth is not relevant to this typology. What matters is that members of the minority group do not interpret their presence in the United States as forced on them by Euro-Americans. Voluntary minorities do relatively well in school, regardless of whether they come from China, Mexico, the Caribbean, or Africa after mastering the language.

Refugees are not immigrant minorities and are not a part of this classification (see Ogbu, 1990). They cannot be in the same category because they are affected by unique factors. For example, they often suffer from broken families and have been prevented from planning either their departure from their country of origin or their entry into their new country. Therefore, they have different psychological and social profiles, the study of which is currently in progress.

Involuntary minorities are those groups (and their descendants) who were initially incorporated into U.S. society against their will by Euro-Americans through slavery, conquest, or colonization. Thereafter, these minorities were relegated to menial positions and denied true assimilation into the mainstream of U.S. society (as were the non-White immigrants). Native Americans, African Americans, Mexican Americans, and Native Hawaiians are examples. The Burakumin and Koreans in Japan and the Maori in New Zealand are examples outside the United States.

I classify Mexican Americans as an involuntary minority group because they were initially incorporated by conquest: The *Anglos* (as Mexican Americans termed them) conquered and annexed the Mexican territory where Chicanos were living in the Southwest—acts that were completed by the Treaty of Quadalupe Hildago in 1848 (see Acuna, 1981; Ogbu & Matute-Bianchi, 1986). Mexicans coming to the United States from Mexico are immigrants.

I have classified Puerto Ricans on the mainland as an involuntary minority group because they feel that they are more or less a colonized group. The United States conquered or colonized Cuba, Puerto Rico, and the Philippines in 1898. Both Cuba and the Philippines later gained independence. For this reason, Cubans and Filipinos coming to the United States come more or less as immigrants or refugees. The status of Puerto Rico is ambiguous: It is neither a state within the U.S. polity nor an independent nation in the real sense. Many Puerto Ricans feel that their "country" is still a colony of the United States (see Ogbu, 1978, 1990).

It is involuntary minorities who do not usually do well in school (i.e., they are the ones who perform low in cognitive and academic tests). To understand why their performance is low, I turn to the types of cultural differences that characterize voluntary and involuntary minorities.

TYPES OF CULTURAL DIFFERENCES

Comparative analyses of cultural differences (i.e., those that minority children in urban industrial societies like the United States and children from non-Western societies attending Western-type schools bring to educational experience) suggest that one should classify cultural differences in the educational context into three types: universal, primary, and secondary.

Universal cultural differences are universal because every child who goes to school must make a transition from home culture to school culture, regardless of whether he or she comes from a middle-class or lower class home, or whether he or she comes from an African-American or Chinese home. The transition involves adjusting to (a) new cultural and language behavioral requirements, (b) new social relations, (c) new styles of language use or communication, and (d) new styles of thinking (Cook-Gumperz & Gumperz, 1979; Scribner & Cole, 1973). This type of cultural difference is not necessarily associated with minority school performance problems. Yet there is now a body of literature (e.g., Laosa, 1978, 1982) indicating that communication and language use at home is closer to that of the school in certain milieus, particularly when mothers have more school education.

Primary cultural (and language) differences arise because members of two populations had their own ways of behaving, thinking, and feeling before they came in continuous contact with each other or before members of one population began to attend schools controlled by members of another population. For example, voluntary or immigrant minorities had their own cultures before they came to live in the United States, and various African peoples had their own cultures before they began to attend schools established and controlled by Europeans or Euro-Americans from the United States in Africa. I illustrate these two situations with the case of Punjabi Indian immigrants in California and the Kpelle of Liberia in West Africa.

Punjabi Indians in Valleyside, California, came originally from Punjab in India. Before they came to the United States, they spoke Punjabi; had arranged marriages; practiced Sikh, Hindu, or Muslim religion; and (males) wore turbans. They still maintain some of these beliefs and practices to some extent in the United States. However, although the Punjabis want to retain these and other aspects of the culture they brought with them, they also try to learn some aspects of North-American culture, including the English language, which they think they need to enhance their chances of achieving the goals for which they came to the United States. Thus, their cultural frame of reference permits them to cross cultural and language boundaries. They do not perceive or interpret learning the selected aspects of North American culture as threatening to their cultural identity.

The other example of primary cultural differences is taken from the study of the Kpelle of Liberia, West Africa, by Gay and Cole (1967). Gay and Cole found that, in the areas of arithmetic, the Kpelle had some concepts similar to Western arithmetic concepts; but the Kpelle system lacked some other Western concepts, such as "zero" and "number." In geometry, the researchers found that the Kpelle did not have many concepts and that they used the few that they had imprecisely. For example, the things that the Kpelle describe as triangles do not look triangular, and the things they describe as circles do not look circular. In the area of measurement, the Kpelle, like Europeans and North Americans, measure money, length, time, and volume, although they do so imprecisely. However, they do not measure weight, area, speed, or temperature.

To conclude, the bearers of primary cultural differences had their different cultural attributes before they came in contact with the dominant group or entered the institutions controlled by the dominant group. In addition, they operate within a cultural frame of reference that also predated their emigration or institutional participation. A cultural frame of reference refers to the correct or ideal way to behave within a culture—attitudes, beliefs, preferences, and practices considered appropriate for members of the culture.

Because their cultural frame of reference predated their emigration, voluntary minorities do not perceive their cultural frame of reference as oppositional to the cultural frame of reference of the dominant group of their host society. Because some behaviors that enhance the attainment of their goals of emigration are similar to those within the Euro-American cultural frame of reference, they consider not knowing how to participate in the cultural frame of reference of their new or host society a barrier to be overcome. Therefore, voluntary minorities strive to participate in the cultural frame of reference of the dominant group without fear of losing their own culture, language, or identity. Basically, voluntary minorities practice what may be called an "alternation model" (Ogbu, 1984) or "accommodation without assimilation model" (Gibson, 1983). Later, I show how this cultural frame permits voluntary minorities to participate in education.

Secondary cultural differences present a different kind of picture. It is not because their cultures lack the concepts and contents found in the culture of the dominant group. Rather, the cultural differences are qualitatively different and lie in the nature of the relationship between the dominant group's culture and the culture of the minorities. The relationship between the cultures of the minorities and the culture of the dominant group is different for voluntary and involuntary minorities. This difference in the relationship is due to the fact that the differences between the cultures of involuntary minorities and the culture of the dominant group arose after the dominant group and the minorities came into the continuous contact, which keeps the minorities in a subordinate position. The cultural differences arose as part of coping mechanisms used by the minorities to deal with the problems they face in their relationship with the dominant group's members and the societal institutions controlled by the latter.

Because secondary cultural differences arise to enable minorities to deal with dominant-group members, they often become a part of boundary-maintaining mechanisms. For this reason, involuntary minorities have no desire to overcome the cultural (and language) differences because that would threaten their cultural or language identity.

Bearers of secondary cultural differences, like bearers of primary cultural differences, have a cultural frame of reference but theirs is oppositional because it was developed in the context of conflict and opposition between the minorities and the dominant group. The oppositional cultural frame of reference includes devices to protect the social or collective identity of the minorities and protect and maintain their sense of self-worth.

One of the devices in the oppositional cultural frame of reference is "cultural inversion." In a broad sense, cultural inversion refers to the various ways in which the minorities express their opposition to the dominant group. In a narrow sense, it refers to specific forms of behaviors, specific events, symbols, and meanings that involuntary minorities regard as not appropriate for them because they are characteristic of Euro-Americans. At the same time, the minorities approve of and emphasize other forms of behaviors, events, symbols, and meanings as more appropriate for themselves because these are not part of Euro-America's way of life. That is, what the minorities consider appropriate or even legitimate for themselves in terms of attitudes, beliefs, preferences, and behaviors or practices are sometimes defined in opposition to the attitudes, beliefs, preferences and practices of Euro-Americans, who are their enemies or oppressors.

Cultural inversion may take several forms. It may be in-group meanings of words and statement (Bontemps, personal communication, July 1969), different notions of time (Weis, 1985), different emphasis on dialects and communication styles (Baugh, 1983; Holt, 1972; Luster, 1992), or an outright rejection of Euro-American preferences or what Euro-Americans consider appropriate behavior in a given setting (Fordham & Ogbu, 1986; Petroni, 1970).

Oppositional cultural frame of reference and identity manifest themselves most explicitly in the domain of communication—vocabulary and speech. As Dalby (1972) noted, African Americans are constantly creating new words in their vernacular to replace vocabulary that comes to be understood and

coopted by Euro-Americans. They appear to perceive a need to remain linguistically

> one jump ahead of Euro-Americans. And one function of black vernacular is
> to strengthen the in-group solidarity of African Americans to the exclusion of
> Euro-Americans—an oppositional identity manifestation—and to deceive, con-
> fuse and conceal information from Euro-Americans in general. (Dalby, 1972,
> pp. 172–174)

Holt (1972) made similar points in her discussion of the reverse meanings
given by African Americans to words used in reference to them by Euro-
Americans, such as the word *nigger*. Used by Euro-Americans in reference
to African Americans, *nigger* has a negative connotation. But when this word
is used by African Americans among themselves, it can mean a term of en-
dearment. A study of African-American adolescents in a high school in
Washington, DC, found 17 different behaviors and attitudes that the youths
avoided because "they are White." These ranged from speaking standard English or "speaking proper" to "being on time" (Fordham & Ogbu, 1986, p. 186).

The oppositional behavior is not limited to children and adolescents; it
is also present among adults. Luster (1992) reported from her recent study
of an African-American community in San Francisco that

> there is continual delineation and reinforcement of behaviors, practices, and
> attitudes that are "Black" (and appropriate) versus those that are "white" (and
> inappropriate). "Acting white" is an acknowledged and identifiable practice with-
> in the community. The women who were both observed for more than a year
> and then interviewed considered "speaking proper" or using the standard Eng-
> lish an attempt to disassociate oneself from the race; an attempt to demonstrate
> superiority; an act of betrayal. It angered and disgusted the community. (pp.
> 138, 147)

Thus, there is a co-existence of oppositional cultural frames of reference
guiding behaviors, in selected areas of life, as far as involuntary minorities
are concerned. One cultural frame of reference is appropriate for Euro-
Americans but not for involuntary minorities; the other is appropriate for
involuntary minorities. Furthermore, the perception of what is appropriate
or inappropriate for minorities is emotionally charged because it is intimately bound up with their sense of social identity, self-worth, and security. Therefore, individuals who try to behave in the nonappropriate way or who try
to behave like Euro-Americans (i.e., those who try to "cross cultural boundaries" in the forbidden domains) may face opposition from other members
of their minority group. Their behaviors may be interpreted as "acting White"
or "acting Anglo," and they may be further accused of betraying their own

people or as "trying to join the enemy." The individuals trying to cross cultural boundaries or pass culturally may also experience psychological conflict, or what DeVos and Wagatsuma (1967) called "affective dissonance," partly because their sense of social identity may lead them to feel that they are, indeed, abandoning or betraying their people, and partly because such individuals may not be sure that they would be accepted by Euro-American people if they succeeded in learning how to act White.

Oppositional social identity is closely tied to oppositional cultural frame of reference. This is clearly the case with respect to speech. In the African-American community, as noted earlier in Luster's (1992) study, speaking standard English or "talking proper" is viewed as the prime indicator that someone is acting White or wants to be White. Speaking properly produced criticism and sometimes hostility. The people did not regard "proper English" as a part of Black culture but something that African Americans have to learn or "take on." Those who spoke standard English for some reason had to defend themselves against criticism. Such people were observed to feel a sense of engaging in a forbidden practice that is culturally interpreted as an attempt to deny self. Luster concluded from her ethnographic study that "the community's oppositional stance toward 'talking white' was quite consciously linked to resisting white demands that blacks must become more like whites in order to be acceptable" (Luster, 1992, pp. 149–150).

The difference between the cultural frame of reference of voluntary minorities and that of involuntary minorities may be illustrated with the situation facing a Euro-American man from the United States who wants to go to Paris for vacation but does not yet speak French. Using the perspective of voluntary minorities, the would-be vacationer knows that in order to have a "successful" vacation in Paris he has to learn to speak French. Therefore, he embarks on learning to speak French. In so doing, the man from the United States knows that he is not giving up his native language, does not want to give up his native language, and, most importantly, does not think he is giving up his native language. Instead, the Euro-American from the United States thinks he is learning French as an additional language that he needs to accomplish a particular objective, namely, to have a successful vacation in Paris. The process of learning here is perceived, experienced, and interpreted as additive.

So it is with immigrant minorities learning English and other aspects of North-American cultural frame of reference for school or job success. What the immigrants are able to do is to separate the attitudes and behaviors they consider belong to the cultural frame of reference of the public schools, which they need to learn in order to succeed in school, from the attitudes and behaviors that symbolize membership in the dominant group, which is not their objective.

From the perspective of involuntary minorities, the Euro-American from the United States about to go to Paris for vacation would think that once he starts learning French he would lose his English language—his cultural and social identity. He thinks of his action as intended to displace or replace the language and identity he already has with French ones. Therefore, he is afraid even to try. Then, as I show later, there are social and psychological pressures against his learning a language that may change his identity and position in the group (Ogbu, 1989b).

INSTRUMENTAL AND RELATIONAL RESPONSES TO MINORITY STATUS: CONSEQUENCES FOR COGNITIVE AND ACADEMIC PERFORMANCE

How do minority status and cultural frame of reference affect cognitive and academic behaviors of minorities? This question is best answered in two parts.

The first part has to do with how American society and the public schools contribute to the low cognitive and academic performance of the involuntary minorities. I have discussed this part of the problem elsewhere (Ogbu, 1978, 1982), and do not treat it here.

The second part is the consequences for cognitive and academic performance of the minorities' own responses to their treatment. This is the theme of this and the following sections. In this section, I focus on instrumental and relational responses and their consequences. In the next section, I discuss the consequences of their cultural responses or their cultural frames of reference and identities.

At the instrumental level, voluntary and involuntary minorities respond differently to discrimination in jobs and other barriers. Voluntary minorities tend to respond in ways that do not discourage them from working hard in school toward school success; the response of involuntary minorities tends to lead them in the opposite direction.

Voluntary minorities possess what I termed *positive dual frame of reference*: They tend to compare their present selves or situations with their former selves or with their peers "back home." When they make these comparisons, they generally conclude that they are better off in the United States than they were "back home" or than their peers "back home," even when they are allowed only marginal jobs. They may think that their menial jobs and discrimination are only temporary. Furthermore, voluntary minorities tend to interpret their exclusion from better jobs and other positions as the result of their status as "strangers," because they do not speak English well, or because they were not educated in the United States.

Therefore, these minorities tend to believe that education offers the best chance to get ahead in the United States, and they try to behave accordingly, sometimes even in the face of enormous barriers. Voluntary minorities do not necessarily come from societies where the folk theory of getting ahead (i.e., people's notion of how members of their society or group "get ahead") stressed education or hardwork syndrome (i.e., the habit of working hard to achieve a goal). However, they believe that their children will have better opportunities in the United States. In fact, many claim that they make sacrifices to give their children an "American education."

In contrast, involuntary minorities do not have such a positive dual frame of comparison. Because they do not have a "homeland situation" to compare with the situation in the United States, they do not interpret their menial jobs and lower wages as "better." They also do not see their situation as temporary. On the contrary, they tend to interpret the discrimination against them as more or less permanent and institutionalized. Although they "wish" they could get ahead through education and ability like Euro-Americans, they know they "can't." Consequently, they develop a folk theory of getting ahead that differs in some respects from that of Euro-Americans.

However, the situation is, paradoxical for minorities like African Americans. When questioned directly, they may declare, like Euro-Americans, that in order to get ahead one needs a good education or good school credentials. By contrast, their actual strategies or behaviors for getting ahead do not support the middle-classlike folk theory as do those of the voluntary minorities. Indeed, intensive ethnographic interviews and observations reveal that African Americans, for instance, do not really believe that they have the same chance to get ahead as Euro-Americans with similar school credentials. Further, African Americans try to change the rules by attacking the criteria for school credentials and employment, and then employ several alternative strategies for getting ahead. Among the survival strategies developed by African Americans are "collective struggle," "Uncle Tomming," "hustling," and the like (Ogbu, 1981, 1985).

At the instrumental level, the treatment of involuntary minorities and their responses contribute to their low performance on intelligence tests and academic work in some specific ways. First, excluding involuntary minorities from the more desirable techno-economic, social, and political roles that demand and promote Euro-American middle-class cognitive skills, as well as excluding them from middle-class education through segregation and inferior education, deny them the opportunity to develop ways of speaking, conceptualizing, and thinking like Euro-Americans. Over generations of such treatment, they developed other ways of speaking, conceptualizing, and thinking, which have been demanded and enhanced by their menial and unskilled jobs and inferior education. Thus, involuntary minorities make a cognitive adaptation to their ecological niche, not an adaptation to a Euro-American ecological niche. The cognitive tasks posed by the two niches are different.

Generally speaking, because involuntary minorities and middle-class Euro-Americans make different cognitive adaptations to different ecological niches, involuntary minorities and middle-class Euro-Americans differ in cognitive skills. However, the measurement of IQ has traditionally been based on the sampling of Euro-American cognitive skills. That is, IQ tests are constructed to tap primarily those cognitive skills and strategies that are functional for Euro-Americans, rather than those cognitive skills that are functional for involuntary minorities. Of course, there is some overlap because Euro-Americans and involuntary minorities are human groups and have a certain degree of common participation in U.S. institutions, but the overlap would have been much greater had there not been generations of barriers in opportunity structure against the minorities.

Thus, the lower test scores may be partly due to cultural and cognitive differences caused by stratified opportunity structure in education and the techno-economic domain (i.e., due to "cultural bias"). It can be argued, of course, that voluntary minorities face the same "cultural bias" and yet perform better on those tests. Why involuntary minorities are less able to overcome the cultural bias in IQ testing and other situations is examined later.

Although involuntary minorities have been largely excluded from White middle-class education and jobs for generations, they appear to have been involved in other cultural activities in their own ecological niche that required and promoted middle-class types of conceptual skills, abstract thinking, problem solving, and decision making. Indeed, involuntary minorities in the United States and other urban industrial societies may possess the same mathematical concepts and other cognitive skills that make up the IQ test items, but it does not necessarily follow that they are able to translate these attributes into high IQ test scores. Why?

Part of the reason is that doing well on IQ tests and academic tasks at school historically did not bring to involuntary minorities the same rewards that these accomplishments brought to their Euro-American peers (Ogbu, 1974, 1978). Consequently, the minorities became ambivalent or skeptical that good school credentials or high test scores were sufficient to enable them "make it." Hence, they developed an alternative folk theory of "making it" that has not encouraged a strong tradition of "effort optimism" or persevering effort at scholastic tasks and test taking. Even today, the legacy of this is that involuntary minority children do not appear to take IQ tests seriously enough to try for the best scores they can get. For instance, psychologists who test the children have observed that, in non-test situations, African-American children communicate with their peers, solve problems, and use concepts in ways typical of children who have IQ test scores of about 10–15 points higher than theirs (Jensen, 1969).

The relationship between the minorities and Euro-Americans who devise and administer IQ tests also affects the minorities' performance on the tests. For instance, voluntary and involuntary minorities differ in the degree of trust they have for Euro-Americans and the institutions controlled by Euro-

Americans. This degree of trust affects the test performance of the two types of minorities differently.

The relationship between the schools and minority communities may raise similar educational problems for voluntary and involuntary minorities. But the two types of minorities tend to interpret and respond to these problems differently. Three factors appear to account for the ability of voluntary minorities to overcome barriers in school–community relations and thereby do well in school. First, many voluntary minorities see public schools as offering an education far superior to the education available to them in their homelands. Therefore, even when these minorities are attending an inferior school in the United States, they tend to think that the school is of higher quality than it actually is. Their frame of reference for assessing public schools is the quality of education in their homelands, not the quality of education in Euro-American suburbs.

Second, some voluntary minorities believe that they are treated better by U.S. public schools than they would be treated by schools in their homelands. In ethnographic studies, voluntary minority students and parents often express both surprise and appreciation for the fact that they do not have to pay school fees and that they receive free textbooks and other supplies.

Even when the immigrants recognize, experience, and resent prejudice and discrimination in school, as in the case of Punjabi Indians in Valleyside, California, they appear to respond in ways that do not discourage them from doing well in school. They rationalize the prejudice and discrimination against them by saying that they are guests in a foreign land and have no choice but to tolerate prejudice and discrimination (Gibson, 1983). Punjabi parents impress this attitude on their children and place the responsibility of doing well in school on the children. Gibson described the Punjabi strategy as follows:

> Punjabis rarely blame the educational system, or the teachers for a child's difficulties. Responsibility for learning rests, in the Punjabi view, with the individual. Punjabi are *not naive* about institutional and social barriers to success. They simply persevere, seeking ways to overcome obstacles in their path. Punjabi children are taught to do their best and to hold themselves accountable for their failure. If children fool around, squandering educational opportunities, they bear the consequence. (p. 149)

The overall impression from analyzing ethnographic studies of voluntary minorities is that they teach their children to accept, internalize, and follow school rules of behavior and academic enterprise. Voluntary minority parents and communities seem to emphasize to their children the importance of acquiring job-related skills, proficiency in the English language, and basic skills in reading, writing, and math. They also tell their children that to succeed in these, they must follow the advice of teachers, school counselors, and other school personnel about rules of behavior and standard practices for academic success.

Ethnographic research (e.g., Luster, 1992; Ogbu 1974, 1978, 1989a, 1991) has indicated that the perceptions and responses of involuntary minorities to the educational system are strikingly different from those of voluntary minorities. To begin with, involuntary minorities do not have the voluntary minorities' dual frame of reference that leads to favorable evaluation of the segregated and inferior education they think they are receiving. They compare their education with the education of Euro-American children in the suburbs, a comparison in which they always find the latter to be "better" for no justifiable reason, except discrimination. Furthermore, involuntary minorities interpret their treatment by the public schools within the context of overall enduring conflict between them and Euro-Americans and the institutions controlled by Euro-Americans. Thus, African Americans, for instance, interpret their initial exclusion from the public schools, and subsequent segregation and inferior education, as designed to prevent them from qualifying for desirable jobs. Consequently, African Americans have devoted a considerable part of their "collective struggle" toward compelling Euro-Americans and the schools they control to provide them with "equal" and "quality" education.

One result of the enduring conflicts between involuntary minorities on the one hand, and Euro-Americans and the institutions like the schools they control on the other hand, is that the minorities appear to have developed a deep distrust for the public schools. African Americans more or less believe that they cannot trust the public schools to educate their children as they educate Euro-American children (Luster, 1992; Ogbu, 1974). A similar sense of distrust is found among Native Americans and Mexican Americans (Gibson & Ogbu, 1991; Kramer, 1991).

Another consequence of this distrust and conflict is that involuntary minorities have more or less come to interpret school rules and practices differently from the middle-class Euro-Americans and voluntary minorities. As has been mentioned, voluntary minorities tend to endorse school rules and practices much in the same way that middle-class Euro-Americans do: as necessary, desirable, and compatible with their educational goals. However, involuntary minorities interpret these same rules and practices as impositions of Euro-American culture that do not necessarily meet their real educational needs. Furthermore, involuntary minority children define school rules and practices as "White" and therefore not particularly acceptable to them. Because of the conflicts and distrust that exist in the involuntary minorities' relationship with the schools and school personnel, and because of skepticism over school rules and practices, it is probably more difficult for involuntary minority parents and communities to teach their children to accept, internalize, and follow school rules and practices that lead to academic success and social adjustment in school. Furthermore, it is probably more difficult for the children, especially as they get older, to accept, internalize, and follow the rules than it is for children of voluntary minorities (Ogbu, 1984).

CULTURAL FRAME OF REFERENCE AND CULTURAL IDENTITIES: CONSEQUENCES FOR COGNITIVE AND ACADEMIC PERFORMANCE

The last major factor contributing to the differential performance of the minorities is the twin phenomenon of cultural frame of reference and cultural identity. This twin phenomenon makes it difficult for some minorities to cross cultural and cognitive boundaries.

Voluntary minorities have a cultural frame of reference that enhances symbolic responses conducive to academic striving and success. Specifically, they have a nonoppositional cultural/collective identity and cultural frame of reference vis-à-vis Euro-American identity and cultural frame of reference. As noted earlier, this enables minorities to perceive, define, and respond to the cultural and language differences they encounter in school and society as barriers to be overcome in order to succeed in school and eventually get a good job when they leave school. Thus, in our current and past ethnographic studies, we find that, among voluntary minorities, parents are also going to adult or night school to learn English because they believe that knowing how to speak English will help them get jobs. Some parents and other adults in the community are participating in programs to learn how to behave appropriately in the U.S. workplace because they think that to keep their jobs and get ahead they have to know how to behave the way U.S. employers want them to behave.

For this reason, parents tell their children to learn the English language and to learn the cultural behaviors required at school. I must emphasize that voluntary minority parents do not ask their children to give up their own language and culture or to learn the U.S. language and culture because the latter are "better," but because they are tools for succeeding in school. Likewise, voluntary minority parents do not think that learning standard English and U.S. culture is bad for their children.

The definition of cultural and language differences as barriers to be overcome enhances the school success of voluntary minority children. It encourages them to approach learning the cultural and language behaviors very instrumentally as tools to be mastered and used to achieve something; they do not see the acquisition of the cultural and language behaviors as something detrimental to what they already have, to their own cultural and language identity. Voluntary minorities practice what Gibson (1983) called a strategy of accommodation without assimilation. That is, although voluntary minorities may not give up their own cultural beliefs and practices, they are willing and may actually strive to play the classroom game by the rules and try to overcome all kinds of difficulties in school because they so strongly believe that there will be a pay off later. With this kind of attitude, voluntary minorities are able to cross cultural boundaries and do relatively well in school.

In contrast, involuntary minorities possess an oppositional cultural frame of reference and oppositional collective/social identity that make it difficult for them to maximize their IQ test scores or scholastic achievement by adopting the strategies or behaviors that work for Euro-Americans. Both oppositional cultural frame of reference and oppositional identity make it more difficult for involuntary minorities to cross cognitive boundaries (where there are differences in culturally defined cognitive skills) and to translate their cognitive attributes into high test scores (where there are similarities in cognitive skills due to similarities in cognitive demands of cultural tasks). Thus, the special problem of involuntary minorities is that they do not merely differ initially with the dominant group in cognitive skills, as do voluntary minorities. Their special problem arises from the nature of their own responses to their initial terms of incorporation into a dominating society and subsequent treatment, namely, their formation of collective oppositional identity and oppositional cultural frame of reference.

Involuntary minorities develop an identity system (i.e., a social/collective identity system) that they perceive and interpret as oppositional to the social identity system of a dominant majority. They also develop a cultural frame of reference or ideal ways of behaving in selected areas of life, which they also perceive and interpret as oppositional to the cultural frame of reference of the dominant majority.

Oppositional cultural frame of reference is applied selectively by involuntary minorities. The target areas appear to be those traditionally defined as prerogatives of the dominant majority, first by the majority itself and then acceded to by the minorities. These are areas long believed that only the dominant majority could perform well in, and few minorities were actually given the opportunity to try or were rewarded well when they succeeded. They are also areas where the criteria of performance have been established by the dominant majority, competence in performance is judged by the majority or their minority representatives, and reward for performance is determined by the dominant majority according to majority criteria. Intellectual performance (IQ test scores), scholastic performance, and performance in high-status jobs in mainstream economy represent such areas.

More specifically, it appears that the oppositional identity and oppositional cultural frame of reference have produced a cognitive orientation, whereby minorities consciously and unconsciously perceive and interpret learning certain things or acting in certain ways that they associate with their "oppressors," their "enemies" (e.g., Euro-Americans), as threatening and therefore "resisted." In other words, it appears that involuntary minorities perceive and interpret standard attitudes and behaviors in IQ and other test-taking situations as falling within the cultural frame of reference of Euro-Americans, not that of the minorities. To them, expressing such attitudes and behaviors may mean "acting White," which is not appropriate. I suspect that these minorities have a certain degree of self-doubt that they can actually compete successfully or do well in areas regarded traditionally as "White domains."

More specifically, involuntary minorities tend to perceive schooling as (a) a linear acculturation process, (b) an assimilation process, or (c) a displacement/replacement process. Too often they equate school rules and practices that enhance academic achievement with the norms and cultural practices of the dominant majority (i.e., with the cultural practices of their "oppressors" or "enemy"). In the United States, some define school knowledge as "White" knowledge, not minority knowledge; and some interpret the behaviors that lead to academic success as a symbol of White or "acting White."

Because involuntary minorities subscribe to the displacement/replacement model of schooling, they do not make a clear distinction between the rules and practices that enhance academic success and the rules of behavior and practices of the dominant culture. In the United States, they think and fear that adopting school norms will "displace" their own minority cultural norms, behavior practices, and language and identity, and replace these with Euro-American norms, Euro-American behaviors, and Euro-American language and identity.

Among involuntary minority students in the United States, there are social pressures against "acting White" both at school and in minority communities. Individuals who adopt attitudes and behaviors that enhance academic success or who are actually doing well in school may be ridiculed and criticized by their peers as "acting White" or as "thinking they are White." Their peers apply discouraging pressures on them by calling them names like "Uncle Toms" (Petroni, 1970), "brainiacs" (Fordham, 1985; Fordham & Ogbu, 1986), or "gringos" (Matute-Bianchi, 1986), and by excluding them from peer activities.

Family and community members also participate unknowingly in the social pressures against adopting the attitudes and behaviors that enhance academic success. For example, in the family and community, people tend to make uncomplimentary comments about "talking proper" when an African-American child is speaking standard English rather than using ethnic dialect. There is a psychological pressure in the form of "affective dissonance" against adoption of appropriate academic attitudes and behaviors. The individual student may be unwilling to adopt attitudes and behaviors that promote school success or to excel academically for fear of peer criticism and loss of peer

support, and from genuine belief that his or her actions may actually constitute "acting White."

The situation creates a dilemma of choice for involuntary minority students: If a student believes and chooses the assimilation definition of schooling, he or she may indeed succeed academically but suffer peer criticism or
ostracism, as well as suffer from "affective dissonance." On the other hand,
if the student believes the assimilation model but rejects it by refusing to "act
White" (i.e., adopt behaviors and attitudes that enhance school success), then
he or she will not likely do well in school. The dilemma is that by defining
schooling as a linear acculturation, involuntary minority students feel that
they have to choose between academic success and maintaining their minority
identity and cultural frame of reference. However, there are some ways that
students can and do avoid this dilemma: They adopt "secondary strategies"
toward their schoolwork (Ogbu, 1988). Secondary strategies are over and
above the conventional strategies of adopting proper academic attitudes, hard
work, and perseverance. Instead, they are strategies that provide the context in which the minority youth can practice the conventional strategies.
Examples of secondary strategies among African-American youths include
"camouflaging" (disguising one's true academic attitudes and behaviors), "cultural passing" or "emulation of Whites" (adopting Euro-American behavior
or trying to behave like Euro-Americans), "accommodation without assimilation" (when in school, behaving according to school norms, but at home
and in the community behaving according to the minority-group norms; this
strategy is more common among voluntary minorities), and "clowning" (acting like a fool, jester, or comedian).

CONCLUSION

The people who have most difficulty with IQ tests and academic work are
involuntary minorities. This is not merely because they possess a different
culture or a nontechnological culture and socialization process. Although one
cannot equate IQ tests and academic achievement, both are based on tests
given by the dominant group, and therefore both elicit a common approach
from involuntary minorities based on their adaptation to minority status.

In other words, it is not simply that IQ tests are culturally biased against
them, because the tests are also biased against voluntary minorities. It is equally important to consider the responses that involuntary minorities have made
to their forced incorporation and subsequent treatment, especially their formation of oppositional identity and oppositional cultural frame of reference.
These phenomena cause the minorities to interpret IQ test scores consciously and unconsciously as detrimental to their cultural and personal well-being,
and thus they refrain from maximizing their test scores.

As noted earlier, IQ tests discriminate against voluntary minorities, like Asian Americans. However, the latter interpret the cultural differences in the tests as barriers to be overcome and not in a manner threatening to their identity. This interpretation enables them to prepare for the tests and maximize their test scores.

A part of the solution to the problem of low academic achievement and low IQ test scores among involuntary minorities lies in recognizing the historical, structural, and psychological bases of their "resistance" and helping them develop a nonthreatening interpretation of the tests and test taking. For involuntary minorities, the problem is not that of discontinuities in cognitive socialization. Rather, it is one of "crossing cognitive boundaries." Any proposed solution must begin with an understanding of those boundaries.

ACKNOWLEDGMENT

An earlier version of this chapter was prepared for a workshop of the National Institute of Mental Health on continuities and discontinuities in the cognitive socialization of minority children in Washington, DC, June 1991, organized by Patricia M. Greenfield and Rodney R. Cocking.

The preparation of this chapter was supported by the University of California faculty research funds and by grants from the California Policy Seminar, Carnegie Corporation of New York, W. T. Grant Foundation, Russell Sage Foundation, and The Spencer Foundation.

REFERENCES

Acuna, R. (1981). *Occupied America: The Chicano's struggle toward liberation.* San Francisco: Canfield.

Alland, A. (1973). *Human diversity.* Garden City, NY: Doubleday.

Baugh, J. (1983). *Black street speech: Its history, structure and survival.* Austin, TX: University of Texas Press.

Brookover, W. B., & Erickson, E. L. (1965). *Society, schools, and learning.* Boston: Allyn & Bacon.

Closs, M. P. (Ed.). (1986). *Native American mathematics.* Austin, TX: University of Texas Press.

Cole, M., Gay, J., Glick, J., & Sharp, D. W. (1971). *The cultural context of learning and thinking.* New York: Basic Books.

Committee of Correspondence on the Future of Public Education. (1984). *Education for democratic future: A manifesto.* New York: Author.

Cook-Gumperz, J., & Gumperz, J. J. (1979). From oral to written culture: The transition to literacy. In M. F. Whitehead (Ed.), *Variation in writing.* Hillsdale, NJ: Lawrence Erlbaum Associates.

Dalby, D. (1972). The African element in American English. In T. Kochman (Ed.), *Rappin' and 'stylin' out: Communication in urban black America* (pp. 170–188). Chicago: University of Illinois Press.

Dasen, P. R. (1974). The influence of ecology, culture and European contact on cognitive development in Australian aborigines. In P. R. Dasen (Ed.), *Culture and cognition.* London: Methuen.

Dennis, W. (1970). Goodenough scores, art experience, and modernization. In I. Al-Issa & W. Denis (Eds.), *Cross-cultural studies of behavior* (pp. 134–152). New York: Holt, Rinehart & Winston.

DeVos, G. A. (1973). Japan's outcasts: The problem of the Burakumin. In B. Whitaker (Ed.), *The fourth world: Victims of group oppression* (pp. 307–327). New York: Schocken Books.

DeVos, G. A., & Hippler, A. (1969). Cultural psychology: Comparative studies of human behavior. In G. Lindzey & E. Aronson (Eds.), *Handbook of social psychology* (Vol. 1, pp. 323–417). Cambridge, MA: Addison-Wesley.

DeVos, G. A., & Wagatsuma, H. (Eds.). (1967). *Japan's invisible race: Caste in culture and personality.* Berkeley: University of California Press.

Fordham, S. (1985). *Afro-Caribbean and native Black American school learning in Washington, D.C.: Learning to be or not to be a native.* Unpublished manuscript.

Fordham, S., & Ogbu, J. U. (1986). Black students' school success: Coping with the burden of 'acting white.' *The Urban Review, 18*(3), 176–296.

Gartner, A., & Riessman, F. (1973). *The lingering incantation with I.Q.: A review of Arthur R. Jensen's educability and group differences.* Unpublished manuscript.

Gay, J., & Cole, M. (1967). *The new mathematics and an old culture: A study of learning among the Kpelle of Liberia.* New York: Holt, Rinehart & Winston.

Gibson, M. A. (1976). *Ethnicity and schooling: A Caribbean case study.* Unpublished Ph.D. dissertation, University of Pittsburgh, PA.

Gibson, M. A. (1983). *Home-school-community linkages: A study of educational equity for Punjabi youths* (Final Report). Washington, DC: National Institute of Education.

Gibson, M. A. (1991). Ethnicity, gender and social class: The school adaptation patterns of West Indian youths. In M. A. Gibson & J. U. Ogbu (Eds.), *Minority status and schooling: Immigrants versus involuntary minorities* (pp. 167–198). New York: Garland.

Gibson, M. A., & Ogbu, J. U. (Eds.). (1991). *Minority status and schooling: Immigrant versus involuntary minorities.* New York: Garland.

Greenfield, P. M. (1966). On culture and conservation. In J. S. Bruner, R. R. Olver, P. M. Greenfield, J. R. Hornsby, H. J. Kenney, M. Maccoby, N. Modiano, F. A. Mosher, D. R. Olson, M. C. Potter, L. C. Reich, & A. Mc. Sonstroem (Eds.), *Studies in cognitive growth* (pp. 225–256). New York: Wiley.

Greenfield, P. M. (1984). *Mind and media: The effects of television, video games, and computers.* Cambridge: Harvard University Press.

Harker, R. K. (1977). *Cognitive style, environment and school achievement.* Palmerston North, New Zealand: Massey University, Department of Education.

Holt, G. S. (1972). "Inversion" in black community. In T. Kochman (Ed.), *Rappin' and 'stylin' out: Communication in urban black America* (pp. 152–159). Chicago: University of Illinois Press.

Jensen, A. R. (1969). How much can we boost IQ and scholastic achievement? *Harvard Educational Review, 39,* 1–123.

Kramer, B. J. (1991). Education and American Indians: The experience of the Ute Indian tribe. In M. A. Gibson & J. U. Ogbu (Eds.), *Minority status and schooling: Immigrant versus involuntary minorities* (pp. 287–308). New York: Garland.

Lancy, D. F. (1983). *Cross-cultural studies in cognition and mathematics.* New York: Academic Press.

Laosa, L. (1978). Maternal teaching strategies in Chicano families of varied educational and socioeconomic levels. *Child Development, 49,* 1129–1135.

Laosa, L. (1982). School, occupation, culture and the family: The impact of parental schooling on the parent child relationship. *Journal of Educational Psychology, 9,* 791–827.

LeVine, R. A. (1970). Cross-cultural study in child psychology. In P. Mussen (Ed.), *Carmichael's manual of child psychology* (3rd ed., Vol. 2, pp. 559–612). New York: Wiley.

Luster, L. (1992). *Schooling, survival, and struggle: Black women and the GED.* Unpublished doctoral dissertation, Stanford University, School of Education.

Matute-Bianchi, M. E. (1986). Ethnic identities and patterns of school success and failure among Mexican-descent and Japanese American students in a California high school: An ethnographic analysis. *American Journal of Education, 95*(1), 233–255.

Matute-Bianchi, M. E. (1991). Situational ethnicity and patterns of school performance among immigrant and nonimmigrant Mexican-descent students. In M. A. Gibson & J. U. Ogbu (Eds.), *Minority status and schooling* (pp. ???). New York: Garland.

Mayeseke, G. W. T., Tetsuo, O., Beaton, A., Cohen, W., & Wisler, C. (1973). *A study of the achievement of our nation's students* (Department of Health, Education, and Welfare, Publication No. OE 72-131). Washington, DC: U.S. Government Printing Office.

Ogbu, J. U. (1974). *The next generation: An ethnography of education in an urban neighborhood.* New York: Academic Press.

Ogbu, J. U. (1978). *Minority education and caste: The American system in cross-cultural perspective.* New York: Academic Press.

Ogbu, J. U. (1981). Origins of human competence: A cultural-ecological perspective. *Child Development, 52*, 413–429.

Ogbu, J. U. (1982). Cultural discontinuities and schooling. *Anthropology and Education Quarterly, 13*, 290–307.

Ogbu, J. U. (1984). *Understanding community forces affecting minority students' academic effort.* Unpublished manuscript, The Achievement Council, Oakland, CA.

Ogbu, J. U. (1985). A cultural ecology of competence among inner-city blacks. In M. B. Spencer, G. K. Brookins, & W. R. Allen (Eds.), *Beginnings: Social and affective development of black children* (pp. ???). Hillsdale, NJ: Lawrence Erlbaum Associates.

Ogbu, J. U. (1987). Cultural influences on plasticity in human development. In J. J. Gallagher & C. T. Ramey (Eds.), *The malleability of children* (pp. 155–169). Baltimore: Brooks.

Ogbu, J. U. (1988). Diversity and equity in public education: Community forces and minority school adjustment and performance. In R. Haskins & D. McRae (Eds.), *Policies for America's public schools, teachers, equity and indicators* (pp. 127–170). Norwood, NJ: Ablex.

Ogbu, J. U. (1989a). Cultural boundaries and minority youth orientation toward work preparation. In D. Stern & D. Eichorn (Eds.), *Adolescence and work: Influences of social structure, labor markets, and culture* (pp. 101–140). Hillsdale, NJ: Lawrence Erlbaum Associates.

Obgu, J. U. (1989b). The individual in collective adaptation: A framework for focusing on academic under performance and dropping out among involuntary minorities. In L. Weis, E. Farrar, & H. Petrie (Eds.), *Dropouts from school: Issues, dilemmas, and solutions* (pp. 181–204). Buffalo: State University of New York Press.

Ogbu, J. U. (1990). Minority status and literacy in comparative perspective. *Daedalus, 119*(2), 141–168.

Ogbu, J. U. (1991). Low school performance as an adaptation: The case of blacks in Stockton, California. In J. U. Ogbu & M. A. Gibson (Eds.), *Minority status and schooling: A comparative study of immigrant and involuntary minorities* (pp. 3–33). New York: Garland.

Ogbu, J. U., & Matute-Bianchi, M. E. (1986). Understanding sociocultural factors: Knowledge, identity, and school adjustment. In *Beyond language: Social and cultural factors in schooling language minority students* (pp. 73–173). Sacramento: Bilingual Education Office, State Department of Education.

Parliamentary Select Committee on Immigration and Race Relations. (1972–1973). *Education: Vol. 1. Report.* London: Her Majesty's Stationery Office.

Petroni, F. A. (1970). Uncle Toms: White stereotypes in the black movement. *Human Organization, 29*, 260–266.

Posner, J. (1982). The development of mathematical knowledge in two West African societies. *Child Development, 53*, 200–203.

Price-Williams, D. R., Gordon, W., & Ramírez, M., III. (1969). Skill and conservation: A study of pottery-making children. *Developmental Psychology, 1*, 769.

Saxe, G. B., & Posner, J. (1983). The development of numerical cognition: Cross-cultural perspectives. In H. P. Ginsburg (Ed.), *The development of mathematical thinking* (pp. 291–317). New York: Academic Press.

Scribner, S., & Cole, M. (1973). Cognitive consequences of formal and informal education. *Science, 182*, 553–559.

Segall, M. H., Herskovits, M. J., & Campbell, D. T. (1966). *The influence of culture on visual perception.* India: Bobbs-Merrill.

Shimahara, N. K. (1991). Social mobility and education: Burakumin in Japan. In M. A. Gibson & J. U. Ogbu (Eds.), *Minority status and schooling.* New York: Garland.

Slade, M. (1982, Oct. 24). Aptitude, intelligence or what? *New York Times*, p. 22E.

Taylor, M. J., & Hegarty, S. (1985). *The best of both worlds: A review of research into the education of pupils of South Asian origin.* Windsor: National Foundation for Educational Research-Nelson.

Vernon, P. E. (1969). *Intelligence and cultural environment.* London: Metheun.

Vernon, P. E. (1982). *The abilities and achievements of Orientals in North America.* New York: Academic Press.

Weis, L. (1985). *Between two worlds.* Boston: Routledge & Kegan Paul.

Wigdor, A. K., & Garner, W. R. (Eds.). (1982). *Ability testing: Uses, consequences, and controversies: Part 11. Documentation.* Washington, DC: The National Academy Press.

19

ECOLOGICALLY VALID FRAMEWORKS OF DEVELOPMENT: ACCOUNTING FOR CONTINUITIES AND DISCONTINUITIES ACROSS CONTEXTS

Rodney R. Cocking
National Institute of Mental Health

The following discussion explores ways to deal with a major dilemma raised by the chapters in this volume. The dilemma is how to generalize from the individual research projects to a model of child development, still preserving the individual cultural variables and individual cultural interpretations of the studies of these chapters. The dilemma for the behavioral scientist is how to look for developmental commonalities and their variants without distorting the culture-specific and, hence, ecologically valid research.

The organizing framework, therefore, considers culture, societal context, and mechanisms by which culture and context are preserved or mutated in the developmental process. **Generalization** and **transfer** become critical criteria for comparative research models. How these two criteria operate, either as indices of continuities or as evidence that a cultural variable has a different meaning in a contrasting societal context (discontinuities), are raised to point out that variables have different meanings within varying developmental frameworks, and that the benchmarks of development also vary. Generalization and transfer, however, are not meant to imply that the research models should test the "strength" of context-dependent behaviors or culturally derived learning in other circumstances.

This chapter asks what is to be learned about human development by looking beyond Euro-American children and Western cultures and, further, what is to be learned about development within Western cultural contexts by considering the cross-cultural roots of minority child development. This chapter argues that the challenge for developmental theory is to devise organizing frameworks that can account for developmental change, cultural diversity, and contextual variation in a model that presents development as multidetermined (Cocking & Greenfield, in press).

When culture is used as an organizing scheme in psychological research, it is generally to account for differences between groups. The questions raised by the chapters in this volume address how culture can be invoked to demonstrate continuities in development; and alternatively, where societal context operates as a moderator variable, how culture influences behavioral expressions that might be interpreted as discontinuities of development.

The charge in developing a picture of child development that includes minority children is to make clear the dimensions along which cultural differences operate. Developmental differences can be organized in terms of learning and performance differences. Competency models, however, were rejected in the 1960s, when cross-cultural psychology clearly demonstrated that performance differences, used as competency criteria, are fairly easy to demonstrate but are harder to justify as relevant for understanding development or as predictors of behavior (e.g., Piagetian studies, such as Dasen, 1984). Other models that contrast cognition with ecological demands of the culture (de Lacey & Poole, 1979; Nurcombe, 1976) make comparisons: first, within the culture for evaluating relative rates of development; second, between groups on each dimension; and finally, child-by-task interactions are used to extrapolate the contributions of development, individual differences, and culture.

The chapters of this volume allow consideration of cultural influences on development within and across differing societal contexts. To derive models of development from these studies is to stress that each aspect of development is multidetermined. The challenge is to address how the impinging factors work together to produce behavioral outcome, and how these outcomes, although phenotypically different, may have common roots. That is, taken together, the chapters offer insights into both the continuities and discontinuities of behavioral development. The theme of continuities and discontinuities reflects how the culture of origin preserves or continues certain critical features that influence behaviors of the developing generation in a new society, whereas a change in societal context alters other outcomes. It follows that developmental differences may be due to the broader social context in which the cultural heritage (i.e., goals beliefs, values) operate.

The models that guide the research of the individual chapters illustrate the importance of certain comparisons among individuals within the culture of origin (such as the differences in development of street traders and non-traders cited by Oloko, chapter 10, this volume) and as culture bearers in varying contexts (such as language similarities reported by Rabain-Jamin, chapter 8, this volume; Nsamenang & Lamb, chapter 7, this volume; and Blake, chapter 9, this volume, for people of African heritage in Cameroon, France, and the United States, respectively). However, there are some requirements for making such comparisons. The foremost requirement is the establishment of a common language and framework of development. The following discussion presents seven features that need to be considered for drawing comparisons among such diverse data. The rationale for establishing a framework and a research lexicon is not to judge each cultural group against some standard, but for the behavioral scientist to assess the source of observed differences and whether they are due to the phenomena of development or epiphenomena of measurement.

LEVEL OF THE VARIABLE

For researchers who are from different cultures, different perspectives, or different disciplines, the first question is whether there is a common set of processes and, further, whether the operations that are used to measure these processes are comparable. Is it possible to derive a common list of variables that represent critical behavioral processes to enter into a model of behavioral development?

The debate between cross-cultural psychological analyses and indigenous studies is often in terms of differences in meanings of the implied processes or differences in the level at which the variables operate. The kinds of developmental analyses that can account for continuities and discontinuities require scientists to bring consensus to the field through a common language. That is, the first mandate is to obtain scientific consensus for a set of measurement variables that can be specified in terms of level of functioning.

In several of the preceding chapters, language variables were identified as markers of socialization and development. Rabain-Jamin (chapter 8, this volume) shows how certain mother–child verbal interactions have their origins in the African culture from which African-French mothers emigrated to France. This is also shown in comparable mother–child behaviors in the Cameroon studies reported by Nsamenang and Lamb (chapter 7, this volume), that illustrate how children learn communication relationships from mothers' use of affective-marked speech. Blake (chapter 9, this volume), whose language studies follow a U.S. model (Bloom, Lightbown, & Hood, 1975), finds similarities in functional development to the reports by Rabain-Jamin and Nsamenang and Lamb when she shifts from content-based mother–child language interactions to function- and affect-based categories of language. That is, language variables are identified as critical indices of development by both Bloom (1970, 1974, 1991) and Blake (chapter 7, this volume), but there are significant cultural differences in the model of development for determining which behavioral processes will be used as the benchmarks of development.

The value in making comparisons between Euro-Americans and African-American groups even within the U.S. context of development using the criteria of Bloom et al. (1975) as a guideline, these chapters tell us, is that one would have a common yardstick in certain critical areas of language growth. The danger is that one would not see the distinctive cultural goals and values. However, by using the culture of origin as the comparison, not only is the interpretation of development richer because one sees commonalities across societal contexts but the behavioral differences of Euro-American and African-American children can be understood as a product of different practices and values in the socialization of cognition.

The chapters in this volume illustrate that an initial step in looking at the cross-cultural roots of child development is to determine which processes are identified as markers of development and, further, how these processes map onto the variables used to assess development.

INCONSISTENT RESULTS

A second requirement of a model that incorporates continuities and discontinuities into developmental change is to account for inconsistent and uncertain results. This means addressing two opposing types of issues: Whether there is comparability of meaning in variables where inconsistencies occur, and interpreting inconsistent findings within a framework that is driven by an attempt to account for the "universals" of development.

Developmental psychology has a special burden of explaining results that may be or may appear to be inconsistencies. Developmental phenomena are often unstable in early transitional growth periods. Further, developmental psychology often takes a comparative approach to illustrate environmental and situational impact on development or to separate out biological components of development. In both instances, data may show variability. However, apart from these comparisons is the issue of inconsistencies in performance. Both dependent and independent variables may reflect development in ways that are different for children who grow up in different societal and cultural contexts. This is the point of the preceding section about defining variables in terms of processes and developing a common research language to describe those processes (Renninger & Cocking, 1993).

Inconsistencies in developmental data for one culture may be reflective of continuities in another. Cultural groups develop their own criteria and models of development and interpret their own results. For example, studies of the development of representational thought have been shown to produce developmental discrepancies or inconsistencies between subculture populations (economically impoverished and middle-class children; Sigel, 1970; 1986) or within small age spans of comparable socioeconomic status groups within a cultural context (DeLoache, 1993). When comparable cross-cultural studies were conducted in Scottish and African children, cultural norms held but the expected standards of performance were reversed across the populations (Serpell, 1979). The point is that development can be judged by standards of comparison only within a limited framework. One goal of this volume was to address development within a framework broad enough to account for inconsistencies either as developmental discontinuities or with underlying sources of influence beyond the immediacy of the dominant culture and societal context of development. In the latter, inconsistencies within a developmental context may actually reflect developmental continuities that derive from the cultures of origin.

Developmental transitions as markers of important changes in growth are often discovered by inconsistencies in data. Because all children do not progress at the same rate, where data begin to show inconsistencies, developmental differences may be indicating major growth changes. One prominent theory of development posited junctures in development at predictable points, roughly corresponding to ages 2, 7, and 11–13 (Piaget, 1970). Growth of major syntactic structures of English, as another example, shows clear developmental trends when the unit of comparison is a 12-month period (Potts, Carlson, Cocking, & Copple, 1979), but growth curves plotted in 6-month intervals for the same structures less clearly reflect growth over time. The reason for this difference is that the larger unit of analysis washes out the individual differences in development and the considerable inconsistencies across children that is captured in the shorter, 6-month time frame.

What "turns on" a system of growth and what sustains development during critical growth cycles may be reflected in spurts of change that vary across children. Therefore, inconsistencies in development have been enormously important contributors to scientific understanding of individual differences. A model of development needs to account for such individual differences *and* reflect how these individual differences operate within the constraints of culture and societal context. The paradox for this consideration is that the behavioral scientist simultaneously has to account for what is common in development (i.e., the "universals"), as well as what is unique to a culture and an individual.

PATHWAY MODELS

Developmental psychology tries to address why two children within the same family develop so differently, considering their similar biological backgrounds and home environments. For studying these kinds of questions, pathway models focus on *trajectories* of development and stress both *process* and *function*. The same question might be asked across generations of the same family. However, in this case it seems clearer that individuals within the family do not all have the same experiences. These models are important for considering critical processes of development and assessing the impact of each by examining the different trajectories or pathways of development of siblings within the family or generations of the same family (Greenfield, 1993).

One might also ask how developmental models account for the "why so different" or "why so similar" questions when comparing cultures or comparing societal contexts of development and holding the culture of origin constant. Pathway models, or trajectories of development, juxtapose individual development and cultural norms, searching for the junctures of convergence and divergence.

NORMATIVE MODELS

Developmentalists have to know how their data fit with normative cultural models before making comparisons because a good deal of what one learns about a phenomenon comes from a pathology or some detected difference or change. Models based on cultural norms are deceptive because they may fail to account for differences that derive from the subcultures that comprise the larger society represented.

An additional slippery feature of normative models is that time influences the norms in two important ways. First, there are developmental bands, such as childhood and adolescence, that have their own norms and that are often at odds with the societal norms. Second, patterns of behaviors change over time due to unexpected influences, such as the impact of mass media. For example, television had an impact different from radio by showing how other people *behaved*.

An unpredictable aspect of the time factor in models is the so-called "duration-of-effect": Influences may be transitory or permanent. Transitory influences are another complicating factor for developmental analyses because the impact of experiences during development depend on when the influence occurs and how long it lasts. Thus, the *time* dimension is an important moderator of normative models.

In this volume, Oloko (chapter 10) illustrates transitions presently occurring within Nigerian society as women's educational levels rise. The secondary effects impact the women's children and their learning experiences. Likewise, Nsamenang and Lamb (chapter 7, this volume) report on a developmental model for a culture that is in flux as Cameroon becomes increasingly urbanized. Therefore, the chapters in this volume point out that, in looking across contexts for cultural roots of behavioral development, it is important to understand that the comparative contexts also may be in transition. Delgado-Gaitan (chapter 3, this volume) and Tapia-Uribe, LeVine, and LeVine (chapter 2, this volume) point out that the cultural roots that are frozen in time come from an exported culture, whereas the cultures of origin for immigrant groups continue to change.

OUTCOMES AND DEVELOPMENTAL MILESTONES

A concern related to norms of development and the impact of timing on developmental achievements is the concern for the transitory versus the enduring outcomes of development. The importance of this consideration for adopting a model of development and for theory building is in terms of identifying the important variables of cause, influence, or outcome. Are the developmental milestones static, or do they change when the context changes?

As circumstances of immigration change, as they have for Southeast Asians and many Hispanics, behaviors sometimes change to reflect standards of a host culture, and sometimes the behavioral repertoires resist change. Cocking and Chipman (1988) and Cocking and Mestre (1988) speculated that English language competencies differ in Hispanic subgroups on the U.S. mainland (e.g., between Puerto Ricans and Cubans) because of differences in circumstances that initiated immigration. Delgado-Gaitan (chapter 3, this volume) also reports generational differences within Hispanic culture that influence the degree of acculturation (change) versus maintenance of cultural roots (continuity). Therefore, accounting for transitory and unpredictable features of development becomes another problem for developmental psychology to solve.

FACTORS OF VULNERABILITY AND RESILIENCY

Critical periods of development imply both built-in timing "readiness" mechanisms and the associated "on–off" mechanisms. The developmental span of the targeted behaviors, or the period of developmental plasticity, is also a time-bound feature of development. A critical period denotes *when*, in the normative model, development is expected to occur; plasticity accounts for the tolerance limits on the critical period. Flexibility in developmental timing may be due to variation in the environmental features of the child's culture and social context or to factors within the individual—the biological determinants.

With respect to the chapters of the present volume, the issue of flexibility shifts from normative milestones to considerations of the impact of moderator or mediator variables of timing and quality of experience during acquisition of the behavioral norms. Critical periods of development imply that there may be associated risk factors if development does not occur on schedule. The topic of what puts people "at risk" or what makes them vulnerable is broad, ranging from biological predispositions, impoverished environments, lack of cultural identity, malnourishment, to the extremes of sensory deprivation.

The counterpart to pathology models that incorporate risk factors of development are models that identify protective factors that assist the individual in survival and adaptation. Enriched environments have been demonstrated to improve exploratory behaviors and problem solving in domains as diverse as animal learning (Diamond, 1980) and early education (de Lacey & Poole, 1979; Lazar, 1983).

Providing teens with good problem-solving skills may be seen as enhancing protective factors with respect to the wide array of risk-taking behaviors, such as alcohol and drug use, unsafe driving, or unsafe sex (Calvert & Cocking, 1992, 1993; Noell & Ary, 1992). By contrast, avoiding teaching critical-thinking and problem-solving skills to the same groups at the appropriate junctures when their reasoning abilities are developing can be regarded as placing them at risk for dealing with decision-making situations. Thus, protective and risk factors of development may be regarded as important features affecting developmental outcome. Oloko (chapter 10, this volume) attests to the power of informal and formal educational models in affecting developmental outcome for both women and children.

Risk and protective features may be proximal to individuals, such as the risk factors of genetic inheritance that predispose one to disease, or to secondary outcomes, such as performances that are products of learning disabilities. Risk and protective factors may also be more distal to the individual, such as extra-familial cultural patterns of social supports or parent–child interaction styles during learning that teach the child how to consider alternatives and consequences of action as they learn to think about how to solve problems (Sigel, 1993). These social supports for cognitive organization and thinking styles may help the developing person cope with demands of new situations and therefore be regarded as protective factors. That is, vulnerability and resiliency are both constitutional *and* interpersonal factors in models of development.

What is it about socialization and development that puts some people at risk for poor outcomes? What are the protective developmental factors? These questions are particularly important in charting how individuals cope with complex problems that involve knowledge, perception, beliefs, attitudes, decision making, and situational circumstances that are difficult to predict, such as AIDS. Further, these factors relate to issues of pathways or trajectories of development.

A current example of how a complex problem can be interpreted differently by various subcultural groups within the United States is the differential responding to AIDS information. Behavioral change has not been so rapid in African-American groups as in other affected groups because the problem has not been accepted as relevant to their culture. This response to media messages is surprising because African Americans have the highest incidence of HIV (human immuno virus) infection within the United States. Even when high-profile members of the Black community, like Magic Johnson, have appeared in Public Service Announcements, the message and the information have been rejected (Calvert & Cocking, 1993; Kelly, 1992). Others (Mays, 1993) have shown that the messages may be cast too narrowly and may be too individualistic. When messages are framed in terms of the *community*, they receive better response. The general conclusion from the various studies is that comprehension of information is intimately tied to the cultural belief systems that are used to interpret information.

Thus, in behaviors that influence comprehension and interpretation of complex events, skills relating cognitive meaning must be timed closely in the developmental pathway model of cognition. Substantive questions of "How do we account for meaning?" and "How do we account for children's learning to comprehend complex events?" or "How are elements of complex events integrated?" are important. Further, the model will vary by the "meanings" that events carry within cultures. The issue of a common scientific language is extended to account for differences in how particular *events* are regarded within a culture. Thus, vulnerability and resiliency are intimately linked to culture and the conditional or causal reasoning that is part of the culture.

PATTERNS AND RELATIONS OF VARIABLES

Personal relevance is critical to the perception and interpretation of the components that lead to complex behaviors. The closeness of the variables to the individual has been discussed as a factor influencing meaning (Cocking & Renninger, 1993; Sigel, 1993). Personal relevance or personal meaning can be viewed as a within-culture concern, whereby certain events relate more directly to some people than to others. For example, MTV is not equally appealing or personally relevant to all U.S. residents. The ANC means different things to different people within South Africa. Hence, within any complex societal context, there are multiple cultures that interpret events differently. This proximal–distal dimension of variables is relevant for judging how variables operate between cultures—whether the factors influence development proximally through personal interpretation or more distally and subtly as a feature of the cultural context. The point is that variables exist as factors of influence but they do not operate as influences independent of circumstances that are part and parcel of culture and context. In other words, culture and context frame the personal relevance of the variables that enter into the developmental model.

A comprehensive model of development needs to include how the variables are related to, and affected by, one another; in other words, patterns of variables in mutual outcomes. The variables need to be articulated for their relationships to one another and to the individual's behavior. For example, stepwise regression models address how each variable enters into the overall prediction of a particular behavior. In addition, these same variables need to be cast against the cultural backdrop, thereby assessing both proximal and distal functions. The same analyses can be performed within *and* between groups, testing how proximal variables compare across cultures, how distal variables compare, and whether the same patterns of relationships hold for both developmental contexts. Causal modeling, as another example, allows development of multilayered models and two-way causality. The point of such analyses is to determine if the same factors figure into ostensibly similar behaviors and if the sources of influences are similar or different. The ultimate scientific question is whether behaviors can be predicted in lawful ways when cultures and contexts vary. If not, what adjustments have to be made to fine tune the model of behavioral development, or in what ways does the model have to be reconstituted?

SUMMARY

The preceding seven points outlined the scientific issues for building models of development that are less ethnocentric than the models that have guided past research in developmental psychology. These issues include: (a) Articulating the processes and levels of variable functioning in ways that cut across cultures and subcultures and in a language of science that has common meaning, (b) accounting for inconsistent findings within a framework of developmental continuities and discontinuities, (c) going beyond how variables function toward a model of how they influence one another in predicting developmental trajectories, (d) accounting for normative trends and their variations within cultural and individual differences parameters, (e) separating enduring from transitory effects and accounting for transitory behaviors as part of the developmental cycle, (f) specifying patterns of relationships in cognitive and social influences on development, and (g) specifying the vulnerabilities and resiliencies so that the models can account for cultural and contextual features that protect children or put them at risk.

The following discussion is a brief overview of a model based on the premise that the variables that enter into the model change in their relative contributions to behavioral predictions depending on prevailing conditions, such as changes in context during development. Between-group comparisons in such a model are secondary to accounting for the relevance of the variables within a particular group. The model accounts for how both proximal and distal variables function in guiding individual behaviors.

A LENS MODEL OF DEVELOPMENT

Two recent accounts point to the need for psychological literature to address the implications of the *relative* proximal–distal relationships of variables. Flavell, Flavell, Green, and Korfmacher (1990) studied the relationship between young children's cognitive development and what they think about their represented worlds. Specifically, Flavell et al. asked questions about young children's understanding of what they view on television. Flavell et al. suggested that the representation and the things represented can be analyzed along a continuum. These researchers suggested that previous studies have made the tacit assumption that children distinguish between the *proximal* images on a TV screen and the *distal* referents they portray. Development of symbolic functioning within a model that contrasts appearances (internal interpretations) with reality can also be analyzed along a proximal–distal dimension (see Fig. 19.1). In this case, Flavell et al. stated that young children (3-year-olds) whose attention is focused on the salient, proximal image of the TV screen can tell a great deal about what they see; at the same time, because they know little about mental representation, they regard the stimulus as real and palpable, rather than as a *representation* of a distal referent.

Flavell et al. (1990) also found that the specific *context* defined reality for the child's answers with respect to the images and their referents. That is, context-related and context-free queries in child research can contribute to a difference in the way a variable functions. In this case, proximal interpretations of events are literal. Such findings are consistent with Luria's (1932, 1976) classic studies of analogical reasoning, in which it was found that specific instances and personal experience of events overrode generalizable principles based on logic (distal dimension).

A second example of the proximal–distal issue is the difference in findings between comparative cognitive research and indigenous cognition (Cocking, 1993). Performance variables (Cocking & Renninger, 1993) have been shown to yield differences among different cultural groups because of the performer's familiarity with the task or the materials (Baratz, 1969; Serpell, 1979). In comparative psychology, different cultural groups are asked to perform identical tasks, presumably as a methodological control. By contrast,

Salient Image   Representational
Characteristics   Characteristics

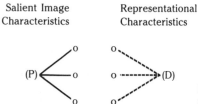

FIG. 19.1. Lens model of proximal and distal variables.

indigenous cognitive studies require the experimenter to determine the specific cognitive ability that is to be measured and then to utilize a task appropriate to that culture. The methodological control in these studies is in terms of *meaningfulness of the task*. The difference between these two approaches to understanding cultural differences in cognition can be analyzed in terms of whether the measurement variable is proximal or relatively distal to the performer. The dependent variable of the comparative psychologist, according to the indigenous model, is psychologically remote or distant to the meaning system of the performer.

One resolution of the differences among models or methodologies is to adopt a different level of analysis. Taking the case of the relationship between representational skills and a cognitive task, one could use the model in Fig. 19.2 to represent the relationships among the component skills of a *proximal* variable under study.

This diagram represents how a developmental psychologist looks at *proximal* relationships among component skills: In this case, a Euro-American child is asked to represent an experience by drawing a picture (Goodnow, 1977) or an African child is asked to build a three-dimensional model (Serpell, 1979). The task is labeled as *proximal* or *distal* to a culture based on where the task lies in the behavioral expectations in that culture. African children whom Serpell studied engage in wire model building and, hence, this representational system is *relatively* more proximal for these children than other representational modes, such as picture drawing. Familiarity with task and materials determine *relative* proximal or distal relationships with the task performers.

The analysis can be used also to address how the components relate to the same variable when cast as a *distal* variable, again to determine the individual component variable relationships to the distal variable and the interrelationships among component variables. In the previous example, this would mean looking at the child's performance on *both* the proximal and distal tasks, such that Euro-American children would both draw and build three-dimensional models, and the African children would be asked to perform both tasks as well. To repeat, in these analyses what is proximal or distal is *relative* to the child's cultural experiences. The previous diagrams present drawing as proximal and model building as distal for the Anglo child. For the African child, by contrast, model building is proximal and drawing is dis-

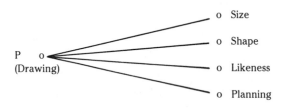

P   o
(Drawing)

o Size

o Shape

o Likeness   FIG. 19.2. Relationships among component skills of drawing as a

o Planning   proximal variable.

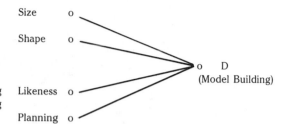

FIG. 19.3. Relationships among component skills of model building as a distal variable.

tal (see Fig. 19.3). The same components of size, shape, planning, and likeness are relevant to both tasks and for both groups to execute the tasks.

The individual component variables each have a relationship to the proximal variable. Further, each has an empirically derived relationship to every other subcomponent, such as coordinating the representational features of shape, size, likeness, and planning relative to one another.

The context of functioning can also determine whether a variable and its components function proximally or distally in the behavioral outcomes one calls performance. Goduka, Poole, and Aotaki-Phenice (1992) found that children from the same culture who were reared in three related, but not identical, contexts performed differently. The study looked at (a) context, (b) correlations among variables, and (c) correlations between family and child variables in comparing physical and behavioral development of African 5- and 6-year-olds who lived in three rural areas of South Africa that are ecologically distinct environments: Homelands, resettlements, and White-owned farms. Simply because the children all grew up in South Africa or that they were Black did not mean that all would have the same developmental outcomes. The essence of the study was that social context affected the culture as conveyed by the family and as it appeared in the outcome measures in child development. The developmental measures showed different patterns across the three environments, illustrating the importance of studying children in multiple environmental contexts ". . . because family characteristics are not associated uniformly across residence areas (Goduka et al., 1992, p. 509). The diagrams in Fig. 19.4 illustrate the contextual difference issue: Using the correlation of a distal parental variable with three proximal child behavior variables, Goduka et al. found that groups within the larger cultural context (subcultures) may exhibit differences among themselves.

Taken together, the two proximal–distal components of the model give an overall picture of the relationship for the same variable as interpreted by the subcultures. The overall relationship between the proximal and distal functioning of the same variable is what Brunswik (1956) called ecological validity. By addressing the subjective and objective meanings of a variable, *context* is defined by its relationship to the event and is accounted for as a contribution to performance. The model in Fig. 19.5 allows for differential interpretations of the meanings of variables and accounts for these differences.

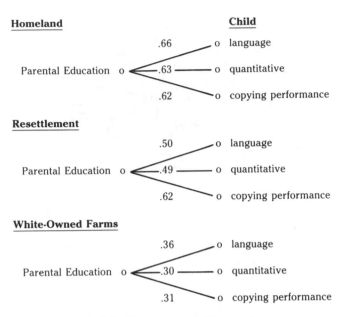

FIG. 19.4. The contextual difference issue.

The proximal–distal differences can operate within the same context. Blake's account (chapter 9, this volume) of different developmental language categories among African-American and Euro-American children in New York City illustrates that overall language competencies are reached through different pathways and in terms of different language skills. In this case, *frequencies* in social and emotional categories of language interaction are different among working-class African-American and working-class Euro-American mothers and their young children, and are indicative of how the mothers differ in their childrearing and management styles (see Fig. 19.6).

The individual chapters in this volume comprise a comprehensive picture of the development of a variety of behavioral phenomena. Together, they

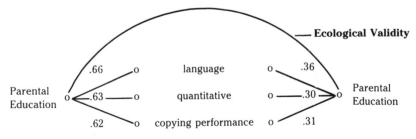

FIG. 19.5. Homeland versus White-owned farms: Differential meanings of variables.

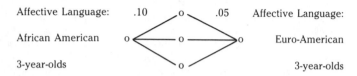

Mothers'
Expressive
Language Categories

Affective Language: .10   o   .05   Affective Language:

African American   o   o   o   Euro-American

3-year-olds   o   3-year-olds

FIG. 19.6. Language interaction among working-class mothers and their young children.

account for differences in development: Differences in performance; differences in encoding, storage, and retrieval of information; and differences that relate in the broadest sense to information processing and problem solving. These phenomena are chosen to represent developmental processes within specific cultural contexts and as interpreted by the individual cultures. The overall picture that this volume has attempted to structure is based on cognitive, social, educational, linguistic, and a variety of human performance domains. The interrelationships of mediating variables, relationships between mediating and dependent variables, and the overall relationship between objective and subjective realities can be made richer by looking across these individual models. What emerges is important in accounting for both competence and performance differences in human growth and understanding.

CONCLUSIONS

The theme of this chapter is the need for an organizing framework to evaluate continuities and discontinuities in development. The chapters in this volume illustrate that evaluating performance or development against arbitrary baselines trivialize almost all dimensions of comparison, whether such comparisons are in terms of developmental change, cultural differences, or performance variations of groups. Such comparisons are also not informative for determining developmental competencies of individuals. This chapter discussed the need for developmental theory to provide models for assessing adaptation and learning in the development of minority children as influenced by culture. In turn, culture was presented as a construct that operates differently in and out of context of the culture of origin. The concluding model was presented to account for varying interpretations of process variables, showing their relative contributions to development *within* a cultural context and to propose a way to frame the emergent properties of the culture and context of development.

REFERENCES

Baratz, J. (1969). A bidialectical task for determining language proficiency in economically disadvantaged children. *Child Development, 40,* 889–901.

Bloom, L. (1970). *Language development: Form and function in emerging grammars.* Cambridge, MA: MIT Press.

Bloom, L. (1974). Talking, understanding, and thinking: Developmental relationships between receptive and expressive language. In R. Schiefelbusch & L. Lloyd (Eds.), *Language perspectives—Acquisition, retardation, and intervention* (pp. 285–312). Baltimore: University Park Press.

Bloom, L. (1991). *Language development from two to three.* Cambridge, England: Cambridge University Press.

Bloom, L., Lightbown, P., & Hood, L. (1975). Structure and variation in child language. *Monographs of the Society for Research in Child Development, 40* (Serial No. 160).

Brunswik, E. (1956). *Perception and the representative design of psychological experiments.* Berkeley, CA: University of California Press.

Calvert, S. L. & Cocking, R. R. (1992). Health promotion through mass media. *Journal of Applied Developmental Psychology, 13,* 143–149.

Calvert, S. L., & Cocking, R. R. (1993). Health communication through information technologies. In L. K. Fuller & L. McPherson Shilling (Eds.), *Communication about communicable diseases.* Amherst, MA: Human Resources Press.

Cocking, R. R. (1993). The interface of cognitive science and educational practice. In *Proceedings of the Third Research Symposium on Limited English Proficient (LEP) Student Issues.* Washington, DC: U.S. Department of Education.

Cocking, R. R., & Chipman, S. (1988). Conceptual issues related to mathematics achievement of language minority children. In R. R. Cocking & J. P. Mestre (Eds.), *Linguistic and cultural influences on learning mathematics* (pp. 17–46). Hillsdale, NJ: Lawrence Erlbaum Associates.

Cocking, R. R., & Greenfield, P. M. (Eds.). (in press). Diversity and development of Asian Americans: Research gaps in minority child development. *Journal of Applied Developmental Psychology.*

Cocking, R. R., & Mestre, J. P. (1988). Considerations of language mediators of mathematics learning. In R. R. Cocking & J. P. Mestre (Eds.), *Linguistic and cultural influences on learning mathematics* (pp. 3–16). Hillsdale, NJ: Lawrence Erlbaum Associates.

Cocking, R. R., & Renninger, K. A. (1993). Psychological distance as a unifying theory of development. In R. R. Cocking & K. A. Renninger (Eds.), *The development and meaning of psychological distance* (pp. 3–18). Hillsdale, NJ: Lawrence Erlbaum Associates.

Dasen, P. R. (1984). The cross-cultural study of intelligence: Piaget and the Baoule. In P. S. Fry (Ed.), *Changing conceptions of intelligence and intellectual functioning: Current theory and research* (pp. 107–134). New York: North Holland.

de Lacey, P. R., & Poole, M. E. (1979). *Mosaic or melting pot.* Sydney, Australia: Harcourt, Brace & Jovanovich.

DeLoache, J. (1993). Distancing and dual representation. In R. R. Cocking & K. A. Renninger (Eds.), *The development and meaning of psychological distance* (pp. 91–107). Hillsdale, NJ: Lawrence Erlbaum Associates.

Diamond, M. (1980). *Neurobiology and mental health.* Discussion at the second workshop of the Jennifer Jones Simon Foundation for Mental Health and Education, Washington, DC.

Flavell, J. H., Flavell, E. R., Green, F. L., & Korfmacher, J. E. (1990). Do young children think of television images as pictures or real objects? *Journal of Broadcasting & Electronic Media, 4,* 399–419.

Goduka, I. N., Poole, D. A., & Aotaki-Phenice, L. (1992). A comparative study of Black South African children from three different contexts. *Child Development, 63,* 509–525.

Goodnow, J. J. (1977). *Children drawing*. Cambridge, MA: Belknap Press of Harvard University Press.

Greenfield, P. M. (1993, February). *The transmission of weaving in three generations of Mayan mothers and daughters*. Paper presented at the meeting of the Society for Cross-Cultural Research, Washington, DC.

Kelly, M. (1992). *A window into Black urban youth. The MEE Report*. Philadelphia, PA: Research Division of MEE Productions.

Lazar, I. (1983). Discussion and implications of the findings of the lasting effects of preschool. In The Consortium of Longitudinal Studies (Eds.), *As the twig is bent: Lasting effects of preschool programs*, pp. 461–466. Hillsdale, NJ: Lawrence Erlbaum Associates.

Luria, A. R. (1932). *The nature of human conflicts: Or emotion, conflict and will*. New York: Liveright.

Luria, A. R. (1976). *Cognitive development: Its cultural and social foundations*. Cambridge, MA: Harvard University Press.

Mays, V. M., Flora, J. A., Schooler, C., & Cochran, S. D. (1992). Magic Johnson's credibility among African American men. *American Journal of Public Health, 82*(12), 1692–1693.

Noell, J., & Ary, D. (1992). Interactive video program to reduce the incidence of HIV in adolescents. Grant funded by the National Institute of Mental Health.

Nurcombe, B. (1976). *Children of the dispossessed*. Honolulu: East-West Centre.

Piaget, J. (1970). Piaget's theory. In P. H. Mussen (Ed.), *Carmichael's manual of child psychology* (Vol. 1, pp. 703–732). New York: John Wiley & Sons.

Potts, M., Carlson, P., Cocking, R., & Copple, C. (1979). *Structure and development in child language: The preschool years*. Ithaca, NY: Cornell University Press.

Renninger, K. A., & Cocking, R. R. (1993). Psychological distance and behavioral paradigms. In R. R. Cocking & K. A. Renninger (Eds.), *The development and meaning of psychological distance* (pp. 19–33). Hillsdale, NJ: Lawrence Erlbaum Associates.

Serpell, R. (1979). How specific are perceptual skills? A cross-cultural study of pattern representation. *British Journal of Psychology, 70*, 365–380.

Sigel, I. E. (1970). The distancing hypothesis: A causal hypothesis for acquisition of representational thought. In M. R. Jones (Ed.), *Miami Symposium on the Prediction of Behavior, 1968: Effects of early experience*, pp. 99–118. Coral Gables, FL: University of Miami Press.

Sigel, I. E. (1986). Early social experience and the development of representational competence. In W. Fowler (Ed.), *Early experience and the development of competence: New directions for child development* (Vol. 32, pp. 49–65). San Francisco: Jossey-Bass.

Sigel, I. E. (1993). The centrality of a distancing model for the development of representational competence. In R. R. Cocking & K. A. Renninger (Eds.), *The development and meaning of psychological distance* (pp. 141–158). Hillsdale, NJ: Lawrence Erlbaum Associates.

Author Index

SUBJECT INDEX